D0679879

FICTIVE CAPITAL

AND FICTIVE PROFIT

FICTIVE CAPITAL and FICTIVE PROFIT

The Welfare-Military State

A Political Economy Based on Economic Fictions

HORACE H. ROBBINS

PHILOSOPHICAL LIBRARY
New York

15 East 40th Street, New York, N. Y. 10016

Library of Congress Catalog Card Number: 73-82164

SBN 8022-2126-2

Printed in the United States of America

CONTENTS

Chapter I—The Welfare-Military State and the Political Economy of Fictive Capital and Profit (A Syllabus of the Book). 7

II—The Independent Capitalist Economy.

Part I—The Independent Capitalist Economy as an Organism; The Structure and the Dynamics of the Organism; The Capital Unit. 47

Part II—Structure and Mechanisms of the Organism; Money, Price, Wage, Profit. 93

Part III—The End of the Independent Capitalist Economy. 165

III—Fictive Capital and Fictive Profit in the Political Economy Based on the Fictive Expansion of Capital. 177

IV—Money, Banking, Inflation.

Part I—Money, Bank Credit Money and Inflation of Bank Credit Money in the Independent Capitalist Economy. 231

Part II—Money and Banking in the Political Economy of Fictive Capital and Profit. 279

V—"Welfare" and "Military" Systems of Distribution and use of Goods. 299

VI—The Welfare-Military State and Government. 337

Part I—Social Structure and Social Change. The "Democratic State." 338

Part II—The Welfare-Military State. 382

Chapter I

THE WELFARE-MILITARY STATE AND THE POLITICAL ECONOMY OF FICTIVE CAPITAL AND PROFIT

(A Syllabus of the Book)

–1–

Early in the 1930's a revolution occurred that changed the political and the economic structure of all nations in which the capitalist economy had been fully developed. A new State and a new form of Government came into being: the "Welfare-Military State" (WMS). This is the State that exists today. This State is a new political form, different from its predecessor, the "Democratic State."

At the same time, a new economic relationship was created, much different from its predecessor, the Independent Capitalist Economy (ICE): The Welfare-Military State is a political economy as well as a political entity. The State is an integral and functional part of the new economic relationship, and the economy is an integral part of the State. This economy is called herein the *political economy of fictive capital and profit.*

This State existed in two main forms: one with a "rationalist" ideology, the other with a "mysticist" ideology. Both are the same political economy, although their respective ideologies represent them as entirely different States. The States with the "mysticist" ideology are mostly defunct, the "rationalist" type surviving and dominant.

The true nature of this State is not socially known; in particular that it is an economic as well as a political relationship. The State appears as a "Welfare State" and as a "Military State," and for these reasons it is so named. The "Welfare" and "Military" aspects are indeed basic components of the ideology and activity of this State. But ideology, immensely important as it is to the existence of this State, reveals the nature of the State only in small part. The real dynamic of the State is found in the economic relationship itself. The Welfare and Military aspects (themselves of a distinctive nature) are functional parts of the economic relationship. Nevertheless, it is the inherent powers of State and Government (State as Polity) that make the economic relationship (State as Political Economy) possible.*

State (WMS) as Political Economy.

An "economy" means the relationship among the individuals in the society in which the material goods are produced and distributed.

In the first place: this State is plainly using an immense and ever increasing part of the goods produced, and is also distributing a great part of the goods produced to a class of individuals who are supported by the State. The State does not appear to be actually engaged in the physical process of production. Nonetheless, this State is actually creating, *causing* the existence of the goods it uses and distributes, as values, just "as if" it were actually engaged in the process of production of these goods for itself, to use or distribute. It is *not redistributing* this mass of goods within the economy: the State is the actual operative force in their production, an integral part of the process of production. The goods would not come into being without the State's action.

In the second place; the creation of this mass of goods as values by the State, has another and deeper significance and importance in this *particular economic relationship.* It is the basis, the cause, the indispensable condition for the production of *all* the other material goods in this economic relationship. And the size and value of this volume of goods created for the State, determines the Level of Production and Income of all participants in the process of production.

Now this is not the "Communist" economic relationship, since

*Refer to Topic 8, Syllabus—on appearances, ideology, actual relationships, dynamics, and interrelationship between social structure and ideology. Ideology—the pattern of socially prevailing ideas concerning the relationship, although false or inadequate to describe the actual relationship, is essential to the existence of the actual relationship, and exists by the same necessity as the relationship.

the actual production of material goods is carried on by "private" units. Undoubtedly there is a semblance to the "Communist" relationship in that the State is the operative force in material production. This semblance is further supported by the fact that a fundamental part of the ideology of this State is that the State must assure and provide for the economic and material needs of all of its members. (State as Polity, below.)

Although the actual production is carried on by private units, this economy is much different from the capitalist economy that ended in 1930. The dynamic of the *entire* production is now in the State; "distribution" differs; the Level of Production is maintained by the State *continuously* at a far higher level. However, superficially, so much is the same, that it is a simulacrum of a capitalist relationship.

"Simulacrum of a capitalist relationship" is the first key to its nature. The whole political economy exists by means of *fictions* simulating real forms existing and required by the capital units. The State creates the fictive forms (of a value equivalent to the goods it causes to be produced for its use and distribution). The individuals and capital units that produce the material goods cannot exist or function without these fictive forms. And the State creates certain mechanisms by means of which these fictive forms can function as though they were real values, and capital, and profit, to individuals and units.

However, just as the creation of the mass of goods for the State has a deeper significance, so do the fictions that the State creates. The economy does not exist for the fictions, and the fictions do not create the economy. By means of these fictions the State creates a *fictive expansion of capital.* The constant expansion of capital is something absolutely indispensable for a "capitalist" relationship in individual capital units. However, because of the nature of the relationship, this can be successfully accomplished through *fictions,* in a State of a certain nature.

This introduces one of the main themes of the analysis that is to be set forth. However, at this point, "expansion of capital," its necessity, and the practicality of substituting a fictive expansion of capital for a real expansion of capital, can have little meaning. Certain lines of analysis must first be developed. (Topics 3-6, of the Syllabus). It is sufficient, at this point, to summarize:

1. The State is the actual cause of the production of the goods it uses and distributes in its Welfare and Military Systems; the goods would not be produced without the State's action.

2. The State creates fictive forms equivalent to the value so produced.

3. Unless these fictive forms are created for them, the separate producing units cannot exist or function: All production in this system is dependent on these fictive forms, and their volume.

When the reasons for the foregoing appear and the dynamic of the political economy explained, it will be seen that the statement above that the economy is a simulacrum of a capitalist economy, is inadequate. It is a new economic system that ultimately emerges.

State (WMS) as Polity:

The political economy is necessarily part of a State, the inherent powers of which make the economic relationship possible. Certain powers of Government are now exercised in a new context and for different purposes. The structure and constitution of the Government arise out of the nature of State as political economy. The new State and Government is visibly different from the "Democratic State" and Government, although the ideology of the WMS ("rationalist" form) utilizes part of the ideology of the "Democratic State." Nevertheless, to some extent, the ideology of the new State does indicate that it is a new political form.

First, as to the new elements of ideology: The State (WMS) is conceived as an association to provide and assure the economic and material needs for all of its members (among other basic political purposes). Furthermore, it is a State conceived to be in a total, constant, ideological war, to preserve itself, and in a posture of constant defence against ideological enemies, requiring the maintenance of an immense armament at all times.

Observe how different this is from the ideology and the actuality of the "Democratic" State. (Ch. IV, Sec. 4.) In the

"Democratic" State the prevailing idea is that man's material and economic needs are not to be provided or assured by the State; and there is a real separation of the political and the economic relationships. (The basic ideology of free man, and compact for a limited Government for limited purposes was actualized into "free economic man" and a separate Economy, uncontrolled by Government.) Furthermore, while the "Democratic" State, like any other State, is an association for the common defense, it is not engaged in a constant ideological war requiring an immense armament at all times. It sometimes wages war, generally for some benefit or necessity of the Economy, but it exists in a world of comparable States, not mortal ideological enemies. There is no actual economic gain to the war of the WMS; quite the contrary. (Contrast and paradox: In the Democratic State the economic dynamic of war will be seen to be the expansion of real capital; in the WMS it will be seen to be the expansion of fictive capital.)

The WMS is in fact an association to provide the economic needs, etc., but the nature of the economic association is not disclosed by the Welfare ideology. The Welfare and Military concepts are dynamics necessary to the creation and existence of this State. But in actuality, neither are quite what they seem. The "Welfare" concept is actualized primarily into the establishment of a new economic class, the Welfare class. The Military class is not like any previously existing military class, nor is this a Military State like any previously existing Military State. Both the Welfare and Military systems are necessary to maintain the political economy, although this is not their political or other apparent purpose. They provide a form of consumption of an immense volume of goods, a "non-capitalist" consumption of goods which have been produced "as if" capital goods, by separate capital units. The producing units and those deriving income through them receive fictive forms created by the Government, as equivalents. (Ch. VI, Part II, the WMS, actual relationship, and ideology; Ch. III, the theory of fictive capital and fictive profit.)

The centralization of power necessary to make the political economy and the Welfare-Military State possible, requires a new Government form. The general form of Government (prototype):

A Chief of Government is the power entity of the Government. He exercises the legislative, the executive, even the judicial power with respect to the political economy, through a great bureaucracy. In fundamental contrast to the Democratic State, the legislative body is not the dominant organ of Government. As part of the legislative power, the Chief of Government has the basic fiscal power—over taxation, borrowing, money and banking, and over expenditure. He manages the entire political economy, "public" and "private" sectors. The Chief of Government controls the foreign affairs of the State, and foreign economic relationships. He controls the armed forces, and can dispose them anywhere in the world.

> (This is essentially the Government of the U.S. The *Presidency* was transformed into the office of the Chief of Government. Presidential Government, not Government by Congress, became the Government of the U.S. (although Congress is an important adjunct of Presidential Government). The Government is not a personal Government of the President, but a Government by the Office of the President. Ch. VI.)

A Chief of Government must be above any economic class, capitalist, labor, or either of the two new economic classes. The Chief manages the political economy in the interest of each of the economic classes and of all of them, each class being dependent on the other, and each necessary for the existence of all. The Chief cannot be the representative of any one class without injuring the political economy and the State. The Chief of Government should be able to control each class, and be controlled by none (ideal form). If the Chief of Government does not control the political economy (as, for example, by failing to maintain an adequate tax system, or by not discouraging excessive *private* inflation of bank credit money and private fictive capital forms) because he is not sufficiently independent of any class—capitalist, Labor, Military, or Welfare—the State and economy can be seriously injured.

The prototype form of Government (but not in ideal form) exists in all WMS's. However, if the ideology of State and Government is of a mysticist nature, it will be seen that the Government exerts greater power over individuals, and utilizes different techniques.

Major Appearances of the new political economy:

A. The goods-money circuit between the Government and the dependent capitalist organism:

The Government advances 200 billion dollars (or 50 billions, or 500 billions) annually, to purchase goods from the private producers, or gives part of this money to individuals who purchase the goods.

Almost all the 200 billions advanced by the Government, flows back to the Government:

Say 85%, or 170 bns. by a "tax." (Note 1, below)

10%, or 20 bns. are borrowed back on the Government's interest bearing bond. (Note 2, below.)

5% does not flow back to the Government, but remains permanently in private hands. This is new money created by the banking system for the Government, on its permanent interest bearing bond: a true inflation of the paper money. (Note 3, below).

Notes: 1. This is the Welfare Military tax, the distinctive tax of the WMS. It is not the tax of the "Democratic State." The tax of the "Democratic State" has a different economic incidence, and a different purpose. Topic 5, the Syllabus, on the W M tax, that creates a fictive profit.
2. This bond is a permanent or continually refunded instrument; it is not the bond characteristic of the "Democratic State." The bond of the WMS is the prototype of the fictive capital form. Topics 4, 5, Syllabus).
3. Inflation is defined in Topic 4, Syllabus. At this point, note that the inflation of the paper money in this process differs markedly from the episodic inflation and deflation of the Democratic State. It is a permanent, continuing inflation of a *new* money form, that can depreciate constantly without deflation.

There is a continual reflux in the circuit, wherein the money received by the capital units from the Government, flows back to the Government, except the newly inflated money.

The prerequisite to the existence of this circuit is the creation of the new money and banking system (Topic 6, Syllabus). The new money form gives the Government absolute power to purchase the goods and cause the production of the goods for the Government's demand; and power to inflate paper money constantly without deflation; and power to create and maintain *at its will* a steadily expanding volume of permanent interest bearing bonds. (Fundamental: the transfer of gold from private hands to the Government is the transfer of power over production from private hands to the Government).

The type of goods purchased will cover the entire productive system—"Welfare" consumer goods, and "military" goods from heavy industry. The purchases will be approximately *congruent* with the sources of the W M tax. (Topic 5, Syllabus).

The goods purchased will never be used as "capital" goods, i.e. to produce other goods; nor will they re-enter the market to disturb current or future production; nor will they be used in such way to disturb the employer-employee relationship in production. (Topic 7, Syllabus.)

There are certain rules which will be seen to govern this circuit:

—Neither the size of the total expenditure, nor the proportions in the return flow,—the "revenue mix" of the Government,—are volitional nor accidental. Practical necessity dictates the size of each. But this "practical necessity" will be seen to be determined by the laws of the political economy. (Ch. III).

—The Government's budget will and *must* always be "unbalanced."

—In the fully developed pefcp, the WM tax *must* always be less than the total Government expenditure for goods.

—If the Government's expenditure for goods is reduced, the W M tax return will fall; the W M tax return will fall as fast as the Government's expenditure falls, and at a certain point it will fall faster.

—The Government *must* borrow, but it cannot borrow sufficiently from non-bank sources; the Government *must* inflate the paper money. The W M tax itself is made possible by the borrowing and inflation.

–The size of the Government expenditure is directly related to the Level of Production and Income, and the proportions in the Government's revenue mix also governs the Level of Production and Income.

B. It can be seen that the Government manages the whole political economy. This management controls not only the Level of Production and the Income, and Money and Banking, but also the major incidents of the so-called "private sector"–wage, price, profit, etc.

In part because of the foregoing goods-money circuit, the Government is seen to be involved in a complex web of management. This is an economy that cannot manage itself; it must be managed. The management requires not only the skills of economic engineering, but the ideal Government structure, i.e., Chief of Government above any economic class and powerful enough to control all.

The capital units, now wholly dependent on the State and Government for existence, must be managed. Because of the nature of this political economy, the inherent dynamics and self-adjusting mechanism of the Independent capitalist economy have disappeared. There is no longer an inherent business cycle. Indeed, there is a constant and inherent instability in price, wage rate and profit rate, at all times. Since there must be an inflation of the paper money, there will be a constant depreciation. The rising price level affects every incident of production. The wage rate must steadily rise. Prices cannot be left uncontrolled without endangering the entire structure. The Government

–Either maintains a system of *direct* legal controls over wage and price, for all sectors of the economy, or

–Maintains a system of informal controls over wage and price; attempting to balance power between unions and employers; utilizing its purchasing power to control large producers; utilizing selective taxation; all to maintain as great a stability as is possible, i.e. a slow steady rise.

Since foreign trade and exchange in a pefc proceeds on a different basis than in the preceding economy, i.e. no longer governed by the expansion of real capital and the business cycle, —trade and exchange cannot proceed without direct national control and international agreement. (Topic 6, Syllabus; Ch. IV).

—3—

The Capitalist Organism. Its Basic Dynamic.

—The organism of the Independent Capitalist Economy (ICE). Its end in 1930, on the failure of its basic dynamic.

—Structure and mechanisms of the capitalist organism.

—The Aggregate Profit of the Organism: the two parts thereof, —Profit A and Profit B.

—The implications of the identity of the new additional capital, the new investment that purchases it, and the *Profit B* created.

—The business cycle of the ICE. The over expansion of real capital.

The analysis begins with two fundamental concepts. The first is that the capitalist relationship constitutes an *organism*.

There are a great number of seemingly independent capital units, each unit (employer, capitalist) advancing *money* out of *capital* to buy goods and equipment for use in further production, and to pay *wages* to labor; producing solely for *sale* (*price*), and solely for *profit*. But that which appears to be a relationship of individuals in separate independent capital units, actually constitutes an organism. It is an organism because all the capital units function as parts of a whole, *and the function of the whole determines the function of each part* (unit).

An organism has its own structure, mechanisms, dynamics. Through its mechanisms, the function and indeed the existence of each of its units and individuals is determined. The units and individuals that compose the organism see themselves as independent units, but actually their economic existence, income, production, price, profit, is determined by the function of the whole (organism).

The organism has a basic *dynamic* upon which its existence and function as an organism, depends (and hence the existence and function of each unit). This dynamic also constitutes its inherent nature. This is the second concept fundamental for the analysis—the nature of the basic dynamic of the organism:

A capitalist organism can exist, and the organism can maintain itself in equilibrium, only if the Aggregate Capital of the organism constantly expands (constant new investment for new additional capital). If the expansion does not or cannot take place, the Level of Production and Income declines in a widening spiral even to the point of total collapse. Corollary: The Level of Production of the organism and the Income of all individuals depends upon and is determined by the existence of the capital expansion and its degree; Level and Income rise and fall spirally as a multiple of capital expansion,—i.e., the new investment.

There is a correlative of this basic law of dynamics of the organism (expansion of capital), and the full meaning of the dynamic appears only when stated with its correlative: The new, additional capital is part of the Aggregate Profit of the organism (the Profit of all the units).

This particular part of the Aggregate Profit is called herein the *Profit B*. (That part of The Aggregate Profit of the organism that represents the personal consumption of the capitalists, or those deriving their income through them, is called the "Profit A"). Why this new, expanded capital is and must be part of the Aggregate Profit (Profit B), an Income of the capitalists—that it is not a "savings"—and that it is the critical factor in Level of Production, and Income of all individuals in the organism, and hence determines the function of all the units, will be examined. But consider, at this point, the implications of the correlation of the dynamics (capital expansion), and capital expansion as Profit B part of the Aggregate Profit, in the context of:

—the capital unit produces solely for profit
—the capitalist organism produces solely for profit

—part of the profit of the organism must have a capital form, that is, be new, additional, capital.
—all units function as parts of the organism, whose function determines the function of each unit.

The End of the Independent Capitalist Economy (ICE).

The (capitalist) organism has a definite span of life; when the organism dies, its parts (units) cannot survive. The organism can live and function only while its dynamic can operate. The organism came into being as an economy (the ICE), because of the immense power of its dynamic, the expansion of capital, which was self-creating and self-sustaining.

But such a capitalist organism *must* reach a critical point when this capital expansion cannot by itself take place. (The capital expansion referred to is the normal and inherent expansion of capital, not the gross overexpansion of capital that is induced by war, inflation, etc., an overexpansion of capital that is itself periodically destructive to the economy). When this critical point is reached, and even the gross overexpansion of capital is no longer possible, the organism (ICE) must enter into a final, and ever widening spiral decline, to its ultimate collapse. (Topic 4, Syllabus—1914-1929 the period of the critical point.) This organism (ICE) came to its end in 1930; it can not be resurrected.* The fact that in the pefcp the same relationship seems to exist in the *units,* as stated at the outset, does not mean that the same economy exists.

Structure and Mechanisms of the Capitalist Organism: The Meaning of the Dynamics, and Its Correlate, Amplified.

Five terms were used to describe the capital unit: money, price, capital, wage, profit. They were used as simple terms, the usage of the practical man. But they are not the simple terms they appear to be, since they arise only out of the structure and mechanism of the organism. Their existence and meaning

*The Democratic State, the political structure characteristic of the period of the ICE, then also failed.

and function in the *unit* flows from the organism.* The terms state the fundamental relationship (structure) of the organism, and it will be seen also that they are its mechanisms. In the mechanism and dynamics of the organism, the terms will appear as *Aggregates*: the Aggregate Capital, the Aggregate Wage, the Aggregate Profit, the Aggregate Price of goods produced and sold.

The Aggregates of the organism are the *primary* forms. It is through them that the function of each unit is determined and controlled. The Aggregates are *not additions* of these forms as they appear in each unit or for the individual. The contrary is the situation: The manifestations in the unit (wages, profit, price) exist and come into being *as parts of the whole*:

–The profit of the particular unit is a share of the Aggregate Profit. This Aggregate is not constituted by adding the individual or unit manifestations in whatever form they appear–entrepreneur's profit, interest, dividends.

–The total price of goods produced and sold by the unit is a part of the Aggregate Price of all goods produced and sold. (Level of production of the unit and profit is determined by the Level of Production of the organism, and its profit.)

–The total wage paid by the unit is a share of the Aggregate Wage.**

*"Money" and "Price," however, will always exist in *any* system of production for sale, i.e., a system of production not for the producer's use, although not necessarily a capitalist system. "Money" and "Price" must then exist in a capitalist organism, since this is a system of production for sale. In the capitalist organism, however, money and price have a distinctive form and nature, which embodies the capitalist relationship. Price, in particular, in the capitalist organism, expresses not only the value of the good in money (and this implies the existence of money) but it also embodies the fundamental wage-profit ratio of the capitalist relationship; it is also a basic mechanism of the organism. (See "Normal Price" Ch. II, Sec. 17.)

**Ch. II, Secs. 15, 16, 17. That the Aggregates are primary—and that individual and capital unit incomes, and prices, etc., derive from them and that the Aggregates are not additions of them—is contrary to all appearances to the individuals and units of the economy. The premises of the

The mechanisms of this organism and the interrelation among the five terms that set forth the fundamental structure of the organism are too complex to be usefully summarized. (Ch. II, Secs. 14, 15, 16, 17). But one fundamental interrelationship, between the two correlative terms, Wage and Profit, need to be mentioned. The premise of Profit is the establishment by the society of an average wage rate at such level that the Aggregate Wage will be a certain fraction of the Net Aggregate Price of Goods sold.

But the *possibility* of Profit implicit in this ratio, does not mean that profit will exist, for the goods must be sold, and at a *Normal* price, i.e., one that embodies this wage-profit ratio. This can take place only if the dynamic is in function: the expansion of capital which will be part of the Aggregate Profit (Profit B). "Normal Price" implies the existence and function of the dynamic of the organism. Normal Price is not itself the dynamic; nor are Wage and Aggregate Wage dynamics of the organism. Through the analysis of structure and mechanisms (Ch. II) it is seen that consumption generally–through the

foregoing, i.e., the organism, its dynamics, etc., are also not within the immediate experience of the unit capitalists. The idea that "organism," "Aggregates," determine production, price, profit, in the unit are furthermore, concepts unacceptable to prevailing, professionally formulated ideology. The prevailing "macro-economics" and "National Income" economics *appear* to be holistic. But they are constructed by adding up parts, accepting all conventional designations and appearances to individuals. The dynamics of this "whole" so constructed, are conceived to exist in the units and in individuals; the economic system is formulated on the basis of the individual volitions, propensities, etc,; and agreeable platitudes—"production carried on for human needs," "production of an individual is equivalent to his income," "savings," and "rewards" for savings. Economic ideology (like all good ideology), is mainly based on appearances, and formulates a system that is "rational," "moral," and agreeable to individuals within the system itself. However, although the prevailing formulations are inadequate to describe the actual nature of a capitalist relationship, or organism, and its dynamics —and therefore incapable of revealing the nature of a political economy based on fictive forms (but rather completely conceal its nature), they are useful as an ideology for a pefcp, and, in part, in its management. In passing: the description of the economy implicit in the "Marxist" ideology—especially that of the "exploitation of labor"—has little relevance to the new political economy, either as analysis of this economy, or as counter ideology. (Ch. VI.)

Aggregate Wage, and the Profit A received by the capitalists, and all derivative incomes, and the money advanced to reproduce capital used up in production, or money, interest, price, etc.—are not the determinants of Level and Income, but consequences or mechanisms of the dynamics of the economy.

Implications of the Identity of: the new, additional capital, the new investment that purchases it, and the Profit B created.

Recapitulation: The new, additional capital goods, the expanded capital of the organism, must necessarily be part of the Aggregate Profit of the organism (part of the profit on the existing capitals). That is to say, the new additional capital goods are goods produced over and above the goods produced for the wage earners (sold to them for the wage advanced), and the goods produced for the consumption of the capitalists (Profit A), and the goods produced to replace those capital goods used up in the production of all the goods. (The foregoing is also the basis of the *multiple* effect of the production and sale of the goods that are the Profit B—on the whole Level of Production and Income, i.e., the necessity for production for the wage earners, and capitalists of their consumption goods to produce these goods, and to reproduce the capital goods used up in the production of all goods, etc., in a spiral.)

The Profit B—the new additional capital goods—is part of the income of the capitalists, as a class. They are not goods that have been "saved", for they have been produced for an effective demand: the new investment for new capital. And they have been produced as and for profit, and the profit exists because of the basic wage-profit ratio of the organism.

But it is the same class in the organism (capitalists as a class) that makes the new investment to buy the new capital goods, expand old capitals, form new ones. The new investment itself then becomes the Profit B (money form) of the producing capitalists. Thus the new investment advanced by the capitalists, returns to them on purchase of the new capital goods, as Profit.

Consider, then, the full meaning and significance of this circuit (which is part of the whole goods-money circuit of the organism (Ch. II, Sec. 5). The capitalists as a class (of the organism) make the new investment, they receive back the money advanced as part of the Aggregate Profit on the sale of the goods. They also receive the new capital itself. Thus there is an identity of the new additional capital, the new capital investment, the Profit B part of the Aggregate Profit.

The foregoing statement—that the Level of Production, the Net Income, the condition of equilibrium, and the existence of the capitalist economy itself, depend on the existence of the expansion of the Aggregate capital, does not yet set forth the entire dynamics of the capitalist economy. There is a direct, inherent, dynamism to expand capital. This direct dynamism is something apart from the desire and necessity for the existing capitals to make the average rate of profit, including all parts of the Aggregate Profit that appear as costs to the individual unit. (Ch. II, Secs. 9, 10, 11.)

The Business Cycle of the ICE: The periodic rise in production, income, and employment, sometimes to "boom" level, followed by a depression.

The law of the dynamics of the organism would seem to indicate that the organism maintains itself in an equilibrium through a constant (normal) expansion of capital. However, this is not what actually takes place in the ICE. In the ICE, there is an inherent tendency to *overexpand* capital (Ch. II, Secs. 9, 11); the business cycle is the consequence of the periodic over expansion of capital. The level of production and employment then rises as a multiple of the additional expansion, i.e., the overexpansion. (Corollary of the basic law on the spiral, multiple increase of Level and Income). This over expansion of capital produces the only real prosperity in the ICE.

The business cycle is mentioned at this point mainly because the overexpansion of capital is usually induced and maintained by two factors: first, war: second, a marked *private* inflation of paper money associated with booming financial markets, land titles, etc., and the creation of private fictive capital forms, and their monetization. These two conditions may be associated. What is taking place, episodically, is not simply the creation of a "market" that supports the existing capitals and the over expanded capitals, or causes a further expansion of capital. The goods purchased through the inflated money and the fictive capital papers, constitute a *fictive expansion of capital*, which itself (and in addition to the real overexpansion of capital which it induces and maintains in the ICE), has a multiple effect on the whole level of Production and Income.

—4—

Fictions, Substitutions, and Their Processes. The Pseudo Profit B. (Preface to the New Political Economy).

The discussion in the preceding Topic concerns the expansion of actual capital. But it was indicated that when the ICE was a dynamic, viable organism, there was an adjunct process (episodic, and invariably a prelude to a cyclic depression) whereby certain material goods were produced for an effective demand, and sold at normal price, yet the goods were not sold and used as capital goods, nor were they produced for the personal consumption of the capitalists—the Profit A part of the Aggregate Profit. The goods produced are comparable to new, additional capital goods, produced "as if" they were such capital goods, because they were produced for an effective demand arising out of money derived from *fictive capital papers*, or money created on such papers (inflated "bank credit" paper money), or money of this nature created on other papers, and in general, entering the goods-money circuit as "profits" not arising out of the production of material goods.

These goods, and the money received for them, being neither a Profit B part of the Aggregate Profit, nor a Profit A part, *are a pseudo Profit B*, because they do not have a *real* capital form. But although they do not have a real capital form (and as capital, function to produce an additional part of the Aggregate Profit), they are effectively represented by a fictive capital paper, representing no actual capital but nevertheless returning interest, etc.; or by an inflated money (which, it will be seen is a "capital" money, that will achieve a capital form in one way or another).

The result of this production for this demand, and the source of this effective demand is not merely an additional "market" for goods, but a fictive expansion of capital in the organism, with all or most of the consequences of a real expansion of capital.

Review, in terms of substitutions and fictions, the discussion in Topic 3, on the implications of the identity of the new additional capital goods (here substitute goods produced for a comparable market or produced "as if" new additional capital goods), the new investment that purchases the goods (here substitute the new investment in the form of the fictive capital paper or money arising from its sale, or inflated money created on fictive capital papers and other papers), and the Profit B part of the Aggregate Profit created (here substitute a pseudo Profit B). The circuit is quite the same, the new "investment" creates the pseudo Profit B, *but* the new investment is not also represented by actual, new, expanded capital, but only by fictive capital paper forms. The latter play the same role in the organism, and hence for the units, as capital papers, etc., representing real capital.

The goods are consumed (by the Government, or personally by those who create the inflated money or the private fictive capital papers, or who obtain possession of them, as a "profit"). That is to say, the goods have a "non capital" consumption, producing no new goods. Yet a "capital paper" survives, or inflated money that will achieve a capital form.

The basic elements of the process of fictive capital expansion (pseudo Profit B), in the ICE are the fictive capital papers and the inflated money. They are called "elements" of the process since neither may result in a fictive expansion of capital. These papers and the inflated money are not created for the purpose of fictive capital expansion, at least not in the ICE. They are created for their own sake, and may create great fortunes. Only under certain circumstances do they act to create a fictive expansion of capital: only if directly or indirectly they create an effective demand for an *additional* production of goods for these forms, (i.e., a production of goods comparable to new additional capital goods, and all other production necessary to produce these additional goods).

Fictive capital paper, and inflated money, exist in a public form, Government created. Both are also privately created. The interest bearing Government bond, or the money created by banks thereon, relatively permanently, and used by the Government as revenue, are the prototypes. These almost always enter into the fictive capital expansion process, since the money raised on this "capital paper" is used to purchase goods, and these goods are usually produced for the Government's demand.

In general, a fictive capital paper is a relatively permanent, valuable, possibly liquid instrument. which does not represent any actual capital or capital money used in the process of material production, yet returns interest at some rate, or effects a transfer to the owner of the paper of some other part of the Aggregate Profit of the organism, or purports to.

"Private" fictive capital papers can also be created, and paper money (bank credit type) can be privately inflated. The "private" fictive capital papers, likewise do not represent actual goods, or money actually used in the process of (capitalist) production. But they, too, are valuable, salable, and return "interest" or a transfer of some other form of the Aggregate Profit to the holder. They can be created on other capital paper, and especially on land titles; or be simply capitalizations of expected profit or interest. They are often created in financial manipulations, mergers, etc. Some of these papers may be almost fraudulent; others represent a reasonably expected future income for future value of some sort. After their creation, they may be injected into the existing capital paper structure and to some extent represent some actual capital. The sophisticated financial mechanisms and markets of the ICE made possible the creation of great quantities of private fictive capital papers, and monetized "profits" on them and on other capital papers, land titles.

Paper Money Inflation.

Paper money inflation has three inseparable characteristics: (a) the *creation* of paper money, (b) to purchase goods for consumption by a Government, or a personal, individual, consumption. (c) the paper money remaining permanently in circulation. This is clear when a Government prints paper money to pay its expenses and buy goods, etc., instead of obtaining the money by taxation or borrowing. It is not so clear when a Government "borrows" its money from its Government bank, or the commercial banks, on its interest bearing paper, and uses the money as above, *and* where the money remains in the circulation,—the bond permanently in the Bank. Yet the identical thing takes place.

While an inflation of bcm (bank credit money) as a revenue for the Government in wartime, in the ICE, was well known to have existed, the episodic private inflation of bcm for a personal consumption was rarely acknowledged. But if private inflation was one of the "mysteries" of the ICE (and of banking), its manifestations and accompaniments were well known, and eagerly sought. The booming stock market, the rapidly rising prices of land titles, creation of mortgages, capital papers on capital papers, mergers and "trusts" that tripled the amount of capital papers, all meant a prosperous economy, with production, income, and employment rising. A great deal of money created for this process, and "profits" from the financial mechanism generally, enters the market to buy goods for personal consumption.*

Further on the process of fictive capital expansion, generally.

The fictive capital paper is a remarkable instrument, even in the ICE. Consider: If real capital goods are to be purchased,

*The nature of the inflation of bank credit money is quite concealed by prevailing economic ideology. The major reason for this is the fact that an inflation of paper money for private benefit has long been practiced, at the same time as Government paper money inflation was attacked. This private inflation was effected episodically by the financial and banking mechanism of the ICE, even while the gold convertible, gold equivalent standard was maintained. Today, popular, professional and political usage of the term "inflation" conceals the essential nature of inflation—the creation of bank credit money for Government and personal consumption. The word "inflation" is used to mean a rise in the price of material goods, and it is given other meanings. (Actually a price rise is a probable, but not even a necessary consequence of the inflation of paper money; there are also other reasons for a price rise. And the *depreciation* of paper money, which, to speak precisely, is the cause of the rise in price of goods, may not even occur if there has been an inflation of paper money.)

and function as capital, the new capital must produce all parts of the Aggregate Profit—entrepreneural profit or dividends, interest, even taxes, etc. But a fictive capital paper, public or private, needs *only* the payment of "interest" or an expectation of such payment to create it and maintain its existence, and this interest need not be (and will not be) even a direct share of the Aggregate Profit of the organism.* This paper can create a fictive capital expansion (representing goods produced for this paper), which, in the organism, serves as well as the production and sale of real capital goods, to maintain the equilibrium or raise the Level of the organism.

Paper money inflated on such fictive capitol paper, or otherwise created, can likewise have this almost "magical" effect. But with respect to inflated money the problem that has to be discussed is how inflated money which becomes part of the pseudo Profit B, does achieve a capital form. This it must do, for it is a capital money, not to be used for the consumption of the capitalists. Among other means, it may enter the financial orbit, and be used in further speculation in the stock exchange, land titles, etc. But if it enters the market to buy goods for production of goods, (a capital use), then at a certain point it must *depreciate*. The depreciation is the means by which it assumes a capital form. (Ch. IV, Sec. 2).

When the ICE comes to an end, its characteristic fictive processes (episodic) also end. The public forms existed in the ICE because the ICE was an expanding organism, and war in support of capital expansion is a policy of State. But if such real capital expansion is not possible (on the end of the ICE), the typical war of the Democratic State-ICE will not recur.

*Refer to Ch. II, Secs. 12 and 16 on the distinction between two forms of interest in the capitalist economy: The prototypical "interest" of a capitalist relationship is interest paid for money borrowed for the production of material goods for sale in this relationship. This interest is a direct part of the Aggregate Profit arising from the production and sale of these goods (a counterpart of entrepreneural profit). The second form is that paid for the use of money not used as capital in the capitalist process of production and sale of goods; it is not a *direct* share of the Aggregate Profit, but a transfer, or paid from some other source, or itself a fiction.

The private fictive processes depended on or interacted with a gross over expansion of capital. (During the 1914-1929 period, the critical period of the ICE, in which it could not maintain itself by the ordinary expansion of capital—Ch. II, Sec. 18—two succeeding episodes took place: a great war; the boom of the 20's really based on fictive forms, and both leading to a great overexpansion of capital. Both maintained the ICE for a while before its ultimate collapse).

The economy—ICE—could not be restored by substituting a fictive expansion of capital for a real expansion, as an artful device. What has to take place is a political and economic revolution, a new State and a new ideology, wherein the goods are not only demanded for certain purposes, and a system of production for fictive forms established, but the power and the mechanisms that make an economic structure of this nature possible, created. It is not a simple substitution of fictive forms for real forms, but the substitution of a *new dynamic*: a State that becomes a distinctive new economic relationship.

–5–

The political economy based on the fictive expansion of capital is created by the establishment of the Welfare-Military State, of which it is an integral part:

—The new State transforms fictive capital paper and inflated money into forms suitable for such a political economy.
—The "fictive profit" form, as part of the pseudo Profit B, can be created by this State.
—The new State creates systems of continual consumption of immense quantities of goods—a non capital consumption. It eliminates a great part of the "labor force" from the process of material production.

The WMS maintains a certain relationship in material production of goods—production for sale, for profit, by individuals in separate capital units, on the basis of an extremely advanced technology and on a large scale. Because of the inherent nature of such a relationship in production, the units can exist, maintain their internal relationships and relationships to each other, after the end of the ICE, only if, as a regular course, as a continuous process, and on a large and ever expanding scale, the State creates fictive forms, and a non capital use of an immense quantity of goods. Although the goods the units produce for these forms, are produced only for fictions of capital and profit, they must be produced, if the units are to exist at all. These fictive forms constitute a fictive expansion of capital for the units as a whole (for a dependent capitalist organism) which substitutes for a real expansion of capital, necessary for such a relationship in separate capital units. But the whole level of production—including the consumption of wage earners and capitalists alike—depends solely on the State's effective demand, and the fictions it creates. The political economy then, the economic relationship, is the inherent, necessary consequences of the State's existence, its nature, mechanisms, ideology.

The State's use and distribution of the goods *must* be of such nature that the goods are completely removed from the consumption and use of the capital units, i.e., a non-capital consumption. The apparent dynamic of the State is the use to which it puts these goods.

This political economy is a simulacrum of a capitalist economy; the fictions are simulacra, although they have an absolute adequacy and reality for units and individuals. But the political economy created, is plainly not the capitalist economy that existed (in the ICE up to 1930). By the creation of a simulacrum, a *new* economy is in actuality created. The "capital units" themselves become creatures of the State.

It is not the fictive forms or processes that create the new political economy; it is not a system created by fictions. The economic and political revolution creates an economy that utilizes these forms to create a certain relationship in production and distribution of material goods. The fictions and their processes are its necessary mechanisms. Certain of these fictive forms existed in the ICE, but their use and nature therein was much different.

The forms themselves have to be radically changed to make them suitable for the new political economy. Mechanisms are created to make them permanent, assure continuity, assure absolute Government power to create and maintain them, and assure production for the Government's demand (for the fictive forms). The Government bond becomes a permanent or constantly refunded form, constantly expanding in volume; the money inflated becomes a permanent, constantly expanding body of money, never deflated although constantly depreciating. And a new, necessary, fictive form—the fictive *profit* form, must be created.

Part of the pseudo Profit B can have a fictive *profit* form, when the pseudo Profit B reaches and steadily maintains a certain volume, and has become the basis of the whole economy. In effect, *part* of the pseudo Profit B is repossessed by the Welfare-Military tax. The money flowing back to the Government can be used again to create part of the pseudo Profit B. "Fictive Profit" means only that a part of the pseudo Profit B does not have a fictive *capital* form; it does not mean that the Aggregate Profit as a whole—including the pseudo Profit B is not actually in existence, either in money form or representing actual material goods.

The WM tax that creates the fictive profit form has its incidence on the pseudo Profit B (Ch. III, Sec. (1), (3). Such a tax cannot exist in the Democratic State. (The tax of this State usually has its incidence on the Profit A, and is a *transfer* of consumption.) The fictive profit form is unique to a pefcp.

It seems anomolous that there will be a production of goods by private producers comparable to new additional capital goods, for "profit" and a "capital" form, that is essentially fictive to them. The answer is, that in the dependent organism the pseudo Profit B comes into existence as a whole—not a part that has a fictive "capital" form or inflated money, and a part that has a fictive profit form (represented by the W M tax). The rationale of the fictive profit form, then, is that a *part* of the pseudo Profit B can have a fictive *profit* form if a sufficient part has a fictive capital form, and, in actuality there is also a Profit B which by hypothesis has an actual capital form. The volume of the W M tax can increase as the absolute size of the Pseudo Profit B increases. The producers *must* increase their production, and maintain increased production for the Government's demand, in order to keep the fictive capital part of the pseudo Profit B (and the Profit A and Profit B too, which is maintained by the increased Government demand).

In summary a fictive profit form in a political economy based on the *fictive* expansion of capital is practicable, since, if to make a net of 50, the production must be 100, or increased to 150, this will always be done; or, to increase a net of 25 to a net of 50, production must go from 100 to 200, this too will be done. (The "net" refers to units of fictive capital, or inflated money.) This cannot be true in an ICE or a pefcp with respect to the Profit B, no part of which can be taken by tax.

With respect to the unit, the fictive profit form and its practicality, presents little difficulty. The profit of the unit comes into being as an undifferentiated whole (and a large part of this is "Profit A"). The amount of profit is ample for the unit, regardless of the very great size of the W M tax. If it is necessary to double production to maintain the same net profit—the unit will do so. The unit or individual will act to maximize the net return, no matter what the gross must be. It is as though the cost of production increases, and to obtain the same net profit, the scale of production must be increased.

Income, to the individual or unit appears to be reduced by the tax. It is hard for the individual or unit to see that this profit before taxes would not exist if it were not for the Government expenditure and the W M tax. The idea that the unit or individual would have, say twice the income or profit if there were no W M tax, is based on the supposition that the profit before tax would exist. But for *all* the units (the organism) this is not true. Actually, the Profit A and the Aggregate Wage are greatly increased, as a multiple of the pseudo Profit B, and the W M Tax ultimately costs the capitalists (class) nothing.

Further Propositions (from Ch. III):

—When a pefcp is in function, some degree of "constant" real capital expansion is restored, although this is not necessary to maintain the economy. This expansion (Profit B) will be only a small fraction of the pseudo Profit B.

—The principle that the Level of Production and Income is a multiple of the pseudo Profit B plus the Profit B, applies, even though part of the pseudo Profit B has a fictive profit form.

—In this political economy the creation of private fictive capital forms, private fictive capital forms, private inflation of bank credit money, will take place to a certain extent, and this will increase the size of the pseudo Profit B.

–6–

A new money form, and a new money and banking system are essential for the existence of every element and every process of a political economy based on fictive forms. This new money and banking system is not the cause of a pefcp, but it is the basis of the Government's power to create the pseudo Profit B, and the fictive forms that represent it. The two basic elements of the new money form and banking system are:

(a) The sequestration of gold by the Government, and the private possession and monetary use of gold forbidden. A unique money form is then created,—a paper money created by Banks purporting to represent a certain weight of gold, but inconvertible to gold, which is the sole money form (domestic); the monetary gold held by the Government.
(b) The transformation of the Government Central Bank into a Bank that is part of the Government, and controlled solely by the Government and operated for the maintenance of a political economy based on fictive forms. The Central Bank may no longer be governed by the power entities of the organism; the Government uses it as a major instrument to determine the function of the dependent organism. The Government can then create or cause the creation of any volume of bank credit money that it chooses; (the Government determines the "reserves" of the commercial banks—the "reserves" of the commercial banks are the Government's bank credit money). (Ch. IV.)

A monetary system is thus created wherein the Government alone determines the creation and existence of a universal value form for all material goods, and for all capitals and capital goods, and for all capital papers.

With such a money and banking system, the Government can inflate, or cause the inflation of any volume of bank credit money it chooses, and maintain this body of money as a permanent, non-deflating body of money, despite a constant depreciation. (The inflation can include a private inflation, if the Government chooses to permit it.)

—The Government can create and maintain, at its will, independent of any private individual or unit, its interest bearing bonds and notes, as a permanent constantly expanding, constantly refunded, fictive capital form.

—Since the Government has the real power of money creation of the *sole* circulating money form, it can purchase any goods it chooses at normal price. The ultimate meaning of the latter is that goods will be produced for the Government's effective demand; the Government can cause this critical mass of goods to be produced, and be a value, and be part of the Aggregate Profit. Hence, too, this money and banking system is one of the essential bases of the fictive *profit* form, itself (i.e., the basis of an effective tax system).

Gold. The transfer of the fundamental economic power from private individuals to the Government.

In effect, the acquisition and sequestration of gold (and forbidding the private use of gold as money, in the buying and selling of material goods, or the buying and selling and creation of capital papers, or the buying and selling of the paper money itself, or as a private bank reserve) is the effective transfer of power not only over money, but over material production itself, from private hands to the Government. The real basis for the independence of the ICE and the private power of the capitalists, was the private possession of gold.

But the monetary unit of the pefcp is still a weight of gold and the standard of price, and gold is still the measure of value. (Ch. II, Secs. 14, 17 on the nature of Money, and Price.) Gold is money in the pefcp; but only the Government possesses this money (except in certain instances in foreign exchange). The production of goods and the banking system are ineluctably on a gold basis at whatever the equivalency of the paper money to gold actually is, or whatever weight of gold the Government declares for the monetary unit, or whatever the price level of the economy in this unique paper money form of the pefcp. (Ch. IV.)

The private possession and use of gold is a mortal danger to an economic system based on fictive forms. It can destroy the system itself and the ever increasing volume of fictive capital papers, as well as the money and banking system. This brings up a major problem of the political economy: The Government can protect the domestic economy by sequestering gold, etc., and insulate the pefcp from any threat by gold; but there is one necessity for the use of gold that may threaten the system. Gold is the international money. Paper money that finds its way abroad may have to be redeemed in gold. And foreign nations and foreign individuals may use gold—and foreign held paper money—speculatively, or hostilely. Or, because of domestic necessities in foreign trade, the domestic power over gold and paper money may be threatened. (Ch. IV, Part II.)

The problem of gold and foreign exchange has to be considered in the context of the trade among political economies based on fictive forms. To begin with, international trade and international exchange proceed on a different basis than in the ICE. The dynamics of inherent capital expansion, the business cycle, are gone. In the pefcp, the *domestic* level of production is determined and maintained by the level of Government expenditure (and the tax–borrowing–inflation mix in Government revenue), i. e., not the dynamic of the ICE. Yet there must be a foreign trade. Certain goods must be purchased abroad because the goods themselves are essential for the function of the national political economy, at whatever level the Government determines the economy shall function. The goods are necessary for the productive and distributive systems, and possibly for the welfare and military systems. Trade therefore is essential for the existence of the political economy, and the level of certain political economies may be absolutely dependent upon their imports and exports. An equivalent value of goods must be sold abroad to obtain the foreign exchange needed to purchase goods abroad. And, in this context too, the inflated money of each national political economy, crystallizing as the Pseudo Profit B, will be seeking investment, and this will include foreign investment.

In each national political economy, the same fictive processes are proceeding, but the several elements in the process (the fictive capital forms—public and private, the inflation of paper money—public and private, the tax rate and its volume) are mixed in different proportions in each national political economy. The degree of inflation and degree of depreciation of the paper money differs in each national economy; the domestic price level in each may be moving upward at a higher or lower rate than others.

Before considering the immense difficulties of foreign trade and exchange in this context (even in an equilibrum), note that any continuous purchase abroad in excess of sales abroad (by the nationals of any pefcp), assuming for certain reasons this is possible over a period of time, is inherently injurious to the pefcp. The Government (of these individuals purchasing goods abroad at a higher level than material goods are purchased by the individuals of the foreign countries) cannot obtain by *tax* or *borrowing*, that part of the Aggregate Profit of the producers of the goods, necessary to maintain the domestic goods-money circuit, at the given level of production, Aggregate Profit, and Wage Profit Ratio. Foreign producers of goods cannot be taxed (by the domestic Government), nor are they likely to lend part of their Aggregate Profit abroad. In the pefcp then, a significant imbalance in purchase of goods abroad must result in increased inflation at home (i.e., the proper tax—borrowing—inflation mix is disturbed). Inflation is a consequence of trade imbalance as well as a cause. (Counterbalancing force: the special situation wherein U.S. paper money is held abroad as bank reserve, and as a fictive capital form of foreign political economies.)

The basic rule then is that each political economy *must seek* an equilibrium in the trade of goods, and an equilibrium in the foreign exchange. Each Government must utilize every means that it can to maintain this balance, including all the standard techniques of a pefcp, of exchange controls, export import quotas, the devaluation of its monetary unit. Actually no political economy (possible exception, the U.S. for a time) can do this by itself; there must be at least a regional cooperation, and an international cooperation. Certainly some cooperation is absolutely essential for a reasonably high trade level.

But whatever the techniques and subtleties and skills of management, fundamental disequilibrium (in foreign trade and exchange) will always exist in every pefcp. The inescapable difficulties can only be ameliorated by international cooperation and regional cooperation. Yet, unilateral control over the gold weight of the monetary unit, over foreign exchange, and trade restrictions, must be retained, and sometimes exercised. It is possible that the "Special Drawing Rights," a new, recently created international fictive capital form, may resolve some of the problems.

While no pefcp can maintain the established gold weight of its monetary unit in international trade and exchange indefinitely, the U.S. could do so for a much longer time than any other political economy. The U.S. money was unique, because of the size and power of the political economy, and its possession of the great mass of gold. The paper money of the U.S. became the "paper gold" of the political economies, and as a reserve money it became a fictive capital form for the foreign political economy. The unique position of the U. S. paper money was of great advantage to the U. S., but it placed its paper money in a position of danger, both domestically and internationally.

–7–

"Welfare" and "Military" System of Distribution and Use of Goods, in the WMS.

In this political economy the great volume of goods that the Government acquires, although produced as if new, additional capital goods, must not be used as capital goods, i.e., used for the production of other goods. They must be wholly consumed without other material goods resulting. And they cannot be used in such a way that the capital-labor relationship in the dependent capitalist organism of the pefcp will be disturbed, i.e., as consumption goods by capitalists, but especially not by "labor." The private employment relationship at the customary wage levels, must be maintained, and the availability of labor for such employment must continue. Nor may the goods be permitted to re-enter the market, since they will destroy the market for current and future production. And yet the goods must be used in a way deemed socially desirable and necessary: no program of direct physical destruction is permissible.

The "Welfare" and "Military" systems of distribution and use conform to the requirements of a political economy based on the fictive expansion of capital. But it would be absurd to speak of the "Welfare" and "Military" systems of distribution and use as being devised for the political economy, just as it is unrealistic to speak of the fictive forms as being devised to be substitutes for the real expansion of capital, etc. "Welfare" and "Military" ideologies are of the essence of the State, and the basis for its existence. These ideologies are the dynamic for the production of the goods, and their purchase, and their use.

But Welfare and Military ideology itself, becomes transformed in the actual State and Economy, by the creation of systems of distribution and use of goods suitable and necessary for a political economy based on fictive forms. A Welfare class is maintained, utilizing the goods produced for the State; an immense, always expanding Military establishment is maintained for a State engaged in ideological warfare and defense, but avoiding actual war. (Refer to Chapter VI and Topic 8 below on the nature of the social process: that ideologies that create and maintain a State, and the structure and form of the State itself, become transformed into forms suitable for the needs of the actual economic relationship.) Nevertheless, the ideology has its own vitality and dynamic. Welfare ideology, among other things, in part realizes the long history of human efforts to ameliorate poverty, illness, and old age.

The main purpose of the analysis of "Welfare" and "Military" systems of distribution and use, as they function in *actuality,* is to examine them in the light of the general laws of distribution and use of goods of this political economy (Ch. V, Sec. I). It is not easy to administer Welfare expenditures to conform with the laws of the political economy. If ideology alone is followed, considerable damage can result. Most of the "Welfare" expenditures are to a Welfare class—individuals not engaged in material production or economically useful to the economy except as consumers, and this class is carefully delimited. In general a subsistence or below subsistence level must be provided. A necessary part of the Welfare class is a large group of unemployed, but employable individuals. How large this can be is a difficult political economic problem. In general, no political economy based on fictive forms can properly maintain "full employment" without injuring the mechanisms of the economy. The unemployable, children of the Poor, the "Poor" generally, including some marginally employed, and large parts of certain social classes, para welfare groups (Veterans), are others that make up the class. One of the most important groups is the "old age" group that is "retired." Certain types of distribution, of great cost, may seemingly not be limited to a class, but here it will be found that the goods and services would not be produced in such volume, and could not be paid for privately, and the production and consumption takes place mainly because of the nature of the political economy.

The Welfare system of distribution and use cannot be used alone; if an adequate Military Program is not in existence, the welfare program must be supplemented by an extensive public works system of expenditure (much larger than the conventional "public works" of the Democratic State). But even the latter is an inadequate substitute for a military program of expenditure. Such a program seems essential to secure a high Level Welfare Program (as it is essential for a high level economy). In general, the type of goods purchased by the Government and its distributees must be such that all capitals of the dependent organism are producing for the Government and its distributees. The purchases must be congruent with the sources of the WM tax.

Little needs to be said of Military and para Military programs of use and distribution of goods. These programs are suitable for the needs of the political economy, and fulfill all requirements with respect to non-capital use of goods, non interference with employer-labor relationships, etc. The defense requirements of the WMS (in which an immense, technologically advanced military establishment and armament is constantly maintained) requires a high level of production. Every sector of the economy is drawn upon, especially the essential heavy "capital" goods industries. The equipment itself obsolesces rapidly, even if not actually destroyed in warfare.

But the Military Program must be operated without a large scale all out war. This would destroy the pefcp. War itself may be utilized if it is carefully restricted to the Little War. All actual war must be highly restricted, not only for economic reasons, but political reasons. The Little War that achieves nothing in military terms, may be useful ideologically (as well as economically). Furthermore the Little War lays the foundation for immense future welfare benefits.
(Ch. V, other related forms of use and distribution of goods: exploration of space; man on the moon; research and development in military and atomic technology. Other modes of Welfare expenditure: foreign assistance, etc.).

–8–

The syllabus presents a political economy, the true nature of which is socially unknown. The ideas that prevail socially (ideology), both economic and political, are inadequate to describe it. Yet this ideology

–is essential to the existence of the State, and the political economy,
–is explicable through the nature of the actual relationship.

The ideas are themselves phenomena of the relationship, existing by the same necessity as the relationships, and by the same necessity as true ideas. In the WMS-pefcp, ideology and fictions have an execptional role as functional parts of the relationships themselves.

It is the inherent powers of State and Government (wherein ideology is obviously so important an element) that make a political economy based on fictive forms possible. But this is not to be understood as meaning that the political relationship creates the form of the economic relationship. The dynamics are actually in the economic relationship, and it is this relationship that shapes the form of the political relationship.

Structure-ideology-dynamics, the nature of the political relationship, all require further analysis, to set forth the entire nature of the WMS and the pefcp. The procedure (Ch. VI) is to first examine *generally*, the relationships constituting the social structure and the nature and necessity of ideology; the laws of the interrelationship among the several relationships, and ideology; the process of social change; and then to apply the analysis to the WMS-pefcp.

Defined generally: the four relationships in a modern society, —the economic relationship, political relationship (State and Government), "family" relationship, "Church" relationship. Each relationship is a necessary one in society. An ideology, ideas descriptive and imperative, socially prevailing—is a necessary part of each relationship and of the society. Man functions in the particular relationship through an ideology of a definite form and content. The ideology makes it possible for the actual relationships to function. The ideology does not disclose the nature of the relationship, and indeed, this need not be known for the relationship to function. Utility and power alone are the necessary requirements of ideology.

However, ideology is always found to be related to the actual relationship. It is at least "congruent" with the relationship, but more often directly supportive, or a functional part of the relationship itself. The whole social ideology is an interconnected and coherent pattern. This cannot be seen until the actual relationships are stated. The reason for the interconnection appears in the general laws of a social structure.

The two basic laws of social structure are:

I. In a particular social structure, all relationships and all ideas socially prevailing, are congruent and consistent with and support the existing *economic* relationship. The political relationship, the "family" relationship, the "Church" relationship will be found to have a certain form. The ideology of each relationship will be found to have a certain content—ultimately congruent with and supporting the economic relationship.* In a particular society, all relationships and ideologies will be consistent with each other. (The actual political relationship cannot be known or described, unless the actual economic relationship is known; this is often true of the other relationships.)

II. A *natural selection* operates in the society, choosing the elements appropriate for each relationship, and selecting or emphasizing ideas appropriate for the relationship. The underlying dynamic of this natural selection is in the prevailing economic relationship. (Note: the specific economic *relationship,* not economic motivation generally, is what is referred to). This dynamic force operates even though the true nature of the economic relationship is not socially known, nor the nature of the other relationships, nor the actual role of the ideas that will prevail socially. In the process of selection of elements and ideas, useless and incongruous elements, and incongruous ideas, are rejected or socially ignored. The economic motivation of the upper class of the particular existing economic relationship plays a significant role in this process of natural selection and maintenance of relationships, ideas, etc.

The *pragmatic test* (in choice, or rejection of elements, ideas) is *utility* for the function of the economic relationship, and the effectiveness of its function.

Social Change. (in general).

From the foregoing laws of social structure, the following law can be deduced:

The whole social pattern (economic relationship, political

*While an ideology is generally false or inadequate to explain or describe the actual relationships in the society, the socially prevailing religious ideology and related ethical ideas—usually part of a "Church" relationship—may seem to include the true ideas of God, man's conduct, etc. However, when true ideas become part of the socially prevailing religious ideology in any particular economic-political structure, by certain processes they are transvalued so that they can be used to support and maintain the existing economy and political structures of the society, and the ideology as a whole follows the general laws of congruence, utility, natural selection. It is not the power of the idea as true idea that makes it part of the socially prevailing ideology.

relationship, "family" relationship, "Church" relationship) and the whole ideology of the society, will change if the economic relationship changes; and conversely, the society will not basically change if the economic relationship does not change.

The power of a *new* economic relationship, then, is central to the *possibility* of a social change. But this dynamic creates only the possibility of the success of the new economic relationship and a consequent total social change. There must also be an effective revolutionary ideology and movement seeking to create a new political relationship (sometimes a new religious ideology). This ideology and movement must be able to establish a new State and Government (sometimes a new Church). Needless to say, the State, etc. finally established will be something different than the revolutionary ideology contemplates. But the new State, etc. will be congruent and supportive of the new economic relationship.

In the process of social change, then, ideology and movement have a more active, dynamic role than in the established social structure, where, necessary as ideology is, its content is simply determined by the existing economic relationship. When the new economic relationship is established it will dominate the social structure, and as stated above, will shape all other relationships, and the content of all ideologies.

The central dynamic force of the new economic relationship:

A new economic relationship may become the prevailing economic relationship (displacing the existing economic relationship, or succeeding to it), if it is more productive of material goods than the existing economic relationship, or rival economic relationships. But it is not general productivity alone that constitutes its dynamism. Economic relationships almost invariably have an economic class structure (of a type wherein there is a power possessed by the upper economic class to obtain part of the current material production because of individual or group ownership of some property form), and it is more important that the new economic relationship would result in a wealthier and more powerful new upper economic class, than that general productivity be greater, although both seem to exist together. Superior productivity in general, and particularly for the new upper economic class, is the *dynamism* of the new economic relationship to effect a change from an existing economic relationship.*

Assuming the existence of both a dynamic for economic change, and a revolutionary ideology and movement (neither of which separately can be effective), nevertheless there is still no determinism that the economic and social change will take place. The dynamism is not a determinism. And stated negatively: no political movement inconsistent with the existing economic relationship, and not supported by a new dynamic economic relationship, can succeed. Unlike the "determinism" that exists within a social structure once the economic relationship is established, the process of social change is indeterminate, and there are many variables, including chance.

Economic Dynamism for a WMS-pefcp. Movements and ideologies that led to the WMS.

Upon the collapse of the ICE, there was a powerful economic dynamism for the establishment of the WMS and its political economy in those countries where the Independent Capitalist Economy had been fully developed. It was far stronger an economic dynamism than that towards a Communist economy and State. The WMS-pefcp in its fully developed form (i.e. embodying both the "Welfare" and "military" systems of distribution) is more productive generally than any other reasonably possible economic relationship; specifically it is more productive than a Communist economic relationship, *and* it provides for the existence of an upper economic class based on property rights.

There were effective ideologies and movements that led to the WMS, once its economic dynamic came into existence. The "fascist" ideology and movement is most clearly to be discerned. This ideology, with its mysticist concepts of State, Government, leader, and an economy absolutely subject to the

*This means that it will be rare that there will be an economic dynamism for a "Communist" economic relationship. But it may exist under certain conditions. Yet even with a strong economic dynamism, a strong movement, there is no determinism that it will succeed.

State, was suitable for a WMS, of the more aggressive, warlike type. This ideology could not succeed while the ICE was viable. Of course, the actual State and the actual economy (the WMS, the pefcp) that eventuated were not those described by the ideology. In other countries, an ideology for a "Welfare" State, utilizing some elements of the ideology of the "Democratic State," but influenced by Socialist concepts, was the moving force. (And, again, the State and economy that came into being were much different than the ideology.) However, the latter was effective for only a political economy with a low level of production. The full form—the Welfare-Military State, did not develop until the conflict with the aggressive fascist States. The WMS with the "rationalist" ideology became the dominant form. They were not only ultimately more powerful, but immeasurably superior in their humanity. The United States, as a WMS, embodying (and in part fulfilling) the best elements of the ideology of the Democratic State, represents a polity and economy superior to their predecessors, and to any existing State and economy.

–9–

The Political Economy Based on Fictive Forms, and the Welfare-Military State, must come to an end.

This political economy, this State, are mortal, as were the ICE and the Democratic State. The political economy must reach a point (called the absolute economic critical point) where there can be no real capital expansion, but rather a contraction of the Aggregate capital sets in, *and* the pseudo Profit B must begin to steadily decline, the fictive forms losing their value and utility, finally becoming inadequate to create the pseudo Profit B. Once the fictive expansion of capital fails (or declines to a very low level), the inevitable downward spiral with a continuing contraction of the Level of Production and Income, means an inadequate production for all economic classes—capitalists, labor, Welfare, Military. As the Level declines the Welfare demands increase, but the goods available become less.

The most striking manifestations of the inherent disorder are first, the decline in the return of the W M tax, and this will not only be in its volume, but in its rate, as an attempt is made to increase the profit rate; the second, which parallels the tax decline, is the great increase in the creation of fictive capital papers, which must result in an increased *inflation* of the paper money. The compulsion of the Government to increase the inflation will lead to a malignant inflation, which will destroy the value and utility of the fictive capital papers, and ultimately the existing money form.

However, because of the nature of the WMS and the national societies in which the WMS exist, and the passions of the ideologies of all national societies, it is not likely that the WMS will fail quietly. It is more likely that a war, possibly thermonuclear, will bring about an abrupt end. The danger of thermonuclear war arises not so much from the existence of the WMSs, but the prospect of their collapse. It is conceivable that preceding such a catastrophe, the entire system of production may be converted into a system af production for military use conducted by the State directly. In any event, the existing political economy must end, and with it the existing political structure. The end of the political economy and State can be hastened by inept management; it can be delayed by skilled management; it is not likely to be averted.

The nature of the social order that will evolve when the WMS-pefcp comes to its end, cannot be predicted. Assuming a technology even further advanced over the present, a still greater overpopulation and overutilization of the natural environment, and the divisive international structure, there can be no return to any prior social order.* In particular, the ICE—Democratic State, or the capital unit, cannot exist; the society

*The social consequences flowing from a pefcp, obscure the future. The pefcp is a major cause of overpopulation and over utilization of resources. Furthermore, it leads to the constant escalation in size of a welfare class, and a great population on the periphery of this class. While most of the cultural changes are simply new ideological forms resulting from the economic-political change, they include elements destructive to basic human values.

envisaged by the Marxist ideology of the 19th century, or any older ideal, is no longer possible.*

The course of social change is ultimately indeterminate. Society may be moving towards some change the nature of which the history of past societies cannot inform the present. While it is hard to conceive that the economic relationship and powerful economic motivations therein, will not, as before, govern the form of the social structure and its ideologies, it is not impossible because of absolute necessity, that a different dynamic will determine the form of the society.

Abbreviations Frequently Used:

ICE	Independent Capitalist Economy
Pefcp	Political Economy of Fictive Capital and Profit
PE	Political Economy
BCM (bcm)	Bank Credit Money
GCRB	Government Central Reserve Bank
Aecp	Absolute Economic Critical Point
Recp	Relative Economic Critical Point

*Caution: the existing Communist societies are much different than represented by their ideologies, which are adaptations of 19th century Marxist ideology.

Chapter II

THE INDEPENDENT CAPITALIST ECONOMY

Part I

The Independent Capitalist Economy as an Organism.
The Structure and the Dynamics of the Organism.
The Capital Unit.

(1) The "Independent" Capitalist Economy. (ICE)

The capitalist economy described in this Chapter is the "Independent" capitalist economy (ICE). The word "independent" has two connotations herein. The first refers to the essential nature of this economy. The Aggregate capital is *self-expanding*: the capital is able to expand itself to an extent sufficient, as will be seen, to enable this capitalist economic relationship to exist as an independent economy. The second connotation is, that as an *economic* relationship, it functions independent of and apart from the State (although the State and Government are necessary for its existence). The Government does not manage the Economy.

The word "Independent" thus contrasts this economic relationship with the "dependent" capitalist organism of the Welfare-Military State. This latter organism is not one apart from the State, but is an integral part of the State; the State is a political economy.

The Independent capitalist economy existed for several centuries (until approximately 1930). In any period of its existence, the same basic relationship of individuals (in the capital unit, and in the system as a whole) is always found. However, the period of the ICE usually referred to in this Chapter is its terminal one:—technologically highly advanced, with large scale capital units (the highly "concentrated" economy), functioning with a fully developed financial and banking system. The structure of the capitals, and the financial institutions of this period differ somewhat from the earlier ICE. (Section 13.)

Although the independent and the dependent systems are fundamentally different organisms and have fundamentally different dynamics, there is a similar relationship of individuals in the *capital units* engaged in the production of material goods, and in the buying and selling of material goods, in each. Although significant changes in the basic forms (capital, money, profit, wage, price) take place in the dependent organism, in the managemnet of the dependent organism by the WM State, these forms must be managed as forms of the capitalist relationship, or as fictions thereof.

(2) The 'Capital Unit' is the basic unit of the structure of the capitalist economy. The relationship of individuals in the capital unit is the same as the relationship of all the individuals in the capitalist system, in the production and distribution of material goods.

The production of material goods is carried on by a great number of separate, independent *capital units,* each producing a particular good.

The individuals who comprise the unit have a distinctive relationship to each other. Five terms—money, capital, wage, profit and price—are used to describe the relationship of the individuals in the capital unit. The terms are used in the following summary description of the capital unit in a simple sense, as they appear to the practical man in everyday affairs. But the terms will ultimately be seen to be far more complex. (Actually, these forms arise only out of a general relationship in a particular *system* of production and distribution of material goods, and only in this general relationship, or system, do they exist for *unit* and individual. As will be seen in the succeeding sections, the terms describe the *structure* and the *mechanism* of a system, or more precisely an organism composed of these separate units, and only as elements of a system are they meaningful in describing the structure and mechanism of each unit.)

Summary description of the relationship in the capital unit:

The capitalist (owner of the capital unit) advances money (out of *capital*) to buy materials and equipment necessary for the production of goods, from other capital units. The capitalist hires labor, for a *wage* (which also is money advanced out of capital) to work in the process of production. The capitalist owns the goods produced, and sells them at a *price*, above their cost of production, and the price, if it is "normal" returns a money *profit*, at a certain rate based on the whole amount of capital used by the unit in the process of production.

Corollary Statement, 1:

Each unit produces goods for *sale*, i.e' for use or consumption by others, (not produced for use or consumption by the producing unit, or for consumption in common by a producing group).

Sale implies the existence of the money form, as a *value* equivalent, and the payment of a money equivalent for the value produced.

The wage earners buy necessaries with their wage, from the capital units; the capitalists buy necessaries with part of their profit, from other capital units; the capitalists buy goods necessary for the process of production from other capital units.

Corollary Statement, 2:

Each unit produces goods solely for profit. The purpose of the production is not the goods in themselves (as for their use for the consumption of the capitalists, or the consumption of the wage earners), but for that part of their *money value* that constitutes profit.

Corollary Statement, 3:

The productive process in the capital unit is distinctive: first, the laborers act in concert, with all physical processes of production subdivided among them (division of labor) always to an increasing degree; second that mechanical power and not human power is used, and all processes are mechanized and automated as far as possible.

The manufacturing unit is used herein as the prototypical capital unit. In mining, agriculture, communications, transportation, retail and wholesale trade, the pattern of relationships is comparable.

The capital unit is the basic unit of the whole relationship, and the relationship (system, structure, organism) can only exist if there are separate capital units. That is to say: the capitalist relationship as system is not one of some hypothetical, single, great collective capital, in which a body of labor is hired by a collective "capital" for a collective "wage" with the collective capital making a "profit"; price being some artificial concept determined in a collective system of distribution. A great number of *separate* capital units is of the essence of a capitalist relationship of individuals in each unit.

(3) All the capital units function as parts of a system; actually as parts of an 'organism,' inasmuch as the units function as parts of a whole, and the function of the whole determines the function of each individual unit.

.1 The relationship appearing in the unit must necessarily be or have been established as a *general system* of production of goods. The system will be constituted by a great number of separate units in each of which the relationship of the *system* prevails. (The system relationship is primary, but separate units are the essential nature of the system and relationship). The terms money, capital, wage, profit, price, that describe the relationship in the unit, derive their meaning and function in every unit, from their meaning and function in the system.

(a) A system is implicit in the nature of the relationship of the individuals in the capital unit; a system is implicit in the necessary relations of each unit to the other.

(b) All individuals in the economy relate to each other through money—the general form of value of material goods, —and this includes the buying and selling of services.
(c) In particular, the individuals in the unit, and the units, must function through a *general market.* The goods-money circuit among all the individuals and units, in the general market, is based on an *effective demand* arising out of the system of production, and the supply of goods arises out of the same system of production. (Sec. 5, below).

.2 The capitalist organism then, is a relationship of individuals (in separate capital units) wherein the capitalists advance money for goods and wages for employees, for production of material goods, for *sale,* at a *profit.* The sale is to other units, or individuals who obtain their income by way of wage and profit through the unit that produces the good (or transferees of these incomes).

The goods are sold at a price that contains the profit. The Aggregate profit is the value of all goods produced (Aggregate Price), minus the value of the capital and wage used up in the production of the goods produced; (or profit may be conceived as part of the value of the particular good in excess of the cost of the capital used up in the production of the good, including the wage). In this organism, and in every unit, production is not and cannot be carried on for the goods themselves (i.e., for the use of the goods by the producers or the wage earners) but solely for a value to be obtained by sale. And further, necessarily, production in the organism and each unit thereof is carried on *solely for profit*—not for the return of the value advanced in the production.

The four Aggregates

Aggregate Capital
Aggregate Wage
Aggregate Profit
Aggregate Price (normal) of the goods produced and sold

in their inherent interrelationships, generally state the *structure* and *mechanism* of the *organism.*

The goods-money circuit in the general market, and the formula of the Level of Production and Income, in this circuit (Sec. 5), is the primary description of the structure and mechanism of the organism.

An equilibrium of goods produced and goods purchased in the general market (in this goods-money circuit) means that the constituents of the effective demand are the same as the money advanced for the production, plus the Profit. (Stated alternatively: the Aggregate Price is Normal).

.3 But Profit, (Aggregate Profit, and hence Profit in each unit part of the organism) has its origin solely in the relationship in the *organism.*

The formulary structure (Aggregate Capital, Aggregate Wage, Aggregate Profit, Aggregate Normal Price of goods produced and sold) is based on a *ratio* in the organism, between Aggregate Wage and Aggregate Profit, that is, a certain proportion in the Net Aggregate Price of goods produced and sold (the wage-profit ratio). The establishment and maintenance of this ratio in the organism is the essence of the relationship in the organism (and hence in each unit of the organism). That is to say, an *average wage rate* must be socially established at a certain level. The Aggregate Wage, then, is advanced at such average rate that the Aggregate Wage will be only a certain percentage of the net value of the goods sold (in equilibrium), and hence a certain ratio to Aggregate Profit. This is a *definite* and determinable percentage in the organism. The usual wage-profit ratio in the organism, in the later ICE is about 1 to 2. (Secs. 15, 16, 17).

If the goods produced by the organism can be sold at a price in which the established wage-profit ratio exists, the Aggregate Price is said to be normal.

Fundamental Inference: given the wage-profit ratio, profit is always *possible,* but the goods must be sold at normal price. But the normal price demands an equilibrium, and the conditions of the equilibrium depend on the dynamics of the organism (below).

.4 The Aggregates of the organism (Aggregate Capital, Aggregate Wage, Aggregate Profit, Aggregate Price) are the *primary* forms, structurally, etc., in the organism, and hence each unit of the organism, functions through these Aggregates. The Aggregates *are not additions* of these forms in each unit, but the unit manifestations exist and come into being *as parts of the wholes*. (Each unit's function in production, price, wage, profit depends on and is controlled by the Aggregates of the organism).

- –The profit of the particular unit is a share of the Aggregate profit
- –The total price of goods produced and sold by the unit is a part of the Aggregate Price of all goods produced and sold. The normality of the Aggregate Price determines the normality of the price of all goods sold by the unit, i.e., normal profit, and the normality of the price of the particular good. (Level of production of the unit is determined by the Level of organism, as to volume, value, profit).
- –The total wage paid by the unit is a share of the Aggregate Wage, and is determined by the Aggregate Wage. (The average wage rate is determined in the organism). (Sections 15, 16, 17.)

.5 The *organism h*as its own fundamental law of function; this is herein called the dynamism of the organism. (The dynamics of the organism is thus the dynamics of every unit of the organism, although this is never apparent to any particular unit.) The fundamental law of function (dynamism) arises out of the inherent nature of the organism and the relationship in the organism. The fundamental law is:

> The organism can exist, and the organism can maintain itself in equilibrium, only if the Aggregate Capital constantly expands (constant new investment for new, additional capital); the Level of production of the organism, and the Net Income of all individuals, depends upon and is determined by the existence of the capital expansion, and its degree.

The nature of the organism is to produce goods for new, additional capital. Production for profit means production for new, additional capital. The profit can and must be in part goods that become capital, and as capital, will produce profit. Production of new capital does not take place if profit is not possible, and profit declines or disappears if new capital goods are not produced and sold. Corollaries: If the organism is not in equilibrium (capital expanding), the Level of Production and Income will always spirally contract (Sec. 8); there is no stable Level in the organism.

.6 The basic law of the organism determines the existence, and governs the function of each unit of the organism, and the economic existence of every individual. (The units function as parts of the whole, and the function of the whole determines the function of each unit).

(4) Continued: To demonstrate the basic dynamic of the organism, it is necessary to assume a stability and normality of each element of structure and function of the organism. In actuality, such stability and normality are not usually present because many forces, including the inherent cyclic nature of capital expansion and the Level of Production and Income of the organism, and monetary manipulation, are changing price levels, wage rates, profit rates, etc.

It has been stated that "Money" "Capital" "Wage" "Profit" and "Price" not only state the relationship and structure of the organism (as "Aggregates," and in the relationships between the Aggregates, as in the Wage-Profit ratio, the "Normal" Price—Normal Aggregate Price and Normal Price of the individual good), but they also embody the mechanisms of function of the organism (and hence of each unit).

The exposition of the foregoing is in Part II of this Chapter. The amplification of structure and mechanism is essential to fully understand the dynamics of the organism. Indeed, it is in such exposition that the true nature of the dynamics most clearly appears. However, there is a constant variation in the function of each element, and the variations in each cause variations in the others, and the actual situation is complex.

It was determined that the best course in the presentation would be to set forth the nature of the dynamics first (particularly since this is the fundamental basis for the analysis of the pefcp) with a minimum of discussion of the terms by which structure and mechanism are described, and to *assume* the simplest situation—of equilibrium, of stability, normality, adequacy, of each. (Whole systems of economics are based on variations in each form, on "supply and demand" schedules, etc., which only conceal the basic structure, mechanism, and dynamics of the economy). It may be necessary for the reader to refer to the sections on Money, Wage, etc. in Part II, in connection with the following further discussion of dynamics of the organism, particularly of the goods-money circuit of the organism (Sec. 5) and the identities of the Profit B, the new investment, and the new expanded capital. (Sec. 7).

Assume that money is gold, and the monetary unit a specific weight of gold—the dollar during the ICE was 1/20 an oz. of gold, 9/10 fine—and that *gold is privately owned.* Assume the existence of paper money instruments that represent the monetary unit, especially the characteristic paper money form of the capitalist relationship—bank credit money created by commercial banks and a Government bank. Assume further:

That the paper money represents in the circulation, the weight of gold it purports to represent;

That the supply of monetary media is adequate for the needs of the production and distribution of material goods;

That the banking system is adequate and functioning properly;

That there is no inflation, and no depreciation of the paper money. (Secs. 12 on why "money" appears to be a dynamic, and 14, and 17, generally).

Further assumptions:

That the price level is stable

That the Aggregate Price of goods sold is Normal:

—Hence, the Wage-Profit ratio of the Net Aggregate Price of goods sold is the conventional one prevailing in equilibrium.

—Hence, there is normal price of individual goods in all or most sectors of the economy.

All of the foregoing imply an equilibrium in the general market of the organism, which, as stated in Sec. 8, means that capital is expanding, and that the phase of the business cycle is not affecting price level, wage rate, profit rate.

(Refer to Sec. 17 generally: The price of a good is its exchange value stated in the prevailing monetary unit. That which affects the monetary unit, or its paper representative, affects the price level, and hence the price of each good. However: In a capitalist economy, price is not only a mechanism of valuation and exchange, but also the mechanism of function of all relationships in production in the organism and the unit—wage, wage rate, wage-profit ratio, the Aggregate Profit and the rate of Aggregate Profit. With respect to the fundamental wage-profit ratio, refer to Secs. 15 et seq.: The basis for and the premise of "Profit" in the organism lies in the establishment of the average wage rate of the organism at a certain ratio to the Aggregate Profit with respect to the Net Aggregate Price of goods sold. The Wage Profit ratio is considered here in equilibrium; hence the further premise of the existence of Profit is the proper function of the organism, i.e. the expansion of capital so that the goods will be sold at normal price).

The Level of Production of the capitalist organism is properly measured only by the Aggregate Price of goods produced and sold. Income, in the organism, is measured only by the Net Aggregate Price of goods produced and sold (Aggregate Wage plus Aggregate Profit). There are many incomes directly derivative from the Aggregate Wage and the Aggregate Profit.*

The Aggregate Profit is that part of the value of the material goods produced and sold—the Aggregate Price of goods produced and sold, over and above the cost of all materials used up in the production plus the Aggregate Wage advanced. The Aggregate Profit can only be conceived as representing a definite *value* of material goods. Anticipating the discussion in the following sections: The Aggregate Profit always consists in part of the value of new, additional capital goods. This part is called

*The Aggregate Price of all goods sold is not the "Gross National Product" and the Net Aggregate Price is not the "National Income" in the current statistics. These statistics purport to measure something different than the value of all material goods produced in the organism, or their net value.

the *Profit B* part, herein. The part of the Aggregate Profit that is the income of the capitalists expended for goods for their personal consumption is called herein the *Profit A*.

The Aggregate Profit is not received by units and individuals as such; neither are the Profit A or the Profit B received as such entities. The Aggregate Profit is received as Entrepreneur's profit, Interest, Rent (in part) Taxes (in part). There are also derivative incomes from each share of the Aggregate Profit.* (Sec. 16)

(5) The general market of the capitalist economy; The goods-money circuit, and the nature of the Demand, and of the Supply, in the general market. The formulae of the Level of Production and the Net Income, in the goods-money circuit.

.1 *The general market of the capitalist economy.*

A system of production by separate, independent, privately owned capital units, each producing a specialized good for sale, for an equivalent value, must function thru a general market. A general market is as necessary for the capital units as it is for individuals producing specialized goods for the consumption of others, where there is private production for exchange of equivalent value. (*non*capitalist, private production). It is necessary for the same reasons: *exchange* and *valuation* are necessary in such economic relationships.

Exchange is the simpler concept of the two: if each unit, or each individual, produces a specialized good, the producers not only have no use for the product, but they have to acquire necessary goods from other units (or other individual producers), for use in production, and also for the personal consumption of

*"Aggregate Profit" is not the same as "profit" in the National Income statistics. "Profit" in these statistics may include profits arising out of financial transactions, the inflation of paper money, transfers, etc. Shares of the Aggregate Profit can appear as "Wages" in these statistics.

the producers. The general market in a system of private ownership, production for exchange, is indispensible for this purpose. But *valuation*, or more precisely monetization, is a fundamental aspect of the exchange, in such an economic relationship. For in such a system the purpose and essence of the exchange is theoretically the exchange of goods for equal value.* Money is the social form of value: the goods sold are valued at a given amount of money. "Price" is the statement of the exchange value of goods expressed in the prevailing monetary unit.

It is in the market that what is socially valued (in exchange) is determined, and the amount of such value is determined. Not all goods produced have value, or actually have the value as might be indicated by their cost of production. To repeat: exchange, *and* valuation, are necessary in a system where the producers are private individuals, or capital units.

But there is a decisive difference in the goods-money circuit, and the supply-demand constituents, in the market of the capitalist economy, as well as in the valuation ("Normal" price, Section 17). In the simpler (non capitalist–individual producer) system of production for exchange, there probably will be an exchange of value equivalents; furthermore, the flow of goods to purchasers, and the flow of money to the individual producers, etc. is a simple and direct circuit, individual producers being individual consumers. Each individual obtains means to buy by selling (assuming all goods are of equal value).

But this is *not the goods-money circuit of the capitalist economy*. And, again, the price of particular goods, in a capitalist economy is not necessarily their value, for price must be viewed in a *profit* system of production, i.e. normal price, that contains the average rate of profit.

*Exchange for equal value is not always the situation in the capitalist economy. It will be assumed, for the moment. In the capitalist economy, *normal* price of a *particular* good implies only the prevailing entrepreneural profit rate in the particular capital sector producing the good, and this rate may be much different from other sectors. (Section 17—Price.) Normal price of particular goods is based on particular profit rates, not equality of values.

.2 The goods-money circuit in the market of the capitalist economy: What constitutes "goods": and "money": The constituents of "supply" and "demand"; money advance and money return, in a circuit.

Where production and sale is by capital units, the goods-money circuit—the flow between the seller and purchaser—of the goods and money, is of a distinctive nature. The circuit itself evidences the nature of capitalist production, as system or organism. The dynamics, the basic law of the organism is manifested in the circuit. Furthermore, the *formulae,* or *equations* stating the "Level of Production" and "Net Income" are found in this circuit.

As to the "Goods", (Supply produced by all the capital units):

In the capitalist economy, a great part of the goods are produced for use in further production. These are called capital goods. The major part of these goods are "*Producer goods*" but *part of the consumer goods* are also capital goods. These latter are the consumer goods that must be purchased by the wage-earners for their consumption, (with money advanced out of capital for wages). The remainder of the consumer goods are produced for the consumption of the capitalists (and those deriving their income by transfer of these various shares of the Aggregate Profit).

Of the producers goods, some are of a relatively permanent type, others are materials used up immediately in the process of production, being converted into other forms of goods. (It may also be noted that some consumer goods are relatively durable, others not).

This classification is essential in examing the *demand,* both as to class of *purchasers,* and their *money source.*

First, as to *purchasers* who constitute the demand. There are three classes:

Capitalists, who buy *producers* goods of all types for use in production.

Capitalists (and also those who derivatively receive a part

of the Aggregate Profit, from the capitalist in return for personal services, or for other reason), who buy consumer goods for personal consumption.

Wage earners, who work in the *process of material production* (and those who derivatively receive part of Wages paid in material production, for personal services to wage earners, or for other reasons) who buy consumer goods for personal consumption.

As to the *money source*, of the purchasers:

The general rule is that in all constituents of the demand, the ultimate source of the money will be found to be an *advance* from the capitalists, viewed as a *class* (i.e. not viewed as individual capitalists), but the advance is not wholly out of capital. The concept of the circuit, implies the *return* of this money advanced, by means of purchase of the goods from the capitalist owners (as a class). (After the process of production, it is the capitalists, as a class that owns the goods—both producers goods, and consumer goods.)

The money *advance* (that constitutes the effective demand in the circuit) is, as has already been indicated, made in certain definite forms, and these are the very forms that characterize the capitalist system of *production*. Equally important (a) they are made in certain definite proportions—see below, and (b) the *return* crystalizes in these same forms and proportions. The "forms" and sources are:

I. Capital (money) advanced by capitalists—their own money, or borrowed money capital including newly created bank credit money: This purchases the producer goods, including fixed capital goods, materials, replacement goods. (This is the major part of the effective demand in the general market).

II. Capital as new investment—also an advance of capital money, that serves to purchase the *new*, the *additional* goods, the *expanded* capital. This actually is used to purchase not only producer goods—additional fixed capitals, material, etc., but possibly as additional wages for additional wage earners (who purchase consumer goods).

III. Money that the *capitalists* advance to buy consumer goods for their personal consumption. This is an advance by capitalists as a class, (not out of capital). However, to the *individual capitalist it appears that it is an expenditure after realization of profit* (See below, further on "profit" as advance and as return). Include in this advance, an advance on behalf of all those who derive income thru the profit received by capitalists, for personal services, or other reasons. This also appears to individuals as an expenditure *after* receipt of the money.

IV. Purchases by wage earners employed in material production, of goods for personal consumption. This is actually capital money, advanced to the wage earners by the capitalists. Include in these monies, the money received by those who render personal services to wage earners, or obtain the money for other reasons. Include also possible new investment for wage earners employed by the new additional capital.

The *return* of the money advanced by the capitalists (as a class)—the completion of the circuit—is accomplished *by sale of goods by the capitalists* to each respective class of purchasers. (Hypothesis, for the sake of simplicity, is that the sale takes place at normal price):

I. The capital advanced for the producer goods used up in the current production, is recovered. This will include a certain share of the value of the fixed capitals (depreciation).

II. The capitalists (as a class) recover the money capital advanced for the purchase of the new, additional, capital goods. This is returned as part of the Aggregate Profit, that part called herein, "Profit B." (Sec. 7, following, on this critical aspect of the circuit, and the identities of new capital, new investment, Profit B). Note that the return is not to the individual capitalists, or necessarily to the same individuals who advanced the new capital money, but to the capitalists as a class.

III. The capitalists recover the money they themselves advanced to buy goods for their personal consumption. This is returned as part of the Aggregate Profit, herein called "Profit A." (This will include monies advanced to others by the capitalists for personal services rendered, etc., and used to buy goods for personal consumption).

IV. The capitalists recover the money they advanced to the wage earners as wages (i.e. also part of capital advanced). This will also include monies transferred by wage earners to others for personal services, etc., and used to buy goods for personal consumption.

A further explanation of "Profit" as advance, and as return:

As stated, the foregoing must be viewed in the general circuit, and in the economy as a whole, not from the individual's point of view.

It *appears* that profit is received first, and then part is expended for goods for personal consumption (of capitalists). This may be true in individual cases, in the day to day function of units and individuals. But it cannot be true in the organism as a whole. The money profit (here consider, for the moment, the Profit A), comes into being after the sale of the goods But the sale of this part of the consumers goods cannot be effected in the organism unless the money to buy the goods is first *advanced* by the capitalists. This advance is then recovered when the capitalists sell the goods, and it can then be advanced again. The fact that the "*Profit B*" part of the Aggregate Profit is first advanced, is much clearer, for this is the *new investment* for the new capital goods. (What is not so clear is that it is returned to the class that advances it).

The origin of the actual money to buy all the goods produced and sold in a capitalist system has always been a vexatious theoretical problem in economics since the value of goods produced and sold is *always* considerably greater than the money advanced in the production of the goods (i.e. capital advanced including wages). But there is no real difficulty. The money necessary to purchase that part of the goods whose sale will constitute the Aggregate Profit is simply advanced, and since the goods belong to the individual capitalists, the money advanced flows back to themselves as "Profit" as they purchase their own goods (individual producers, individual purchasers).

To the individual capitalist, it seems that he makes his purchases with the profit he has received, but this is an impossibility for the organism as a whole. Necessarily in the organism the money to buy all the goods must be first advanced, as capital and as wages and the money that will constitute the profit.

Since the process of production takes place simultaneously at many levels, and the interchange of goods is continual and at many levels, the actuality of advance and recovery and advance again is concealed.

.3 The formulae of the Level of Production and Net Income in the goods-money circuit.

The Aggregate Price of the goods produced and sold represents the Level of Production of the organism; the Net Aggregate Price of the goods, is the Net Income of the individuals in the economy, and is equivalent to the sum of the Aggregate Profit and the Aggregate Wage.

The foregoing statement of the Level, and Net Income, appears in the goods-money circuit in the market of the capitalist system:

Aggregate Price of goods sold = Capital advanced for materials, equipment, etc., used up in the current production of the goods.
plus Aggregate Wage
plus Aggregate Profit
(Profit A plus Profit B)

Net Aggregate Price of goods sold = Aggregate Wage
plus Aggregate Profit
(Profit A plus Profit B)
= Net Income of Individuals.

These are *equations in the circuit*, and nothing more, for they do not state why the *effective demand* (which is constituted by the three elements) is of the size it is as a whole, or the proportions of each element, or why the Aggregate Price or Net Aggregate Price are of the size they are. Nor should there be any inference that the equations state the existence of a self sustaining circuit, at any Level of the economy, i.e. that the sale of the goods returns the money advanced; or that the money advanced will effect the sale; or that production creates its own demand and the means to purchase it. For, as the basic law of the organism indicates, it is one element of the effective demand, the *new* investment for new and additional capital goods (which becomes the Profit B part of the Aggregate Profit) that determines the size of the entire Aggregate Profit (i.e. it determines the size of Profit A), the Aggregate Wage, and ultimately the amount of capital advanced in current production, and the proportions of the elements of the whole.

With further respect to the statement that the equations: Aggregate Price = Effective demand = some of Capital advanced, plus Aggregate Wage plus Aggregate Profit, are not self-sustaining:
It is only when the Aggregate Price is "normal" (which means that an equilibrium exists because of the new investment for new Capital goods, and hence too, the Wage-Profit ratio is normal, and the ratio between Profit A and Profit B is normal), that the equations, or formulae describe a situation, or describe a circuit in which effective demand is "determining" the Level of Production: the Production is creating the effective demand. That is to say, *only then* is there the self energizing, continuous circuit. But it is an illusion that the formulae or equations can be, in the absence of these conditions, descriptive of a continuity or a dynamism of the capitalist economy, and that the Level is being created by and maintained by an "effective demand." Sale itself, Aggregate Price itself (disregarding for the moment all monetary factors affecting price level) all depend on the proper proportions of Effective demand, and the factor or element determining these proportions, and not simply on overall volume of effective demand.

(6) The basic law of the organism (the expansion of capital) restated and amplified. Its full meaning appears only when stated with its fundamental correlative: That the new, additional capital is 'part' of the Aggregate Profit of the organism (the "Profit B" part).

.1 The essential nature of the system, or organism, and its dynamism, is the production of material goods for new, additional, expanded capital. The Aggregate capital must always be expanding for the system to function. Equilibrium in the market depends on the existence of capital expansion, and the existence of capital expansion constitutes normal function.

If the Aggregate capital cannot expand, it will contract, and as capital contracts, the entire Level of Production and the Net Income enters into a spirally increasing decline (not a decline measured solely by the amount of decrease of the new additional capital) and this continues until capital expansion can take place.

The Level of Production and the Net Income are determined by the existence of and degree of capital expansion. The Aggregate Wage, and the part of the Aggregate Profit that represents the consumer goods that are produced for and purchased by the capitalists (Profit A) are dependent for their existence and volume solely on capital expansion(Profit B).

.2 The new, additional (expanded) capital is part of the Aggregate Profit on the existing capitals; more dynamically stated, part of the Aggregate Profit arises out of the sale of these particular new capital goods that constitute the new, expanded capital. This part of the Aggregate Profit determines the existence of the Aggregate Profit as a whole, the size of the capital advanced, the Aggregate Wage, the Level of Production, and the Net Income as a whole.

Alternative statement: the *new investment* that constitutes the effective demand for the new capital goods, itself becomes part of the Aggregate Profit on the existing capitals; (Sec. 7 on the identity of the new investment, the Profit B and the new additional capital). Further statement, in terms of dynamics—the Profit B comes into existence because of the new investment; new investment takes place because the capital is profitable, i.e., will produce capital that will produce profit. *Corollary* of .1 and .2: The Aggregate Profit expands as the Aggregate capital expands.

The statement of the basic law of the expansion of capital, *and* the correlative, that the new, expanded capital is part of the Aggregate Profit of the existing capitals, are essentially inseparable. Their full meaning appears when they are considered together.

To begin with, in the capitalist economy, production is for *profit*, in each unit, and in the organism *Profit* is the sole purpose of production. Any material good can be produced and sold at a profit if there is a demand for it at the price that returns the profit: new capital goods can (a) be sold at profit and (b) so far as the organism is concerned, constitute part of the profit of the organism. The limit on the production of such goods is the new investment which will be made; i.e. whether the new capital goods themselves will return a profit. (It must always be assumed that if new capital goods are produced and sold, then in the process of production *in the organism* as a whole, the existing capital that has been used up in the production of the goods is reproduced, the wages advanced are recovered, and the goods necessary for the consumption of the capitalists are also produced. This is the meaning of production at profit).

If the profit on the existing capital will in part be constituted by the new, additional capital—since the new investment becomes part of the Aggregate Profit—it is necessary, if the new capital goods are to be purchased, that capital expansion will continue. That is to say, for part of the profit to become capital, the capital must be able to produce profit, (which requires continued capital expansion). Thus the profit exists because part of it, as capital, will also produce profit.

The statement, then, that production in each unit is for profit, and that production of the organism is for profit, should not be understood to mean, simply, that profit is the *incentive.* No doubt, for the unit and the individual, profit is a necessary incentive, but the possibility of profit lies in the dynamics of the organism: the expansion of capital that creates the profit. The question then is, not incentive, but that which creates the profit, and the answer is the need and desire for the new capital itself, provided the new capital is profitable. (Secs. 9, 10, 11, this Chapter).

To repeat: The existing capitals (the organism) will not function profitably, if capital expansion (part of the profit) is not taking place; the new capital part of the profit, will not come into being unless, as new capital, it is profitable. (That is to say the new capital itself can produce for capital expansion, and capital expansion is taking place, there thus being profit on existing capitals.) In other words, the conditional possibility of all profit is that profit on the profit itself (its capital part) is possible. The possibility of the existence and continuance of the system is the existence of profit; capital expansion is the nature of the system.*

It must be inferred from the foregoing that the Level of Production and the Net Income are not governed and determined by consumer needs, or the effective demand of consumers, i.e., the demand of the wage earners—the Aggregate wage, or the demand of the capitalist for consumer goods—Profit A. Nor can the ICE, in itself be converted into a consumer economy. So far as the individual capitalist is concerned, his needs for consumer goods are of significance, but nonetheless he undertakes production for profit, and profit is not determined by his personal needs. The desire of capitalists for consumer goods is not a dynamism of the system. Production of consumer goods depends on the profitability of their production and the existence of profit in the organism. The latter requires the existence of capital expansion. — It will be seen that to approach a satisfaction of consumer needs in the ICE, there must be a marked overexpansion of capital, i.e. a boom. (Sec. 11)

Part of the goods produced are purchased because they are needed or desired for personal consumption. However, most goods produced are sold for one purpose only: to be used in further production of material goods. They are the "capital" goods, (fixed, capital goods, and materials used up in further production). And it is their possible and actual use as capital (i.e. to be used in production to make a profit) that enables these goods to be sold, i.e. to have a value. The existence of a major part of existing capitals depends on the sale of these goods as capital goods.

*Refer to Sec. 16.2, where this is restated in terms of the actual shares of the Aggregate Profit that the individual or unit receives—the entrepreneurs profit, interest (insofar as it is a direct share of the Aggregate Profit) taxes, rent, etc.

All capital goods are produced as and for capital goods. They are not "savings"; capital goods and capital do not come into existence because of the non consumption of goods. This is true of the capital goods used up in production, and of the new additional capital goods. To obtain additional capital goods, the capitalist advances capital and wages to produce these additional capital goods, and this will be done if the product can be sold as capital goods (used as capital goods), which means that their use in production is profitable. Capital goods–replacement capital or new, additional capital–are themselves produced for profit, and they are sold because the goods can be used to make profit.

(7) Recapitulation, and necessary inferences, on

(a) Identity of—the new additional capital
—the new capital investment
—the Profit B part of the Aggregate Profit

(b) That none of these are "savings"

(c) That there is an internal circuit of Profit B—new capital investment; that the capitalist as a class, receive the Profit B and the new additional capital, although the same individual investors generally do not

(d) That "savings" of Wages, Profit A (not offset by deferred expenditures), have a minor effect on the circuit, and little significance in the basic dynamism.

The new additional capital is constituted by certain material goods produced and sold. These are mainly producers' goods, but there are some additional consumer goods for additional wage earners, although the last is not necessarily the situation. It is the sale of this part of the production for new capital, that will result in the Profit B part of the Aggregate Profit. As a corollary: this part of the Aggregate Profit comes into being as money, only when and if the goods are purchased for this new additional capital.

The money that is advanced to purchase the goods, is called the new capital investment. This is capital money, owned by the capitalists, existing ones, or new ones. Under certain circumstances the money may be bank created for the purpose of purchasing the new capital goods.

On the purchase of the new capital goods, the new investment (money) becomes part of the *income* of the capitalists producing the goods (part of the Aggregate Profit, the Profit B).

But this *income,* the Profit B, must necessarily have a capital form or assume a capital form. It could have been directly spent by the individual capitalist, presumably "out of profit" to expand his capital, and the income then clearly appears as a capital form, but in any event the new investment as a whole itself has purchased capital goods either directly or indirectly, and the income has a capital form. On the return of the money (Profit B) to the capitalist as a class the money resumes its role as money capital, and is not spent by them for consumer goods. The consumer goods are purchased by money advanced and returned as Profit A.

As a class, the capitalists who make the new investment are those who receive the Profit B, as entrepreneur's profit, interest, etc. The conclusion is that *the new investors as a class obtain the new capital goods, and as a class receive back the money advanced to buy the new capital goods.* The identity of new capital goods, new investment, Profit B, is also the identity of the class of owners, investors, recipients of the Aggregate Profit. Within the class, the capital money circulates as capital among individuals as investors and recipients of the Profit B, by loan, transfer, purchase of new capital papers, etc. This is most clearly seen in the function of the financial institutions and financiers. (Section 16, on the Aggregate Profit and its several distributive forms).

Since the money for the new capital is advanced and returned along with the new capital itself (within the class of capitalists in the organism), and the goods are produced as and for new capital for this effective demand, the doctrine of "savings" of either the new capital or the new investment, is false and irrelevant so far as the organism is concerned, with respect to its dynamics, mechanism, (or the failure of its dynamics). Nor is "savings" a proper or acceptable basis in the formulae of the Level of Production, or Net Income (i.e. consumer goods plus "savings").

The whole Aggregate Profit is the result of the use of capital and labor in the process of capitalist production at an established wage-profit ratio. (Secs. 15, 16, 17, that the premise of profit is the establishment of the average wage rate at such level that the Aggregate Wage will be a certain fraction of the Net Aggregate Price of the goods produced and sold). Goods that constitute the new, expanded capital are part of this Aggregate Profit of all the capitals of the organism. The production of these goods is undertaken because the goods themselves can be used to produce a profit in a capitalist relationship, and are themselves a profit in the organism. The individual unit produces the goods (that will be new additional capital) because they are profitable to produce and will be purchased. These goods are no more a "savings" for the unit than for the organism. It is immaterial to the unit what the ultimate use of the goods produced and sold will be. (A unit may be producing goods that will in their entirety be used for new and expanded capital but as in all capitalist production, an exchange takes place among the producers of capital goods and consumer goods, etc. so that ultimately, in the system as a whole, the new capital goods appear as the Profit B).

Actually, capital goods are constantly being produced in the organism to replace capital goods used up in the production of other goods. These goods are certainly not the result of "savings." At the same time all these capital goods are being produced, including the new expanded capital, the capitalists and wage-earners are necessarily producing goods for their own consumption—values equivalent to the Aggregate Wage and the Profit A. This must be the situation if all the goods are being sold at normal price.

A further note on "Savings"

"Savings" may be the source of wealth in a non-capitalist economy, and savings may affect the goods-money circuit of such an economy, and also may affect the Level of production. That is to say, in a non-capitalist economy, where private production and sale for value prevails, if individuals sell without buying (i.e. saved their income), it is true that the Level of production will decline. This means only that the individuals in the economy do not want the volume of goods produced. But in the goods-money circuit of the capitalist economy, the purchasers of new capital goods are not consumers. The failure to buy such goods is not a manifestation of savings, but of failure of the dynamism to expand the capital. That is to say, the goods produced cannot function as new capital.

In general, the capital goods produced are not suitable for personal consumption. However, it may be argued that the existing capital goods could have been used to produce consumer goods for the consumption of the capitalists, rather than produce new, additional capital goods (Profit B to become Profit A). Thus the capitalists could consume more, rather than "save", i.e. by not consuming goods that could be produced for them (i.e. in place of new capital goods). Thus, theoretically, the economy could function at any desired level, and "furnish employment" to all who desired it; and thus a high level, full employment economy could exist.

But such a re-arrangement of capitals to produce additional consumer goods for capitalists (in place of production of goods for sale for new, additional capital) cannot be accomplished in a capitalist relationship. The effective demand will exist for the new capital goods, or not at all. Money (Profit A) is advanced to buy consumer goods, if the production of the capitals at a profit, is generally such as to afford a Profit A, and this depends on the existence of the Profit B. A capitalist relationship cannot be transformed into a consumer economy for capitalists (certainly not for the wage-earners), except by the techniques of fictive capital, fictive profit, etc., and this will require a political and an economic revolution.

However, these questions arise: in the internal money circuit of Profit B and new investment, does "savings" make the Profit B (money form) available for new investment? Is the refusal to invest the specific Profit B, that has come into being as money, the cause of a decline in the Level, etc. The answer generally is in the negative. The Profit B will not exist unless the new investment is made first. The failure of Profit is not the cause of the cessation of capital expansion; it is its consequence.

Assuming a properly functioning money and banking system

in the ICE, the money to invest for new capital for material production will be available if the use of the goods will be profitable.

When the Profit B does come into existence as money, the money will achieve a capital form, and it does so by the new investment for new capital goods directly, or more usually by becoming capital paper representing the new investment. The profit as money may be accumulated as gold or a paper money form, temporarily.

Effect of nonexpenditure ("savings") of individual income normally used for personal consumption—Wages of those employed in production of material goods; Profit A.

Net savings (in the whole organism) by wage earners, where the wage earners retain part of their income, as money or as unused deposits, means that a part of the production of consumer goods will not be purchased. In actuality this is not a common situation. Deferred expenditures commonly balance out current savings. The average wage probably no more than covers the actual real expenditure (Section 15). If there are Net savings, more often than not the money is used to purchase some fictive capital forms, rather than real capital, or moves into the orbit of money used in the financial mechanism. Some of this money will move into consumption through certain activities of the financial mechanism, creating a pseudo Profit B (Sections 12, 16, and Chapter III.)

But if consumer goods production must decline if there are actually any Net savings of wages, certain capitals will have to stop producing an equivalent value of consumer goods. This will also mean a decline in Profit A, but it does not mean a significant decline in the Level of Production and Net income which is occasioned by the decline in new investment and capital expansion generally.*

*If these savings are actually invested in the purchase of new capital, assuming that capital is expanding, there is simply a shift in the source of money for new capital expansion. And some wage earners may enter the class of capitalists. Anyone who owns goods or money that is used in the capitalist productive process can be regarded as a capitalist. Anyone with

Savings of Profit A is a difficult concept. Profit A has been defined as that part of the Aggregate Profit that is usually expended for consumer goods at the given level of the Aggregate Profit. It is a relatively discrete sum, as a minimum. If there is any tendency to reduce such consumption i.e. not advance the money to purchase consumer goods, the production of consumer goods must decline as in true net nonconsumption by wage earners. Again this is not a significant decline in the Level of Production and Net income. It is the decline in the new investment for capital expansion that causes the spiral decline.

In actuality the consumption by capitalists and wage earners alike is quite stable at any given Level of Production, and if anything, tends to exceed normal consumer income, when deferred expenditures are included, rather than the contrary. As pointed out above any real net savings from such incomes, in one way or another finds its way back to the purchase of consumer goods, and, as will later be pointed out, the purchase of consumer goods through the pseudo Profit B, even though episodic in the ICE, establishes a fairly high Level of consumption.

In general, then, money saved out of consumers' income is of little significance in the availability of money capital for capital expansion, although it may be some significance in the money capital generally for the creation of fictive capital forms, etc.

(8) "Equilibrium" of the capitalist organism means: capital is expanding, the Level of Production and the Net income are rising. In the ICE there cannot be a stable Level of Production and Net income. If capital does not expand, the whole

money can become a capitalist. However, the class, generally, is constituted by those who to a significant degree own capital and to a significant degree receive part of the Aggregate Profit for the use of the capital and by virtue of ownership of capital. (Exclude the small saver for deferred consumption who receives interest or some other form of return.)

The discussion of savings in the text relates to the organism as a whole, and not to individuals. Savings is of importance to individuals, to provide for necessary future expenditures, and it may be the means of enabling the wage earner to become a capitalist, or one who obtains income through fictive capital papers.

Level of the economy will enter into a spirally increasing decline that will not end until capital expansion is resumed. Capital expansion, and its degree determine the Level of Production and the Net Income. Hence, there must be a continuing new investment to buy new, additional capital goods (and create the Profit B) if the capitalist economy is to exist; if at any time capital expansion will not be resumed, the economy will not be able to function at a socially acceptable Level of Production.

It has been noted that in the organism as a whole, the production of the new, additional capital goods (constituting the Profit B) means the parallel production of *consumer* goods equivalent in value to: (a) the wages of those engaged in the production of the new capital goods, and the wages of those producing the consumer goods for the wage earners; and (b) the Profit A received by capitalists producing the new capital goods, and producing all the consumer goods relating thereto. Furthermore there will be the production of goods for capital replacement (used up in the production of the new capital goods); the production of these goods also requires the production of consumer goods for labor and capitalists engaged in the production of the capital goods. So the "effective demand" in the market as a whole is far greater than the demand constituted by the new investment for the new capital goods, and the volume of goods produced is far greater—involving both consumer and producer goods. This is the first aspect of the basic law of the organism, i.e. that the level of capital expansion determines the Level of Production and Net Income (i.e. they are determined by the size of Profit B).

Generally, the Net Aggregate Production (Net Income) in the later ICE is somewhat more than three times the volume of the new investment (Profit B). (Wage-profit ratio approximately 1-2; the Profit A is greater than the Profit B). This is sometimes called the multiplier, although the prevailing theory of the multiplier is confused by its association with the doctrine of "savings." (That is, the idea that the new investment becomes "saved" by degrees, and thus fails to exert further effect in maintaining the Level of Production). But the new investment is really returned by "degrees" to the class that advanced it, becoming Profit B. Whether there will be another advance, whether of the same or other money, is not prevented by "savings," but depends on the possibility of the constant expansion of capital, i.e. purchase of additional capital goods which can, as capital, return part of the Aggregate Profit.

This multiple effect of new investment for new capital on Level and Income can be very great if there is an unusual rise in capital expansion, particularly the expansion of capital due to war, inflation, etc. (Secs. 9, 10, 11, following). The periodic decline or failure of capital expansion (Sec. 11, the inherent cyclic nature of the ICE), likewise has an inverse multiplier effect. The decline or failure of new investment and capital expansion results in a decline far greater than the immediate loss of the market for the new capital goods; as indicated above the increasing spiral loss in market for consumer goods, replacement capital goods, etc. immediately sets in.

The effect of the cessation of capital expansion on Level and Income have further consequences, beyond the immediate spiraling decline in the market, and these consequences are themselves necessarily spiralling. The capitalist organism, and each capital unit functions for profit. The requirement that each unit show a profit (entrepreneur's profit) as well as pay all other shares of the Aggregate Profit which have a higher priority than entrepreneur's profit, determines whether the unit can or will continue to exist. If the unit fails because it cannot make an entrepreneur's profit, or pay interest or taxes, the whole production of the unit ends, and there is no wage advanced and no replacement capital purchased. A failure in effective demand for capital goods in the organism as a whole, not only affects the Aggregates directly; unit sales based on other units demand, can cause serial failure, and each failure has a spiral effect on Aggregate Wage, Aggregate Profit, capital advanced. Any particular unit's production may be theoretically salable at a price that returns a profit, in the light of the general demand in the market, but there is no orderly demand in the market that can be allocated to any unit. For example, ten units can fail in a market that could well sustain five.

If the Aggregate capital were a single capital, with a single Aggregate Wage, a single Aggregate Profit, and an ordered market in which goods were simply interchanged, it is conceivable that there could be an ordering of production in an equilibrium, and an ordering of Aggregate Wage, Aggregate Profit at a given level. In such a system, it is conceivable that a fairly high level of consumption be provided, assuming the owners of the capital had a demand for consumer goods high enough to employ a reasonable number of wage earners. But this is not the capitalist organism; there can be no such order in an organism constituted by separate capital units, each producing for profit. The unit can collapse on failure of profit or ability to return other shares of the Aggregate Profit that appear as costs to the unit. The collapse of units severally affects the other units. This is an effect induced by the general failure of capital expansion, and is in addition to the spirally increasing loss of market for capital goods and consumer goods. This effect is of particular importance in a boom situation, where there is a marked overproduction of capital goods.

The effect of unit failure in increasing the spiral decline should also be considered in connection with the general structure of individual capitals in the organism: one part of the organism is constituted by capital units producing capital goods, the other part by capital units producing consumer goods. Each part depends on the other for interchange, and for market. Unit failure in one sphere markedly affects the other sphere, in addition to the general decline in the total demand.

In the concentrated economy (Sec. 13), the powerful sectors can often maintain a degree of profit, whereas the other sectors cannot. But this does not mean that the powerful sectors can maintain a sufficient market for the weaker consumer goods sectors, for the total production in the powerful sectors must also spirally decline.

In addition to the serial effect of collapse of units because of failure to make a profit and pay other shares of the Aggregate Profit appearing as costs in their function, the continuing and spiral decline has a general effect that results in individual bank failure. This reacts on the ability of other units to function (units that may even still be profitable), with a further and spiralling decline in the market, etc.

(9) "Constant" capital expansion. "Variable" or episodic capital expansion.

The foregoing propositions,—that the Level of Production, the Net Income, the condition of equilibrium, and the existence of the capitalist economy itself, depend on the existence of the expansion of the Aggregate capital, do not yet set forth the entire dynamics of the capitalist economy.

(a) There is a direct, positive, inherent, dynamism to expand capital. This direct dynamism is something apart from the desire and necessity for the existing capitals to make the average rate of profit, including all parts of the Aggregate Profit that appears as costs to the individual unit. It is true that the foregoing implies that the existing capitals as a whole must sell goods that in part can only be sold if they are purchased for capital expansion, and that the Profit B is constituted by such sale. But the direct dynamic goes beyond this:

(b) This direct dynamism expresses itself in *two* ways: ***First,*** there is what is called herein "*constant*" expansion of capital. This arises out of the nature of the capitalist relationship itself, and the constant advance in technology that reduces the cost per unit of goods, and expands the scale of production and the capital; at the same time the area of the dominion of the capitalist system is expanded. There is a compulsion on each capital and on each sector of commodity capital to ultilize new technology to maintain its competitive position, create new commodities; capital must be expanded for this purpose (constantly increasing the use of materials in production, new machines, new equipment, new installations). The consequence of the constant expansion of capital is the full growth and development of the system (Sections 10, 18 below).

The *second* type of capital expansion is an *episodic* marked increase of capital, expanding or paralleling old ones, that takes place usually because of the existence of special conditions (in particular, paper money inflation, war or preparation for war, boom psychology induced by these and certain other causes—Sec. 11, below). New capital is formed that would ordinarily constitute an *overexpansion* of capital (and reduce the profit rate) but for certain reasons this is not immediately apparent. One of the reasons is that the episodic expansion itself is for a time being self-energizing, (Sec. 11, below). Generally, certain special conditions (war, inflation) provide a "market" for these new capitals, as well as existing ones, which "market" *in part.* will be seen to be in the nature of a fictive capital expansion. But in general: variable expansion is a periodic overexpansion of capital, an expansion beyond the "constant" type of expansion, and this soon becomes evident in the existence of a general overproduction of goods which will not be purchased.

Variable expansion has a profound effect on the function of the economy. It raises the whole Level of Production and income as a multiple of the Profit B (general law of dynamics) and results in prosperity. But this expansion and this prosperity must inevitably come to an end, and when it does, a spirally increasing fall in the whole level of production will follow, and this even causes the "constant" type of expansion to halt. The spiral fall in the level is only halted at some point, by the possibility of resumption of constant expansion. The business cycle is inherent in the capitalist economy (ICE), because variable expansion is inevitable.

It is in connection with variable expansion of capital, that the fictive expansion of capital episodically becomes important in the ICE (Sec. 11).

The distinction between constant and variable expansion is of great importance in the analysis of the end of the ICE (Section 18).

(10) Continued: The "constant" expansion of capital.

As indicated in the foregoing section the "constant" expansion of capital has two main aspects, which are interrelated. First, there is the creation of new capitals in new areas, the establishment of new industries for capitalist production (include transportation, communication, manufacture, etc), and the full capitalist development of an area. New populations, new products, new industries are all brought within the ambit of the relationship. The second aspect is the constant change in existing capitals because of advances in technology, the constant change in methods of production that change the scale and nature of the existing processes. Such technological change in effect requires a great expansion of the capital in use. Each of these two aspects require a constant new investment, whether by the entrepreneurs themselves, or investors, promoters, financiers, generally. (Caution: the term "constant" does not mean that the capital expansion of this nature cannot be temporarily interrupted by the depression phase of the business cycle).

The term "constant" expansion of capital thus also means the growth and full development of the capitalist economy. The dynamics of "constant" capital expansion is the very dynamics of the existence, development, and supremacy of the capitalist economy. The growth and development of the capitalist economy implies and requires the constant addition of new capital to the existing capital.

Technological development and capital expansion.

The constant capital expansion required by technological development in production, including the development of new products, in actuality is compulsory for the individual unit and capital sector if the unit wants to continue in business and make the average rate of profit.

Technological improvement generally reduces the cost of production. It may be the improvement will be undertaken by a unit to increase its profit, since, at the prevailing price in the sector, the reduction in unit cost will mean a higher profit. But because of competition, price will tend to decline, and practically speaking, as soon as one unit reduces cost of production, every other unit in this sector *must* do so also. If a superior product requiring new capital investment, supersedes another product, all producers will seek to compete. Capital will flow to sectors with a higher than average profit (assuming mobility of capital).

Technology then, not only offers a means of increasing profit temporarily, but in the long run forces a general capital expansion, to maintain each unit's relative position in the market. The new investment required is not only for new machinery, buildings, and other installations, but there is a relatively great increase in the volume of materials that must be purchased for the total output, for the advancing technology means that an increased volume of materials can be processed with the same amount of labor. There is an absolute increase in the scale of production, and the size of the unit generally increases also. (It will be seen below, that one of the results of advancing technology is the tendency of the unit to be of an enormous size and the tendency of the smaller units to disappear. Size results both from absolute growth or merger with smaller units).

It is not only competition *within* the commodity sector that forces the expansion of capital as the technology advances. The same forces operate in each commodity sector as a whole as against every other commodity sector since each will seek a larger share of the Aggregate Profit than the other sector. The other sectors *must* then advance technologically, and expand the capital and increase new investment to maintain the same relative position. (Some sectors never succeed at this, and continue with a higher unit cost as well as a lower price and a lower profit rate, a situation that compounds its difficulties resulting from the greater price power of other sectors.)

The consequence of great unit size, and concentration, resulting in principal part from technological advance, itself affects the further development of the technology and new capital investment. The great unit is in a position to utilize and develop technology and increase efficiency. In addition it has the advantage of price power, etc.

Creation of new capitals, and new industries, in old areas and new areas.

The capitalist relationship itself, and advancing technology are also a dynamic for this type of "constant" expansion. The capitalist system of production has so powerful a dynamic to supersede any other relationship in production, that it will spread to and dominate any non-capitalist area. This aspect of "constant" capital expansion may involve a revolutionary change in the existing mode of production in the new area or the new development. The introduction of modern means of transportation, and communication, and new industrial processes, is irresistable. The advancing technology spreads the system; it also completely changes the structure of any pattern that exists. While the capitalist relationship is itself dynamic, it is its advancing technology that makes it so powerful.

The establishment of new industries in old areas and new areas requires a constant new investment. Superficially, the sales by existing capitals of the goods necessary, appears simply as a way of making a profit, recognizing of course that this market (for new capital goods) is essential for their existence. And there is a great deal of pressure by these existing capitals to obtain and expand this market. But the real dynamic is in the *new* capital formation itself—the new industry, the penetration of old and new areas. The new capital is sought for its own sake. (Refer to Sec. 18, as to consequences in the organism, of the "constant" expansion of capital, the development of the advanced technology, and the worldwide development of the ICE).

(11) Continued: The "variable" or episodic expansion of real capital, in general. This overexpansion of capital is usually induced and maintained by certain special circumstances. Certain of these special circumstances (war, inflation) result in a fictive expansion of capital and a pseudo Profit B represented by fictive capital papers and inflated paper money. This "fictive expansion" tends to increase further the real capital expansion—variable expansion—or at least sustains the new capital for the time being without further real expansion. In the ICE this is an episodic and temporary condition, always ending in depression.

—The business cycle is inherent in the ICE, and is the result of the episodic overexpansion of capital which must come to an end.

.1 Overexpansion of capital, in general. The special conditions that induce and maintain it.

The course of a capitalist economy (ICE) is not that of the equilibrium maintained by the "constant" expansion of capital (which, as stated, is the essential dynamic of the economy). There is usually an episodic *additional* expansion of capital (which, pursuant to the general law of dynamics, raises the Level of Production and income as a multiple of the Profit B). The Level and Income then is considerably higher than that ordinarily existing by virtue of the "constant" expansion of capital. But this additional expansion is actually an overexpansion of capital and must end. On its cessation, a depression follows in which the "constant" expansion of capital falls, or stops entirely for a time. The level of the economy will decline until the constant expansion of capital revives. This is the business cycle of the capitalist economy (ICE). In short, *all* capital expansion in the ICE, is periodic.

(Before proceeding: assume as a premise that the motivation of individuals to acquire capital, new capital or old existing capitals, is always present, a motivation necessary fo rall capital expansion, constant or variable. But the motivation itself is effectual only when the new capital is or can be profitable. The condition of profitability, i.e. the capital expansion itself, is the subject of this part of the Chapter).

Overexpansion of capital viewed in one specific commodity sector, and in the economy as a whole (especially in the concentrated economy).

(Refer to Section 13, on the pattern of capital units in the organism: Sector structure; number and size of the capital units in each sector; "Concentration" and disparate degrees of concentration among the several commodity sectors).

If an overexpansion of capital takes place in *one* sector alone, (usually accompanied by a marked increase in the number of production units), the consequence of an increase in production beyond the extent of the market of that particular sector is soon apparent. There is a fall in price, reduction of or termination of profit, and even a great accumulation of unsold goods, that may cause many capitals to fail. Nevertheless, a variable expansion of this nature is often found in certain sectors, despite the quickly felt consequence. It will occur where these conditions prevail: there are a large number of producers; the capital that a producer needs is relatively small; the general market of the sector is uncontrolled. These conditions are typical in agriculture. In agriculture, in most countries, overexpansion and overproduction are almost inevitable. It is hard to stop. Years of poverty, subnormal wage rate, etc. will follow before there is a readjustment of the capitals, and price level.

In the unconcentrated capitalist economy (all sectors unconcentrated i.e. the earlier ICE), the tendency to variable expansion may assert itself in several sectors at the same time, as soon as the economy seems to be in an upswing. When this occurs, the situation is different than where the overexpansion takes place in one or two sectors, for the overproduction does not make itself felt so quickly in any one sector. The variable expansion in each or in several sectors creates a demand in the other sectors, and the variable capital expansion in the organism as a whole can proceed with the temporarily self energizing effect described below, wherein the overexpansion of capital in several sectors itself provides the market for the new capitals in the sector. But the problem of market for the new capital, produced by all these new capitals, very soon presents the same insuperable difficulty for the organism as a whole.

In the highly concentrated economy of the later ICE, the situation is somewhat different. The concentrated sectors effectively resist any production beyond the immediate market of the sector (resist overproduction), and this means an effective resistance to variable expansion within the sector itself, *unless there is a variable expansion throughout most of the economy.* There must be a general incitement to the variable expansion affecting the whole economy, with all the concentrated sectors participating together. Because of the firmer control over entry into the sectors, and control over volume of production, the expansive movement that once could sweep each sector in the "competitive structure" does not get so easily started. A more general and powerful inducement is required in the concentrated economy, such as inflation and war, or some sort of financial manipulation.

It may be stated, as a general rule, that in the late, developed, concentrated economy, *only* inflation and war, or manipulation in financial markets creating large volumes of fictive capital papers, can induce and maintain a variable expansion of capital of any significant degree.

The temporarily self-energizing effect of variable capital expansion (general, throughout the economy).

The variable expansion itself has a temporary self energizing, or self sustaining effect. The new investment furnishes a market not only for existing capitals (Profit B), in addition to that supplied by the investment for "constant" expansion, but for a time furnishes a market for the capital goods produced by the *new capitals*. The increased consumer demand may incite additional capital expansion, etc. A continuing variable expansion, in short, is the basis for some further variable expansion, although this cannot, by itself continue. Once the new capitals are all functioning, the scale of production becomes such (production of new capital goods), that an investment on a still greater scale is required. This can ordinarily only be met (if the variable expansion is to continue) by war or inflation or both. (below) If these are not available, then the overexpansion of capital—the essence of the variable expansion of capital, becomes apparent, and there is an overproduction of goods. The ever widening spiral decline sets in.

The self-energizing, self-sustaining effect of an initial variable expansion, in the absence of the other reinforcing conditions, *must* be temporary, unlike the situation of a "constant" expansion, where there is a true "circularity". That is to say, that as long as "constant" expansion continues, the economy is in an equilibrium. And this is unlike the situation of "variable" expansion, which is overexpansion of capital and means an overproduction of capital goods. This can take place for the moment only because of the capital expansion itself (or because of the fictive capital expansion). The problem of market for the new capital created because of technological advances, and new development in new areas et., i.e., ("Constant" expansion) is resolved by the continuing development of the system, the technological development, new products, etc. (at least until such time that the organism finds "constant" expansion impossible because of size and technology of the capitals). The additional new capital goods produced are purchased because of the constant expansion itself. This is what is meant by the circularity of constant expansion, for it maintains the equilibrium even though on an ever expanding scale.

But this is not true of variable expansion—overexpansion. It cannot possibly maintain itself beyond the temporary self-energizing effect, or insofar as it is maintained by fictive processes. During the ICE, however, the belief existed that *all* capital expansion energizes itself continually. This is related to the belief that the Independent capitalist economy could continue as an indefinitely expanding system.*

The special conditions that initiate, maintain, or increase a variable expansion of capital:

(a) Paper money inflation (especially bank credit money), public or private.
(b) War, or preparation for war.
(c) Impetus from a sharply rising Level of Production, after a depression: psychology of a coming boom, especially an anticipation of war, inflation, etc.
(d) Marked territorial or population increase.
(e) An extraordinary technological advance, or new product.

As will appear, the first two are the primary causes. Nevertheless, the latter three factors have triggered a variable expansion of capital. Expansionist psychology is extremely important, not only for the entrepreneur, but especially in the later ICE (where new investment is centralized in the financial-banking mechanisms) the psychology leads to the creation of new capital papers. If money can be made in creating (and manipulating) new capital papers, even if in reality the entrepreneural profits will be small or even questionable, these papers will be created. A variable expansion will then take place, and the Level of the economy will rise.

Expansionist psychology has many subtle ingredients. It may not have any realistic basis, yet it may be effective to raise the Level of the economy. In the ICE it was deemed treasonable

*This theory has its counterpart in another popular idea: that the ICE could become a "consumer" economy, with minor revision. It is believed that in the capitalist economy production creates its own equivalent in "purchasing power." This is untrue. The economy can function in equilibrium only if new investment is constantly made to purchase part of the production, i.e. create the Profit B.

But these concepts were much utilized in the early days of the pefcp, especially in the "pump priming" doctrines, when it was thought that the Government expediture was needed only to get the system "started" and it would then continue in a self generation of purchasing power at the higher level.

to do or say anything that would discourage it.* It would be an error to think that the boom was not universally desired. The size of the working class in the ICE was such that the overexpansion of capital was essential to provide a reasonably good level of employment. Even those who knew that the prosperity would be temporary, hoped to benefit in some way before the boom collapsed.

.2 Nature and mechanisms of the fictive expansion of capital, and the pseudo Profit B, in the ICE. That in the ICE fictive capital expansion is an episodic adjunct of the overexpansion of real capital.

Recapitulation: Two major "special conditions," war and inflation of the paper money seem to be essential to induce and maintain a large scale variable expansion of real capital. These conditions have their effect principally by creating a fictive expansion of capital, the creation of a pseudo Profit B, represented by fictive capital papers and inflated money. The Profit B of the real capital expansion and the pseudo Profit B together have a multiple effect on the whole Level of Production and Income. Nevertheless, in the ICE, it is in the expansion of the Profit B, that the fictive expansion has its major effect.
(The material in this subsection on the mechanism etc. of the fictive process in the ICE, was placed in the Syllabus, as Topic 4. Since it is a restatement of the analysis more fully developed in Chapter III and Chapter IV, with special reference to the limited and episodic use of this process in the ICE, a repetition at this point would encumber the text).

.3 The business cycle is the result of the episodic "variable" expansion of capital, and the adjunct fictive capital expansion,

*The economic doctrine of the ICE emphasized measures that would incite a "variable" expansion of capital, and warned against anything that might prevent it. The list of things that "discourage" expansion, decrease "confidence," includes unions, higher wages, Government control or "interference," taxes, etc.

if any. Since variable expansion is inherent in the ICE, the cycle is inherent. Constant expansion of capital is so affected by the business cycle that it tends to become cyclic also.

Variable expansion of capital, and its inevitable termination, are the cause of the business cycle. This is the characteristic sequential alternation of the Whole Level of Production and Income, from depression, to prosperity, to depression. While variable expansion and its termination are the basic cause of the cycle, the cycle itself seriously affects the constant expansion, and consequently both seem to be periodic. That is to say, the overproduction, decline in profit rate, fall in prices, etc. halts new investment of any sort for the time being. However, in the highly protected sectors of the economy, a degree of constant expansion tends to continue despite depression. The alternation of the business cycle also affects re-investment for replacement capital.

While the cycle is in essence an alternation in the degree of capital expansion, it appears more clearly as a marked alternation in the Level of Production and Income. (Refer, elsewhere, to price and money aspects).

Depression Phase of the Cycle:

In this phase, the Level is a declining one, for in the ICE, unlike the pefcp, there is no static condition possible. Price has usually declined from normal price; the Aggregate Profit is reduced in volume and in rate and is still declining. Entrepreneural profit has disappeared in many sectors of the economy. An increasing quantity of capital papers, including banking capitals, are destroyed. The failure of banking capitals causes the failure of many entrepreneural capitals. Unemployment is severe and increasing, the wage rate declining, and Aggregate wage sharply reduced.

Recovery:

The recovery is not only the cessation of the decline, but is a *rise* in the Level and Net income. The recovery in the ICE almost always begins at a higher level than the preceding cyclic recovery. That is to say the business cycle is not an alternation around a fixed level, but an alternation of depression and prosperity, on a constantly ascending scale of the Level of Production and income. The constant expansion establishes an expanding system, and the depression that sharply lowers the Level and Income nonetheless always leaves the Level and income higher than before. However, there are usually an increasing number of individual capitalists and wage earners that suffer severely in the depression.

The recovery is due to the restoration of constant capital expansion which had, at least in great part, been terminated by the depression. At the beginning of recovery, the Level of Production has shrunk to such an extent that there is no gross overproduction of capital, i.e. the expanded capitals resulting from the variable expansion have failed, or have reduced their scale. Furthermore, since the rate of profit has fallen, a lower rate of profit is acceptable to new capitals. And a depression itself encourages the type of capital expansion required by improved techniques, so as to cut costs of production. Smaller capitals have been forced out, and the other capitals tend to increase in size and scale of production. Opportunities for new businesses accumulate during the depression, and the replacement of depreciated machinery and installations, which has been deferred, will take place. The reach for new markets that was suspended during the depression, reasserts itself. The fact that the wage rate has been lowered may also be of some importance.

As the recovery progresses, and equilibrium is restored, the Level of Production and Income begins to rise. And employment of course, increases as does the Aggregate Wage and the volume of the Profit A. Even without the revival of a variable expansion at this point, a Level will ordinarily be reached that is higher than at the same point in the prior business cycle, because of the constant expansion of capital. Among other things it will be found that the size of the existing capitals and the Aggregate Profit are all increased.

At some point in this recovery, a variable expansion may take place. It is true also, that the recovery may be initiated by causes that induce the variable expansion. It may be noted, that in recovery, a fairly high degree of unemployment may continue.

During the ICE, the *depressed* phase of the cycle (not the

boom stage) was the object of much concern. Many suggestions were made to "even out" the cycle, by some control of the expansion, but these were quite futile. No proposal to restrict expansion could ever be accepted. However, a limited control over overexpansion of capital was implicit in the concentration of some sectors of the economy. Trade associations, cartels, private agreements also operated in many sectors of the economy to limit expansion beyond the current market. These could in no way prevent the variable expansion induced by the financial mechanism, war, etc.

(12) The several reasons why it appears that "money" and "interest" per se, are the primary dynamics of the capitalist organism (ICE), or the primary dynamics of capital expansion therein; why it appears that wage rate, price, individual volitions and propensities, are the dynamics of the organism.

(a) "Money," "interest," "banking," (also wage rate, Aggregate Wage, price, price level, etc.) *appear*, to capital units and individuals, to be the dynamics of the economy, because these forms, being essential parts of the structure and mechanisms of the organism, reflect the dynamics of the organism. The function of the organism does actually control each unit, and hence these elements *appear* to be the ultimate dynamics. (The nature of the organism and the true dynamics of the organism are not apparent to the individual and unit).

(b) Statement of the general rule:
The supply of money, the rate of interest, the banking system (insofar as it creates money for the *production and sale of material goods*) are not in themselves basic factors in the dynamics of the Level of Production and Income in the ICE. And money, banking, availability of money, etc., are neither dynamic or determinative of the expansion of real capital, which is the actual dynamic of Level and Income. Money and banking are essential parts of the structure and mechanisms of the capitalist system. The prototypical form of interest in the capitalist economy, a direct share of the Aggregate Profit, is an essential form (Sec. 16). But neither

such interest, or any other share of the Aggregate Profit, are in themselves the dynamic of the system. They come into being as shares of the *primary* form, the Aggregate Profit, and the existence and size of the shares of the Aggregate Profit are determined by the dynamics of the organism. Sec. 16).

(c) But up to this point the dynamic described has been the expansion of *real capital.* But because of the possibility, episodically, of a fictive expansion of capital and the creation of the pseudo Profit B., and the creation of fictive capital papers and the private inflation of bank credit money, "Money" in general, the banking system, the interest rate, appear *generally* to be a dynamic of Level and Income, in the ICE. But these fictive processes are temporary and episodic in the ICE. These episodes support the *appearance,* to units, and individuals, that money and banking are the fundamental dynamics of unit function and system function.

It is easy to mistake the mechanisms and structural elements of the system, for its dynamics. Money, and bank credit money, are essential elements in the functioning of the economy. There must be an adequate supply of bcm, at an average interest rate somewhat below the average entrepreneural profit rate (Sec. 16). Further: the establishment and maintenance of the average wage rate at the Level of the prevailing wage-profit ratio (in equilibrium), is the essence of the capitalist relationship. (Sec 15). Price and market are essential mechanisms of the economy. (Sec. 17) All the elements of the organism will necessarily reflect, in their function, the basic dynamic operating, and any change in the dynamic (capital expansion or failure of capital expansion) may cause change in price, wage rate and Aggregate wage, supply and availability of money, interest rate etc.

To the individual and the unit in particular, money, price, wage, seem to be the dynamics that determine the level of the economy. Certainly they dominate the function of the unit. Prices that are too low seem to be the reason that the unit fails to make a profit. Or certain costs seem too high: wages, taxes, interest rates. Difficulties can appear to the unit as an inadequate volume of money (i.e. a decline in effective demand, or a decline in new investment or a price level that is too low).

However, money, the banking system, and interest and interest rate (herein a payment for the use of money without regard to the source of the payment) are factors in the episodic fictive processes, and the private and public inflation of bank credit money. And hence they become of importance episodically with respect to the Level of Production and Income; *and*, during the time the episodic processes are in function, they have an effect on price, price level, and wage rate.

The "quantity of money"and the availability of money, and the banking system and process, interest and interest rate are of significance in the creation of fictive capital papers, the inflation of bcm, and the monetization of "profits" of existing capital papers, new capital papers, land titles, etc. This money, in part, moves into the goods-money circuit, creating the Pseudo Profit B. (Ch. III)

But it is an error to generalize, then, that money, and etc., are the basic dynamics of the Level of Production, in the ICE. The episodic existence of the fictive expansion of capital (and the role of money, banking, etc. therein) should not be permitted to obscure the fundamental basic dynamics. Furthermore the true nature of Profit, Price, Wage, in the structure and system should not be obscured by the episodic role of "money" in the inflation that may occasionally take place in the ICE.

It is true that the consequences of the fictive forms and inflated money do episodically have an effect on Price, price level, Aggregate Price of goods sold, wages and wage rate, through their effect on the level of production, and possible depreciation of the paper money. But again, it is erroneous to generalize from these episodes, in the ICE, that the "quantity of money" or certain other monetary factors are fundamental in determining wage, wage rate, price, normal price. (Further discussion in Part II, this Chapter).

Part II

Structure and Mechanisms of the Organism
Money, Price, Wage, Profit

(13) The pattern of the capital units in the organism. Capital papers.

.1 Sector structure; number and size of the capital units in each sector; "Concentration" and disparate degrees of concentration among the several commodity sectors.

The capitalist organism is constituted by a great number of specialized, separate capital units. However, the capitals must be viewed first, as functioning within their particular commodity sector (include transportation, etc., as sectors).

The pattern of capitals in each sector changes, as the capitalist economy develops; likewise, as the system develops, certain sectors achieve unusual power. (Sec. 18 on the consequences of the constant expansion of capital, etc.). These changes have a marked effect on unit function, although the basic nature of the organism is not changed. Furthermore, the development of the financial mechanisms and institutions, significantly affect unit and sector function.

In *all* periods of the ICE, the commodity price is the sector price. To each unit in the sector, the production, price and technology of the other units in the *sector* seems the dominant aspect of the unit's existence (rather than the function of the organism as a whole). The unit is first in competition within the sector for a share of the sector's market. The unit may lower price, improve technology, etc. as a means of increasing profit or its share of the sector market; the unit may be compelled to follow other units in the sector in these respects.

But in the *whole* market, the commodity *sectors* compete with each other for their share of the whole effective demand. It is the *commodity sector as a whole* that obtains a share of the whole market. While the unit obtains part of the whole effective demand, it is as part of the sector's share. The commodity price is the average sector price. Each unit in a sector tends to sell at approximately this price, and each unit then obtains its part of the Aggregate Profit that the sector obtains.

The capital units in the different sectors do not have the same capital structure. In some sectors, the unit functions with a great amount of capital and a far advanced technology; in other sectors there is a much greater amount of labor used for each unit of material goods produced, and the technology may be backward. This will be of importance in the establishment of normal price in the sector, the sector rate of entrepreneural profit, and even the wage rate. (Secs. 15, 16, 17.)

"Concentration" and disparate degrees of concentration among commodity sectors.

In certain sectors of the economy (later ICE) production tends to become "concentrated" in a very few large scale units, highly advanced technologically. Control of the sector, entry, and the formation of new capital, is centralized; financial instituitions and mechanisms are related to this centralization of control. The importance of this in the full development of the ICE will be discussed elsewhere. (Sec. 18). At this point, the effect on price, wage, profit etc. needs to be mentioned. The price, profit, etc. aspects of sector concentration are particularly significant because, in the later ICE, some sectors continued to be composed of a large number of relatively small units (agriculture, etc). There is a disparate degree of concentration among the sectors.

The concentrated sectors can establish a higher price for the commodity they produce, and obtain a higher rate of profit than the nonconcentrated sectors, and the large units in the concentrated sectors have a higher than average profit rate. When cyclic decline occurs, and the market is contracting, the concentrated sectors have another advantage. They can reduce production in an orderly way, and maintain price, and might even still make a profit instead of a loss, whereas in the nonconcentrated sectors, the usual collapse of price and demand means widespread failure.

The effect of this price and profit differential goes deeper than appears. The concentrated sectors obtain a relatively greater part of the money constituting the whole effective demand (a greater part of the whole Income) because of their price power, and this is at the expense of the nonconcentrated sectors, whose profit rate is *pro tanto* reduced by the greater profit in the concentrated sectors. In disequilibrium the condition is worse. The relatively low price and profit rates of the nonconcentrated sectors are a consequence of the power over *price* and profit of the concentrated sectors. What is added in some sectors is taken from the others. (Partial exception: If the episodic inflation and the episodic creation of fictive capital papers is in process in the ICE, the concentrated sectors may be able to obtain all the inflated money, etc., as part of their generally higher profit, without further reducing the profit of the nonconcentrated sectors. Price and profit, of course, will be substantially higher than in the other sectors.)

The consequences of such higher prices and profit rates and correspondingly lower profit rates in other sectors, affects wage rates. Wages in the concentrated sectors can be higher than those in the nonconcentrated sectors, not only because of the higher profit rates but because the concentrated sectors can pass on a wage increase by higher prices. This further reduces the profit of the weaker sectors and also forces their wage rates down.

The power of the concentrated sector may be such that the sector can function at a profit in periods of depression, where the weak sectors are subject to business failure. A considerable degree of prosperity can exist despite depression in one sector. The prolonged depressions in agriculture in the ICE did not have a major effect on the organism as a whole.

Nevertheless, the basic law of the organism still prevails; the function of the organism will ultimately determine unit and sector function no matter how powerful the sector, and how well it can protect itself at the expense of other sectors. In a profound or prolonged depression, or the situation where the organism becomes unable to function because capital expansion cannot resume, the great units will not be able to function.

In summary: The effect of concentration, and disparate degrees of concentration among the sectors, markedly affects the units and the sectors, but it is generally not of major significance in the basic dynamics of the organism. Concentration tends to make for a more orderly economy, for it restrains gross overproduction of goods in a sector, an overproduction which the market cannot absorb and which is destructive to the units in a sector. Most national economies in the later ICE, in some way or other must make some arrangements either by private agrement or with Government assistance to restrain excessive production and competition.

Progressive concentration, a phenomenon which is in part the consequence of the "constant" expansion of capital, plays a part in the onset of the relative economic critical point, at which point the capitalist organism cannot function as an "independent" economy (Section 18).

The financial system of the later ICE; financier's profit.

Besides the manufacturing, transportation, etc. capital units, the capitalist organism contains banking and financial institutions (commercial banks, Government Central Reserve Bank, Investment banks, savings banks, insurance companies, and financial markets). The function of the banks will be considered in Chapter IV.

The financial system had a significant part in the development and concentration of the capitals. Furthermore, in the later ICE the financial institutions exerted a direct control over unit function and sector function. They may even exert inter-sector control.

An aspect of the financial system that is of great importance in the analysis is its role in (a) expansion of capital, the creation of and the acquisition of the Profit B, and, (b) the creation of fictive capital papers, and the inflation of paper money.

The financier plays an important role in the later ICE as the agency for new investment in new capital goods. But he also has other roles. (Section 16 on "financier's profit.")

.2 Capital Papers. (Capital represented by a capital paper; Profit B, as new additional capital, represented by a capital paper.)

Fictive capital papers, private form and public form, not representing an actual capital.

In the later developed capitalist economy (ICE)—large scale unit, concentrated sectors, financial system, the capital paper is a fundamental instrument in the function of the organism.

The term "capital paper" is used herein to designate an instrument, "stock" type, or "bond" type, or "note" type, that:

(a) represents goods or money used in material production and distribution, in a capitalist relationship, and which entitles the owner to a share of the Aggregate Profit of the capitalist organism, by way of entrepreneur's profit, interest, or other form of the Aggregate Profit.

(b) represents a "capitalization" of a regular, expected *income* but does not represent capital goods or capital money used in the process of production of material goods, in an economy where the capitalist relationship in production prevails. General example: the sum of $5 payable annually from a source that is not a direct share of the Aggregate Profit may be represented by an "interest bearing" capital paper, worth say $100. This paper may be bought and sold, and represent a liquid value of $100. Such papers may have their origin in a loan of money to an individual or Government, where the money is expended for personal consumption or Government consumption —*not expended* for capital goods for the production of material goods. They are, of course, privately created in many other subtle ways. (The papers considered herein are the permanent or relatively permanent forms, not the short term form that will soon be cancelled on repayment). The return on these papers does not arise directly out of the use of the money as capital—part of the Aggregate Profit—but is a transfer, in some way or other of part of the Aggregate Profit on the Aggregate capital, or may be inflated money, or some other money. The public form is the Government bond or note; this is the prototype of the fictive capital paper. The private form is created by individuals or units. (Ch. III; IV.)

The fictive capital papers that are principally considered in this book are those that enter the process of fictive capital expansion, and are suitable for this purpose. There are other fictive capital papers which do not enter into the process of fictive capital expansion (Ch. III). Certain of these latter papers may be injected into the existing capital paper structure and to some extent later come to represent some actual capital. In the early ICE most of such paper was almost fraudulent, but in the later ICE such paper was often based on a more reasonable expectation of future income or future value.*

All capital papers become of increasing importance as the capitalist economy develops:

(a) In the later ICE, most capitals are represented by capital papers. Ownership, control, management, expansion of capital, function through capital papers. The financial institutions and financial mechanisms are based upon them. In particular, centralization of control of capitals, and centralization of the expansion of capitals (Profit B) is effected through capital papers.

(b) Profit B resulting from new investment for new capital, is usually constituted and effected through capital papers.

(c) Bank credit money, the characteristic money form of the capitalist economy is almost entirely based on capital papers.

(d) Fictive capital papers privately created, become episodically important to the later ICE with respect to the level of production and income. They are also important elements of "financiers profit" even though they do not enter the process of fictive capital expansion. To some extent they also can become integrated into the whole capital paper structure.

Amplification on capital papers representing actual capital goods used in the process of production of material goods, and capital money:

Capital goods are material goods used, or to be used, in the capitalist relationship for production of material goods. They are

*The history of the "watered stocks" and fictive capital papers generally, of the late 19th and early 20th century in the U.S. can be read almost as a prologue to some aspects of the political economy based on the fictive expansion of capital. The great masters of the fictive processes (private form), some of whom manufactured fictive papers of good quality, were J. P. Morgan, Andrew Carnegie, Jay Gould, Daniel Drew, the Vanderbilts and the Rockefellers. There were many others.

of two classes: "producers" goods, and "consumer" goods. The former are in part "fixed" capitals—machines, buildings, installations, etc., and the materials of all types used up in the productive process and converted to other goods. In the organism, part of the "consumer" goods are capital goods. These are the consumer goods which are to be purchased by the wage-earners who are engaged in the production of material goods, their wages being an advance out of money capital by the capitalists. The remainder of the consumer goods are produced for the consumption of the capitalists, or those deriving their income through them. In the economy as a whole there is a great body of goods in circulation, in inventory, or in storage, which are part of the Aggregate capital of the economy, but not all goods in circulation will be sold for use as capital.

Money to be used to buy goods for production and pay wages (in the capitalist relationship) is money capital (capital as money). Capital as goods cannot be separated in practice or in concept from capital as money. All capital goods must at one time have had a money equivalent form, and after the productive process, even the fixed capitals return slowly to the money form. All money can become capital and all money can be used as capital.

(14) Money, generally. Money in the ICE.

.1 *First principles.*

- Money arises out of the nature of the relationship in production of *material goods*; it must be itself a *material good.* (There must be "money" in the ICE, and the pefcp)
- Money is gold, in the ICE (and in the PEFCP)
- The monetary unit is a specified weight of gold.
- The monetary unit may be represented in the circulation by a paper instrument, as symbol, or as promise to pay the gold weight on demand.
- There are two main types of paper money; Treasury notes; and bank credit money, currency, and "deposit" form.
- Price is the exchange value of a material good stated in the

monetary unit. (The monetary unit as a standard of price). The fundamental nature of money is best seen in the analysis of the "price" of goods.

Money arises out of the nature of the relationship of individuals in the production of material goods. Furthermore, the fact that money is a *material* good—one material good, chosen conventionally and legally to represent and measure the value of all material goods—also arises out of the nature of the relationship in the production of *material* goods.

The relationship in production that gives rise to money, is one where material goods, or at least a considerable part of the goods produced, are produced not for the consumption of the producers, or the common consumption of a group of producers, but by private individuals, or even groups, *for exchange for other goods of equal value*. Where the person who produces the goods, or owns the goods produced, customarily alienates it, but for a *value equivalent* only, possessed and offered by another person, and a production for exchange for equivalent value, (which implies a private production, or at least a private possession), there will be a money form. A money commodity will be selected. The money commodity becomes the universal value equivalent, of all goods produced, and is the universal measure of value.*

It is plain that in the capitalist relationship, all material goods are produced to be sold for money, as universal value equivalent. Furthermore, capital is advanced as money to buy goods; wage is advanced as money; the goods produced have a money value and profit is realized as money. In the capitalist relationship there is a series of money "ratios" in the money advanced for production and in the money representing the value

*The exchange of a specific commodity for another specific commodity—barter—indicates a relationship where there is an occasional exchange of products, rather than production for exchange by individuals specializing in the production of a single good. The existence of the money form—*one* good representing the value of *any* good—indicates a more widespread system of production for exchange. It is where there is a fairly large number of individuals so producing for exchange of some sort (and, of course, this need not be a capitalist relationship), the separation of one commodity, (or more) takes place, and this commodity becomes the socially accepted, socially designated general equivalent of value.

of material goods produced. The capitalist relationship is inherently and necessarily on a "material good" standard; if the money commodity is *gold, capitalist production and all the relationships and ratios are ineluctably on a gold basis.* This is always the situation, whatever paper forms representing gold may be created, and used in the circulation of the goods, and in the money advanced and returned in their production.

For many years, gold has been the money commodity. Why it was chosen need not be of present concern. Gold would not have become the money commodity unless it were a material good first, and had the same quality of value as all other material goods.

The monetary unit is not to be confused with money itself. The monetary unit is a weight of gold. The dollar is .888671 grams of fine gold; a British pound is 2.13281 grams of fine gold; a French franc is .160 grams etc. The weight is first conventionally and then legally established, and it can be changed conventionally and legally.*

The actual gold monetary unit, as *medium of exchange*, and as *means of payment* can be represented by a symbol, or a paper form; (note that the measure of value, is still gold itself, and the monetary unit always is a specified weight of gold). The paper form represents the monetary unit. It is necessary that this symbol, or paper form, be socially acceptable in place of the actual gold unit, in the general circulation. These symbols, or paper forms,, usually completely displace gold in the general domestic circulation in the ICE. The paper instrument is usually a promise to pay the money it represents on demand; the promise itself circulates as the money media. The "Government" or the "Bank" that creates and issues these media, is believed to be "good" for its promise, and it is generally believed that the Government or the Bank have the money or the ability to get the money to make the promise good.

These paper representations of the gold monetary unit need not be a physically circulating instrument—currency—but can be a promise to pay, represented by a book entry in a bank's book; these are used as money media by "checks" that effect their

*The weights stated have been changed since the foregoing was written.

transfer in the banks' books, from person to person, as means of purchase and payment. They are called "deposits".

The paper money form can represent in the circulation the weight of gold it purports to represent; under certain circumstances it can circulate representing a lesser weight of gold than it purports to represent.

If the paper money form is generally accepted at its purported gold weight, and is directly or indirectly convertible to gold on demand, it may be considered to be the equivalent of the gold monetary unit in the circulation. Paper money that is gold equivalent is much superior to gold itself as a medium of circulation and means of payment. "A currency is in its most perfect state when it consists wholly of paper money, but of paper money of an equal value with the gold which it professes to represent." Needless to say, the paper money substitutes for gold because gold is money; the money commodity and the monetary unit must first have been established. The printing of the paper form, or the creation by banks of promises to pay money, do not create the money form, the money commodity, or the monetary unit.

Paper money circulates in the political unit wherein it is created. It is a creature of a political system and a legal system. If it is sometimes overlooked that it is *gold* that is money, it becomes plain in international exchange and trade, wherein the paper form must on request be converted to gold. Gold is the international money.

Paper money forms:

The Treasury Note
Bank Credit Money of the commercial bank (deposit form, currency form). (BCM)
Bank Credit Money of the Government bank, or Government Central Bank (deposit form, currency form).

The classic paper representation, or symbol, of the monetary unit is the Government's Treasury Note. It is a promise to pay the monetary unit it represents, to the bearer, on demand. There were two types: one represented an amount of gold actually in the Treasury. However, most notes were simply promises to pay gold that the Government did not actually possess (although it may maintain a percentage of the gold).

If the Treasury Note circulates as though it were gold at the gold weight it purports to represent, it is said to be gold equivalent; it will probably then be actually convertible on demand. It is inconvertible if the Government states, either before or after issuance that it will not pay the gold on demand. Inconvertible Treasury Notes are probably (but not necessarily) not equivalent, in the circulation, to the weight of gold they purport to represent. The private owners of gold can buy such paper money for less than its purported gold weight(depreciation)

The distinction between BCM of the commercial banks, and that of the Government bank, or the Government Central Reserve Bank, (GCRB) is of great importance. The first is called the private type; the second, the public type. The public type, *currency form*, is in reality the national (Government) money. Sometimes it is issued by what seemingly is a privately owned "Government" bank. The currency form (public) is gold convertible (ICE), and legal tender, but in effect the book entry "public type" is presumably convertible to the currency form, and the book entry forms must and will be created and managed as though they also were direct obligations of the Government.

In effect (a) it is the public form of paper money that the commercial banks, the creators of the private type of BCM, promise to pay, or gold, and (b) the public type of BCM is the "reserve" of the commercial banks. (Further: Chapter IV on money and banking, and on gold equivalency and gold convertibility of the public and private types of BCM).

The term *gold standard* as commonly used, means that not only is gold the money commodity, and that a certain weight of gold is the monetary unit, but also that the paper money that represents the weight of gold, is *convertible to gold* on demand. Where BCM is the usual money media, the private BCM issued by commercial banks is convertible on demand to the public currency form (currency issued by the GCRB). However, if the public currency is convertible to gold on demand, all the BCM may be deemed to be convertible.

Devaluation is the reduction by the Government of the weight of gold of the monetary unit.

Depreciation, herein refers only to paper money. (It is not the same concept as devaluation). Most simply stated, it means that the paper money form comes to represent in the circulation less than the weight of gold it purports to represent. (The monetary unit *may* then be devalued by the Government to conform to the depreciated value of the paper form). The price level rises as the paper money depreciates. This is most clearly seen in the case of Government printing press money depreciation, where sooner or later a two price system for goods is established, paper money price and gold money price. But while BCM also depreciates when it is inflated, it cannot properly be said that the depreciated BCM is worth less than the weight of gold it purports to represent, unless there is a hyperinflation. (See Chapter IV on this)

Deflation is the reduction of the volume of paper money forms. (Treasury Notes can be cancelled or repudiated; BCM can be cancelled by several means, including refusal to make new loans, bank failure, etc.) On devaluation or deflation the price level may rise, or fall, or remain the same.

*.2 The price of goods stated in the monetary unit. The Monetary unit as the standard of price of material goods.**

To simplify the discussion:

(a) Assume gold to be privately owned, and that it can be used in the purchase and sale of goods; that the paper money forms in the circulation represent the weight of gold they purport to represent, and are convertible to gold on demand. (Caution: this is not the money form and money system of the pefcp).

*Throughout this book, the term "price" is used only with reference to the price—the exchange value of *material goods*. The term is not given such uses as: the "price of money" (interest); the "price of labor" (wage); the "price of land" (rent or capitalized rent) or for the "price of services" generally.

(b) The discussion following relates to price, the monetary unit, in the exchange and valuation of material goods, generally, (i.e. not a discussion of price in the capitalist relationship, specifically). The general principles of money, price, valuation, are of course, applicable to and indeed basic for the consideration of price and normal price in a capitalist economy. That is to say, the monetary aspects of price, and price level, are always implicit in normal price (the price in the capitalist economy embodying profit at the prevailing wage-profit ratio). Nevertheless, it will simplify a general price-money analysis, if normality of price in the capitalist relationship is considered separately. (Section 17.) Normality is generally not a monetary question at all (although inflation and depreciation of paper money *may* have some effects on normality).

Further: so that the discussion of price and the monetary unit can proceed without the complications introduced by changes in the dynamics of the economy, assume an equilibrium in the market, (normal price).

The price of a good is its exchange value stated in the monetary unit (a weight of gold). The fundamental principle of price is that the exchange of goods for money is not a *barter*, where one good is exchanged for another good of equal value, for the use of the person seeking the exchange. The good is not bartered for a weight of gold as an object of equal value (the value of each, determined, let us say, by the actual cost of production of the good, stated in labor time or uniform average "wage units"). Barter is not the nature of money; money is more than a material good, although it must be a material good and always remains a material good. But money is also the social form and expression of all commodity value generally; it expresses the value in exchange that the society will place on a good at any one time. The general, effective social demand values the good, vis-a vis all other goods.

It is not a question at all of the value equivalencies of two specific commodities (gold and the good being sold), or the cost of production of these two commodities. The same commodity can at one time sell for $35.00,–one ounce of gold, and at another time for $70.00, two ounces of gold. The cost of production of any good, may not change at all. The amount of money the purchaser may pay for the good may at any time change.

By using the money form, the socially accepted expression of value, purchasers put a price on goods that varies as the social value, and the social demand changes. (Whether production will be carried on at the demand price is another matter). Some goods produced may have no money value at all; some are so overproduced that their unit value is far less than the cost of production.

If the good is in social demand, and the price of the good at any one time is its cost of production (at the general price level prevailing, i.e. the price of all goods), the price should rise or fall as its cost of production rises and falls. But it may not, if the social demand for the good also changes.

Actually, in the price of any particular good, or of all goods at any one time, the cost of production of gold is irrelevant. The stability of gold value should be assumed. In any event, at the time of the price change, the cost of production of gold is constant.*

So then, price is not a ratio between the value of goods and the value of gold. Furthermore, assuming an equilibrium in the market, price is *not*

- the result of supply and demand of goods
- a ratio of quantity of goods to quantity of money or the supply and demand for money

*It is true that at certain periods where there is a great change in the volume, and cost of production of gold, this may have some influence in changing the general price level. When this happened gold was, physically, a major media of exchange, and the barter at the mine is of sufficient volume to have an effect on the general price level. This was long ago; cost of production of gold today is practically of no significance on the price level (especially in the PEFCP).

Note in this connection, as stated elsewhere, that the weight of gold in the monetary unit can be halved by Government devaluation, without any appreciable effect on the domestic price level.

The gold producers may suffer if the price level doubles or triples and the monetary unit still contains the same weight of gold. Their cost of production, in terms of the goods they must purchase and the wages they pay, must rise. However, it is possible that their cost of production may not rise, because of technological advances, or they may use slave labor functioning at a far below subsistence level.

The goods enter the market with a price, and the money enters the market with a value.

The nature of Price and Money appear when imbalances between supply and demand for goods, or concepts of "supply and demand" for money, are eliminated. Refer to the discussion on Normal Price (the capitalist economy in equilibrium) in Sec. 17. Note also that equilibrium means more than that supply and demand are in balance. In the capitalist economy it implies the proper proportions in the demand, i.e., the new investment, etc.

Change of Price, of the particular good, or of prices of all goods:

In the change of price, the nature and function of money is particularly well seen. Disregarding for the moment, the change in the prices of all goods (general price level) because of the depreciation of paper money:

The price of a particular good changes as its cost of production changes, and as the social demand for the good changes.

The prices of *all goods* (the price level) can change as the cost of production changes; and as the general effective demand changes.

The price of all goods can move from one-half its original level, to twice its original level; and there is no connection whatsoever (as in a barter concept) to the cost of production of the gold, or the cost of production of the specific good. (And the weight of gold in the monetary unit can be changed by Government action at any one point, without affecting the price level, or the price of any particular good.) The same good, to repeat, can be priced at x, or 2x of gold, where there is no change in the cost of production of the good; the general price level can be x or 2x in gold with no change in the cost of production.

The general price level changes (again disregarding for the moment, price level changes due to the process of depreciation of the paper money which is the major reason for price level change) because of changes in the general demand, vis-a-vis the existing supply. If the overall demand starts to fall steadily, faster than overall supply can be reduced, then the price of all goods, and each good will be expressed in a relatively lesser weight of gold. Again, this is the function of the money form. Each good does not necessarily fall in price, but a general decline in demand almost always affects the price for the particular good, and hence its price.

(Example, from Sec. 17: the depression phase of the business cycle, where demand contracts because of the end of capital expansion, and then spirally contracts further as production itself declines. These are the general price level declines that are part of the mechanism of the system, i.e. result from the dynamics of the system. Do not confuse the fall in the Aggregate Price of goods sold, with the fall in the price level).

Rise in price level because of depreciation of the paper money (after a certain degree of inflation).

Prefatory: Refer to comments in Chapter I, Topic 4, and Ch. IV, on the confusion resulting from the use of the word "inflation" to describe a rise in the price level. Inflation is defined as a certain process in the creation of paper money. Paper money *may* depreciate because of the inflation, and the price level will rise. When the price level rose because of the inflation of Government printing press money, the concept of depreciation of this paper money was quite clear. After a certain degree of inflation, the paper money did not represent the weight of gold it purported to represent in the circulation. Prices of goods were higher in paper money than in gold. But a *mild* depreciation of bcm, on the inflation of BCM, raises the prices of goods in *gold price* as well as in paper money price, during the process of the inflation. A two price system does not take place except in a hyperinflation. It cannot be said that the BCM does not represent the weight of gold it purports to represent. (Chapter IV)

As a general rule, if the price level rises to any extent, the monetary factor is to be suspected first, generally the depreciation of the paper money, or possibly in the change of the monetary unit (although the latter is not always of great importance, especially over the short term). But depreciation may also be interacting with the effect of a rise in demand due to a variable expansion of capital in the ICE. It is extremely hard, in practice, to distinguish to what extent the several factors that affect the price level, are operating. (Note also, that the depreciation of paper money, etc. may be concealing the decline that takes place in the unit value of goods, over the long term, because of technological advance. If prices are stable over a long period, it is probable that there is a depreciation of the paper money).

It is not the price level itself but the *change* in the price level in the ICE* that affects the economy, and, even more important to the economy than the change in the price level, are the *causes* that result in price level changes. Except in the later pefcp, and in instances of uncontrolled paper money inflation in the ICE, it can well be assumed that whether the price level is x, or 2x, or 3x in gold, is quite immaterial. Money and gold function as standard of price and measure of value, equally well in different weights of the unit, or in multiples of the same unit weight.

Furthermore, normality of price, the most important aspect of price in the capitalist economy, can be established at any price level. Normality is always determined on a *given price level;* the *change* in the price level affects normality, wage rate, profit rate, indeed all relationships and ratios. The "given price level" is itself a point in a history of almost constant change, and constant re-adjustment. There are short term movements, and long term movements. In summary: It is paper money depreciation that has most significantly affected price levels; and the change in price level has then affected all the ratios and relationships of the capitalist economy. See elsewhere, on the popular doctrine that change in the general wage rate causes general price level changes (false in the ICE, rarely true in the pefcp).

*In the pefcp, the domestic price level has a great significance in foreign trade; the Government may reduce the gold weight of the monetary unit, and thus, in terms of *foreign* currency the price level falls.

.3 Bank credit money, private and public forms, must always be viewed in its primary context, as money created for the production and sale of material goods in the capitalist relationship, even though it is created for other purposes. It is always tied to the actuality of material goods, and hence to gold. But the analysis of gold equivalency, and gold convertibility must take into account not only the dynamics of the capitalist relationship in the production of goods (the expansion of capital and the business cycle) but also the fictive processes that may be episodically present in the ICE.

The discussion of Money and Price (Sec. 17, on Normal Price) in this Chapter is a necessary part of the analysis of the structure, mechanisms, and dynamics of the capitalist relationship, specifically the ICE. But it must be wholly incomplete without a discussion of the banking system and banking process, viewed as part of the capitalist organism. This is deferred to Chapter IV, since the main thrust of the analysis of the book is towards the fictive processes. The questions of gold equivalency and gold convertibility, cannot, even in the ICE, be adequately considered apart from the banking process, inflation, and the fictive forms and processes, although the subject is *always* concerned with the price and value of *material goods.*

The idea of the "creation" of money.

It is an illusion that "Money" is something created, *ex nihilo,* by the Government, or by the "Bank", by printing press, or stroke of the pen. In the first place, money and gold as money, and the monetary unit, must have been socially established, before the paper money representative form. The paper money form serves in only one of the functions of money, i.e. as a medium of payment; gold, and a specific weight of gold, are the measure of value, and the standard of price. Secondly, the system of production must exist in which there is a production for exchange of value equivalents. The private individual producers must be willing to use this paper money as a value equivalent: That is to say—it is the *acceptance* and *utilization* of these paper forms by private producers and individuals that causes this paper to be money. Thus money is not "created" by a simple *unilateral* act of Bank or Government.

This acceptance is only under certain conditions, and the acceptance is not necessarily at the gold weight the paper purports to represent, or declared by the Government to represent. The acceptance must not only be by the first person to whom the money is transferred, but by all succeeding transferees, who also determine what weight of gold is to be given to the paper form in the circulation.

The volume of paper money at the gold weight purported to be represented, that can be created by the Government, is not in the power and control of the Government, but depends on the volume that can be used in trade, or more precisely, in capitalist production, if it is to circulate at the gold value it purports to represent. Nor is this volume in the power of the "bank" (at the gold weight purported to be represented by the paper money); it depends not only on the level of production but also on the volume and rate of Aggregate Profit of the organism.

The Treasury Note is issued on the faith, credit, and power of the Government (its power to borrow money and levy taxes) to make good its promise. That is to say, further, there is something more than an ex nihilo act, even at the very outset. The Bank's creation is also made on its faith and credit, but this credit is essentially based on a specific asset, and on the bank's assets generally. The condition of acceptance of bcm is ultimately the value of the assets on which it has been created. Consequently the productive activity of the economy at a profit (equilibrium, capital expansion) will be the ultimate basis for its acceptability. It is true that the capital papers on which bcm are created may be fictive, or the money a pure inflation, and the bcm may still be as "good as gold". However, their equivalency to gold depends on the dynamics of the economy. (The analysis continued in Chapter IV.)

(15) "Wage." (Paid to labor by capitalists in the production of material good.)*

—The Wage-Profit ratio in the Net Aggregate Price of Goods sold

—The establishment of the average wage rate in the capitalist organism

—The Aggregate Wage of the organism; the Level of employment; wage in the capital unit.

.1 Recapitulation and amplification on the basic structure of the capitalist organism, expressed in terms of "Wage" "Profit" and "Price" (as Aggregates of each and interrelationships between Aggregates); "Wage" is always the correlative of "Profit;" the fundamental Wage-Profit ratio in the Net Aggregate Price of goods sold.

The basis for, and the premise of Profit in the organism lies in the establishment of the average wage rate of the organism at a level so that the Aggregate Wage will be a fraction of the Net Aggregate Price of goods sold. The Wage-Profit ratio in this Net Aggregate Price is normally established in an equilibrium; hence

*(a) The term "wage" is used herein only to refer to the money advanced out of capital to hire labor to engage in the process of production and distribution of material goods, in the capitalist relationship.

In ordinary usage "Wage" is money paid to *any* employee for his services. But most of these "wages" are not advanced out of capital, are not recovered by the sale of the goods produced, and there is ordinarily no correlative of profit. There are many other incomes, classified as "wages" that are not included. Many employees (including Government employees) produce "services" which are conceived to be part of the National Income and the Gross National Product. A considerable part of incomes classified as "wages" are part of the Aggregate Profit itself. In the capitalist relationship, care must be taken to exclude from "wage" in the wage profit ratio, all wages except those paid for material production and distribution.

(b) The wage is a *Cost* to the capitalist, being advanced out of capital and recovered by him by the sale of the goods. It is not income to the capital unit, but one of the several costs recovered; the remainder of the sale price after all costs, is the profit. But Aggregate Wage must be considered part of the Net income of the individuals of the system. The wage should not be considered as representing a share of the goods produced that belongs to the Wage earners. When the goods are produced they belong to the capitalists; the wage earners buy goods from the capitalists with their wage.

the further premise of the existence of Profit is the proper function of the organism, i.e. the expansion of capital so that the goods will be sold at normal price, the Aggregate Profit then coming into being.

The following has been explicitly or implicitly stated in the discussion of the nature of the organism and its dynamics, and the goods-money circuit. The economy is one in which labor is employed by capitalists, who advance a wage out of capital for the production of goods, at a profit, through sale at normal price. The employment relationship is of the essence of the relationship.

It is fundamental that the average wage rate for the organism be *socially* established at such level that the Aggregate Wage advanced represents only a certain part of the net value of the goods produced in the organism—the net Aggregate Price. Assuming an equilibrium, in the later Independent capitalist economy the ratio of Aggregate Wage to Aggregate Profit is approximately 1 to 2.

The first question to be examined is how the *average* wage rate of the organism is established (.2 below). "Supply" and "Demand" for labor do not establish the average wage rate.

The analysis of "Wage" must be made for the organism, not at the level of the unit or sector of the economy. Furthermore, the primary study is not of the variations in wage rates from time to time, or in sectors of the economy, or the wage rates of the several types of labor employed. The analysis of wage and wage rate must be at a given *price level.* (Sec. 17, .1h, a general summary on price level). The wage-profit-normal price relationship must be examined at a given price level, or extraneous factors obscure the real relationship.

The *real wage* is what the money wage will buy at any given price level. The significance of wage and wage rate (a) to the wage earner is what part of the goods constituting the net Aggregate Price of goods sold, the wage will buy; (b) and to the capitalists, what part of the net Aggregate Price of goods sold they have to pay the wage earners.

It does not follow that the establishment and maintenance of the average wage rate means that Profit will come into being at all, or at its normal level. The actual size of the Aggregate

Profit and its rate depends on the dynamics of the economy, i.e. the expansion of capital and the size of the Profit B.

The wage rate is not part of the basic dynamics that determines the Level of Production and the Net Income. Changes in the wage rate are not even a significant factor affecting Level and Income. The size of the Aggregate Wage—in appearance a vital factor in the size of the effective demand and the volume of consumer goods produced—is only a *consequence* of the Level of Production, which is determined by the dynamics of the organism. Unemployment is not only consistent with prosperity, but in the ICE a moderate degree of unemployment was economically desirable. The standard of living (the real wage) is also of little significance to the function of the organism (ICE).

But in stating the foregoing, it must be understood that the basic premise of the system and organism, is the establishment and maintenance of the average wage rate at a certain level (wage-profit ratio), and the existence of a class of laborers who will work at the average wage rate.

Changes in the wage rate do occur (.3 below), particularly since the price level changes frequently for monetary reasons. (There are other reasons for change in the average wage rate). But wage rate changes take place in a narrow range, and slowly, and they do not essentially or material change the wage profit ratio, at the equilibrium condition, at a given price level. The wage profit ratio must not be seriously disturbed by any marked rise in wage rate if the capitalist relationship is to exist.* The structure of the society and the economy and all ideology maintains this wage profit ratio.**

*Among other consequences: if the ratio is seriously disturbed, Profit B will fail; if Profit B fails the system will fail, i.e. if capital expansion fails, the system will fail. A revolutionary rise in the average wage rate will end capital expansion permanently. A corollary of the foregoing is that a marked rise in wage rates cannot substitute for capital expansion (the capitalist economy cannot be converted into a consumer economy). The maintenance of the wage-profit ratio is of equal importance in the pefcp. In the pefcp if the pseudo Profit B cannot come into being, the WMS will fail.

**The ideology of the capitalist economy has many doctrines useful for this purpose. Examples: that wage increases are the cause of the price rise; that wage rises cause "inflation"; that depression and business failure are caused by rising wages, or union activity, etc.

.2 In the ICE, the Average Wage Rate is established for the economy as a whole on the basis of average actual cost of subsistence, or what is socially regarded as subsistence of laborers.

There is a wide range in the pattern of wage rates of all individuals engaged in the production of material goods in the capitalist relationship, from the wage rate of the unskilled manual laborer in the weakest sector of the economy, to the most skilled salaried professional employee in the most profitable sector of the economy. But an average wage can be stated, and an "average" type of labor for which the average rate is paid, can be assumed. The greater part of the laborers, and the labor, will be found at a certain mean (as to type of labor and as to wage rate).

This basic average wage rate is established at either the *actual* cost (at the given price level) of basic physical maintenance—food, clothing and shelter, and the reproduction of the average laborer—*or* what is socially regarded as constituting the physical minimum maintenance. The socially prevailing concepts of what is minimum physical maintenance have almost as great a force as the actual minimum for physical maintenance. Since there is a considerable range in types of laborers and labor, some more costly to produce, maintain and reproduce than others, certain specific wage rates will be above the average, and others below the average.

This basic actual cost of subsistence, (or what is socially accepted as a basic level of subsistence) differs in national economies. It may change from time to time in each national economy. Certain economic factors enter into both the actual cost of subsistence and the social concept of what subsistence is. Natural resources, the environment, the land, the population mass vis-a-vis the land area, all affect this. It seems also that technological improvements in production (of consumer goods) change the basic cost of subsistence, and also social concepts of what subsistence is, (Below, that technological improvements may also reduce money wages at a given price level). Certain cultural factors and political factors also affect the concept of what basic subsistence is, and these can also change from time to time.

The minimum for physical subsistence and reproduction was the basis of the average wage rate in European countries in the 19th century, and it was the socially accepted standard of the wage rate. It is likely that the level was somewhat below human subsistence for a part of the working class (the wage rate for child labor). However, despite the fact that many children were destroyed, the labor force, on the whole reproduced itself and expanded.

A subsistence level of this nature is not willingly accepted. A coercion, direct and indirect, is necessary to maintain such a wage rate. It is not too much to say that economic, political, and religious ideology was directed towards the maintenance of the wage level at minimum subsistence, (particularly in the nineteenth century). Economists maintained that lowering the wage rate was a positive good; that the lower the wage, the more that could be "saved" and capital expanded—the ideology that "savings" was the source of capital. Economists taught that the labor fund could not provide a higher wage and even that to pay more than a subsistence wage was socially injurious, in that it would encourage a propagation that would outrun the food supply. The nineteenth century wage earners and the other poor, were almost outside the social order. It was the period in which the concept of "exploitation" could effectively be formulated into a revolutionary economic doctrine.

In America the situation was somewhat different. A minimum subsistence level was not socially accepted, although it did prevail in many parts of the economy. Political doctrine, religious doctrine, the existence of free land, raised the socially accepted standard of subsistence, and the average wage rate. The existence of slavery also probably tended to raise the social standard of subsistence, and the average wage rate, rather than lower it.

The wage rate *and* the real wage, generally tend to rise above subsistence level as productivity increases. That is to say, advancing technology generally raises both the money wage rate and the real wage. However, it is hard to say how much the average money wage rate actually did rise in the twentieth century (before the end of the ICE) because the price level was rising, although even despite the general price rise, real wages did rise.

With respect to the wage rates of employees not engaged in

the production and distribution of material goods, in the ICE—(employees engaged in rendering personal services, most employees of the Government, certain financial institutions, etc.): In general, their wage rates parallel the wage rates in material production, in comparable types of work. However, in certain spheres the socially accepted concepts of "subsistence" are higher, and in some it is lower. The wage of the "clerk" rarely rises above subsistence. The subject of wage patterns in all these types of employment is a complex one, and need not be considered further herein.

Summary:

(a) The premise of the existence of the capitalist system is that there will be free laborers available for hire—a class of individuals, (not independent farmers, independent craftsmen, or individuals incapable of entering into a private contract of employment).
(b) That the average wage rate will be such that an Aggregate Profit of a certain size (and rate on the total capital employed) is *normally* returned on the sale of the goods produced, when the economy is in equilibrium. The normal ratio of Aggregate Wage to Aggregate Profit is 1 to 2. Such a ratio is, course, by no means true for all units, or all sectors of the economy.
(c) The basic average general wage rate is not established by the "supply and demand" for labor.

.3 Principal Causes of Change in the general average wage rate. The effect of these changes on the organism, and on the capital unit.

The average wage rate does change, although slowly. And the real wage tends to rise as productivity increases; furthermore the socially accepted standards of subsistence rise as productivity increases. The essential points, however, are:

(a) The change in the average wage rate is never such that it significantly changes the established wage-profit ratio (at equilibrium).

(b) Most wage rate changes are illusory, being a readjustment to price level changes, i.e. a change to restore the wage-profit ratio at a given price level.
(c) If the cost of production falls because of technological advance, and yet the price level remains the same (because of counteracting depreciation of the paper money), the wage rate may remain the same, yet the real wage increases.

The principal cause of change in the average wage rate is the change in the general price level that takes place because of *monetary* reasons (inflation, and depreciation of paper money; in the earlier ICE also devaluation and debasement of the monetary unit). The rise in wage rate under such circumstances does not ordinarily change the wage-profit ratio. But in the actual situation, there will be found to be other forces operating, beside the price level change, and these forces may result in an absolute increase in the wage rate, or they may resist a rise in the wage rate necessary to restore the wage-profit ratio. That is to say, price level changes because of monetary reasons are often part of an economic situation that includes certain other factors, which in some way also affects wage rate. It is not easy to ascertain what all the forces operating are, the effect of each, and the direction in which they are operating. It would be best to consider some of these aspects separately:

(a) Changing price levels due to monetary reasons. (As stated above, this is the main reason for change).
(b) Changing price level in the business cycle.
(c) Variations in supply and demand for labor, particularly for certain types of labor. (Repeated, from .2 above: It is not "supply" and "demand" for labor that establishes the basic average wage rate. In the establishment of this rate, the realistic hypothesis is that the supply always exceeds the demand. It may be that for certain particular types of labor —highly specialized labor—demand is a significant factor in establishing the rate, but even here the effect of scarcity should be viewed as a determinate of what multiple of the average rate will be paid.) The variations in supply and demand referred to, are the *gross* disturbances in the busi-

nes cycle (war or serious depression); mass migration to industrial areas, or from one country to another.

(d) Advancing technology that reduces the cost of production of consumer goods (possibly the increased productivity of labor generally.) This raises the real wage, and may affect the money wage. It may also affect social ideas of the level of subsistence.

(e) Unions: collective activity of wage earners to raise wage rates.

(f) The acquisition by a commodity sector of such power over price that the sector can pay a relatively higher wage rate. (Secs. 13, 17.)

None of these factors should be considered as acting separately; almost always there is a conjunction of factors, and two factors may operate in opposite directions.

Restatement of the general rule on effect of a rise in the price level because of paper money depreciation (or possibly a change in the monetary unit): The money wage rate will slowly rise to maintain the wage-profit ratio, and the real wage. There is a lag, since wage rates rise more slowly than prices. The money wage *follows* the price level (other things being the same). Whatever the appearances are to the individual or the individual unit, the rise in wage rate is not a cause of the rising price level (except in rare circumstances in the pefcp, and then only to a very limited extent).

The average wage rate as affected by change in the general price level in the business cycle, and variations in demand for labor in the business cycle:

The Price level may rise in boom conditions, i.e., a demand exceeding the current supply of goods. This is often accompanied by a paper money inflation, and it is then hard to determine to what extent the rising price level is due to the depreciation of paper money. But in any event, the wage rate tends to slowly rise since the general price level is rising, but, again, the wage rate rises *after* the price level rise, and before this rise, Profit and Profit rate are temporarily higher.

If there is a fall in the price level in a depression, the wage rate will fall, and here the response is faster than on the rising price level. The main readjustment of the Wage-Profit ratio in depression, however, is the sharp decline in the Aggregate wage, through the reduction in the number of laborers.

The average wage rate may be slightly affected by increase in demand for labor during boom periods, and likewise by greatly increased unemployment during depressions. But other things being the same (and here the general price level is the most important consideration), demand and supply changes in the labor market do not significantly affect the basic average wage rate.*

Reduction of Cost of Production of Consumer Goods; Cost of Production in general:

The general rule is that the *money* Wage does not increase as productivity increases, (reduction of cost of production of any type of good, consumer good or capital good) other conditions being the same. (The idea that money wages rise as productivity increases is part of a fairly recent ideology, and it is rarely true even in the perfcp)** However, changes in the price level because of monetary reasons, so often co-exist with changes in productivity, that it often seems that money wages increase because of productivity increases. What is happening in practice is that the price level rises, either offsetting or more than offsetting the decline in costs; hence there are more goods at the same or higher prices, hence wages must increase to maintain the wage-profit ratio.

*Chapter VI: In the PEFCP where war may cause a marked rise in capital expansion and production, and at the same time a withdrawal of great numbers of laborers from the work force, and an *actual* shortage of labor, there is a tendency toward a real rise in the Average Wage Rate, but this can be controlled by the Government.

**Only under certain special circumstances in the PEFCP, can the wage rise cause a rise in prices, and possibly this price rise again cause a wage rise— i.e., the so called wage price spiral. It is an unusual situation; the basic rule is that wages follow the price level in the PEFCP as in the ICE.

The *real* wage may increase as labor productivity generally increases, and the cost of consumer goods declines. There is no certainty, however, that the real wage will increase, because the *money* wage rate can then fall, although generally speaking, the *money* wage tends to remain stable. But other factors, resulting from productivity increase, may cause some rise in the average wage rate.

If, thru advancing technology, productivity increases with respect to *consumer* goods—and this will include the means of their production— then the *money wage rate* should ordinarily fall, if the real wage is to remain the same. That is to say, since the actual or socially accepted cost of maintenance falls, the money wage rate should fall. (It may be that a reduction is necessary also to maintain the wage-profit ratio, if the Aggregate Value of the goods produced falls because of the decline in the cost of production). However: (a) Actually, the *social standards of subsistence* will be rising as the technology advances, and the money wage rate (at the given price level) tends to remain the same, with *real wages* rising; (b) it is probable that the price level is in its usual long-term rise (because of the usual monetary depreciation), and as the cost of production declines, the rising price level counteracts the tendency for price to fall (because of technological advance) so that the commodity price tends to remain the same, or even rises. So, given a decline in the cost of *consumer* goods because of increasing productivity, rising social standards of subsistence, and rising price levels, the average money wage rate will not fall and more likely will rise; hence, *both* real wages rise and money wages rise.

Restatement of the basic rule that an increase in productivity, other things being the same, does not increase the money wage rate; rather the money wage rate should fall if the real wage rate is to remain the same; if the money wage rate remains the same then the real wage rate is rising. Note that increasing productivity increases the "Real" profit but not necessarily the money profit, unless capital expansion is at the same time increasing the level of production. The same factors that obscure the consequences of increased productivity with respect to Wage will be operating on price, for although price should fall as productivity increases, the price level can remain stable, or rise (because of monetary factors.)

Price level changes and productivity changes must be considered particularly in the context of the other factors:—changes in supply and demand for labor, the business cycle, pressures exerted by unions and employers, (below) changing social standards of subsistence, etc. (all of which may be moving in different directions).

There is another factor that should be added to this complex of variables. We have been considering *average wage rates* and average real wages, in the *organism* as a whole. But certain sectors of the economy* which have great price power, can usually pay higher than average wages, because they can pass on additional costs in price. (See elsewhere, that this reduces the profit of other sectors, and will also usually reduce *wage* rates in those sectors.) So the average wage of a *sector* must also be considered in the foregoing.

Labor Unions.

The union does not achieve a significant role in the ICE in effecting change in average wage rate, although late in the ICE, the union had some influence in narrow sectors of the economy.** In these few sectors the union was able to raise wages to current subsistence level, and in some cases something above a subsistence level. The net economic effect was to raise the average wage rate very little, but it must be conceded that the unions had some effect in changing social concepts of what subsistence was.

The subject of union pressure to raise wages must be con-

*Even towards the end of the ICE, labor had acquired little political power. It could not obtain Government assistance to unionize, or raise wages. On the contrary, the Government's power was not infrequently exercised for employers, to lower wage rates, and to prevent unionization.

**In the pefcp, the labor union achieves its truly important and necessary role. Power to increase wage rates is essential in an economy where the price level steadily rises. Nevertheless, the Government now has a profound interest in maintaining the wage-profit ratio, as great an interest as the capitalists, for the pseudo Profit B may not come into being if the labor unions assume too great a power. The Government counterbalances the unions' power; otherwise it must itself directly fix wage rates.

sidered, first, in the context of the constant individual and collective pressure of *employers*

to resist wage rate increases
to force the wage rate down.

Every individual capital in the organism (a) seeks to reduce costs of production—cost of production of course includes the Aggregate wage paid for the given value of goods produced; (b) each capital resists any increase in costs which will tend to reduce or destroy the entrepreneural profit at the given level of production. It is to be recalled that the entrepreneural profit is only a part of the Aggregate Profit; other parts exist as *costs* to the producer, and are institutionalized in the system as costs. Thus the entrepreneur has the burden of not only assuring himself of his profit, but of assuring the existence of other parts of the Aggregate Profit as a whole. The individual unit struggles against any effort to raise wage rates, for its own existence, and at the same time it is protecting the recipients of taxes, interest, rent, etc. With respect to resisting wage increases, the entrepreneur properly receives the support of recipients of other parts of the Aggregate Profit.

There is another aspect to wage as cost (a cost that the employer constantly seeks to *reduce*), which makes the problem of union activity to raise the wage rate, more complex.

Labor can be made more productive through technological improvements. The wage rate can remain the same, yet the total wage or number of employees can be reduced. (In the more powerful sectors of the economy, the tendency is to cut wage costs by technological improvement; in the weaker sectors the tendency is to cut wages. These tendencies are causally related. The stronger sectors can raise the price of goods. This reduces profit rate in the weaker sectors, inducing the employers in these sectors to reduce wage rates, or resist a rise to levels comparable to those in the stronger sectors.)

Union efforts to raise wage rates in an economy that is disparately concentrated (and an economy—ICE—where unionization is very unequal among the several sectors), has uncertain and unpredictable consequences on sector prices and sector wages. The interests of many groups, and individuals in different sectors seem antithetical. Nonemployers, such as farmers and small business men were anti-union, feeling that it was to their interest that the lower wage rate be maintained. Consumers who receive income derivative from recipients of Profit A—this includes many wage earners outside the sphere of material goods production—opposed wage increases to those engaged in material production. Their economic interests seem opposed to "labor." (The popular belief is that a rise in wages causes a rise in prices.) However, where the wage-earner outside the field of material production finds that his wage depends on the general average wage rate, he tends to support the union.

.4 The Aggregate Wage. The Level of employment.

Recapitulation: The Aggregate Wage represents the sum of all wages paid to individuals employed in the production of material goods. It is the average wage rate multiplied by the number so employed. Aggregate wage is a consequence of the Level of production (given- a. the existing wage rate, and b. the state of the technology insofar as it determines the number of laborers necessary, per unit of goods produced). A more general statement: The Net Income, of which the Aggregate wage is a part, is the consequence of the Level of Production. Aggregate Wage is not a cause or determinant of the Level of Production, although, seemingly, as part of the effective demand it is a cause of the Level. In summary, the Aggregate Wage, determined by the Level of Production, is thus determined by the level of new investment for new capital goods (Profit B).

As to wage rate, and state of technology:

The general rule is that over the relatively short period, changes exert no significant influence over the size of the Aggregate Wage; each had best be regarded as almost constants. The truly variable factor is the number employed, and this is determined at any one time by the Level of Production.

The average wage rate tends to remain stable, and even with a rising price level, the wage rate rises more slowly than the price level rises. Likewise, over the short term, the number of employees required by the state of the technology can be considered fairly constant, although if the entire period of a cyclic episode is considered, there will be some change—reducing the number of laborers necessary. But the main change in any cyclic period is the Level of production, rather than the technological change.

Over a long period of time, technology reduces the number of laborers required per unit of material good. Furthermore, there is almost invariably a price level rise due to monetary unit depreciation, and of course the Aggregate Wage is affected by these two factors. But again, these do not affect the organism's function thru the Aggregate Wage. Actually over the long term there is an increase in the number of laborers, not the decrease caused by technological advance. The long term steady increase in the number employed is solely the consequence of the constant increase in the Aggregate capital. The marked variation in the number employed in the business cycle is the consequence of the change in the Level of Production, itself a consequence of capital expansion and contraction. But at any point, while technology determines the number of employees per unit of goods produced, technology is not the cause of significant change in the Aggregate Wage (just as change in the wage rate is not). The Aggregate Wage, to repeat, is dependent on and determined by Level of Production; and the cyclic changes in the Level determine the cyclic rise and fall of the Aggregate Wage.

Long term changes in wage rates and technology, on the one hand tend to increase wage rate and hence Aggregate Wage, and reduce the number employed and hence the Aggregate wage, but the latter is overwhelmingly counteracted by the increase in number because of the greater increase in the Aggregate capital.

Price level rise due to monetary factors, may result in a rise in the wage rate (to maintain the same wage-profit ratio) and hence Aggregate wage tends to rise as the price level rises. This type of increase in Aggregate Wage and wage rate does not affect the Level of production, and is a consequence of other factors.

With respect to Wages of those employed outside the sphere of material production (not included in the Aggregate Wage):

For the greater part, their volume is dependent on the size of the Aggregate Profit, since a major part of these wages are derivative from Aggregate Profit. To a limited extent they are also derived from Aggregate Wage.

These "wages" do not affect the size of the Aggregate Wage, or the number of employees (being a consequence of the Level and normality of price). Caution: the place of the Aggregate wage, and the great volume of "wages" received outside the sphere of material production in the *pefcp*, require a somewhat different analysis than in the ICE.

(16) "Profit."

—The Wage-Profit ratio in the Net Aggregate Price of goods sold

—The Aggregate Profit of the organism; Rate of Aggregate Profit

—Constituent parts of the Aggregate Profit.

.1 Recapitulation:

"Profit" is the correlative of "Wage" in the capitalist relationship in production of material goods. See recapitulation on "Wage" in Section 15.

The Aggregate Profit is a basic structural entity of the organism; it also contains the dynamics of the organism. But it is the Profit B part that is the dynamic element, determining the size of the Aggregate Profit itself, the size of the Aggregate Wage, the amount of capital that will be advanced as a whole, and hence the Level of Production and Income.

The Aggregate Profit must be conceived as representing a value of material goods: that part of the Aggregate Price of all goods produced and sold, minus the cost of the capital used up in the production, which includes the Aggregate Wage advanced.

The Aggregate Profit is not received by units and individuals as "Aggregate Profit," nor is the Profit A part (consumption of the capitalists) received as such an entity; or the Profit B part (representing, the new expanded capital), received as such an entity. The Aggregate Profit is received by units and individuals in certain forms—shares of the Aggregate Profit—entrepreneur's profit, interest, etc. These shares of the Aggregate Profit each contain (with the exception of the tax of the Democratic State) part of the Profit B, although the share received by any *specific* individual or unit, may not contain part of the Profit B.

But the Aggregate Profit comes into being as a whole. It does not come into being as an addition of its parts or shares, as if the parts and shares came into being first. Each capital unit obtains a part of it (entrepreneur's profit); other individuals or institutions obtain a distributive share of it. Some of these distributive shares, received by individuals or institutions, may appear as *costs* to the capital unit.

.2 *The size and rate of the Aggregate Profit. (Rate of Aggregate Profit in the mechanism of the organism and the unit; Price and Normal Price of particular goods express this Rate.)*
—The rate of entrepreneural Profit
—The component parts of the Aggregate Profit, received by units and individuals:
Entrepreneur's Profit; Interest; Taxes; Rent; "Financier's Profit."
—The dynamics of the organism reconsidered in terms of the distributive shares of the Aggregate Profit.

The absolute size of the Aggregate Profit is of importance in three ways:

(a) It is one of the factors that determines the *rate* of the Aggregate Profit (the percentage of the Aggregate Capital that the Aggregate Profit represents). This rate is a basic mechanism of the organism, and in each unit's function. (Refer to Normal Price.)
(b) The size of the Aggregate Profit sets forth the limits of the sum of the distributive parts of the Aggregate Profit; entrepreneur's profit, interest, etc. These are shares of the whole; the whole is not an addition of the shares.

(c) The size of the Aggregate Profit reflects the dynamics of the organism. (The Profit B part determines the size of the Aggregate Profit as a whole.) The size of the Aggregate Profit will reflect the whole Level of Production—the capital advanced, the Net Income (Aggregate Wage plus Aggregate Profit). With respect to (c) it is to be noted:

A. The size of the Aggregate Profit rises and falls in the business cycle;

B. The size of the Aggregate Profit increases absolutely as the Aggregate Capital increases.

The rate of Aggregate Profit is the percentage of the Aggregate capital represented by the Aggregate Profit. Practically, this rate is difficult to ascertain. (The size of the Aggregate capital itself is hard to determine; it cannot be ascertained from capital papers). And to determine the Aggregate Profit, the Aggregate Price of goods produced and sold would first have to be determined (for the Aggregate Profit must be stated in terms of the price of goods produced and sold), and from the Aggregate Price there would have to be deducted the cost of the capital used up in the production, to arrive at the Net Aggregate Price: and from this the Aggregate Wage paid. All these elements are hard to determine.

Nevertheless, the rate of Aggregate Profit is real and demonstrable, constantly making its presence felt in the mechanism of organism and unit: always expressed in the *price of every material good sold,* and in the *rate of the entrepreneural profit.*

A: In equilibrium, the *average* rate of entrepreneural profit closely follows the rate of Aggregate Profit, but at a *lower level.* (The average entrepreneural rate is much easier to ascertain than the rate of Aggregegage Profit). The entrepreneural profit is but one part of the Aggregate Profit, although a major part, in the *ICE.* Other parts of the Aggregate Profit—interest, most taxes, rent—appear as *costs* to the capital unit. Hence the whole net profit of the unit (the entrepreneural profit) will be less than the hypothetical share of the Aggregate Profit of the unit.

Both the entrepreneural profit rate and the Aggregate Profit rate are percentages of capital employed (in the case of the capital unit, the rate on all capital employed by the unit, not the capital used up in the production of the goods sold alone). The total price of the goods sold (in equilibrium) if normal, will reflect the rate of Aggregate Profit of the organism; but although this is the price the unit receives, the net return to the unit is always reduced by the other "costs" that represent other parts of the Aggregate Profit. However, it is by selling the goods at the normal price—reflecting the rate of Aggregate Profit—that the unit can recover all these "costs."

B. The rate of Aggregate Profit (in equilibrium) is of fundamental significance in the determination of the *normal* price of all goods, and of particular goods. The normal price is that price that embodies the prevailing wage-profit ratio of the organism as a whole, and the price that is based on the prevailing rate of Aggregate Profit. Normal price—as applied to the *Aggregate price* of goods produced and sold means that the economy is in equilibrium, the wage-profit ratio is at the usual level, and the Aggregate price of goods is such that the rate of Aggregate Profit is at the normal equilibrium rate. Normal Aggregate price of goods is a consequence of, or rather a statement of, the fact of equilibrium.

As to the normal price of the *particular goods*: the rate of Aggregate Profit (in equilibrium) is fundamental in establishing the normal price of particular goods. The normal price of the *particular* good, is the cost of the capital used up in its production, (including wages), *plus* the *rate of Aggregate Profit,* in equilibrium, and *all the capital* of the unit producing the particular good. To repeat: the normal price of the *particular* good returns all parts of the Aggregate Profit, as well as the entrepreneural profit, and of course, all the capital used up in production. Hence, again, the entrepreneural profit rate, in equilibrium, although it follows the Aggregate Profit rate, must always be considerably lower, so that all other parts of the Aggregate Profit are found in the normal price.

Caution: the foregoing statements, of the average rate of entrepreneural profit, its relationship to the rate of Aggregate Profit, the normal price of goods reflecting the rate of Aggregate

Profit, are all concerned with averages in the organism as a whole. In the later ICE, certain sectors of the economy have the power to "fix" prices. (Sections 13, 17.) The entrepreneural profit of these sectors will be higher than average. Other sectors of the economy must then have a lower than average rate of entrepreneural profit; this follows from the laws of Aggregate Prices and Aggregate Profit.* Thus, in the later ICE, each sector may have a different "normal price." Note also, with respect to different normal prices in the sectors, that since the normal price reflects the amount of capital the unit employs in the production (and not the amount of wage-labor alone), different sectors employ different amounts of capital for each unit of production. If the capital invested is higher than other sectors, the normal price will be higher than the other sector. That is to say, price and normal price in the capitalist economy does not reflect the cost of labor alone, but the capital involved in the production as a whole, and allocates part of the Aggregate Profit to the price of the good. (The wage-profit ratio in a sector is not the significant ratio in determining price.) Thus:

—the wage-profit ratios of each sector differ
—entrepreneural profit rate of the sectors differ
—normal price differs in each sector
—capital invested per unit good produced,
differs in each sector

Recapitulation, and amplification on Entrepreneur's Profit, and its Rate.

The profit obtained by the capital unit producing (transporting, distributing) material goods, consists of that part of the total Price of the goods produced and sold by the unit, remaining after *all costs,* including capital used up, wages advanced,

*That is, since the Aggregate Price and the Aggregate Profit are a definite limited amount, and all the particular commodity prices are parts thereof, a price in a sector that obtains a higher than average rate of profit, will result in prices in other sectors that return a lower than average rate of profit.

and other costs to the unit, which may include other parts of the Aggregate Profit, such as interest, rent, taxes.*

The entrepreneur's profit is stated as a *rate* on the basis of the *whole* capital invested in the unit.

Rates of entrepreneural Profit differ markedly in the various commodity sectors of the economy (the higher rates existing in the more concentrated sectors because these sectors have a great power over price). Since the various sectors share in the Aggregate Profit, if some sectors can obtain higher than an average rate, the profit of the weaker sectors is *pro tanto* reduced. Some sectors may have a rate of entrepreneural profit as high as or higher than the rate of Aggregate Profit.**

There is, however, an *average* rate of entrepreneural profit for the organism. In equilibrium, it closely follows the rate of Aggregate Profit.

The rate of entrepreneural profit reflects at once how the organism is functioning. If the volume and rate of Aggregate Profit begins to decline because of cyclic depression, (failure of capital expansion) the rate of entrepreneural profit declines, and it declines faster than the rate of Aggregate Profit, because the other shares of the Aggregate Profit are less vulnerable, and have a greater priority of payment, being costs to the unit.

In a disequilibrium, (depression) the falling rate of entrepreneural profit reflects both the fact that the price of goods tends to be below normal, and the fact that the effective demand has begun its spiraling decline. Demand and price may be inadequate to the point that entrepreneural profit disappears; it may not even be possible to pay all fixed costs, or even return the wage and capital advanced. But even if the unit is able to pay all costs (including other shares of the Aggregate Profit, such

*All entrepreneurs' profits are part of the Aggregate Profit. In the sequence of production of raw material to finished product (including transportation, wholesale and retail trade, etc.), the entrepreneural profit of the supplier appears in the value of the goods purchased for further production and sale, to each purchaser in the sequence.

**Differences in rate of entrepreneural profit were, in the earlier ICE, an important mechanism in the function of the economy. Capital would tend to move from the sector with a lower rate to a sector with a higher rate. In the later ICE this is of much less importance, since most sectors are highly controlled as to entry, etc.

as interest, rent, taxes), the failure of entrepreneur's profit may result in the termination of the unit, thus terminating all other parts of the Aggregate Profit that the unit might have been able to pay.

New investment (creation of a new capital or the expansion of an existing one) normally requires the existence of the entrepreneural profit at the prevailing rate, on the new capital. (The ability to pay interest alone, or other parts of the Aggregate Profit is not sufficient; interest is only one part of the Aggregate Profit. The new investment may be lost, as to principal, if interest is the only part of the Aggregate Profit that can be paid on the new investment.)

But entrepreneural profit, and its rate, are not the dynamics of capital expansion, or the dynamism of the organism, any more than interest is. The existence or possibility of entrepreneural profit, or interest, on new capital is a consequence of the existence of new investment for new capital itself; it is not a cause of the new investment. That is to say the precondition for the existence of the entrepreneural profit for the unit on existing or new capital is the fact that Profit B is coming into being, in the organism, i.e. capital expansion Entrepreneural profit is the individual incentive; but it is the dynamics of capital expansion that makes the "incentive" possible.

In connection with the foregoing, it would be useful at this point, to restate the law of the dynamics of the organism in terms of the distributive shares of the Aggregate Profit. The general statement was that the dynamics of the system lies in the Profit B part of the Aggregate Profit (new investment in new capital goods) and not in the Aggregate Profit as a whole. The size of the Profit A (as well as the Aggregate wage and the capital advanced) are dependent on the Profit B. Likewise then, the dynamics of the system is not in the sum of the distributive shares of the Aggregate Profit. *A fortiori,* the dynamics is not in any one of the distributive shares of the Aggregate Profit, entrepreneural profit, interest, etc.

To begin with the Aggregate Profit as a whole (Profit A plus Profit B) has come into being because the new investment has been made. Likewise then, the distributive shares as a whole have come into being (assuming an equilibrium) because the new investment has been made, i.e., because Profit B exists.

Further: the new investment has been made because it is expected that the new capital purchased will return its proportionate share of the Aggregate Profit as a whole—(read also then, its proportion of all shares of the Aggregate Profit). The basic premise of this is that new investment will again be made, so that the proportionate share of the Aggregate Profit on the new capital will come into being (read also then, that all distributive shares of this part of the Aggregate Profit will come into being).

But is is necessary to add that the existence of the Aggregate Profit as a whole (Profit A plus Profit B) on existing capitals (read also, payment of *all* shares of the Aggregate Profit) is a necessary condition to the reasonableness or the existence of the expectation that new investment will be made to enable the new capital to be profitable, i.e., return its share of the Aggregate Profit (read also, return all parts of the Aggregate Profit).

The point is that an expectation is not sufficient. Unless the new investment is actually made to enable the Aggregate Profit on existing, or new capitals to come into being, it will not. And the payment of all distributive shares is dependent on the actuality. Certainly the *incentive* of any or all distributive shares of the Aggregate Profit is essential for a new investment, but the expectation does not mean that these distributive shares can or will be paid. *A fortiori,* the incentive of interest, for example, neither means that all shares of the Aggregate Profit will continue to be paid, or that the interest itself will be continued to be paid. The existence of all shares (because the new investment has been made) does not mean that new investment will continue to be made.

The "incentive" of entrepreneur profit, or of interest, or of taxes, or of financier's profit, etc., are neither the reason for the functioning of the economy in equilibrium, nor the reason the new investment is made. (See, below, however, that payment of *interest* alone, on a fictive capital paper, may affect the Level of production, and may cause new investment for actual capital expansion etc.)

.3 Shares of the Aggregate Profit received by units and individuals—other than Entrepreneur's profit:
Interest. The rate of interest.

(Also considered: Interest that is not a direct share of the Aggregate Profit; interest on money or capital paper not representing goods used in the process of material production.)

Rent (as a direct share of the Aggregate Profit).

Taxes (insofar as they are a direct share of the Aggregate Profit).

Financier's profit (referring to that part of the Aggregate Profit created by the inflation of paper money, and certain fictive capital papers—the pseudo Profit B).

Derivative incomes (from each share of the Aggregate Profit). Transfers of income. Priorities and preferences of payment of each share.

A. Interest, and the Rate of Interest, in the capitalist economy.

Interest is money paid for the loan or use of money, and is a percentage of the principal, for a time period. (Assume the promise to repay the money loaned—the principal.) The loan or use of the money can be for any purpose. The money may be created by a bank for the loan for interest; the repayment of the principal to the bank cancels the money.

Fundamental distinction: the two forms of interest in the capitalist economy:

(a) The prototype interest form in the capitalist economy is interest paid for money borrowed (include money newly created by a bank) *for the production of material goods for sale* in the capitalist relationship, i.e. buy goods for further production, pay wages, distribute the goods. This includes money borrowed or created as new, additional capital. The interest is *part of the Aggregate Profit* resulting from the production and sale of these goods. It is a direct share or part of the Aggregate Profit. It is a counterpart form of the entrepreneural profit. This does not mean that the prototype interest form and entrepreneural profit are interchangeable or alternative forms. Interest is a necessary form for a share of the Aggregate Profit.

(b) The interest that is paid for the use of money that is *not used as capital* in the capitalist process of production and sale of material goods. The interest is not a direct part or share of the Aggregate Profit arising from the capitalist production and sale of goods. The interest (also a percentage on the money loaned for a time period, with promise to repay the principal) may be a derivative from some income arising from Aggregate Wage, Aggregate Profit, part of the capital itself, or a monetization of an existing capital paper, or the money may be itself created by the banking system, etc. These loans are mainly personal consumption loans, or loans for Government consumption. This interest form may be called the "original" interest form, surviving in an economy characterized by capitalist production.* Fundamentally, this interest is a *transfer* of wage, Aggregate Profit, or paid from some other source. (In precapitalist economies, this type of interest was called "usury").

With respect to the prototypical capitalist interest form, (a) above: Interest as a direct result of the Aggregate Profit in material production exists because of the fact that in the capitalist economy all money can be used as capital (to purchase goods to be used in the process of production and to pay labor a wage). In fact, money is an absolutely essential form in the capitalist process of production and circulation of goods. The goods produced must have or achieve a money form. Money, per se, then, when used as capital, is able to obtain part of the Aggregate Profit.

Interest is a necessary form of the Aggregate Profit, furthermore, because bank credit money is essential to the function of a capitalist economy, and interest is the only practical way for the bank to obtain part of the Aggregate Profit. Existing money capital tends to become centralized in banks and financial institutions. These institutions (individuals also) often will only invest for interest, and will not invest in production or distribution as direct participants because of the relatively greater security of the interest bearing type of capital investment.

*In older economic systems, where money was borrowed to buy goods for resale (the goods produced in a noncapitalist relationship) interest has a quasi-capitalist form, but it is not the prototypical form of the capitalist economy, where the goods are produced in the capitalist relationship. Loans on land, in precapitalist days, were often a means of obtaining, through interest, a part of the produce of the land, i.e. a counterpart of "rent."

The prototypical *rate of interest* in the capitalist economy (an average of a range of rates) is the average rate of interest for money so used in capitalist production. This average rate of interest in the capitalist economy becomes the basic interest rate of the economy; it is related to and usually governed by the average entrepreneural profit rate, or such rate in the specific commodity sector.

Interest usually appears as a *cost* to the unit enterpriser who borrows money for the process of production and sale, including money for fixed capital used in production.

With respect to interest on "non capital" use of principal:

The distinction between the prototype interest form and rate and the "original" interest form and rate is not always recognized, and for certain reasons in economic ideology, the distinction is not emphasized. The idea is sometimes advanced that any interest is a "property" of money, and that it is immaterial if it is loaned for the production of goods, or for other purposes. In the capitalist economy, the interest rate from money loaned for a non-capital use is to a great extent governed by the prototypical interest rate. It was once determined by private or public necessity, and these aspects still continue to have influence (on such loans in the capitalist economy).

Special mention should be made of interest on the Government note or bond, in the ICE (Democratic State). This interest is generally paid out of the tax revenue, and the tax is for the most part a share of the Aggregate Profit (below). Thus the interest on these Government papers *seems* to be a direct share of the Aggregate Profit. But it is a transfer of part of the Aggregate Profit from one group of capitalists to another, i.e., to those that hold the Government bonds. The interest is not a share of Aggregate Profit arising out of the use of this money in the production of material goods. (Further on this in Chapter III.)

There are certain other interest payments in the ICE which do not quite fit in to either of the two categories mentioned, i.e., the prototype form, which is a direct part of the Aggregate Profit, the principal being used for the production and circulation of material goods; or the second form, the loan for personal or Government consumption.

These other interest payments are on money created to deal in capital papers, land titles, etc., and on capital papers themselves created on the basis of other capital papers. (Refer to discussion on these papers, in Ch. IV.) These interest payments are so closely related to the function of the capitalist system itself, that the interest will be called herein an *adjunct form* to the prototype form. These interest payments are important not because of the interest itself, but because of the implications of the transaction as a whole to the economy. The essential point is that, in part, this "adjunct form" of interest is not only not a direct part of the Aggregate Profit arising out of the use of the money in production of material goods, but is part of a fictive process.

The ultimate *economic source* of the interest paid, and the nature of the *use* of the money borrowed, are the means of distinguishing the three interest forms discussed: the interest as share of the Aggregate Profit in material production; the "original" interest form—on money borrowed for personal or Government consumption; the adjunct types of interest in a capitalist economy. Interest other than the prototype form is usually a transfer of wage income, or a transfer of some part of the Aggregate Profit, or paid out of capital itself, or by inflated money, or by a fictive capital paper.

The several forms of interest, the rate of interest, considered in connection with the dynamics of the organism:

(a) General Rule: The interest on loans, investments, reinvestments in material *production* and sale—a direct share of the Aggregate Profit—plays no primary dynamic role per se, in the Level of Production of the Net Income; the rate of interest on money so used is not of primary importance—supply and rate and availability of money being a consequence of the equilibrium or the disequilibrium resulting from capital expenditure or its failure. (Assume an adequate banking system. Refer to Sec. 12 on "Appearances" of dynamics of money, interest, banking.)

It is expected that the interest on the principal will be paid, just as entrepreneural profit is expected on the new investment, as well as all other parts of the Aggregate Profit. The offer or actuality of interest does not mean that a new investment or a reinvestment will be made. As stated in the preceding subsection the dynamics of the organism is not found *in any one* of the distributive shares of the Aggregate Profit. Entrepreneural profit, interest, etc., are essential individual incentives, without which the system would not function, but their existence at any one point, altogether or separately does not mean that new investment will continue.

It is true that it *appears* that a new investment may be made because interest is paid on it, or it is expected that interest will be paid on it. Consequently, it appears that the availability of money itself and the interest rate have dominant importance in the Level of Production and the Net Income. (Assuming that it is recognized that the principal, the new investment, becomes part of the Profit B on existing capitals, it is true that when the principal, the new investment, does become part of the Profit B and the capital is expanding, the entrepreneural profit will come into being, as well as interest, taxes, etc., on existing capital.) However, the new investment will not have been made simply because it pays interest (although it appears that the investors advance the money because of interest) but because the loan itself, the principal, the new investment, itself will function so as to return all the parts of the Aggregate Profit. A rational investment is based on the whole quality of the loan for use in material production, and in material production this means more than the ability to pay interest. (Note again that the ability of the new investment to pay all parts of the Aggregate Profit requires also that there will be continued new investment to buy the production of the expanded capital.) To repeat: interest alone on new investment for capital for material production is not sufficient for such investment. This is the essential distinction in the role of interest in the creation of fictive capital paper, *where interest alone is sufficient for the creation of such papers.*

It might be inferred that if interest can be paid on new investment for material production, that it can reasonably be expected that all other parts of the Aggregate Profit will be paid. Possibly this is true in the public utility field, where public authority guarantees all parts of the Aggregate Profit of the capital. But generally, the new investment requires the reasonable expectation that all parts of the Aggregate Profit will be returned. This depends on the existence of, and continuance of capital expansion in the economy as a whole.

It may be noted that even if interest can be paid on the new investment, this may possibly mean that the interest is being paid out of pre-existing profit (i.e. not on the new capital invested), and the net result is to reduce the rate of entrepreneural profit.

(b) Interest and interest rate in the creation of capital paper and bank credit money, which are not created as capital for the production of material goods.

Recapitulation: The Level of production and the Net Income (production of material goods) may be significantly affected in the ICE, episodically, by the inflation of bank credit money, public, or private, or the creation of certain fictive capital papers. Simply by the payment of interest alone, a fictive capital form can be created and money inflated. If a pseudo Profit B is created—or an overexpansion of capital induced (Profit B), the Level of Production and the Net Income will rise. The principal, as "new investment" constituting part of the pseudo Profit B, need not be able to pay entrepreneur's profit, nor the other parts of the Aggregate Profit. And there need be no further expansion of capital to make this "investment" possible (as in the case of an investment in real capital goods).

The general rule stated in (a) then, must always be considered in the light of the possibility of paper money inflation and creation of fictive capital forms which will raise the Level of Production, as a pseudo Profit B. Episodically, the creation of money, the availability of money, interest and interest rates can become of great importance in the dynamics of the ICE. The supply of money, rate of interest for money used in material production and capital expansion, needs always to be studied in the banking system as a whole. At the same time the function of the banking system is profoundly affected by the financial mechanism, the creation of money for the financial mechanism, and for fictive capital papers, and inflation.

In the actual function of this economy (ICE), money and banking and interest and interest rate must be examined in a larger context than the advance of money for material production, whether as new investment or re-investment. And the function of the banking system and the banking process itself moves in a much larger context than the creation of money for material production, in an *equilibrium*. The role of money and interest then must be examined in the whole context, each aspect of which interacts upon the other:

episodic fictive capital formation
episodic inflation of bank credit money
the variable overexpansion of capital
the inherent business cycle, the depression
the effect of depression on the banking process, the problem of gold equivalency of the paper money unit, bank liquidity and solvency, the flight of gold in foreign exchange, and the role of the Government Central Reserve Bank. (Refer to Chapter IV.)

General comments on interest rate: In equilibrium, the prototype interest rate (that on money in the production of material goods) is the dominant rate. It is actually two rates: the bank rate, and the non bank rate. These are closely related. The non bank rate is usually for money itself on deposit. In the ICE, the bank rate is almost entirely on short term commercial paper; the non bank rate is generally for longer term paper, and is higher.

In equilibrium, the basic average interest rate will generally be lower than the average entrepreneural profit rate. It would appear that the difference between the rates diminishes as the ICE develops, although both tend to fall. However, the pattern of interest rates and the actual pattern of entrepreneural profit rates exhibit a considerable range in the different sectors of the economy, and they are not congruent. In some sectors of the economy, the interest rate may be higher than the entrepreneural profit rate. In sectors which have a low or uncertain profit rate, the interest rate may be very high (ICE). Generally speaking, in the ICE, sectors of the economy with the highest price power pay the lowest interest rates; the weaker sectors pay the highest interest rates if they can borrow at all.

An interest rate may be excessive, reducing the rate of entrepreneural profit to such extent that capital expansion will not proceed. However, this is generally a consequence of the failure of the dynamics of the system, and not its cause. This is not to say that there cannot be an inadequate or incompetent banking system, or that in some sectors of the economy the banking facilities are inadequate. However, it is typical in the ICE for the weaker sectors of the economy to be adversely affected by the scarcity of loan capital and excessive interest rates.

In general, in the later ICE, lowering the interest rate does not by itself ordinarily raise the entrepreneural profit rate. Even if it does, capital expansion cannot be activated by this means. If a rapid cyclic rise is in process, lowering the interest rate may induce further expansion. (The rise in entrepreneural profit rate because of rising price level and lag in rise of wage rates, is probably more important than the reduction of interest rates). In general, the rate of interest will have more significance in re-investment rather than in new investment.

In disequilibrium (decline and depression) or disequilibrium resulting from a boom, or where there is a considerable inflation of paper money and creation of fictive capital forms and a marked speculative rise in capital papers and land titles, not only is the rate of interest in material production *not* the dominant rate, but the latter rate too, is affected by the entire monetary and banking situation, and the function of the financial mechanism.

B. Taxes. (ICE, Democratic State.)

Prefatory: The tax, as W M tax, becomes of profound importance in the WMS—pefcp, and is considered in Chapter III. In the ICE, the tax as a whole is not of great significance in relation to the total income. (Taxation is of political importance in the "Democratic State" and in the establishment of this State; Ch. VI. Sec. 4.) The reason that the tax of the Democratic State is considered in Ch. III, Sec. 2.2, is that the purpose is to contrast the nature and especially the incidence of this tax with the W M tax.

The present discussion is concerned with three main points:

(a) Most taxes in the ICE-Democratic State have their ultimate economic incidence on the Aggregate Profit.
(b) But, unique among the shares of the Aggregate Profit, the tax falls on the *Profit* A part, and not on the Profit B part of the Aggregate Profit.
(c) Some taxes of the Democratic State, however, are not part of the Aggregate Profit but represent an actual cost of production of material goods.

As set forth in Chapter III, the term "economic incidence" designates the part of the income, i.e., Aggregate wage or Aggregate profit on which the tax *ultimately* falls. "Personal incidence" is used to indicate the person on whom the tax *ultimately* falls. The word "ultimately" is used in both connections because the first incidence of the tax is usually shifted.

The difficulty in recognizing that most taxes (ICE) are a part or share of the Aggregate Profit arises from the fact that the immediate incidence of the tax might seem to be on either wage or on capital, or on material goods as a cost of production or distribution. The fact is that these taxes are shifted; in particular the tax on wages is almost in its entirety shifted to the Aggregate Profit. Even some direct income taxes are shifted. What appears to be a tax on property, or on capital, really has its ultimate incidence on the Aggregate Profit.

The *fundamental principle* of taxation of the Democratic State: the tax may not take capital or capital coming into being (Profit B) but only part of the *income*. In effect, then, the tax of the Democratic State falls on the Profit A. The tax is essentially a *transfer* of consumption from one group to another. (Contrast the W M tax which falls on the pseudo Profit B and is not a transfer of consumption.)

As to the exceptions to the rule that the tax is a share of the Aggregate Profit, refer to Chapter III. i.e., tax as payment by entrepreneurs and others (as a forced payment) for material goods produced for them by the Government, or for certain labor furnished by the Government necessary for the private production of material goods (roads, harbors, communications, education of wage earners, etc.). Certain of the expenses for activities undertaken by the Government may be met by a tax on the wage earners, but the benefit constitutes an addition to wage not paid directly to the wage earner but paid by a tax on the Aggregate Profit or a cost of production of goods.

In summary: the tax in the ICE is a share of the Aggregate Profit. The tax does not reduce the Aggregate Profit. To the individual and the unit who are receiving some part of the Aggregate Profit—entrepreneurs' profit, interest, etc.—the tax appears as a reduction of their income or share. The greater part of the tax revenue flows in a goods-money circuit between the Government and the ICE, which is part of the whole goods-money circuit of the organism.*

C. Rent.

In the capitalist economy the rent of land or natural resources becomes a share of the Aggregate Profit, and it is a significant share. Distinguish the usage of the term "rent" herein from its common usage, wherein "rent" usually includes other elements: cost and depreciation of improvements, labor, cost of management, profit on improvement and structures, taxes, etc.

Rent will not be discused herein, particularly the complex problems of differential advantage in production, or rent determination of various types of lands, etc., since the subject is not of particular relevance to the general discussion. The essential point is that "rent" is a share of the Aggregate Profit obtained because of certain power; it is not a reduction of the Aggregate Profit. Rent may appear as a cost to the entrepreneur. Rent is a share of the Aggregate Profit that has a higher priority than any other share of the Aggregate Profit except taxes.

Some further comments may be made: The amount of rent does not follow from the price of the land; the price of land is a "capitalization" of the amount of rent. In the ICE, the

*The *tax rate,* as the term is commonly used, is not a rate or percentage of the Aggregate Profit. However, even in the ICE, the total tax share of the Aggregate Profit could be stated as a percentage of the Aggregate Profit. This rate would be of little significance in the ICE; it is of great importance in the pefcp.

rate of interest has a marked effect on the price of land, but this is not so much the situation in the pefcp. Rent paid by wage-earners (referring to rent in the pure sense) is also usually, but not necessarily, a part of the Aggregate Profit, although it is a part obviously not obtained by the entrepreneur. The rent paid by capitalists for the personal use of land, or for certain types of business, is a transfer of a share of the Aggregate Profit.

D. Financier's "Pseudo B" Profit (episodically existing in the ICE. The inflated money and fictive capital forms that become part of a pseudo Profit B).
"Financier's Profit" considered generally. (The several sources of such "profit.")

There is a certain share or part of the Aggregate Profit that is episodically created in the ICE: the part that comes into being as a pseudo Profit B. It will be called herein (as a share of the Aggregate Profit) "financier's pseudo Profit B." The term is an imprecise one because those other than financiers may be the recipients of this pseudo Profit B. In particular, if there is a public inflation as well as a private inflation, with large volumes of Government bonds created (wartime), these papers and the inflated money, as pseudo Profit B, do not particularly flow to the financiers, as a class.

It will be useful to digress at this point to consider "financier's profit" generally, as a whole. This will clarify the nature of the specific part of "financier's profit" now under discussion—the pseudo Profit B that episodically is created in the pefcp. It is also useful to review the role of the financier in creating part of the Profit B, generally.

"Financier's profit," considered generally, includes certain parts of the Aggregate Profit (beyond the episodic pseudo Profit B). There is also certain income ("profit" to the financier) that is not part of the Aggregate Profit at all. The several parts of "financier's profit" are:

(a) A part of the Profit B, arising from the fact that the financier advances new investment for new capital. The financier is part of the "capitalist class" which advances capital, receives

the Profit B, and the new capital itself (Sec. 7, identities). The Profit B is received in the form of shares of the Aggregate Profit: entrepreneur's profit, interest, etc.
(b) The financier may be the agency through which the new investment for new capital goods is made. The financier may take a percentage of the Profit B in one way or another, and thus obtains part of the Aggregate Profit, as new capital.

With respect to (a) and (b) above:

The financier plays an important role in advancing money for investment for new capital. He may possess the money himself, or assemble it, or have it created by banks for such use by him. He is a *personal* "dynamic" in the expansion of capital, assuming, of course, that the expansion of capital is possible. It is he who seizes the opportunity for a lucrative new investment (here referring to the actual expansion of capital, not the manipulation of capital papers, or the acquisition of other persons' capitals, etc.)
(c) Income from "services" rendered to capitalists generally, whereby some part of other capitalists' income, via entrepreneural profit, interest, etc. is *transferred* to the financier. (See following subsection, referring to incomes derivative from the various shares of the Aggregate Profit).
(d) Income from existing investments: direct shares of Profit A and Profit B paid out as entrepreneur's profit, interest, etc., on existing capitals owned and acquired by the financier. This is simply the return to capitalists, stated herein to a certain group of capitalists.
(e) The direct acquisition of existing capitals, capital papers (including fictive capital papers) that are owned by others. There are various techniques of acquisition. These activities are highly profitable, but this "profit" is not part of the Aggregate Profit at all, but may appear as "income" under one heading or another in National Income statistics.
(f) Profit from the creation of fictive capital papers, that do not enter into the goods-money circuit (not part of the Aggregate Profit).
(g) Finally: monetized fictive capital papers and inflated money that becomes part of the Pseudo Profit B. This is the "profit" principally considered at this point.

The individuals or groups who arrange for or create private fictive capital papers and the private inflation of paper money, which enters the goods-money circuit, obtained this part of the Aggregate Profit (Pseudo Profit B) in the form of material goods. This special group, herein called the "financiers" receive this share of the Aggregate Profit as actual material goods for consumption. As stated, the term "financiers profit" is not entirely suitable, since other than financiers are beneficiaries. The essential point is that the "profit" as pseudo Profit B essentially arises in the sphere of "finance."

With respect to (f) listed above—fictive capital papers created by the financiers—and (e) capital papers and capital acquired by various devices, including bank credit money created thereon, *none of which enter into the goods-money circuit of the organism:* these are indeed a considerable part of the income and wealth of the financial groups. They become the means of acquiring shares of the Aggregate Profit by way of entrepreneur's profit and interest—(d) above.

But the capital papers thus created or acquired may also be used when monetized, to purchase consumer goods, the money and the capital papers themselves becoming part of the pseudo Profit B. This is the financier's profit" under discussion—the direct share of the Aggregate Profit constituted by creation of the Pseudo Profit B. It may be noted in passing, that a certain part of this expenditure may be through "foundations" and charitable institutions that are established with great amounts of these fictive capital papers (among other assets). The expediture of this money is of importance to the economy, but here again it cannot be said that the "financiers" who have created the papers, the money, etc., are the actual beneficiaries. Furthermore, (see below), a significant part of this money flows to the professionals in the financial mechanism, lawyers, etc., and a staff of "wage earning" assistants.

E. Incomes derivative from the various shares of the Aggregate Profit. Incomes, or payments that are in appearance shares of the Aggregate Profit, but are not truly part of the aggregate Profit.

Many individuals receive part of the Aggregate Profit as *transfers* from the recipients of entrepreneural profit, interest, taxes, financier's profit, or as payments deducted as "costs" before these payments are received. The money transferred may appear as *wages* (not to individuals engaged in the process of production of goods), or as professional fees or some other type of personal, or business income. The services paid for may be quite necessary for those paying for them, as a personal service to the capitalist, or a business service in acquiring the part of the Aggregate Profit. (The latter is not to be confused with the actual cost of production of the material goods). It has been noted above that a part of the financier's profit is likewise obtained by transfer, again appearing as professional fees and wages, or deducted as costs for these services necessary to the financial mechanism.

Payment for services for the management and safe-guarding of capital papers, or capital per se, is a cost that is also such a transfer or deduction (from a share of the Aggregate Profit). This cost is not to be confused with actual management costs in the production of material goods. However, the distinction is difficult to make in practice, for financial interests and industrial management often coalesce, and the financial management aspect may predominate in the duties of the prime managers.

The costs—in wages and professional fees, etc.—of dealing in capital papers, land, etc., may also be a transfer of part of the Aggregate Profit and here again, the transfer of part of the financier's profit (above) is an important element.

Certain payments that appear to be parts of the Aggregate Profit, or possibly appear to be derived from a share of the Aggregate Profit, are actually a true cost of production of material goods. An example is that of a part of bank interest. The banking system must include a charge in its interest rate for the labor and materials necessary to maintain the bank credit money system, which is necessary for the capitalist system of production. This is a true cost of production and sale for the whole system, and in one way or another, it is a cost that must be charged against all capitals. The cost is far less than the cost of producing and using gold (if it were possible to produce all the gold needed for the circulation of the goods) but it is an appreciable cost. It becomes greater towards the end of the ICE, when the use of bank checks spreads even among the ordinary consumer, although this is in part paid for by a direct charge on the users of the checks. The cost of bank notes continues to be paid thru interest, but actually, in the later ICE, and of course especially in the pefcp, this is paid for by taxes (indirectly thru part of the interest on Government bonds, the interest on which is an important part of the income of the Government bank and the commercial banks). Caution: the major part of the interest paid to banks is a share of the Aggregate Profit.

With respect to certain activities of the Government, paid for by taxes, which activities are a true cost of production of material goods, and not a part of the Aggregate Profit (the service being delegated to the Government), see Ch III, Sec. 2.

F. Relative proportions of several distributive shares of the Aggregate Profit; Priorities of payment.

In equilibrium, the major part of the Aggregate Profit will be constituted by entrepreneural profit. The entrepreneural profit, however, is most vulnerable in a depression, and its relative volume is the first to decline. (But depression affects the rate and volume of entrepreneural profit in some sectors more than others. Sectors with great price power and control over production are often able to maintain a fairly high rate of profit, although the volume of profit absolutely declines.)

Interest has a greater security and stability, and has a priority over entrepreneural profit. However, the rate of interest is generally lower than the rate of entrepreneural profit. (Note that in certain sectors of the economy, for example agriculture in the ICE, the rate of interest may be higher than the rate of entrepreneural profit.) While the rate of interest may not necessarily decline in a depression (indeed it may increase) the total sum paid in interest does decline.

In general, the relative share of each distributive part of the Aggregate Profit *in the ICE,* is determined by certain institutional patterns and powers, and in these, historical factors are important (the background of land tenures, the history of the development of the banking system including monopoly, the political developments, international factors, the rate of development of the national economy, and of the various capitals, etc.)

General priorities: taxes have the first priority. Rent has a high priority. Interest has a priority lower than tax or rent, but higher than entrepreneural profit.

The relative proportions of the distributive shares differ in equilibrium and in disequilibrium (depression). In a boom, especially with inflation and the creation of fictive capital papers and large paper profits, the relative distribution is again somewhat different. It is then, as has been noted, that the size of the "Financier's Profit" becomes significant.

(17) The Price of goods in the capitalist economy: The Aggregate Price of Goods sold The Normal Price (Normal Aggregate Price; normal price of the particular good). Price Level.

.1 Recapitulation and Amplification on "Price."

(a) The subject has two aspects; they are economically inseparable, but need to be considered separately to simplify analysis.

A. Price, and Normal Price, in the structure and mechanism of the capitalist relationship (organism, and each unit).
B. Monetary aspects of Price, and Price Level. (Money, Price, exchange and valuation of material goods.)

The first cannot be understood except within the whole context of the second—of money and the general price level. Yet the second, by itself is a wholly inadequate basis for examining price *in a capitalist economy.* (The second may have meaning, by itself, in a non capitalist economy where valuation and exchange are taking place).

(b) Corollary, or alternative statement: Price is not only a mechanism of valuation and exchange, but also a mechanism in the function of the relationships in production of the capitalist system itself (with respect to wage rate, wage-profit ratio, the Aggregate Profit, and the rate of Aggregate Profit). It has a fundamental role in the function of the organism, and of each unit.

(c) Aggregate Price of all goods produced and sold (the total value of the goods produced in the capitalist organism) is a primary price concept in the structure and function of the organism:

A. The Wage-Profit ratio is a proportion in the Net Aggregate Price of goods produced and sold. The Net Aggregate Price is the Aggregate Price less the cost of the capital goods used up in the production of the goods. Aggregate Wage, and Aggregate Profit are shares of the Net Aggregate Price of goods produced and sold.

B. The Level of production is measured only by the Aggregate price of goods sold; and the Net Aggregate price is the sole appropriate measure for stating the Net Income; neither the Level of Production nor the Net Income can be measured (in a capitalist economy) by the *volume* of physical goods produced, whether characterized as consumer goods, or consumer goods plus new capital goods. Price of goods sold is the measure because the system is one of production for value and for profit, and the value and profit can be determined only in the market. The market exists not only for the purpose of exchange for consumption, but for an exchange for further production (in a system the purpose of which is a production of a value that is itself profit, i.e., Pseudo Profit B, and capital).

C. *The Aggregate Price of goods sold, and its normality at any given price level, controls the function of all the units,* with respect to the volume and value of production, and the normality of the price of the particular good. (Subsection .2 below; see further in (h) below, that all relationships and the *Aggregate Price and its normality,* must be examined on the basis of a given price level.

(d) Normal Price is the essential price concept of the capitalist relationship, in describing the structure of the organism, and the function of the organism. Normal Price contains profit at a certain ratio to wage—the normal wage-profit ratio of an economy in equilibrium. When Price is normal, the Profit B is coming into being as part of the Aggregate Profit (new investment, capital expansion).

The *price of the particular good* is normal when the price represents the cost of the capital used up in the production of the good, including the wage, *plus* the rate of Aggregate Profit of the organism in equilibrium, on *all* the capital in the unit producing the good. The normal price of the particular good thus includes certain parts of the Aggregate Profit that are "costs" to the unit (Sec. 16). In the actual capital structure of the later ICE, normal price in each sector may differ because of the power of certain sectors to obtain a higher than average rate of ent repreneural profit. (Subsec .2, below.)

Note also, with respect to different normal prices in the sectors, that since the normal price reflects the amount of capital the unit employs in the production (and not the amount of wage alone), and different sectors employ different amounts of capital for each unit of production, normal price in each sector will differ. Thus. if the capital invested in a sector is higher than in other sectors, the normal price will be higher than the normal price of other sectors. That is to say, price and normal price in the capitalist economy does not reflect the cost of labor alone, but rather the whole capital involved in the production, and the pricing process allocates the aliquot part of the Aggregate Profit to the price of the good. (The wage-profit ratio in a sector is not the significant ratio in determining price.)

(e) But the *normality* of the Aggregate Price is not the dynamic of the capitalist economy but is a *consequence* of the functioning of the basic dynamics of the system itself. The dynamic is manifested through the mechanism of price and the pricing process.

(f) The Price of a good is its exchange value stated in the prevailing monetary unit. "Price" and the pricing process are inherent in the capitalist relationship, as mechanisms of valuation and exchange of goods (as in any system where goods are produced for sale).

The monetary unit, as a specific weight of gold, is the standard of price of goods. Money has a value as it enters the market for goods, and goods have a price as they enter the market.

The price of a good, or the price of all goods, can change:

—overall supply changes

—over all demand changes

(both of these being usually consequences of the business cycle, as capital expansion exists, or fails.)

—the supply or demand for a particular good changes.

In any of these instances, this does not mean that the monetary unit changes in value: the function of money as standard of price is to reflect and express the changes in the market value of goods.

But there can be a change in the whole price level—the price of all goods, because the monetary unit changes in value, or its paper representative form changes in value. In particular, if the paper money depreciates, the process of depreciation will raise the price level. (See Ch. IV, that BCM depreciation may raise the price level in terms of gold, unless the depreciation is of such extent that there is a paper money price level and a gold money price level.)

Thus, the price level can change for two reasons:

As a result of the dynamics of the economy affecting the level of production and the effective demand

Because of monetary reasons, particularly the depreciation of the paper money

There may be a close relationship between the circumstances that precede either cause, and each may interact on the other.

(g) Assuming no depreciation of paper money:

The price of a particular good changes as its cost of production changes, and as the social demand for the good changes. The price of *all goods* (the price level) can change as the cost of production changes; and *as the general effective demand changes.*

Distinguish a rise or fall in the *Agregate Price* of goods sold, from the rise and fall in the *price level.* The Aggregate Price can rise or fall with the price level unchanged; the price level can rise or fall with the Aggregate Price of goods sold unchanged. Generally, a marked fall in Aggregate Price means some fall in the price level—an inherent mechanism of the economy.

The reasons that cause the change in the general price level—and the change in the general price level itself—affect the price of the particular good, *in addition to* the variation in the cost of production of the particular good and change in demand for the particular good. A general decline in demand almost always affects the demand for the particular good, and hence may affect the price of the particular good.

(h) General recapitulation on *price level:*

A. All relationships of the capitalist economy, and all its basic elements, have to be viewed and examined on the basis of a *given price level* (to understand the relationship, eliminate extraneous factors that may conceal the relationship, and the interrelationship). Thus

The Average Wage rate
The Aggregate Price of all goods produced and sold
The Normality of the Aggregate Price
The Price of the particular good
The Normality of the Price of the particular good
The Wage-Profit ratio
The Aggregate Profit
The effective demand, and its components, and their proportions

are to be examined on the basis of a given price level.

B. However, *changes in the price level*—due either to 1. the dynamics of the economy, or 2. monetary factors—immediately affect all relationships, and all elements and all ratios, especially the normalities of the relationship or element. Note however, that when the change in the price level arises out of the dynamics of the economy, the change is primarily a consequence of function, and the changes in the relationship or ratio are primarily manifesting the dynamics of the economy. But change in the price level because of monetary factors affirmatively affects the elements, the normality, etc.

At a given price level, the economy seeks a normality of price. Normality can be achieved at any price level, and the price level per se, is not of great importance. But change in the price level significantly affects the function of the economy.

C. Corollary, and alternative statements: The price level affects the size of the Aggregate Profit, but Aggregate Price can be normal at any price level.

D. The rise in the price level because of paper money depreciation often obscures the price level changes that are taking place for other reasons. For example: there should be a long term fall in prices because of technological improvements that reduce the cost of production. However, on the contrary, over the long term there is a rise in prices. This rise in prices is due to repeated inflations and repeated depreciations of paper money, which have a permanent effect on the price level, even if there is some fall in price subsequent to a deflation of the paper money. The price rise more than balances the tendency of prices to fall. (Amplification of subsection (h) in .3, below.)

Note: One of the principal causes of confusion in concepts of price and price level is the inflation of paper money, and the probable (but not necessary) depreciation of the paper money form. The confusion existed in the ICE, where inflation was only episodic, and the depreciation that may have resulted, cured by the cyclic depression. But the confusion is greater in the pefcp, where inflation must be constant, and there is no deflation, and no cyclic depression, and a constant depreciation. Inflation in the ICE may affect the Level of Production and Income, *and*, during the time the inflation is proceeding, the change in the Level of Production and Income, may affect price, price level, and wage rate, *apart from* the effect of the possible depreciation of the paper money.

These effects invite erroneous generalizations having to do with "quantity of money" and Income, etc., determining price level *and* Aggregate Price, or wage rate and Aggregate Wage.

.2 The Aggregate Price of goods sold, and its normality at a given price level, as controlling the function of each unit, with respect to volume and value of production, and the normality *of the prices of the particular good. The situation where certain*

sectors have such price power that they can get higher than the average rate of entrepreneural profit in the price of their goods.

Assume a given price level, and assume that it is not being affected by paper money depreciation. The discussion covers both equilibrium (capital expanding, wage-profit ratio normal, supply and demand in equilibrium) as well as disequilibrium (termination of capital expansion, supply in excess, demand in downward spiral, wage-profit ratio abnormal). In the latter instance, the price level will probably decline, requiring certain further adjustments, but the effect of price level *change* because of the disequilibrium or from paper money depreciation, will be considered in the following section.

The Aggregate Price of the goods sold at a given price level is equivalent to the capital advanced and used up in the production of the goods, including the wage, and the Aggregate Profit. The capital advanced, the Aggregate Wage, the Aggregate Profit, are, of course, the effective demand (Sec. 5).

If the wage-profit ratio is normal, (which must mean an equilibrium, capital expansion, etc.) then the Aggregate Price is normal. The Aggregate Price is not normal, if the Aggregate Profit is less than that expressed in the normal wage-profit ratio.

But in any event, the Aggregate Price represents the total value produced, whether the price is normal or not. The same volume of goods can have a higher or a lower price—assume again a stable price level—and the same volume of goods can be more or less profitable.

The Aggregate Profit can be stated as a percentage of all the capital used in the production. This rate is an extremely important rate, since production for each unit is for profit on the capital invested, and the price of the particular good, and the total price of goods the unit sells will be controlled by this rate. (Sec. 16.)

Each unit shares in the whole effective demand, obtaining a part of this effective demand, at the given price level. The price of goods sold of all the units, is the Aggregate Price. At the given price level, all the units cannot have a higher Aggregate Price (than the whole effective demand)—in the ICE. Each unit also obtains a share of the Aggregate Profit; the price of all goods includes the whole Aggregate Profit.

The unit seeks, and indeed must have a *normal price* on the particular good. This is equal to the capital it advances and uses up in the production of the particular good, including the wage, *plus* the rate of Aggregate Profit on *all* the capital the unit uses in the production of the good.

But, on the average, (disregarding differences in sector price power) it can only get this normal price for the particular good if the Aggregate Price is normal. (Note that the unit obtains its entrepreneural profit by normal price of the good it sells, and the return of other parts of the Aggregate Profit which appear as costs to the unit.)

It is not to be assumed, however, that in obtaining normal price, the wage-profit ratio of the sector, in equilibrium, is the same as that of the organism. Some units use a great deal of capital and little labor in producing the good: a normal price for such sector will contain a greater part of the Aggregate Profit than those sectors that use little capital, and more labor. The result is that the wage-profit rations of the sectors differ. (Sub sec. .1(d), above.)

The functioning of the units, then, as to the volume of their production, their rate of profit, are determined by the Aggregate Price and the Aggregate Profit, and the normality of the Aggregate Price. (Thus the condition of equilibrium—the capital expansion, the normal wage-profit ratio, determines absolutely the unit function.)

Normal Price and the actual market price:

Consider first, the normal price of the particular good in an economic structure where each sector of the economy obtains the same rate of the Aggregate Profit (i.e., not the disparately concentrated economy of the later ICE). Note again that the wage-profit ratio in each sector may differ from the average because of different proportions of capital and labor used in each sector.

As stated, the normal price of the particular good is a definite price (i.e., cost of production plus rate of Aggregate Profit in equilibrium; assume also average efficiency in production). The normal price is not a price determined by "supply and demand." Supply and Demand determine the Aggregate Price, (at any given price level) but do not determine the *normality* of the Aggregate Price. Normality of Aggregate Price is the result of the whole context of the nature of the supply and the nature and proportions in the demand. (sec. 5.)

While the normality of the Aggregate Price determines the normality of the price of the particular good (normality of Aggregate Price determining the level of function of the unit and its profit), it does not determine the *actual price* that the unit will obtain. The actual price will be determined by supply—demand (which does not determine normality). It is up to the unit, and the commodity sector to regulate the volume of its production, and its efficiency of production so that it does not produce more than is salable at the normal price, nor at a cost above the average. If it produces in excess of the demand at normal price, it will not be recovering its costs, or make its entrepreneural profit: the actual price will be too low. Production should not be undertaken unless it is expected that the normal price will be obtained. However; while it has been stated that supply-demand do not determine the normal price of the particular good, but may determine actual price, *normal* price always assumes that a social demand exists at this normal price. The determination of whether a particular sector or unit thereof is producing socially demanded goods (to obtain its part of the whole effective demand), and in such volume that sale can be at normal price, is made in the market. Some goods produced may have no value at all; others are so overproduced that the unit price cannot contain its aliquot share of the Aggregate Profit. (Sec. 14, on one of the basic functions of price in a capitalist economy.)

In the later ICE some sectors of the economy have the power to establish a market price that obtains a part of the Aggregate Profit at above the average rate of Aggregate Profit (in equilibrium). These are the highly concentrated sectors of the economy, in a pattern where some sectors are not concentrated. (Refer to Sec. 13.) But it was noted that if some sector can establish a price which returns a greater than average rate of entrepreneural profit, the consequence of this is to force down the entrepreneural rate of profit of the non-concentrated sectors (and even force down wage rates). The normal price of these sectors then, is lower than it would otherwise be, and the market price may be still lower. The fact that the normal price of these sectors must be lower follows from the basic principle that since the Aggregate Price and the Aggregate Profit are a definite, limited, amount, and all the particular commodity prices are parts of the Aggregate Price, a price in a sector that obtains a higher than average rate of profit, will result in prices in other sectors that return a lower than average rate of profit. (Certain exceptions: episodic inflation and creation of fictive capital papers: the concentrated sectors because of their price power can obtain a higher profit rate by capturing this increase in the Aggregate Profit without diminishing the profit and profit rate of the other sectors.)

However, the situation *seems* to be that certain sectors establish a market price that becomes its normal price without being controlled by the normality of the Aggregate Price. Nevertheless, this does not mean that the price and volume of sale at this price is not ultimately being determined by the Aggregate Price, and the normality of the Aggregate Price. The fundamental law of the organism still operates and the concentrated sectors are not free of the basic law of the organism. The higher normal price of the concentrated sectors is simply at the expense of the other sectors. That is to say, in the organism as a whole, the rate of Aggregate Profit and the volume of Aggregate Profit, and the existence and size of the capital expansion, and the size and proportions in the whole effective demand are not determined by the units, no matter how powerful the price power of a unit or sector. The Aggregate Price cannot be raised to create or increase profit or the profit rate. (Refer to Ch. III, however, on the importance, in the pefcp, of a price control to prevent the powerful units from raising prices to such extent that the Government is forced to inflate money, etc.)

Thus the general principle stated at the outset, that the normality of the Aggregate Price of goods sold, will ultimately determine the normality of the price of the particular good, and the function of each unit, is operative in a disparately concentrated economy, viewing the organism as a whole. The fact that certain sectors of the economy have a greater control over price than other sectors, and can thereby secure a higher profit leads to the erroneous idea that in the organism as a whole, price controls profit and the size of the market, the effective demand, the Profit rate, and hence expansion and contraction of capital. But the concentrated sectors are only seemingly free of the compulsion of the basic law of the organism.

.3 *Price Level Change:*

a. As a result of depression, or because of a boom in the business cycle.

b. Caused by paper money depreciation.

c. Caused by technological advances in production of material goods over a period of time.

(Effect on Aggregate Price of goods sold, and normality: Effect on Prices of Particular Goods, and Normality. Effect on wage rates, wage-profit ratio, Aggregate wage, Aggregate Profit; the distributive shares of the Aggregate Profit and rates of these distributive shares.)

(Restatement of the effect of changes in wage rate, wage-profit ratio, Aggregate wage, Aggregate Profit, on *price level and Aggregate Price of goods sold; on prices of particular goods.)*

The following is a further amplification of "Price Level" summarized in .1(h) above, with particular respect to *change* in the price level; and amplification of .1(g) above, as to change in price of goods, assuming no depreciation of the paper money.

Even though the price level at any given point is of itself not of great importance in the ICE, provided *normality is established or re-established* with respect to the Aggregate Price, the wage-profit ratio, etc., nevertheless a *change* in price level is of great importance. In the first place, a general fall or general rise of prices in the business cycle is one of the mechanisms of the function of the organism, and one of the means by which all units are controlled. In the second place, the change in the price level resulting from paper money depreciation (i.e. not primarily arising out of the mechanisms or dynamics in the production of goods), will itself affect the function of the economy, since ratios must be readjusted. This is a serious matter, since rates and ratios are not easily re-adjusted uniformly throughout the economy, particularly when there is a wide disparity of power among the sectors of the economy, and disparities of power among groups of wage earners, etc. Finally, a rising price level in itself may have a dynamic effect on the Level of Production and the Net Income.

The subject is one of great complexity since so many factors are operating at the same time, and not always in the same direction. It is difficult to separate cause from effect. The discussion must be simplified by focusing on one factor at a time, although it may well be that the actual net price level change is the result of other factors. The major distinction should be between (a) price level changes that result from the operation of the dynamics of the system of production, which change then has certain consequences on all the elements of the system; and (b) price level change principally from paper money depreciation, the change in price level then causing certain changes in all elements of the system, and under certain circumstances, affects the Level of Production.

In the discussion, the principle set forth in .2 above, with respect to the control exerted by the Aggregate Price of goods sold, and its normality at any given price level on the function of each unit, is of course, always relevant.

(a) The general fall of prices in the depression phase of a business cycle.

It is not possible to separate entirely the fall in the price level in depression, from certain monetary factors, especially in the later ICE. It is probable, in the later ICE, that there has also been a depreciation of the paper money during the previous boom— i.e. price rise due to depreciating paper money. (Chapter IV.) This depreciation is cured by the depression, wherein a considerable volume of the paper money is destroyed. Furthermore, because of bank failure, and other failures, an excessive amount of the paper money may be deflated, and there may be a shortage of paper money. The decline in prices may thus have a monetary cause, as well as the rapid decline in demand for goods.

Confining attention to the production-demand aspects: in the depression there is a general fall in demand before production can contract, *and* a spiral fall in demand as production contracts. Aggregate wage and consumer demand falls spirally, and the market for replacement capital also. Both Aggregate Price and price of particular goods decline.

It should be noted, too, that not *all* prices will necessarily fall, because some sectors have sufficient control of production and price to contract their production quickly, and even to maintain their price despite a sharp decline in other prices, wages, etc.

The Aggregate Price, of course, declines in size because of a reduction in production, but also because the price level falls. Furthermore, the Aggregate Price will unquestionably be not normal, because Aggregate Profit is declining very rapidly. It is true that the Aggregate Wage is being reduced, but this follows the decline in the Aggregate Profit. The wage-profit ratio becomes unbalanced.

The wage rate tends to decline as a consequence, as one of the means of restoring normality to the wage-profit ratio. But the main means of adjustment is the more rapid fall in the Aggregate wage because of the decline in the number of employees. Nevertheless, if the price level is lower, the wage rate will tend to decline.

It should be repeated again that the decline in the Aggregate Profit is not the consequence of fall in price level, but its cause; the fall in the Aggregate Wage and the wage-rate is for the most part a consequence of the fall in the Level of Production, in part a consequence of the decline in the price level; this is a mechanism of the system.

Furthermore, the declines in the various distributive shares of the Aggregate Profit are also the consequence of the depression, and not of the fall in prices, and this is true of the rates also. The entrepreneural profit rate is the first to fall. The unit and the individual attribute loss to the fact that prices are too low, but the real causes are elsewhere.

As indicated in .2 above, the function of each unit is responsive to the decline in the Aggregate Price, the associated decline in the effective demand, the decline in the Aggregate Profit to such point that the Aggregate Price is not normal. The fall in in the Price level as well as in the effective demand reduces the production and profit of each unit, even to the point of loss of entrepreneural profit or failure of the unit as a whole.

The decline in price in general, means that the price of the particular good falls below the normal price, although as indicated in .2 above, this is not true in all sectors of the economy. Certain sectors have enough power to maintain normal price. But whether normal price is maintained or not, there is a marked decline in effective demand and production, and the loss of entrepreneural profit is due more to the decline in production than the lower price.

When the cyclic depression ends, the price level is lower. Normality may be restored at the lower price level. And this will mean lower wage rates, lower Aggregate wage and Aggregate Profit. This does not mean that on the restoration of capital expansion that ends the depression, the lower price level of the depression may not rise somewhat. To some extent this lower price level was the result of gross over production, in some sectors, and the price must and will rise.

If the price level is rising because of boom conditions (the opposite situation to the failing price level in a depression) it is difficult to separate the monetary factors that raise price, from the demand factors that raise price (the sharply increased demand for new capital goods, possible Government demands for war goods, etc.) The extra demand occasioned by the inflation of the paper money is itself one of the demand factors. It is however, certain that under such certain circumstances the price level will rise because of depreciation of the paper money.

In this rising price level there is again a disequilibrium, and since the profit rises faster than the wage, the wage-profit ratio is distorted. The attempt is soon made to raise the wage rates.

(b) The rise in the price level because of depreciation of the paper money. (Ch. IV, inflation of bank credit money; theory of depreciation.)

The major cause of a significant price level rise in time of peace, in the ICE, is paper money depreciation; this is the result of a preceding or concurrent paper money inflation. In war time there will also be a general price rise due to excessive demand and temporary shortages of goods, as well as the depreciation of the paper money.

If the price level rises because of the depreciation factor, then, just as in the case of price level rise due to demand factors alone, the wage-profit ratio becomes unbalanced, the Aggregate Price of goods, and the price of most goods, are not normal.

Wage rates tend to rise to restore the wage-profit ratio to its usual ratio, but since wage rates rise more slowly than prices, for the time being the rate of Aggregate Profit is higher than normal. This tends to increase the variable expansion further; if the economy is expanding, depreciation of the paper money encourages the expansion. However, if the economy is in a decline, the depreciation does not encourage expansion. (*In the ICE,* depreciation of paper money and depression do not ordinarily go together, since the depression results in the deflation of the paper money. (Ch. IV.) However, in the pefcp, a decline in the level of the economy, with continuing depreciation, and rising prices, is common.

One of the more important consequences of price level rise because of paper money depreciation is the inevitable conflict resulting from labor's effort to re-adjust the wage rate. (Section 15, above.) In the ICE, the power of labor was markedly inadequate, and wages advanced, if at all, far more slowly than prices. The normal wage-profit ratio was more likely to be restored by a depression that deflated the paper money, and caused a decline in the price level, than by rise in the wage level. The depression, of course, reduces the number of wage earners, also tending to restore the overall wage-profit ratio.

(c) Price level decline caused by long term technological advances in the production of material goods.

The general price level should decline over the long term because of the reduction in the cost of production of the goods as the result of technological advance in the process of production. (Furthermore, since this is accompanied by a very great increase in the capital involved, the Aggregate Profit rate of profit falls, and the normal price of the particular good is thus also reduced.) However, with rare exceptions, this long term decline in prices because of improved technology is not manifest, except possibly in periods of depression when the cyclic fall may hasten improvement in technology in an effort to overcome the falling profit, and reduce the cost of production.

Prices do not decline, because there is a countervailing long term rise in prices (as well as episodic price rises in the business cycle) due to the long term general depreciation of the paper money which despite periodic deflation, generally causes an ever rising price level. Thus the slow general rise of price over the long term wholly obscures the effect of the fall in the cost of production.

Restatement of the effect of change in the wage rate, wage profit ratio, change in the shares of the Aggregate Profit, *on* Price Level, and Aggregate Price of goods sold; on prices of particular goods (from Sections 15, 16):
Assuming no change in the price level because of depreciation of the paper money, the basic rule is that in the ICE a rise in the average wage rate does not affect the Aggregate Price, *nor* the general price level. Assume also that productivity of labor is constant. A rise in the average wage rate means a fall in the Aggregate Profit, not a rise in the Aggregate Price. It is the wage-profit ratio that changes. In the organism, a fall in the average wage rate increases the Aggregate Profit.

Changes in the distribution of the Aggregate Profit, i.e. in the proportions of interest, entrepreneural profit, taxes, rent, in the ICE:

In the organism, changes in the proportions of the distributive shares, through changes in rates, do not affect the Aggregate Price, or the Price Level, unless they should have some effect on capital expansion, which may then affect the normality of the price.

This is of particular importance with respect to the ideology (in the ICE) that taxes raise the price level as a whole, whereas, at a given price level, taxes are generally a share of the Aggregate Profit, and the tax is a reduction of some other distributive share of the Aggregate Profit.

However, changes in interest rates and taxes will affect the individual *unit,* and the price of some *particular* goods, just as a change in wage rate can affect the individual unit.

Corollary: prices (in the organism) cannot be raised to increase the Aggregate Profit.

PART III

The End of the Independent Capitalist Economy

(18) The "constant" expansion of capital, and the advanced technology in production, must and will bring the ICE to a "critical" point, wherein it cannot continue to function as an independent organism. (The relative economic critical point; the socially critical point; the absolute economic critical point of the capitalist relationship.)

.1 Summary of the consequences in the organism of the "constant" expansion of capital, the development of an advanced technology, and the worldwide development of the ICE.

(a) The Aggregate capital attains an immense *size;* likewise the Aggregate production, in value (the Aggregate Price of goods produced and sold) is of great size, as is the physical volume of goods produced. One of the most significant aspects of the foregoing is the great size, in value, of the Profit B part of the Aggregate Profit. Furthermore, this value (Profit B) represents a great volume of goods. It is further significant that there is a relative increase in the size of the Profit B in relation to the Profit A. The relative increase in Profit B is related to the development of marked concentration in the "capital goods" sectors of the economy.
(b) In general, most sectors of the economy have a highly concentrated structure (Sect. 13). The control over price, in the concentrated sectors, and the higher profit rate of these sectors, and the lower profit rate in the other sectors, are of significance also in the process set forth in (a). In the economy as a whole, the number of capitals relatively declines. But the number of Wage Earners increases greatly.
(c) The development of a distinctive financial and banking structure parallels the growth of sector concentration. Most

capitals tend to be represented by paper capital forms. The financial institutions assume control of major capital units either directly or indirectly, and this control may extend to the whole sector; there may even be a centralized financial control over several sectors. The financial group begins to acquire much of the new capital. The control of new investment (the formation of Profit B) becomes centralized. The central bank becomes a necessity. On the one hand this financial and banking structure becomes indispensible to assure variable expansion of capital (overexpansion) in a concentrated economy, and the concomittant creation of private fictive capital papers, private inflation; on the other hand this financial and banking structure seeks to force the overexpansion of capital, and fictive capital expansion, to maintain the existing capitals' value and the Level of Production.

(d) Necessity for variable expansion, induced and maintained by fictive capital expansion, and paper money inflation, to maintain equilibrium in the later ICE, at a reasonably acceptable level:

In the late ICE because of the great size of the Aggregate Capital, the *possible* volume of variable expansion and hence the possible Level of Production and Income increase greatly (i.e. while production can be very great, productivity is still far greater). But the basic points are:

A. A very considerable overexpansion of capital becomes necessary, if any significant degree of prosperity is to exist. This overexpansion depends more and more on fictive processes, inflation, etc. The volume of *constant* expansion that is ordinarily possible becomes less and less able to sustain an organism of the size of the fully developed capitalist economy.

B. *To maintain a constant expansion itself a variable (over expansion) of capital is necessary, i.e. the constant expansion is at relatively too low a level to maintain capitals of the size existing.* Profitability declines to such extent without the overexpansion of capital that the possible constant expansion is threatened.

C. Because of the extent of the episodic variable expansion and the paralleling fictive capital—inflation activities of the financial and banking structure, the cyclic swings become more violent, and a depression becomes more widespread and more destructive.

(e) The average rate of entrepreneural profit tends to decline in the ICE as the rate of Aggregate Profit decline (relatively greater increase in the Aggregate Capital). However, in the concentrated sectors there may be no decline, or a lesser decline in the rate of entrepreneural profit than in other sectors. (Note that the *total* entrepreneural profit in the concentrated sectors increases greatly). Furthermore, the decline in the cost of production is greater in the concentrated sectors, and since these sectors can maintain price, its entrepreneural profit rate does not decline at once. But ultimately it must also decline. The effect of the declining rate of profit effects the *nonconcentrated sector so that* entry into these sectors is very hazardous. Entry of new capital (outsiders) into the concentrated sectors is hazardous for a different reason.
(f) The average wage rate apparently increases because of the rise in the price level resulting from paper money depreciation, but the wage-profit ratio in the organism as a whole is probably the same. It is even possible that the profit part increases. But *real* wages probably increase because of greater productivity and the decline in the unit value of goods.

.2 *The relative economic critical point of the capitalist organism (ICE). (The "absolute economic critical point," distinguished. This is not reached in the ICE, but can be reached in the pefcp.) The "socially critical point" of a failing economy.*

The following is a summary statement of the relative economic critical point (recp) of the capitalist organism—ICE: When
the size of the Aggregate Capital (the result of "constant" expansion)
the size of the Profit B (new, additional capital)
the long term decline in the unit value of the commodity
the decline in rate of Aggregate Profit (existing and new capital)
have reached the point that the new, additional capital goods

produced in any equilibrium condition, cannot be purchased for any "constant" type of capital expansion that is possible, and such constant expansion would simply exacerbate the situation, i.e. a greater decline in the rate of Aggregate Profit would result and a further decline in unit value of the commodity, *and* there is no longer a possibility of a variable expansion of capital induced or supported by war, inflation, etc., then the organism cannot maintain itself, and a final depression, that is *non cyclic,* will follow, without recovery.

The depression that must then follow is a profound one, and the greater part of the Aggregate capital, as well as most of the capital papers, will be destroyed. It is unlike the cyclic depression The Level of Production formerly existing will never be restored to any point near its former height.

The depression may be accompanied by or end in an economic collapse—financial, monetary, banking, industrial—rather than a recovery to some extremely low level of production. The collapse is the most likely course if there has been, in the recp, some episode of great variable expansion based on a war or inflation or the creation of fictive capital forms. etc. It is extremely unlikely that there can be any "recovery" from such a collapse. (Below, .3—the actual situation.)

The recp then, in any of the three following situations will probably result in a *socially critical point*—defined below—where the existing economic relationship is not socially viable, and another and more productive economic relationship will supersede it, given certain conditions (Chapter VI).

These three situations are: the depression and stagnation of the recp, which is *non-cyclic*; the low Level of Production in which a low level equilibrium and a small constant expansion is possible; a depression plus an economic collapse and a panic in the recp when there has been a preceding immense variable and fictive capital expansion.

Theoretically, the depression of the recp, or a following low stagnant Level of Production may not result in a socially critical point. That is to say assuming the long continued spiral shrinking of the Aggregate capital, *without* a money and banking collapse or panic. and assuming a reasonable degree of social stability, the restoration of an equilibrium even at some very low level might permit an ICE to continue, at least to the absolute economic critical point (aecp)) It would be fairly certain however, that there would have to be a considerable degree of political change. It might be argued, however, that the small rate of constant expansion might not be feasible in view of the widespread destruction of capital. But it is not useful to consider further the hypothetical possibilities, because in actuality, the recp is not reached in a slowly declining economy and a low stagnant level. What actually happens is that a great war intervenes, and an immense inflation; actually there were two great periods of variable expansion which not only reversed the depression but led to a great temporary prosperity. The great prosperity and over expansion of capital and the great inflation, etc., created a situation where the capitalist economy must collapse rather than proceed to deep depression in a slow decline.

The socially critical point is that point in the ICE where (a) production is at a very low level, the volume of profit very low and only the largest capitalists are operating at a profit; most capitals are not operating at a profit and are failing, and there is a very large and increasing class of capitalists who have failed; (b) the professional and managerial classes have a markedly reduced income and the majority of them are unemployed; (c) a third or more of the wage earners are unemployed and the number is increasing; (d) it is believed that there will be no improvement under the existing relations in production and there is, or there is believed to be, an alternative economic relationship of greater productivity, income and the distribution thereof. In short, material production is inadequate for the major part of the population, especially the capitalists, and those deriving income through them.*

Definition of the absolute economic critical point (preliminary)

The word "relative" in the RECP is used to distinguish that

*The *cyclic* depression of the ICE does not bring on a socially critical point. There must be more than poverty and unemployment. The economy, and the society too, can get along well with a high degree of unemployment. The Marxist ideology (Ch. VI). stated that a cyclic depression could produce a socially critical point, but this was not true. The essential prelude to a socially critical point in the ICE is the recp, and probably the economic collapse that actually took place.

critical point from an absolute economic critical point. An AECP is a theoretical concept, meaning that no capital expansion can take place because technology is reducing the cost of production to such a point that capital will either not expand or will shrink as production increases. The capitalist relationship becomes impossible to maintain because, even worse than in an RECP, there can be *no* market for the new capital goods produced even at the lowest level of production, and the rate of profit and the volume of profit is declining, and any further capital expansion involving technological advance must cause the rate and volume of profit to decline further.

This absolute critical point does not occur in the ICE,, nor does it have to exist to end the ICE; the RECP will suffice. But the tendency toward the AECP again becomes active in the PEFCP, where there is again an Aggregate capital of great size, and one that is expanding, and the technology is developing further (all on the basis of a pseudo Profit B.).

Amplification, on the fall in the rate of Aggregate Profit, and rate of entrepreneural profit, and the absolute increase in the Aggregate Profit (preceding the recp, or the aecp.)

As indicated in .1 above: There are two parallel tendencies in the advanced ICE, with respect to the size of the Aggregate capital, the Aggregate Price of goods sold, the Aggregate Wage, and the Aggregate Profit: (a) the reduction in the cost of production of each unit of material goods; the value (price) of the goods declines, because constant technological improvement is inherent in the capitalist relationship. (Caution: because of paper money manipulation and other monetary manipulation, this is completely concealed: the *price level rises*, so that it appears that values rise.) The Aggregate Price of goods sold would then *tend* to fall, and the Aggregate Wage and the Aggregate Profit *tend* to fall as the technology advances. Because of the declines in the Aggregate Profit, the rate of Aggregate Profit will consequently *tend* to fall.
(b) But the Aggregate Capital actually always increases ("constant" expansion of capital)—and despite the *tendency* in (a) above, for the Aggregate price of goods sold, the Aggregate

Wage, and the Aggregate Profit to fall, they *absolutely* increase in volume, despite the fall of the rate or profit. The rate of profit falls because the Aggregate capital increase faster than the Aggregate Profit. Furthermore there is a change in the ratio between Profit A and Profit B, the latter relatively increasing; as the industrial units become fewer in number and greater in size, Profit A diminishes.

The rate of constant expansion may have been increasing, but it can never possibly increase enough to keep up with the growth of the economy, even if the growth due to variable expansion is limited. As has been stated, in the last stages of the ICE, the economy is totally dependent on an overexpansion of capital to maintain an equilibrium, constant expansion being totally inadequate.

The recp, (which actually brings the ICE to an end when the depression deepens into a collapse for certain reasons, and a socially critical point is reached) does not mean that technology cannot further reduce the cost of production of goods, or that new industries cannot be created, or new products come into being, or new areas be developed, or that millions upon millions of individuals are not in need of material goods, or that the Level of Production, as a technical matter, cannot be expanded to meet any of these needs. The recp means that the technological advance and development, and the capital expansion cannot take place on the basis of a capitalist relationship in an ICE. The aecp means that none of these things can take place in *any* capitalist relationship and that the fictive forms will not enable these things to take place or maintain the capitalist relationship. Since the expansion cannot take place the capitalist relationship cannot exist. There is an inability to maintain profit on the existing and new capitals on the relative degree of capital expansion (relative to the size of the existing capital), or in the pefcp, the inability to maintain even the existence of a fictive expansion.

.3 *1914-1929: the period of the relative economic critical point of the ICE. The Great War. The two great over expansions of capital during this period (in the Great War, and in the final "boom" in the U.S.)*

In the fifty years before the Great War of 1914-1918, the full development of the ICE took place.

In the course of the world wide development of the economic system, several new national economies achieved major status. Certain national economies established an economic dominion over relatively undeveloped parts of the world. These dominions were of great importance to their national economies, in the effort of the national economies to maintain a degree of capital expansion absolutely necessary for the domestic economy. The national economies and Governments competed for opportunities to expand capital.

The half century period was a troubled one. There were recurrent serious depressions and financial crises that resulted in widespread distress and in the ruin of many. There was labor conflict and a degradation of large parts of the laboring class. The units in nonconcentrated sectors of the economy found increasing difficulty in surviving. The accumulation of immense fortunes, and political corruption seriously weakened the ideology of the Democratic State. "Socialist" movements caused much concern. However, they were not in themselves significant.

In 1914, the recp was clearly recognizable. The size and productivity of all the capitals in the developed capitalist nations had reached such level that new investment for constant expansion was grossly insufficient to maintain an equilibrium except at a low level of Production, including investment in existing undeveloped areas. The course of the national economies for several years had been erratic, and in most there was a great degree of dependence on production for war purposes, to maintain normality.

The recp must be viewed in the actual political and international situation at this time, i.e. the several fiercely competing national economies, rather than abstractly, as though there were one single great capitalist economy, highly advanced, and unable to maintain an equilibrium. In the actual situation, the recp could not really take the course of a decline into low level stagnation. Capital expansion of any type, all important for domestic survival (of the economy and the State) was a matter of intense concern to each national power. "Expansion" groups became the dominant forces in the several Governments, overriding all other groups.

A world war on the inception of the recp, has two aspects. First, is the possibility of destroying the rival as a national economy, either as a "preventive" measure, or to take over all areas of dominion (control markets for constant expansion) acquired by the rival. The rival's domestic economy might also be destroyed, making the rival an economic dependent of the dominant national capital. The other aspect is the immense variable expansion that the war itself must bring to each national power. Indeed, as long as the war goes reasonably well, and is not too prolonged and destructive, ("attack" the basic military doctrine of each nation), there could be great prosperity.

The war was effective in delaying the effect of the recp. Despite the fact that there was a military and political miscalculation (that a short war could be waged and won), there was widespread prosperity. The war itself was a popular war in all the warring countries, and it relieved the economic, social, and political stresses of the recp.

Prosperity was produced by the war itself, not by the victory. The idea that the recp could be reversed by taking over a rival's dominions or a rival's economy was a vain one. Even a quick victory for either side could not have been effective.

There were two major unforseen consequences of this war. First the Russian economy reached a socially critical point and the Communists seized power. The second was that the period of prosperity that was to come after the war for the successful warring powers, was achieved only by the United States, which entered the war later. The other victors, as well as the defeated nations had to turn to the United States to save themselves from the socially critical point that their economy was entering, something which the war itself could not do.

The period of prosperity in the United States, the second great period of variable expansion in the recp, indeed not only postponed the depression of the recp but was able to postpone the socially critical point of the European economies.

The remarkable variable expansion that took place in the U.S. after WWI, was, first, the result of the war, and of the loans to rebuild or sustain the European economies. But the real basis for the boom was the extraordinary development of the financial system, and a related private monetary inflation through the banking system, to a degree that had never been reached before. (Ch. IV.) There was an immense real capital expansion. Furthermore new capitals were formed, and old ones expanded because the new capital papers themselves became the things of value; capitals could be created because their paper forms would constantly sell for a higher price. And capital papers were then created upon the basis of these papers, their values increasing in the booming stock market. The great sums of money made on all these papers was in part fed back into the economy in the purchase of consumer goods. A genuine private inflation was in being. (Ch. IV on techniques of private inflation *despite* a gold standard, and its consequence.) The results and the technique were the basis of the belief that a new economic system had been devised, unhampered by the limitations of ordinary capital expansion and the business cycle. It was thought that a permanent high plateau of prosperity had been reached. This belief was held by high Government officials and professional economists, as well as the business men, financiers, and bankers. That this new era was based on the full development of private fictive paper and bank credit money inflation and a variable capital expansion based on a pseudo Profit B—all of which had to be *temporary* and all of which were in fact only the ultimate stage of a recp—was not recognized.

Summary: during the period of the recp, 1914-1929 there were two periods of great variable capital expansion. The first was in the Great War; this was effective in prolonging the life of the ICE. The second episode, really a sequel to the first, laid the basis for the total collapse.

.4 *The Great Depression and collapse, 1929-1932. The socially critical point in the recp is reached, and the ICE comes to an end.*

The collapse of the stock market in 1929-1930 was the critical factor terminating the boom and the great capital overexpansion, real and fictive. The financial system and the inflation had been the main forces behind the real capital expansion, and when these could no longer function, the great structure of paper capitals collapsed, and with this collapse the whole economy failed. The Level of Production and Income at once entered into a precipitous decline. (It may be noted that the prosperity existing was unequally distributed; the non concentrated sectors of the economy were already in trouble before the collapse. There was also substantial unemployment. The economies of other nations were already stagnant, and sustained only by the prosperity of the U.S.)

It was stated in subsec. .2 that theoretically, in the absence of a great boom based on financial and monetary manipulation, it is conceivable that a long steady decline into depression *might* permit the ICE to continue, with a very low level of constant expansion restored, and with a draconic control over a poverty stricken society. A small capitalist class could be maintained.

But the extent of the overexpansion of capital, the volume of fictive capital paper and inflated money that had been created, and some of the financial techniques that had been used, made a collapse of the system inevitable rather than a depression alone. By 1932 no banking capital could withstand the test of solvency, and liquidity was soon thereafter lost. (Ch. IV, (3) on the end of the banking system in the catastrophic depression). The Government central Reserve Bank in itself could not thereafter maintain a banking system, except on the basis of an inconvertible paper money, and even on this basis, the GRCB could not maintain an ICE.

Extensive as the depression and collapse were, if they had proceeded further in 1933 the result would have been the destruction of the economic and political organization of the society. But the socially critical point had been reached, and the ICE came to an end and the pefcp had its inception.

Summary note: (a) The final depression and collapse of the capitalist economy (ICE) in the recp is qualitatively and quantitatively unlike the cyclic depression of the ICE. Even if the recp had resulted only in profound depression, it would have been a non-cyclic depression, without recovery. (b) The socially critical point of the ICE is unlike the social situation in a cyclic depression. The cyclic depression of the ICE does not really affect the basic fabric of the society: the State, the economic relationship. The ICE remains a dynamic economic relationship, and will recover relatively quickly. Unemployment and poverty may be widespread, but the basic structure of the society is little affected. These conditions are common in relatively good times. Low wages and even below subsistence wages could not bring on a critical point; indeed low wages were characteristic of the vigorous and expanding ICE.

CHAPTER III

FICTIVE CAPITAL AND FICTIVE PROFIT IN THE POLITICAL ECONOMY BASED ON THE FICTIVE EXPANSION OF CAPITAL

(1) The general theory and mechanisms of fictive capital, inflated money, and fictive profit, in a political economy based on the fictive expansion of capital.

—The Government (WMS), through the inherent powers of Government, creates the fictive forms that make a certain relationship in the production of material goods possible, and creates a distributive system necessary and suitable for the goods represented by these fictive forms.

—The real significance of these fictive forms is that a fictive expansion of capital takes place, to substitute for the real expansion of capital essential for such a relationship.

—The entire dynamics of this political economy is in the State, and the State determines the Level of Production and Income; the existence of each capital unit depends on the State. The result is the emergence of a new economy.

—The process of fictive capital expansion and the fictive forms, are also considered generally, in this chapter. However, in the ICE, they function in an entirely different context, with different dynamics. They are an adjunct to the periodic overexpansion of capital.

.1 Premises for the statement of the theory and mechanism of a political economy based on the fictive expansion of capital.

(a) That the Independent Capitalist Economy has ended; its basic dynamic of a self expanding Aggregate capital and the constant creation of Profit B no longer viable; an episodic variable expansion of capital, can likewise no longer take place. (Ch. III.)

(b) That the Welfare-Military State has been established, with its system of distribution and use of goods. The establishment of the State is the establishment of the political economy. The substitution of a fictive capital expansion for a real capital expansion is not a calculated device to maintain a certain relationship in material production, but the consequence of a certain economic and political structure.

(c) That the WMS has established the money and banking structure and mechanisms necessary to create and maintain the fictive forms as permanent forms, at the will of the Government, and give the Government the power to cause the production of goods by the capital units, for its demand. (Ch. IV, Part II.)

(d) Further assumption: Since this political economy requires that the goods represented by the fictive forms have a *non capital use,* i.e. be consumed without further material goods being produced, and that the goods be totally removed from the distributive system of the dependent organism, assume that the systems of distribution and use of the WMS are so conducted that this will be accomplished.

(e) The analysis and the theory of substitution in this Chapter is predicated on the analysis in Chapter II on the nature of the capitalist organism, the basic law of the organism and its dynamics, and the corollaries thereof.

.2 Synopsis (from Chs. I, II, III, IV) on fictive capital papers, inflated money, and certain other money entering the goods-money circuit of the organism as basic elements *in the process of the fictive expansion of capital.*

- *(a) Government bond, Democratic State, ICE, as part of national debt; repayment expected.*
- *(b) Government bond, WMS, a permanent or constantly refunded form, continually used and constantly expanding in volume (the prototype permanent fictive capital paper of the pefcp).*
- *(c) Private fictive capital papers, in ICE and in pefcp. In particular, those which are in some way the basis for*

money that enters the goods-money circuit of the organism for purchase of goods for personal consumption (non capital use of the money).

(d) *Inflated money—bank credit type. In the ICE in a banking system where the paper money is gold convertible; in the pefcp, in the new money and banking system. Both public, and private inflation of the bank credit money, i.e. on public fictive capital papers, and private fictive capital papers. By definition, the inflated money enters into the goods-money circuit of the organism to purchase goods for personal consumption or Government consumption, and the money remains in the organism.*

(e) *Certain other money entering the goods-money circuit for personal consumption of goods; i.e. money that is not an income from the production of material goods or a transfer of such income: in particular, certain "Profits" made on capital papers, realty titles, etc. monetized with existing money or new money. However, a major part of this money may also be inflated money (above). Considered in the ICE, and in the pefcp.*

(f) *The distinction between the "interest" that is paid on fictive capital paper, and the prototype form of interest in the capitalist economy (a share of the Aggregate Profit arising from the use of the goods or money in the process of material production).*

Comments on the foregoing:

(a) and (b)—the interest bearing Government bond:

This instrument has been defined as a fictive capital paper because it represents no actual capital used in the process of (capitalist) production, yet it is a valuable, even liquid paper, returning interest. (Ch. I, Ch. II, Sec. 13.) It becomes part of the fictive capital expansion process when the money obtained through the sale of the bonds, or created thereon by the banking system as an inflation of the paper money, is used to purchase goods by the Government, when the goods are produced for this effective demand, and the goods are wholly consumed by the Government or its distributees, (Subsec. .3 and .4, following).

Refer to Sec. (2) following with respect to the bond of the Democratic State as a fictive capital form, as part of an occasional process of fictive capital expansion. In general, it is an inadequate form in this process.

The Government bond of the *WMS* is really a different instrument, being part of a *system* of fictive capital expansion. It is continually used, of a permanent nature, etc. It is the primary fictive capital paper of the pefcp, the basis of the system, and the basis even of the fictive profit form. Refer to "inflation," below.

(c) Private fictive capital papers.

Defined generally, Ch. I, Ch. II Sec. 13, Ch. IV: valuable, usually salable papers, relatively permanent—not short term notes—that return "interest" or a transfer of some other form of the Aggregate Profit to the holder, created by private person or capital unit, not representing actual capital or capital money used in the process of (capitalist) production of material goods. However, after their creation, they may be injected into the existing capital paper structure and, to some extent, represent some actual capital. They can be created on other capital paper, and especially on land titles; or be simply be capitalizations of expected profit or some other return. They are often created in financial manipulations, mergers, etc. Some of these papers may be almost fraudulent; others represent a reasonably expected future income or future value of some sort.

Some of these papers are created for money that enters the goods-money circuit to buy goods for personal consumption, including the consumption of the large numbers of individuals engaged in the financial mechanism and institutions. Others are sold, and the money or the "profit" then enters the goods-money circuit, for consumption. In both instances, assume a production for the effective demand. Money can be inflated on the basis of these papers, other moneys can be created on them to deal in them, create them. This latter money creation may not constitute an inflation of the paper money.

These papers were created in large volume in the ICE, episodically, and the process continued in the pefcp.

(d) Inflated Money (bank credit type)

Inflation is defined as always having three characteristics: (a) The creation of a paper money—here bank credit money—by a commercial or Government bank, (b) to purchase goods for the consumption by a Government, or a personal consumption—a non capital use, and (c) the money remains permanently in the circulation. Inflation can be public-i.e. created on Government capital paper; or private, created on private fictive capital paper and under certain circumstances on other capital paper, land titles, etc.

The basis or source of a great deal of inflated money (private) arises in the creation of bank credit money for the buying and selling and trading in capital papers, land titles, mortgages, creating additional capital papers thereon, etc. This is not inflation itself, since the money at first remains in the financial orbit and does not enter the goods-money circuit. But a considerable part of this money does ultimately enter the goods-money circuit, as "profit" etc., to buy goods for consumption, and it is then properly to be considered inflated money.

It is to be noted that some inflated money does not ultimately constitute part of the pseudo Profit B (i.e. it creates simply an increased demand that competes for existing production). A fundamental question is how inflated money, that is part of the pseudo Profit B, achieves a capital form (summary in subsec. .4).

(e) Further note: Some of this money may simply represent a transfer of consumption, i.e. a transfer of money that would be spent for consumer goods, and to this extent it is not to be considered a fictive capital form by becoming part of the pseudo Profit B.

(f) "Interest" on fictive capital papers. Refer to Ch. II, Secs. 12 and 16: There is a fundamental distinction between two forms of interest in the capitalist economy: The prototypical "interest" form of a capitalist relationship, which is interest paid for money borrowed or newly created, for the production of material goods for sale in the capitalist relationship; this interest is part of the Aggregate Profit arising from the production and sale of these goods. (Counterpart of entrepreneural profit). The second form is that paid for the use of money not used as capital in the capitalist process of production and sale of material goods; it is not a direct share of part of the Aggregate Profit, but a transfer of wage or some part of the Aggregate Profit from material production, or paid from some other source, or itself a fiction. Refer to note in Sec. 12, that fictive papers can be created simply because of payment of "interest" (second form).

Caution: The fictive capital papers, public or private, are not created for the purpose of fictive capital expansion nor is money inflated for this purpose. Money is inflated for the sake of obtaining the money; the fictive capital paper, if public, is created for the Government's need for revenue; if private, for the sake of acquiring a valuable capital paper.

.3 Fictive capital expansion, examined generally, as a process in the capitalist organism:-ICE or the dependent organism of the pefcp. The process must be examined in the whole goods-money circuit of the organism, and the capital money, capital goods, capital papers circuit therein.

The discussion bypasses, for the moment, questions of adequacy of the particular fictive form, and the context, scope, and significance of the fictive process, i.e. as in the pefcp compared to the ICE.

The essence of the concept of a fictive expansion of capital is first, the production of goods in a capitalist organism for sale for an effective demand constituted by money that will ultimately be represented by (or arises out of) a fictive capital paper, or is inflated money itself which will ultimately assume some capital form. This means essentially that there has been an additional production of goods for the effective demand, and that the production and the purchase are part of a regular consistent course and policy. Second: these goods are necessarily part of the Aggregate Profit of the organism (and the money paid for these goods is part of the Aggregate Profit of the organism, money form). That is to say they are goods produced above and beyond the goods that represent the consumption goods of wage earners and capitalists alike, who are engaged in the production of these goods (sold for money represented by the fictive capital forms) and all other goods, and above and beyond the production of capital goods necessary to reproduce the capital goods used up in the production of all goods. In short, these goods are comparable to goods that will be new, additional expanded capital. They are produced not for the producers consumption, etc. but "as if" they were new additional capital goods. The foregoing necessarily means also:-that the goods themselves have been sold at normal price, at a profit to their producers and in the organism as a whole.*

But although the goods and money are part of the Aggregate Profit of the organism, and are produced "as if" they were new, additional capital goods, they are not the "Profit B" part of this Aggregate Profit, but rather a pseudo Profit B. The goods are not used as capital goods, *and* they do not, as in the case of goods actually purchased for capital expansion (Profit B) belong to the capitalists (as a class) since they are wholly consumed in a non capital consumption. (Ch. II, Sec. 7, on the identities of Profit B, the new investment, the new capital.) In the fictive process, the capitalist receives only the fictive capital paper forms. There is thus this vital difference between fictive expansion and actual capital expansion, although the consequences in the organism are quite the same.

* These goods, of course, although part of the Aggregate Profit and part of the pseudo Profit B, are not all "profit" to the direct sellers to the Government. The goods purchased by the Government clearly do not represent the profit of the *individual* capital unit, since these goods also embody the value of capital used up, wage, and Profit A. Out of the money paid by the Government for the goods, the unit is reimbursed for capital advanced, wages, costs, etc. Only part of the goods sold to the Government by any particular unit may represent the profit of the particular unit. The situation is comparable to the situation in the interchange of goods among units producing consumer goods, and those producing producer goods, where the goods that represent the profit of those units producing consumer goods may become the goods that the wage earner of the units producing producer goods buys, and the goods that represent the profit of those units producing producer goods may be the capital goods of other units. As stated above, in the Aggregate, the goods purchased by the Government will represent part of the Aggregate Profit.

While all units produce goods that may become part of the Aggregate Profit, and become part of the goods purchased by the Government, there is no specific body of goods in the unit representing part of the Aggregate Profit.

If the goods are part of the Aggregate Profit, and are sold at normal price, observe that the whole production will have to be increased to provide for the consumption of both wage earners and capitalists who are engaged in the production of these goods, and to reproduce the capital used up in their production. The basic assumption of normal price is that all the goods are being produced at a profit. It is from the foregoing that the rule is derived that the pseudo Profit B acts in the same way as the Profit B, in resulting in a multiple increase in the whole Level of production. The pseudo Profit can produce an equilibrium in the organism, just as a Profit B does. (Refer to basic law of dynamics of the capitalist organism, and corollary as to Level of production, and multiple effect of Profit B, Ch. II.)

Note particularly, then, that if the goods in question are *not* part of the Aggregate Profit, not being produced for this demand, but that the inflated money or other money arising from the sale of the fictive forms simply competes in the market for the stock of *existing* goods, and thus purchase wage earners and capitalists consumption goods, or even actual capital goods, then the fictive expansion process is not functioning. This possibility must always be considered. Are additional goods being produced for the Government demand? In Ch. IV, it is pointed out that not all inflated money becomes part of the pseudo Profit B in the pefcp, or in the ICE. Production may have reached its maximum at some given point, and the inflated money is simply an additional pressure in the market, resulting in a "demand" price rise.

The fictive capital expansion process can only be seen and comprehended in the goods-money circuit of the organism, and the nature and source of the effective demand therein. It is in this circuit, and particularly the capital money, capital goods, capital paper part of the circuit, that the possibility of substituting the fictive forms for the real capital expansion, can be seen. And if it is possible in the function of the organism, it is possible for each unit and individual part of the organism.

Recapitulation of the fictive capital expansion process in the goods-money circuit of the organism, including the situation where inflated money enters the circuit instead of fictive capital paper directly.

Assume the production of goods for the effective demand arising out of money from fictive capital papers; assume sale at normal price.

The Government bond; publicly inflated money:

Assume, first, that all the money involved has ben advanced by the capitalist producers (class) by purchase of the Government bonds (i.e. the money is not bank created on the basis of the bonds). The Government or its distributees purchase the goods, the money then flowing back to the capitalists (class, not the same individuals). The capitalists then own the bonds, as capital form of the goods produced "as if" new capital goods, but not the goods, as capital. Note that in the comparable situation where the capitalists (class) advance the money to buy new additional capital goods, (or the private capital paper through which the goods are purchased as new additional capital), the money flows back, but the capitalists own the capital paper *and* the new capital goods. In the instant case, the goods are wholly consumed by the Government or its distributees.

(With respect to the interest: This is presumably obtained by Government tax falling on the Aggregate Profit, and is a transfer of part of the Aggregate Profit from one group of capitalists to another. If the organism were simply a collective capital, with a single collective Aggregate Profit, this would be absurd. But since the organism is composed of separate units, the process is feasible.)

The fact that the capitalists (class) do not also receive "capital goods" in the process is not so important as first appears, although it is of considerable significance. That is to say, it is not unusual for new investment to be made in capital papers (representing actual capital) that return only a part of the Aggregate Profit, say, interest or dividends. But at the same time it must be recognized that a new investment in actual capital may return far more than interest: i.e. the shares of the Aggregate Profit, less taxes.

Yet, generally speaking, the Government bond is not an entirely desirable investment, and not only because its rate of return may be lower. Ordinarily an investment for new capital (or replacement capital) is not only more profitable—and may return far more than the "interest" on some new investments, but there are other factors involved. Purchase of the Government bond does not afford control over a capital; it cannot be manipulated to increase its value when there is depreciation of paper money, or through other mechanisms of the financial system. And the other shares of the Aggregate Profit are of importance when the advance of money for new capital is made (especially with respect to financial institutions and financiers, who, in one way or another, expect and obtain more than the interest and entrepreneural profit. Ch. II, Sec. 16, on financier's profit).

So, at the least, there is a competition that the Government paper must meet in the private investors market. The assumption, made at the outset, that the money will flow from the capitalist class directly, is not the actuality.

An inflation is inherently *necessary* in the use of the Government bond in the process of fictive capital expansion. A great part of the money *must* be obtained from the banking system (Government bank, commercial banks) and it will be seen, that for the same reasons that the money will not be directly advanced by the capitalists (class) on the bonds, the money will remain permanently in the circulation, i.e. not cancelled by the capitalists buying the bonds from the banking system).

The money then moves directly to the capitalists for the goods, and remains in their possession. This is now a money capital part of the pseudo Profit B. The question now is how this money achieves a *capital form.* The money is not, just as in the case of the Government bond which is an adequate (fictive) capital form, used for the consumption of the capitalists. The means by which the money achieves a capital form is discussed in the following section.

Private fictive capital paper; privately inflated money:

The sequence in the goods-money circuit is the same as in the Government bond and publicly inflated money, *if* the private fictive capital paper is the basis for the money that enters the goods-money circuit to purchase goods for a personal consumption. (Not all private fictive capital paper is in this category). That is to say, assume the sale of this paper to capitalists (class) by individuals, foundations, Estates, etc. and the money used to purchase goods for consumption (non capital use). The money flows back to the capitalists (class) (Assume also production for this effective demand). The capitalists (class) possess the fictive capital papers, but not the goods as capital. The situation is not exactly the same as with the Government bond, for the process takes place after the sale of the fictive capital paper, and there is no question as to whether the capitalists (class) are willing to purchase the papers. If they are not, the money is not available.

If the papers are created for sale, or it happens that on creation the money acquired is treated as a profit (often in the case of realty transactions, mortgages, etc.) the sequence again follows. Note that a considerable part of this money may be a "business" expense, as for professional services, employees, etc., and this money enters the goods-money circuit for consumer goods. This will involve a considerable outlay.

.4 Inflation of paper money (bank credit type) is not only a necessary mechanism in the process of fictive capital expansion. When accomplished through private fictive capital paper, it tends to act dynamically to effect a fictive capital expansion, and hence raise the level of the economy.
—Preliminary statement of the modes by which the inflated money, as part of the pseudo Profit B, achieves a capital form.

It was indicated in the last subsection that a public inflation was unavoidable and necessary in the process of fictive capital expansion. The capitalists (class) will not or cannot purchase all the Government bonds, either originally, or after the goods are sold. Money must be bank created on the bonds. The Government should, of course, reduce the degree of necessary inflation by a proper tax system, and certain direct controls, which encourage the private purchase of the bonds. However, if the economy is at a high level, this is difficult to do.

In a sense, a public inflation can be considered a dynamic

of the Level of production, if the Government permits it to go beyond the necessary minimum. But if this does take place, it will be seen that there are other factors operating (private inflation). It is best to regard public inflation simply as a mechanism of the basic fictive capital expansion process.

Private inflation. and all related activities, are dynamic, as much in the pefcp as in the ICE. In the ICE (Ch. II, Sec. 11) private inflation, private fictive capital forms, etc. are primary causes of the variable expansion of capital and the boom stage of the business cycle. A similar effect, although to a lesser extent, is produced by a marked private inflation in the pefcp.

In the pefcp, some private inflation and some monetization of paper "profits" is inevitable, because the public inflation results in a depreciation of the paper money, and the prices of existing capitals, capital papers, and real estate tend to rise. This minimal private inflation, etc., is not particularly dynamic. It is the large scale activity in stocks and realty, and the marked private inflation, that produces the dynamic effect on the Level and Income. It also tends to increase the degree of public inflation. (Sec. .7, below.)

Inflated money that becomes part of the pseudo Profit B achieves a capital form in several ways. (Ch. IV, Sec. 2.)

This money is part of the Aggregate Profit, but it is not part of the Profit A and it will not be spent for the consumption of the capitalists; it is part of the pseudo Profit B. The Profit B, money form, is not spent for personal consumption (it is money that has been advanced to buy new, additional capital goods, and returned); likewise the pseudo Profit B is not spent for personal consumption. This is a capital money for the producers of the organism, and it will be used as capital. (Note that it will take some time before the inflated money, used to purchase goods, finally crystallizes as pseudo Profit B. The time lag affects the rate of depreciation).

The summary at this point refers only to the inflated money that is part of the pseudo Profit B. It has been stated elsewhere that inflated money may simply compete in the market for available goods, i.e. additional goods are not being produced for the inflated money. This money too, will depreciate, but the mechanism of the depreciation is different. The actual situation may be a mixture of both, i.e. inflated money that is part of the pseudo Profit B and inflated money that is not.

The "capital money" of the pseudo Profit B will seek a capital use. In the first place, the money may seek investment as money capital in production and sale of material goods. Here, there are two situations. First: there is a real capital expansion proceeding. The money then serves as new money capital, and thus obtains part of the Aggregate Profit of the economy. Insofar as it can do this, there will be no depreciation of the inflated paper money. Almost certainly, in such circumstances, the volume of inflated money will be relatively small, and a fairly strong capital expansion is proceeding.

Before considering the second situation (no capital expansion existing) it may be noted that the money may be put to other "capital" uses wherein it will not depreciate. It may enter the orbit of capital money in the financial markets and mechanisms, and be used to deal in capital papers and land titles, and remain in this orbit without entering the goods-money circuit. The money may also move into foreign investment, purchasing either foreign capital papers or foreign goods for material production abroad. While there may be no domestic depreciation of the money i.e. a rise in the price of material goods, this latter use may give rise to serious problems in foreign exchange, and affect foreign trade, producing a reaction on domestic prices. (Ch. IV, Part II.)

If the volume of the inflated money (part of the pseudo Profit B) is too great for any of the foregoing, or there is no capital expansion, no foreign investment, or it cannot be absorbed in the financial orbit, it will enter the orbit of capital money in use in the existing and prevailing Level of production and sale of material goods. This increases the volume of this body of money, and the inflated money comes into competition with the money available, all seeking a given volume of profit on a given volume of capital goods. This is comparable to the situation of inflated money that is not a part of the pseudo Profit B, but is competing with other paper money for a given volume of goods. In this latter situation the prices of material goods will rise, i.e. the paper money depreciates. The inflated money that is part of the pseudo Profit B likewise depreciates as it seeks to purchase a given volume of capital goods.

Depreciation, under these circumstances is the means by which the inflated money that is part of the pseudo Profit B obtains a capital form. Depreciation creates the fictive capital aspect of the inflated money.

If the inflated money can be absorbed in the process of temporarily monetizing new fictive capital papers (which then move into the goods-money circuit for private consumption) this will induce a further inflation and increasing the probable rate of depreciation.

(Problems with respect to hyperinflation, where none of the situations above are really practicable, are considered elsewhere. The gold equivalency, and gold convertibility of depreciating bank credit money, are also considered in Ch. IV.)

*.5 When a political economy based on the fictive expansion of capital is functioning (i.e. a WMS has come into being), some degree of "constant" real capital expansion will take place. However, the Profit B is only a small fraction of the pseudo Profit B.**

—There may also be a marked rise in real expansion of capital if the Government's expenditure is greatly increased. This is called herein the "reactive" expansion of capital, and it is unlike the "variable" expansion of capital of the ICE.

Prefatory: At this point and in the following subsections of section (1), the discussion is concerned only with the political economy based on the fictive expansion of capital: that is, the WMS as political economy and as polity.

Once an equilibrium is restored by the Government's systems of expenditure and the fictive capital forms and inflated money, i.e. the creation of the pseudo Profit B sufficient to establish equilibrium, the "constant" expansion of capital (technological improvement, new products, new industries) resumes, even at a

* Conversely, in the ICE, the pseudo Profit B is only a fraction of the Profit B. (Repeated: in the ICE, the fictive processes are an episodic adjunct and incitation to the overexpansion of capital.)

relatively low level of production. As set forth in Ch. II, Sec. 9, 10, this is inherent in a capitalist relationship, and compulsory. Thus, as soon as production is generally profitable (equilibrium restored) a modest Profit B will exist resulting from new investment being made for new additional capital goods. (Note that other conditions are necessary; restoration of normal price, perhaps limitation of production, wage and price controls, etc. (Sec. (4). The pseudo Profit B will be found to be far greater in value than the Profit B. This is the meaning of a political economy based on the fictive expansion of capital.

One of the consequences of the expansion of real capital is that the Government must constantly also increase its level of expenditure to compensate for the rising level of production.

The variable expansion of capital (overexpansion of capital) does not ordinarily take place in a well managed pefcp. However, if there is a high level of production, and, because of poor management that permits an excessive private fictive expansion of capital and private inflation to take place, an overexpansion of real capital quite like the variable expansion of the ICE, may take place. It is not entirely the same in nature, since it is wholly dependent on the size of the pseudo Profit B, most of which has been created by the Government. This excessive real capital expansion in the pefcp can also be self energizing for a time, as in the ICE (Ch. II, Sec. II).

There is another form of real capital expansion in the pefcp called herein "reactive expansion" (Refer to Sec. 3, on the several possible levels of the pefcp). The Government can raise the level sharply by a great increase in its purchases, creating fictive capital papers and inflating money for this purpose. This is the consequence of war, or a Little war that has gotten out of hand. Capital expansion must take place to meet the Government's demand, and related demands for new capital goods. In the early stages of the pefcp the reactive expansion of real capital has to be financed by the Government. The Government itself advances or loans money for new capital, or guarantees the expansion of the capital. "Private investment" is of a hybrid type. There is little confidence that the new capitals can be sustained except on the basis of continued Government demand of one sort or another—which means a fully developed pefcp.

There is no inherent business cycle in the pefcp. The level

may rise or decline dependent on the level of Government demand, and the constitution of its revenue mix. Even the rise sparked by the private inflation and creation of private fictive forms is ultimately the result of Government action or inaction. The change of level is not cyclic, and it is not spiral. (Further on this, Section 3.)

.6 Part of the pseudo Profit B (in a political economy based on the fictive expansion of capital, the WMS), can have a "fictive profit" form, under certain conditions. This is a necessary form in a high level economy. Preliminary discussion of the WM tax; its incidence on the pseudo profit B, repossessing for the Government part of the money it expends in its Welfare and Military programs of distribution and use.

The fictive profit form is unique to this political economy; it cannot exist in the Democratic State—ICE. The WM tax is unlike the tax of the Democratic State in its purpose and significance, and in its incidence. The WM tax falls on the pseudo Profit B, and not on the Profit A. (Secs. 2 and 3, below.)

Certain of the basic concepts set forth in subsec. .3 with respect to the fictive expansion of capital, are also necessary in the analysis of the fictive profit concept: goods are produced in a capitalist organism for the effective demand of the Government, i.e. a production of additional goods; these goods are part of the Aggregate Profit of the organism, and the money paid for these goods is part of the money form of the Aggregate Profit of the organism; as part of the Aggregate Profit these goods are goods produced beyond the production for wage earners, capitalists, capital replacement, etc.; the goods are produced "as if" they were new additional capital goods.

However, in the discussion in subsec. .3, the money that purchases the goods will ultimately be represented by a fictive capital paper, or is inflated money which will achieve a capital form. In effect, in the goods-money circuit, the goods are sold for a "capital" form. In the present discussion, the money ultimately received by the capitalists (class), as part of the pseudo Profit B, will not achieve a capital form (or be kept by the capitalists, as inflated money is) but is repossessed by the Government through the WM tax. It is a fictive profit form of the pseudo Profit B.

Now whatever the limitations of a fictive capital paper, or inflated money, it is easily comprehensible that the private producers of the organism will produce and sell goods for such valuable paper, as if they were producing new, additional, capital goods. (All that is required of them is hiring more labor and advancing more capital, the cost of both of which is returned, with a Profit A; there is no question of a "savings" or a nonconsumption.) But it appears anomalous for the production of this additional "as if" capital goods, for a profit that is essentially fictive to them. (Caution: it is a true, actual part of the Aggregate Profit; but it is the Government that actually receives it.) It is true that the goods will be produced and sold for the effective demand—money advanced by the Government, but the hypothesis is that this will be part of the Aggregate Profit, i.e. additional goods produced for this demand. If the producers find that their actual share of the Aggregate Profit that is reduced by the WM tax is the equivalent of this additional production, it would seem that the additional production cannot or will not be undertaken. That is to say, the value of the goods is actually no value to the producers of the organism, as capital goods, or otherwise.

So if the additional production for the Government's demand of goods produced "as if" capital is actually only a fictive profit in the organism, and has not even a fictive capital form, the production of the additional goods will not continue. But the answer is that it is the *whole* pseudo Profit B that is in question, and that the pseudo Profit B comes into being as a whole (along with a Profit B, restored through the function of the WMS). *Part* of this pseudo Profit B does have a fictive *capital* form. The theory of the fictive profit form, then, is that a *part* of the pseudo Profit B can have a fictive profit form if a sufficient part has a fictive capital form, and, in actuality and practice, there is also a Profit B, which, by hypothesis, has an actual capital form. This pattern must exist *as a regular course*. which is to say an established, regular system of Government expenditure, a regularly created pseudo Profit B, and the regular creation of a permanent fictive capital form and a permanent inflated money. In short, a fictive profit form for part of a pseudo Profit B is possible in a political economy based on the fictive expansion of capital.

In actuality, the fictive profit form implies a *marked expansion* of the pseudo Profit B (through marked expansion of the Government's expenditure). As the size of the pseudo Profit B increases, the WM tax becomes practicable, and the volume of the WM tax can increase as the absolute size of the pseudo Profit B increases. The producers must increase their production, and maintain increased production for the Government's demand, in order to keep the fictive capital part of the pseudo Profit B (and the Profit B too, which is maintained or increased by the increased Government demand). The increase in production means an increase in the capital advanced for additional capital goods and additional labor. This is not a "savings" or non consumption by the capitalist producers.

The theory of a fictive profit form in a political economy based on the *fictive* expansion of capital is that if to make a net of 50, the production must be 100, or increased to 150, this will always be done; or, to increase a net of 25 to a net of 50, production must go from 100 to 200, this too will be done. (The "net" refer to units of fictive capital, or inflated money.) This cannot be true in an ICE with respect to the Profit B, or in a pefcp with respect to the Profit B, no part of which can be taken by tax.

Summary: The Government must create a pseudo Profit B of sufficient size to make a fictive profit form possible, and part of the pseudo Profit B *must* have a fictive capital form, or inflated money form, and there must be a degree of Profit B. Since the organism will function under these conditions, the individual and units will.

With respect to the unit: the Aggregate Profit comes into being as an undifferentiated whole, and a large part of this is Profit A. (In the organism, the Profit A cannot be considered in the calculation, because the Profit A comes into being only as a consequence of the existence of the Profit B or the pseudo Profit B.) All that the unit requires is that its goods be salable at a profit (normal price). It is immaterial to the unit what use is made of the goods produced, whether as new capital, or consumption by the Government or private person. If it is necessary to double production to maintain the same net profit, it will be done. The unit or individual will act to maximize the net return, no matter what the gross must be. It is as though the cost of production increases, and to obtain the same net profit, the scale of production must be increased.

Profit or income before taxes, and profit or income after taxes, and the idea of the tax as part of the price of goods, are not new ideas to the individual or unit, although the scale is now quantitatively very different.

Income, to the individual or unit appears to be reduced by the tax (and thus it appears that there is a transfer of consumption, as in the case of the tax of the Democratic State). It is hard for the individual or unit to see that this profit before taxes would not exist if it were not for the Government expenditure and the WM tax. The idea that the unit or individual would have, say twice the income or profit if there were no WM tax, is based on the supposition that the profit before tax would exist. But for all the units (the organism) it is not true that this profit before taxes would exist. Not only would not the unit's gross profit not exist, but the real fund for consumption would not exist either. "Profit before taxes" is an illusion in the organism. It is true that any *one* unit would have a higher profit if there were no taxes, but it is false when stated for all (the organism).

Actually, the Profit A and the Aggregate Wage are greatly increased, as a multiple of the pseudo Profit B, and the WM tax ultimately costs the capitalists (class) nothing. The pseudo Profit B, to the extent equivalent to the WM tax, is created by the Government's action. It is true that taxes can be so increased in the WMS (large scale war) that they will reduce the consumption of some recipients of the Aggregate Wage and the Profit A. It is true also that many taxes, including the WM tax, do reduce the income and consumption of those individuals who derive their wage or income from the Government. (But this latter is a reduction of the actual payment to them; the real question is simply how large a payment the Government wishes to make.)

The principle that the Level of Production and Income is a multiple of the pseudo Profit B plus the Profit B, applies, even though part of the pseudo Profit B has a fictive profit form.

The foregoing follows from the fact that the goods are part of the Aggregate Profit of the organism, and the specific goods themselves have been sold at normal price. All the goods necessary for the consumption of the wagesearners and capitalists, and capital goods that must be produced to replace the goods used up in the total production, have been produced and sold at normal price. The fictive profit aspect of the pseudo Profit B does not affect the general principle. However, the fact that the WM tax may not have its proper incidence, and other malfunctions (Sec. 3, below, on congruence, time necessary to integrate the tax, etc.) may to some extent limit the application of the principle of multiplicity.

The fictive profit form is not only a possible component of the pseudo Profit B but at a high Level of Production and Income is a necessary component.

It would be improper in a pefcp, where a high level of production and Income have been achieved, to utilize the fictive capital form and inflated money alone to create the pseudo Profit B. The rate of profit for individuals would be grossly excessive, and induce a gross over expansion of real capital. Inflation would soon reach the point of hyperinflation. The overexpansion of capital would require a rapid escalation of use of fictive capital forms, which would soon bring the pefcp to an end. (Refer, further, Sec. 3, below.)

In the organism, the fictive profit is an actual part of the Aggregate Profit, and represents an actual part of the goods produced. It is not a reduction of the Aggregate Profit. The concept is properly a concept of the organism only, and means that part of the pseudo Profit does not have a capital or fictive capital form. "Fictive profit" may have various meanings to the individual or unit—as profit before taxes, or as "fictive cost of production." These are not the meanings of the term herein.

.7 In a political economy based on the fictive expansion of capital, the creation of private fictive capital forms, private inflation of bank credit money, and the monetization of certain

financial "profits" will take place to a certain extent, and this will increase the size of the pseudo Profit B. If the private processes are of any magnitude, they will raise the level of production and may increase real capital expansion.

Recapitulation: Because of the public inflation and depreciation of the paper money, the prices of existing capitals, capital papers, land titles, tend to rise, and there is some degree of monetization of "profits" and private inflation. Some of this money enters the goods-money circuit, increasing the pseudo Profit B. The Government, however, may encourage these private processes by inadequate WM tax, inadequate controls, etc., so that they achieve considerable magnitude. When this occurs, there is a marked effect on the Level of production and Income.

In a properly managed pefcp, the Government should always compensate for increased private inflation etc., by reducing the public inflation and the public fictive capital forms in its revenue mix. That is to say, it should in effect substitute private fictive capital forms for the public forms, by increasing the relative proportion of the WM tax (.8, following). However, this is generally not done; rather than compensate for the private inflation, the Government action encourages it.

In the pefcp, far more than in the ICE, this is improper. This political economy is based on a publicly created fictive system, and welfare-military systems of expenditure, and a money and banking system that will sustain all these processes. It should not be abused for private advantage. In the ICE, at least, there is a great degree of risk, because the cyclic depression terminates many of the private fictive forms, and much of the privately inflated money. But in the pefcp, the Government is really supporting and maintaining the private forms and the private inflation. A permanent burden is placed on the system, which can shorten its life. There is an excessive depreciation of the paper money, which continues when the overexpansion of capital ceases, and the level declines. The many difficulties that follow excessive private inflation and the creation of private fictive capital forms, are blamed on the Government's inflation.

.8 The WMS Government's "revenue mix." Proportions of borrowed money, inflated money, W M tax revenue, with respect to
The total Government expenditure
The Level of Production and Income
The type of goods purchased by the Government
The extent of the real expansion of capital (profit B).
The extent of new private fictive capital forms, private inflation.

Refer to Sec. 3, .2, on WM tax and the Level of Production.

The size of the Government expenditure (and the size of the pseudo Profit B) are the first determinants of the possible proportions of the elements in the Government's revenue mix. When the pseudo Profit B is relatively low (low level of production, low "constant" expansion of capital), the Government's revenue for Welfare, etc. expenditure, must almost in its entirety be derived from the fictive capital form and inflated money. Furthermore, since the distributive system is almost essentially "welfare" any considerable WM tax, which will fall on "capital" goods industries, will not be congruent with the type of goods purchased, and the tax will not function properly. (Sec. 3, .1 on incidence of the WM tax.)

When the Level of Production rises markedly (increase in Government expenditure), the WM tax must become a major element in the revenue mix. If the pseudo Profit B were represented mainly by fictive capital paper and inflated money, in addition to the existence of a substantial Profit B, the function of this political economy would be seriously impaired. The inflation would tend towards hyperinflation; the grossly excessive fictive capital paper would cause additional real capital expansion, comparable to a variable overexpansion of the ICE.

The general proportions in the revenue mix are properly established in a relatively stable, high level economy. There is a degree of Profit B, and even a degree of private fictive capital expansion which can be taken into account. Since the pseudo Profit B must in part have a fictive capital form, and since this in part must consist of inflated money, the technical problem is to adjust this part of the revenue mix to the lowest possible level consistent with the maintenance of a high level stability of the Level of Production and Income.

With respect to the overall size of the WM tax (Sec. 3, below):
(a) The total return depends on the Level of the economy, which in turn depends on the total expenditure of the Government and the proportions of fictive capital forms in the revenue mix, plus the Profit B and private fictive capital forms.
(b) In general, the WM tax (and taxes as a whole) must always be less than the expenditure of the Government. The Government's budget must always be unbalanced.
(c) The return of money obtained by means of the WM tax will always fall as fast as the Level of Government expenditure declines, and at a certain point will fall faster than the Level of Government expenditure.

.9 The political economy based on the fictive expansion of capital is a new economy; it has a totally different dynamics than that of the ICE; the distributive system is different; the mechanisms necessary to make the fictive forms effective are not those of the ICE. The political economy is an integral part of a State, the WMS. This State is itself a political economy.

Certain basic processes and mechanisms of this political economy have been outlined. There are yet two fundamental aspects of this political economy that require further examination: the new money and banking system that makes the fictive forms of this political economy practicable; the distributive systems that make the political economy operative. But it is fair to say, even at this point, that a new economic relationship has emerged, a distinctive political economy integral with a State.

This State is itself causing, or creating, the existence of the immense volume of goods it uses and distributes, as values, "as if" it were actually engaged in producing these goods itself. It is not "redistributing" the goods produced; it is an integral operative force in their production. The goods would not come into being without the State's action, i.e. the creation of fictive forms necessary to the existence of the private producers. Thus, in this particular economic relationship, the creation of this mass of value by the State is the basis, the cause, the indispensable condition for the production of all the other material goods produced in this relationship. The size of this value of goods created for and by the Government determines the Level of Production and the Income of all the participants in the process of production, as a multiple of this value.

The whole political economy is a simulacrum of a capitalist relationship, since the dynamic, the essence of such a relationship, the constant expansion of capital, is accomplished by fictions, and the capital and profit forms necessary for such expansion are created as fictions. The State is an integral part of this simulacrum. But the result of simulacrum and fiction, is the emergence of a distinctive new form.

While certain of the fictive forms have functioned episodically in the ICE, they are operating in a new context in the pefcp, and they require new mechanisms to enable them to be created and function in a pefcp, and in effect they become different forms. It is plain too that the scope of the fictive forms and the consumption of goods are different in the pefcp. Consumption resulting from fictive forms in the ICE was for the benefit of a relatively small part of the capitalist class. Even though some billions of dollars might be involved, such consumption could not approach in volume the consumption of the welfare class in the pefcp, which is, furthermore, a continuous consumption.

It is not the processes themselves, when used in the ICE, that prefigure or create the new economy, but the revolution that creates both polity and economy, that utilizes these forms.

(2) The Government bond, Democratic State, in episodic fictive capital expansion in the ICE. (Government bond as part of national debt, not as temporary short term loan.) Public inflation. Repayment of bond, and deflation.
—The tax of the Democratic State (ICE).

Prefatory: A review of the role of the Government bond of the Democratic State in the process of fictive capital expansion (ICE), and the anomaly of repayment of this bond, will be instructive in understanding the significance of the Government bond of the WMS, the basic fictive capital form of the political economy based on the fictive expansion of capital. This latter fictive capital form is part of a permanent. never repaid or constantly refunded body of capital papers, constantly expanding. It is ultimately the basis for the fictive *profit* form. In the ICE, the Government bond is not a primary fictive capital form; it is rarely used in great volume. The private fictive capital forms and private inflation are more important in the ICE than the public forms.

.1 The revenue of the Democratic State, in general. Borrowing and the Government bond. The "repayment" of the money borrowed.

A part of the discussion of the tax of the Democratic State, in subsec. .2 must be repeated in the discussion of borrowing by the Democratic State, since borrowing and taxation are interdependent.

Assume, for the moment, that the Government (Democratic State) is meeting its ordinary expenses by taxation. The canons of the political economy of the Democratic State require this: the Government should not borrow (apart from short term borrowing in anticipation of tax revenues) for its ordinary expenses.* The tax of the Democratic State falls properly only on the Income of individuals or units; it must never take part of the capital, or capital coming into being (Profit B). Actually, it will fall on a particular part of the Income: the Profit A of the Aggregate Profit (Ch. II Sec. 16) whatever the apparent incidence of the tax (.2, following). The tax of the Democratic State must take as little as possible of the Profit A. The part it takes is actually very low relative to the Total Income, because it may be levied only for the proper expenses of the Govern-

* It is likewise a canon of the political economy of the Democratic State that Treasury notes should not be printed to pay for the Government's ordinary expenses, i.e., in place of taxation and borrowing.

ment. The functions of this Government are limited (Ch. IV, Sec. 4) and its expenses are consequently relatively low.*

If, instead of obtaining its necessary revenue by tax, the Government borrowed to meet its *ordinary* needs, it would in effect be presenting its interest bearing capital papers to the be taken by tax. The borrowing and expenditure of the money capitalists, as a class, for the share of the Profit A that should would certainly not be a creation of a pseudo Profit B. A transfer of consumption is taking place (not a production of additional goods for the Government's demand), even though the Government is issuing its bonds to pay for the goods. However, in this discussion, assume that there is an adequate tax for ordinary expenses of the Government.

If a major war occurs, the tax of the Democratic State, even expanded, cannot possibly be sufficient to provide the money to purchase the goods the Government must have. Furthermore, if the Government were to rely on taxation to finance a major war, it is fairly certain that the necessary goods will not be produced for the Government's needs. If production remains approximately the same or rises somewhat, a heavier tax at best might increase the transfer of income from the capitalists and possibly the wage earners; possibly it might take some capital. It is difficult to materially increase the share of the Profit A that the Government can acquire by tax, even in wartime. The real need is an increase in production for Government demand and the means for the Government to acquire the increased production. The tax of the Democratic State, even increased is not the answer.

The *only* recourse is for the Government to borrow the money on its bonds, and inflate paper money on the bonds through the banking system (or print paper money directly). In a reasonably well managed war effort (Democratic State), the

* The later Democratic State does engage in some activities that to an extent go beyond its traditional functions. These activities cost additional money. Nevertheless the basic principles are still applied: the tax must be as low as possible. The ideology relating to taxation and "representation" is based on the determination to control and limit the Government's share of the Profit A.

great profit that would ensue will result in a marked capital expansion, and an increase in the Level of Production sufficient to meet the Government's effective demand. (Assume that the non bank loans are domestic and that there is a sufficiently well organized domestic banking system to permit an effective inflation.)*

The situation becomes one of the creation of a great pseudo Profit B, and an increasing Profit B. The Aggregate Wage is sharply increased (possibly some increase in wage rate), and the Profit A increases. War is immensely profitable in the ICE-Democratic State and causes prosperity and full employment.

It may be inquired why at this point the Democratic State cannot impose a tax comparable to the WMS tax, and recover a part of this pseudo Profit B, granting that the great expansion of capital (Profit B) must remain untouched. But, whatever may be said or even done about "excess profit" taxes, etc. they are simply not effective and cannot be effective in the Democratic State. The tax and tax system of the Democratic State is not able to repossess the pseudo Profit B even in small part. Mechanisms for a tax that will do so do not exist; the political structure and power sources make it impractical for such a tax to be levied or collected. It could not even be effective in time. It may even be that any such tax would prevent the necessary capital expansion in the ICE. Such a tax is contrary to the ideology of the Democratic State, even in war-time.

To finance the war by borrowing means in the Democratic State an inflation to an extraordinary extent. Ultimately for most economies, a ruinous hyperinflation takes place (Ch. IV) which destroys the currency, and the Government bonds also.

It has been pointed out that the use of the Government bond-inflated money as part of a process of fictive capital expansion is actually quite rare in the Democratic State, a situation completely different than that of the WMS tax, pefcp. In summary, the occasional episodic fictive capital expansion in major war of the Democratic State (ICE) is actually thoroughly dissimilar to the continual fictive capital expansion of the pefcp (WMS)

* The Government will seek a foreign loan if the goods it needs are not domestically available, and it has no gold or foreign exchange to buy the goods.

through its military program of expenditure. Although the basic processes seem the same, the basic instruments are not the same.

The anomaly of "repayment" of the Government's bonds—Democratic State (ICE). The necessity for deflation of the war-inflated paper money.
The destructive effects of "repayment" and "deflation" of the paper money.

Prefatory: In the Democratic State, and the ICE, the interest bearing Government bond is not considered to be a permanent form. The concept is that borrowing by the Government is quite the same thing as borrowing by a private person. It is believed that the money is spent for the benefit of the "Government" and the Government must repay the money as soon as possible and pay interest, just as a private person does.

In actuality, the situation is completely different from a loan to an individual or capital unit, whether it is a loan for a *capital* use, or even for personal consumption. To begin with, the Government is not using the money (goods) as a capitalist does, for further production of material goods. And the Government is not a private consumer. Government bonds have also an unusual place among capital papers, being almost liquid, the basis of money creation, and they can be maintained in existence for long periods. But the essential point in the following analysis is that in purchasing goods from the capitalists as a class (i.e. in the organism), essentially with the money borrowed from them, (assume a non bank loan) a pseudo Profit B is created for the capitalists, and the capitalists receive the bonds as a (fictive) capital form of the goods produced and sold to the Government and then wholly consumed.

If the bonds are repaid, observe how anomalous the situation is. The papers are a fictive capital form, representing no capital goods; actually the goods have been destroyed. The goods represent a pseudo Profit B that has once been created. Now the Government is obviously not repaying out of capital assets, as though it were a person (or a capital unit which might have borrowed the money to use as capital and has the capital goods). Bonds are repaid out of the proceeds of taxation (Democratic State). This means, in effect that they will be repaid—

presumably to the capitalists who hold them—out of the *current* income or production of the capitalists (organism). The tax of the Democratic State falls on a particular part of the Aggregate Profit A. Part of the Profit A is transferred to the capitalists—not necessarily the same persons who pay the tax—but, that which was money destined to purchase goods for a current consumption, now suddenly becomes a capital money, the monetization of the fictive capital paper. It can again be noted that this fictive capital paper represents an *old* pseudo Profit B, which is being monetized not only out of current income but current consumer income. And there is another consequence of this. Part of the current production may not then have a market since the consumer income is being converted to a capital money.

The conversion of a Profit A to a capital money is something that cannot practicably be done, except on a small scale, under very special circumstances. It is a destructive process even if there is a surplus in the Government's budget. This is money that should be returned to the goods-money circuit—or part of the current production of consumer goods may not be purchased.

However, such repayment is made on occasion in the Democratic State. It can be made on a small scale without too much disruption of the economy if the economy is expanding fairly rapidly (variable expansion, private fictive capital expansion, private inflation). Under such circumstances the tax of the Democratic State may be picking up some of the "paper profits." The monetization of fictive capital paper may not then seriously disturb the market if this market is expanding. Whatever loss takes place in the goods-money circuit is compensated for by the general expansion.

The money repaid is now a capital money, (not money to be used for consumption), and it must find other investment. This also will not be a major problem in a boom period.

But it is certain that this repayment cannot be done on a large scale or under ordinary economic conditions. In particular the repayment of great war debts to another national economy is not possible. In summary: in ordinary times, even with a somewhat larger scale economy, repayment in any significant amount cannot be made without a depressing effect on the economy; it can be done on a relatively small scale in boom times.

Deflation (of publicly inflated money); Ordinary inflation; hyperinflation. Preliminary note on deflation, generally, in the ICE (Ch. IV).

The subject of repayment of the Government bond, Democratic State–ICE, cannot be separated from that of deflation of the inflated money, (and deflation generally, in the depressed phase of the business cycle in the ICE).

It has been noted that a major war (Democratic State) cannot be undertaken without a paper money inflation, and that often there will be hyperinflation. Even if the inflation is not a hyperinflation, the Government and the banking system cannot maintain a gold convertible standard in wartime.

The situation of hyperinflation need not be considered further at this point. Only repudiation is possible.

But with respect to "ordinary" wartime inflation: A deflation *must* take place in the ICE even before the question of repayment of the Government bond is considered. This is part of the depression phase of the business cycle. After the great overexpansion of capital induced by the war and the fictive expansion of capital, there will be a serious depression, and a major contraction of all paper money and capital papers will automatically take place (Ch. IV). The paper money in its existing volume cannot possibly represent the weight of gold it purports to represent in the circulation.

Repayment of bonds held by banks (in the repayment sequence noted above) is of course, itself a deflationary process. But as stated, if this takes place in periods of prosperity or boom, the countervailing private inflationary processes at work may compensate for this.

.2 *The tax of the Democratic State. (ICE.)*

The term "economic incidence" is used herein to designate the part of the Income of the capitalist organism, i.e. the Aggregate Wage or the Aggregate Profit, and the particular part of the Aggregate Profit (Profit A, Profit B, pseudo Profit B) upon which the tax *ultimately* falls. The term "personal incidence" is used to indicate the person on whom the tax *ultimately* falls.

The word "ultimately" is used in both connections because the first incidence of the tax is usually shifted. The tax may have an apparent economic incidence on wages (in material production), but this is almost invariably shifted to the Aggregate Profit. Most taxes that seem to fall on certain persons, and units are shifted to others. The shift in personal incidence is usually involved in the shift of economic incidence.

(Ch. II, Sec. 17: The tax of the Democratic State, for the most part, (see exceptions, below), is one of the shares of the Aggregate Profit of the capitalist organism. It falls on the Profit A part of the Aggregate Profit. But the analysis of ultimate incidence is of great complexity, i.e. in what way the specific tax, on the specific person, or on a material good, finds its ultimate incidence on the Aggregate Profit.)

The tax of the Democratic State must not take capital; the tax may properly only take Income. What often appears to be a tax on capital, or on property, really has its ultimate incidence on Income, and more precisely on the Profit A part of the Aggregate Profit.* Equally important: not only must not the tax fall on capital in being, but it must not fall on capital coming into being, i.e. the tax does not, and may not, take that part of the Aggregate Profit that is Profit B, created by new investment for additional capital goods. The money that constitutes the Profit B (in the ICE) has its inception as new capital money that purchases the goods from the capital units, and must flow back to the capitalists (as a class) even though it is Income as well as new capital. Actually, viewing the organism as a whole, the tax of the Democratic State is relatively so low, that it is extremely unlikely, except under unusual circumstances, that it will ever take capital.

In examining this economic incidence, the tax (Democratic State) must be viewed as part of the goods-money circuit between Government and the capitalist producers, and this again as part of the whole goods-money circuit of the organism. That is to say, the tax, and the goods purchased for the tax money, cannot be viewed separately. The tax revenue received by the

* The tax may take the money equivalent of fictive capital papers or capital papers representing actual capital goods, but in the organism of the ICE, the tax will be found to falling on current Income.

Government, ultimately obtained from the capitalist producers, is used to purchase goods from the capitalist producers. The circuit is one in which the tax is a transfer of part of the Aggregate Profit (of the organism) from capitalists to Government, the par of the Aggregate Profit viewed as money equivalent of the goods, and the goods themselves.

The problem is how the goods purchased from individual units can be said to represent part of the goods constituting the Aggregate Profit of the organism, and specifically the Profit A part of the Aggregate Profit. The goods purchased by the Government clearly do not necessarily represent the profit of the *individual* capital unit, for these goods also embody the value of capital used up, wage, and Profit A. That is to say, out of the money paid by the Government for the goods, the unit is reimbursed for capital advanced, wages, costs, etc. Only part of the goods sold to the Government by any particular unit may represent the profit of the particular unit. The situation is comparable to the situation in the interchange of goods among units producing consumer goods, and those producing producer goods, where the goods that represent the profit of those units producing consumer goods may become the goods that the wage earner of the units producing producer goods buys, and the goods that represent the profit of those units producing producer goods may be the capital goods of other units. As stated above, in the Aggregate, the goods purchased by the Government will represent part of the Aggregate Profit. The goods the Government purchases are paid for by taxes on *all* individuals and units, and constitute part of the Aggregate Profit. When returned to the individual unit, by purchase of goods, this tax money is part profit to the individual, or unit, and the rest a return of wages, capital, etc.

While all units produce goods that may become part of the Aggregate Profit, and become part of the goods purchased by the Government, there is no specific body of goods in the unit representing part of the Aggregate Profit—or the tax share taken by the Government. The Government will be taxing not only part of the profit of the seller of the goods to the Government, but part of the profit of those that supply goods to this producer, etc. Thus the goods-money circuit between Governmen and organism is complex, insofar as the tax money is derived from all, and then, when returned to specific sellers by purchase of their goods, is passed along to all the others by their purchase of goods necessary for the production of goods purchased by the Government, and becomes part of the Profit of every unit.

Exceptions to the rule that the tax of the Democratic State falls on the Aggregate Profit. (The following is not applicable to the WM tax; however insofar as the tax of the Democratic State continues in the WMS, these exceptions also exist in the WMS.)

(a) The Government (Democratic State) produces certain material goods which are used in production, by the individual entrepreneurs (i.e. roads, harbors, communications, etc.) These goods and facilities are not produced for profit; the Government acts rather as a general agent of all the capitalists in the production of these necessary goods and facilities. The money necessary to produce these goods, obtained by tax, is in a sense a forced payment to the Government as producer. The point is that the tax paid for this production is ultimately a cost for labor and materials of the individual entrepreneurs, a true cost of production of material goods that will be privately produced, reappearing as part of the value of all of the material goods produced.

(b) The Government (Democratic State) undertakes certain activities for the maintenance and reproduction of the wage earners (among others), a portion of the funds spent for education, etc. The payment for these may be derived from a tax on the wage earner, but more likely, it constitutes an addition to the wage—an addition not paid directly, and is paid by tax on Aggregate Profit. It is properly a part of the Aggregate Wage, and a cost of production of the goods.

It may be thought that the exceptions have no practical significance (as to whether this tax is generally a share of the Aggregate Profit) since for the most part, being either a hidden real cost of production, or an increased Wage, this part of the tax is ultimately a reduction of the Aggregate Profit, even if it is not technically a share of the Aggregate Profit. But for reasons that will appear, the distinction must be made.* It may also be noted that the ideology and practice of the Democratic State is to keep these costs at a minimum.

Economic and personal incidence of the taxes of the Democratic state.

The four main classes of taxes of the Democratic State are Property, Excise, Income, and Death. (The last two become of significance only toward the end of the ICE, although a limited income tax was used to aid in financing wars.)

A. Property: Imposed on individual holding real property, land and buildings, used in agriculture, mining, manufacturing, residence (by owner or leased to others), and for various commercial uses. It was also imposed on individuals holding personal property, including possibly capital papers. This tax will be found to have its incidence on the income of the property owner.

B. Excise: On the sale of goods—at the level of manufacture, wholesale, or retail sale. The tax can be on specific commodities, or a general tax on all sales. Include herein also, tax on imports, on the use of railroad, telephone, telegraph, pipe lines, etc., *and* the tax on wages paid in material production.

C. Income: Directly on income of individuals. (Income may be of any sort, including wages in material production, the several forms of the Aggregate profit. Include also so-called "capital gains" as income.

D. Estate, inheritance, gift taxes.

The tax system of the Democratic State is one of haphazard growth. The Government's main consideration is whether the tax is effective to produce revenue, and not its economic incidence. The Government first turns to what is visible and easily reached—property, the sale of commodities. These taxes are long

* It is sometimes stated that since the Government is necessary to the economic (capitalist) relationship, the maintenance of the Government is a "cost of production" of the goods. However, with certain exceptions, the cost of maintaining the Government should not be considered an actual cost of production of material goods. Nevertheless this cost, paid by tax, is a proper share of the Aggregate Profit.

established modes of taxation and are still used. Income taxes and death taxes becomes significant at a later time. The income tax, of course, is the tax of supreme importance in the pefcp.

It is hard to determine the real "economic" *source* of any income. Many incomes are derivative from parts of the Aggregate Profit; some derivative from the Aggregate Wage. The term "wage" that may characterize some incomes, is itself deceptive as to the economic source of the income. The *immediate* incidence of a tax (i.e. on the person or the good on which the tax falls), will not reveal the economic source of the income. Practically speaking, it is necessary to ascertain first the ultimate personal incidence, and then the ultimate economic incidence. Furthermore, in the course of time the incidence of a tax will change. It takes time for the ultimate incidences of the taxes to become institutionalized.

In general: Taxes that seem to have their incidence on *wage* earners (in the production of material goods), are sooner or later shifted to the employer (falling on the Aggregate Profit). That is to say, wage levels will *rise* to include the tax, whether the tax is directly on the wage, or is an income tax affecting the wage, or an excise tax affecting consumer goods that are purchased by the wage earners engaged in the production of material goods. However, the shift of the tax on wages, so that it will fall on the Aggregate Profit, is a far more complex process than a patent rise in the wage rate. Changes in the wage rate may seem to be taking place for many other reasons (Ch. II, Sec. 15), and the change in the wage rate because of tax incidence may be concealed. Furthermore: the price level may be changing, and the real wage and the money wage will change without any apparent change in the wage rate. The situation is further complicated by the fact that a particular capital sector of the economy may have the power to resist a change in the wage rate, or, if such sector does raise the wage rate, it has the power to maintain the same profit rate by shifting the rise in the wage rate (i.e. by the amount of the tax) to the other sectors, because it has the power to raise prices. Other sectors may then be forced to resist a rise in the wage rate. Yet the general rule (the situation in the organism as a whole) is that the average wage rate will rise when the tax falls on the wage of those employed in material production, thereby reducing the Aggregate Profit, pro tanto.

Some taxes on wages, however, and some taxes on Aggregate Profit directly, may become a true cost of production of the individual producer (paying for goods produced by the Government and used by the unit capital in further production). These are returned in the price of goods sold, the price including the added value.

The property tax is usually made use of by local Governments. If the tax is on owner occupied residential property, it is a tax that is not shifted. It is a tax on income. The economic source of the income is usually(in the period under discussion) the Aggregate Profit. If the tax is on leased residential property, it is in part shifted to the tenant, and the tax may in part be paid out of Aggregate Wage, (which may or may not be shifted to the employer). If the tax is on property used in material production, agricultural or otherwise, it is in part paid by the entrepreneur, out of profit. It may also be in part a cost of production raising the value and the price of goods sold (tax as forced payment for goods). However, the problem of disparate control over market price may arise here, as it does in excise taxes, and the producer may not be able to get a price that will cover this part of the tax, and he then pays the tax out of his Profit.

An excise tax, custom tax, if on producer goods, will be likewise paid in part out of entrepreneur's profit, and in part may be a true cost of production, raising value and price. If the excise is on consumer goods, domestic or imported, the purchaser usually pays the tax, and then it is a tax on Wage or Aggregate Profit, and if on wage, is gradually shifted to the Aggregate Profit.

Income taxes are usually ultimately paid out of the Aggregate Profit. Inheritance, estate and gift taxes should be viewed, in the organism as a whole, as taxes on personal savings out of Income, although they may appear to be on capital.

Personal incidence, and the shift of personal incidence, are germane to the analysis herein, only insofar as they may be related to ultimate economic incidence. Personal incidence is, of course, of great importance to the individual. But it has some significance in the general function of the economy. (For example: since the later ICE has disparate degrees of concentration among the sectors, and some sectors have a very much greater price power than others, some sectors can easily shift taxes to other sectors. This may contribute to the difficulties of the weaker sectors). The main concern with personal incidence in the Democratic State, and the shift of incidence, is connected with the principle that taxes should be uniform and equal for each individual. (Note: in the WMS this *cannot* be the theory of taxation). In the Democratic State, a tax system is regarded as ideal if it is proportional.* Actually, in the Democratic State, the tax system was regressive, those with smaller incomes paying relatively more. Furthermore, because of disproportions in power among the sectors and units of the ICE, and the power of recipients of large incomes, the tax fell unequally throughout the economy, and was easily shifted. There were also many exemptions obtained through political favor. However, since the tax is not a significant factor in the function of the ICE, the inequalities do not particularly affect the economy as a whole.

(3) The Welfare-Military tax, creating a fictive profit form for part of the pseudo Profit B. "Economic incidence" of the WM tax on the pseudo Profit B The WM tax as part of the whole revenue mix of the WMS, at various Levels of Production and Income.

.1 The incidence of the Welfare-Military tax on the pseudo Profit B.

Recapitulation: The theory of the fictive profit form is that a WM tax can take part of the pseudo Profit B (that has itself

* Proportional tax system: The same percentage is taken by tax, from each individual or unit, no matter what the income, and the tax falls equally on each individual and unit.

Regressive tax system: The lower the individual income, the greater percentage of the income taken by the tax.

Progressive tax system: The higher the individual income, the greater percentage of the income taken by the tax.

been created by purchase by the Government at normal price of goods produced for the Government's demand) if a sufficient part of the pseudo Profit B has a fictive capital form, and a Profit B (real capital form) exists in some degree. The level of Government expenditure for its welfare and military programs must have reached a certain size, i.e. the pseudo Profit B must be of a certain size. The WM tax does not effect a transfer of personal consumption, since the goods in question are produced "as if" they were new capital goods, and would not be produced except for the Government's effective demand, i.e. would not be produced for the personal consumption of the capitalists. The WM tax must not be of such size or incidence as to take any part of the Profit B or that part of the pseudo Profit B that must be represented by a fictive capital form. There are other parts of the tax revenue of a WMS, since the tax of the Democratic State continues, which is integrated into the economy, and continues to fall on the Profit A—a transfer of consumption. Certain parts of the revenue of a WMS do not enter into the goods-money circuit of the dependent organism at all.

The statement that the ultimate "economic incidence" of this tax must be on the pseudo Profit B is based on the analysis of the goods-money circuit of the dependent organism, and the money-goods-money flow between the capitalist producers and the Government of the WMS, in an established system of welfare and military expenditure, where the pseudo Profit B is established as a regular course, and fictive forms created as a regular course. The basic premise is the fact that these goods are additional goods produced for Government demand at normal price, and are necessarily part of the Aggregate Profit of the organism, being goods produced above the demand of wage earners and capitalists for consumer goods, capital replacement goods, etc. The money received for these goods on their sale to the Government will be the money form of part of the Aggregate Profit. It is not the Profit A part nor the Profit B part which have demonstrably different places (effective demand) in the goods-money circuit of the organism. In summary, given the Government expenditure as a system, all the premises of a political economy based on the fictive expansion of capital, the establishment of the WM tax as a regular course, then the tax must be paid out of the pseudo Profit B, money form.*

The main inquiry is how this incidence is actually accomplished in the organism, *and* with respect to individual and units. As to the latter, the problem of tracing the source of income to the pseudo Profit B, is a difficult and complex one. The shift of immediate incidence is difficult to follow, more so than in the tax of the Democratic State. Individual income in the pefcp, even wage earners income, is always increased by the fictive profit. Personal incidence or apparent personal incidence in the pefcp does not reveal the ultimate economic incidence. The source of the income has to be traced, and the shift of the tax with respect to the source has also to be traced. While the pseudo Profit B does tend to crystallize in the very large incomes, it is true that there can be a marked shift in the actual receipt of the pseudo Profit B, part of which is actually never personally received, but is an income "before taxes."

The four factors affecting incidence of the WM tax in the organism.

There are four factors affecting incidence on the pseudo Profit B and in proper proportion in the organism: the overall *size* of the tax imposed in relation to the size of the Government expenditure; the *congruence* of the tax with the type of Government expenditure i.e. incidence on sectors of the economy from which the goods are purchased; the *progressive* nature of the tax; the time factor in *integrating* the tax into the organism. All of these factors are also directly related to the immediate and ultimate personal incidence of the WM tax.

In general, the total WM tax must always have a definite relationship to the size of the Government's welfare-military expenditure to assure incidence on the pseudo Profit B, and in

* Of course, the goods purchased by the Government, part of the Aggregate Profit and specifically part of the pseudo Profit B, do not necessarily represent the profit of the individual selling unit. There is the usual interchange among units, and it is only when viewed in Aggregates, in the organism, that it can be stated that the goods purchased by the Government are part of the Aggregate Profit.

proper proportion. (Assume this expenditure is large enough to permit a WM tax.) The tax must be less than this expenditure according to general principles stated in Section (1). If the total tax is too high, it may fall on the Profit B, or prevent the formation of the pseudo Profit B itself (insufficient fictive capital form). But absolute size of tax with respect to incidence must be considered with reference to ultimate personal incidence and shift of incidence.

Exemptions, deductions, and power to shift incidence may produce such distortions that the incidence is shifted from the pseudo Profit B, or parts of the pseudo Profit B escape the tax. The tax may seem to be of the proper size, yet these distortions so affect it that it is either too high or too low. Size cannot be considered alone, without reference to the other factors, i.e. congruence, progressive nature, and integration.

The congruence principle (with respect to the incidence, and certainty of incidence, and the safety of the incidence) is based on the nature of the purchases by the Government, and in particular the balance in the Military-Welfare expenditures. The Government cannot impose taxes on all sectors of the economy, and then make its purchases only from part of the economy. Tax source and Government purchase should be congruent. Congruence is best understood through the concept of the general goods-money circuit of the economy. Actually a preponderance of goods should be purchased from the so called "capital" goods industries. However an excessive reliance on military expenditure can injure parts of the consumer goods industries even if they do benefit by sales to those employed in heavy industry.

The WM tax system must be of a progressive nature. There is as unequal a distribution of income in the pefcp as in the ICE. This is not so material (in the function of the economy) in the ICE, since to a great extent the upper incomes are constituted by Profit B—real capital expansion. But in the pefcp, these upper incomes to a considerable extent contain a great proportion of the pseudo Profit B, and the WM tax must reach these incomes.

The different profit rates between the large scale producer and the smaller producer, may be mentioned at this point with respect to the necessity for progressive taxation. But even a progressive tax may not be sufficient for certain sectors of the economy. It is probable that certain selective taxes will be necessary to reach the pseudo Profit B in these sectors. The special excise tax will be found to be essential. Death taxes will be useful in recovering and canceling part of the fictive capital forms without injuring the economy, and they may also be fitted into a tax system that will recover part of the pseudo Profit B.

Generally speaking a proportional, or regressive tax system will not accomplish the purpose of the WM tax, and will injure the pefcp. Again, the problem of certain tax exemptions that particularly affect the very large income, must be resolved.

It takes a period of time in this political economy before the WM tax is properly integrated into the economy and has its full incidence on the pseudo Profit B. A newly imposed tax may have a different immediate economic incidence, but all taxes sooner or later become integrated into the economic structure and shift to the Aggregate Profit, and to a part of the Aggregate Profit. The great variety of consumer taxes, sales taxes, are at first a reduction of individual income (even of wage earners in material production) and might be a reduction of income that would ordinarily be spent for consumers goods. But this is temporary; sooner or later the economic incidence of the WM tax will be on the pseudo Profit B, *if* the Government's expenditure system is of proper size, and in proper balance, and the Government is maintaining the proper proportions in its revenue sources, and the Government is maintaining a proper balance of power in the economy.

Once a tax at a certain rate has been established, and it becomes integrated in the economy, and the necessary shifts of economic and personal incidences have taken place, the tax should not be changed. The economy adjusts to the tax, and incidence also.

Changes in the tax structure, and the immediate incidence of the tax before a shift of incidence takes place, create greater problems in the pefcp than in the ICE, since the tax of the Democratic State is relatively low. Furthermore, some shifts in incidence can be hurtful to some sectors of the economy, since the WM tax is an important "cost" to the unit.

The size of the WM tax and the possibility of a shift to a

weak sector of the economy are among the reasons for the need for controls by the Government over all aspects of private production. In some cases there is a necessity of preventing a shift, and in other cases the necessity of accomplishing a shift (as from wage earners in the production of material goods, to the employer, so that the tax does ultimately fall on the Aggregate Profit). Among other things, the Government must balance powers and equalize powers, and protect weaker sectors, assuring wage earners some power in bargaining. The equalization of powers, of course, should not only be for the benefit of wage earners in material production, but, also for many who receive part of the Aggregate Profit in one way or another, and who have little power to adjust to shifting taxes, (or for that matter, to protect themselves from a steady depreciation of the paper money).

The creation of an effective, balanced tax system for a pefcp is a matter of great difficulty. There are two aspects of this difficulty: economic engineering; and political feasibility. The question of Government power, and proper Government form (Chief of Government *above* any economic class, Ch. VI) is of primary importance. If too much control is exerted over the Government by certain segments of the capitalist class (financial interests especially) certain incomes which consist in great part of the pseudo Profit B will escape taxation, and the tax will have its incidence where it should not. The problems of economic engineering are themselves considerable. They cannot be separated from management problems with respect to the level of production, the elements of the revenue mix, etc.

On the whole, the tax level in the WMS is usually too low. Furthermore, there is a tendency to reduce taxes whenever the level of production dips (below, .2) and it is then difficult to raise the tax. And, to repeat, there is always the problem of certain exemptions and avoidances, particularly an excessive exemption of financial and realty "profits" from the tax. In wartime, the WMS may have to tax part of the Aggregate Wage and the Profit A. However, to make these taxes effective, it is probable that direct controls over the economy are necessary. (Direct controls are necessary for other reasons also.) In the absence of war, it is an error to levy additional taxes, which in their incidence, possible selectivity, or their size, will fall on the

Profit A or Aggregate Wage, for *welfare* expenditure. It is unnecessary for the function of a pefcp; the tax will not have a multiple effect on the Level of the economy; it is unwise for political reasons.

.2 Continued. The WM tax in the Government's "revenue mix," in general; the WM tax at the several levels of production.

The dependent organism can function at several levels:
(a) A low level equilibrium. Probable at the outset of a pefcp, which is principally based on welfare expenditure and some "public works" (Ch. V). The welfare system itself is at a relatively low level.
(b) Low level of production rapidly rising (war situation, or transformation into complete Welfare-Military State). What is involved is the "reactive" expansion of capital, Sec. (1) subsec. .5 above.
(c) High level of production, rising slowly on modest capital expansion. This is the fully developed pefcp, relatively stable. Private inflation and private fictive capital paper creation are strictly controlled.
(d) High level rising rapidly (generally a war situation, and/or uncontrolled private inflation and private fictive capital paper creation).
(e) High level of production, declining.

On the inception of the pefcp, the funds for the Government expenditure (welfare) are derived from the sale of bonds and the inflation of papers money. The pseudo Profit B has an almost entirely fictive capital form. The WM tax cannot even be instituted until equilibrium and normal price have been established. (The Government must act directly to restore normal price, normal wage-profit ratio, limitation of production in certain sectors, etc. in addition to establishing its systems of expenditure. (Sec. 4, below.)
(a) Low level equilibrium. As stated in subsection .1, the pseudo Profit B must reach a certain size before a WM tax can effectively take a significant part of it. However, the WM tax should

at least be instituted at the low level equilibrium even though the fictive profit form cannot constitute any great part of the pseudo Profit B. The necessary procedure is first to increase the Government expenditure. This is a difficult thing to do if the political economy is based on welfare expenditure alone. The WM tax cannot really be substantial because of the necessity for congruence of tax and expenditure, as well as the fact that the size of the pseudo Profit B is inadequate. And expenditure cannot easily be increased. It must be concluded that with a low level economy dependent on a welfare system of expenditure, the Government must rely mainly on borrowing and inflation, and the pseudo Profit B will principally have a fictive capital form.

(b) Where the level is rising rapidly from a low level equilibrium, a situation caused by war or imminent war, there is a great (reactive) expansion of real capital. The economy approaches the developed WMS-pefcp. The full scale WM tax *must* now be introduced. (There must also be controls to prevent the "demand" type of price rise, a consequent spiral in Government expenditure, accelerated monetary depreciation.) The great expansion of actual capital, Profit B, the great increase in fictive capital papers and inflation mean an immense Aggregate Profit which will be disbursed to units and individuals. This is unnecessary to maintain the high and rising level. Such a volume of Profit B and pseudo Profit B with a fictive capital form, will encourage the overexpansion of capital, private fictive capital manipulation, hyperinflation, excessive depreciation, etc.

(c) The High Level economy, slowly expanding. (The fully developed, well managed pefcp.)

The same rate of taxation should be maintained, as in the reactive capital expansion to the high level. This is a hard course to follow. It is a mistake to reduce taxes, particularly since they have become well integrated into the economy, in the rise of the level, and their proper incidence is established. The level of Government expenditure, cannot immediately be sustained at the same level. However, different types of military and paramilitary programs can be introduced, and the welfare system expanded. Public works can be expanded (Ch. V).

The level of production will be slowly rising as the capital slowly expands. This does not necessarily mean a rise in the number of those employed in material production, since the technological advance will reduce the number of employees. For many reasons, then, the level of Government expenditure should expand. This means not only a steady increase in dollar volume, but absolute volume, since the paper money depreciating. The tax return automatically increases, as the money depreciates, and the level of production rises.

(d) High level economy, rapidly expanding.

In the high level economy faced with an actual war (even a little war) a rise in taxes is necessary. (If it is a Great War the tax must be of such size as to reduce the Profit A and the Aggregate Wage.) And if this rise in taxes is not sufficient, direct controls must be imposed to prevent or limit private consumption, and to reduce any private inflation or private fictive expansion of capital. The increase in military expenditure requires a real expansion of capital. The increased Profit B, and the increase in the pseudo Profit B which will have a fictive capital form because of the increase in Government borrowing and inflation, will permit a marked increase in the fictive profit form. It is essential that the Government maintain a WM tax that will make as large a part of the pseudo Profit B as possible, a fictive profit.

(e) The high level economy, declining. The question of reducing the rate of the WM tax, and increasing fictive capital and inflation components of the Government's revenue mix.

Assume that the Government's level of purchase (Welfare, Military) is not declining. (If there is any reduction in this expenditure, the Level of the economy will decline—and the WM tax revenues also. In such instance, the prior Level of expenditure must be restored. This is not so difficult a matter as may be imagined, even if there has been a termination of a Little War.)

But if the Level of production does decline, (Government expenditure stable) recognize, first that this is not a cyclic decline, nor is it a spirally increasing decline. This will remove a considerable amount of apprehension, and apprehension leads to unwise measures.

The first question to be asked is why the Level of the economy is declining.

If, preceding the decline, there had been a modest degree

of capital expansion, (the characteristic condition of the pefcp), and no unusual private inflation and creation of private FC papers, then a modest decline in the Level of the economy may be due to the fact that the Aggregate Profit tends to decline (and the Aggregate Price of goods sold tends to decline—concealed by the depreciation of paper money—and also the Aggregate Wage)—all due to technological advance in the productive process. This also means a relative change in the ratios of real capital expansion, fictive capital expansion, inflation, and the fictive profit component on the pseudo Profit B, which itself affects the Level and the Income. Ordinarily (as in the ICE) the decline in the Aggregate Profit (due to technological advance) is counterbalanced by the expansion of real capital.

Consequently, the situation simply is that the Government has failed to maintain the necessary, steady *increase* in the Level of its expenditure. This means, in essence, an increase in borrowing and inflation, since the tax return will increase if the economy is expanding. Note that the tendency for employment in material production always is to fall, because of technological advances, but this is a separate question. The level of employment may not even rise as the level of production rises.

The second situation to be considered is the one where there has been some preceding extraordinary increase in real capital expansion and in the whole Level of the economy, due to a Little War, usually accompanied by an excessive, poorly controlled private paper money inflation and creation of private fictive capital forms.

The relatively sharp decline in capital expansion—once the expansion of capital for war production has been completed—and the decline in any private fictive capital paper creation with private inflation, will result in significant decline in the level of production and employment. This will be more marked than in the first situation described. But again, it is not a cyclic depression that sets in. There is a decline in demand, but the basic dynamic of the political economy—the fictive expansion of capital, is operative, and the level simply falls to the point where it is supported by the degree of fictive capital expansion maintained by the Government. Actually the level of Government expenditure is not likely to be reduced.

An unfortunate concommitant of the situation is that the rate of depreciation of the paper money seems to increase, and prices rise, despite the decline in the level of production and employment. This is unlike the situation in the ICE, and is an anomaly to the economist. The cause is the excessive previous inflation of the paper money, mostly of a private nature.

It is important at this point to understand that the level of production has been excessively high; that private inflation and creation of private fictive capital forms has gotten out of hand; that taxes have been too low or that their incidence has been escaped. This was not an unwelcome situation to most groups in the economy. A great deal of "easy money" has been made.

The readjustment is not easy. There is a tendency to inflate excessively, and encourage private inflation, to raise the level of the economy, and to reduce taxes, or to take steps to encourage real capital expansion. These steps will lead only to further difficulties. The idea prevails that this political economy should be managed so that the highest possible level of production should be achieved, with "full employment." This is not the nature of this political economy. The erroneous view of this political economy encourages the spread of Little wars. It is true that the Government should maintain a high level of production and employment—much higher than was possible in the ICE. But an excessively high level and an excessive level of real capital expansion are aberrations of a pefcp, and can only shorten its life.

.3 *The tax revenue of the WMS, as a whole. (All taxes.)*
Taxes that obtain money that will be returned to holders of the Government bonds as interest.
The effect of the acquisition of money that appears as "profit" in financial and realty transactions.

The entire tax revenue of the WMS does not enter the goods-money circuit between the Government and the dependent capitalist organism (the large sum returned as interest on the Government bonds and notes being the most important exception).

Of the tax revenue that does enter the goods-money circuit, a part does not create the pseudo Profit B. Most of the taxes previously levied by the Democratic State, and integrated into the economy with an incidence on the Profit A, continue to be levied. This money is expended for some Governmental function. Furthermore, certain taxes and expenditures are a true cost of production of material goods, falling on neither the Aggregate Profit or the Aggregate Wage. (Sec. 2.)

In wartime, taxes may be imposed that may reduce the capitalists personal consumption and may reduce for a time the consumption of the wage earners in material production.

As set forth elsewhere, it is only the WM tax that takes part of the pseudo Profit B, where the Government expenditure does create the pseudo Profit B, that has the effect on the multiple expansion of the whole level of production.

With respect to taxes that appear to fall on wages, in the WMS, note that a considerable part of these "wages" are not wages in material production. These may be

(a) "Wages" that are derivative from Profit A. The economic incidence of the tax on the wage is really on Profit A.

(b) "Wages" or other payments from the Government—assume from the pseudo Profit B. The tax, economically speaking, is simply a reduction of the payment by the Government.

(c) Wages, or other income derived from "profit" made in dealing in capital papers, land titles, private inflation, etc. These taxes may ultimately fall on the pseudo Profit B.

The money obtained by tax, and returned (interest payments) to holders of the Government's bonds or notes, has no real effect on the function of the organism, or the Level of Production. Essentially, it is a transfer of part of the Aggregate Profit from some individuals to others, or even a taking and return to the same individual or unit. It does not particularly affect the goods-money circuit of the organism as a whole. Assume: as in the Democratic State, the levy and return is of the Profit A. The same value of goods are purchased for consumption, although the individual recipients are different. If the transfer is of part of the pseudo Profit B, the return may become a consumer income, and again, since the tax falling on the pseudo Profit B would result in consumption by the Government or its distributees, there is little difference in the goods-money circuit of the organism. If the return of the pseudo Profit B is not spent for personal consumption, there will be some effect on the goods-money circuit. The interest then has to achieve some capital form, which it can do in various ways. (See, elsewhere, on the capital forms that inflated money can achieve).

It is possible that the tax and return may slightly affect the ratio between the Aggregate Wage (of those engaged in production of material goods) and the Aggregate Profit.

It is possible also that part of the interest is not paid by the taxed money at all, but continues as a further accretion of the fictive capital form.

The effect of the acquisition of money that appears as "profit" in financial and realty transactions.

If publicly inflated money becomes part of the pseudo Profit B, it has been stated as a general rule that it will not be recovered by the WM tax any more than the Profit B itself, or that part of the pseudo Profit B that achieves a fictive capital form (Sec. .1, above). The same rule is generally applicable to privately inflated money that becomes part of the pseudo Profit.

It is important to note, however, that a considerable amount of bank credit money will have been created to deal in capital papers, and land titles, etc., and part of this may appear as profit and income to some individuals. It has however, not entered the goods-money circuit (i.e. may not properly be considered to be inflated money).

If the Government, by tax, does acquire some of this latter money (i.e. profit or income in financial transactions that is newly created bank credit money) or for that matter, acquires by tax, private or public fictive capital papers, or their money equivalent, and then expends this money in its goods-money circuit, the economic effect is as if the Government inflated the money itself, for its revenue and expenditure. The money becomes part of the pseudo Profit B, and itself seeks a capital form, etc. This is not to be considered a tax on privately inflated money (which has entered the goods-money circuit of the economy). Of course, some of these "profits" and income that fall into the Government's revenue, thru tax, may not be newly created money, or newly activated money, but may in origin be simply a transfer of existing consumption and, when the Government acquires this money, it is also simply transferring consumption.

But to return to the general rule that inflated money that has become part of the pseudo Profit B, even if privately inflated, should not be taken by tax: if the private inflation is excessive, it is conceivable that some part of this money, appearing in the pseudo Profit B, could be taken by tax. However, it is certainly better policy for the Government to prevent an excessive private inflation of money by an effective tax system (eliminate certain exemptions).

(4) Government management of the Level of Production, price, wage rate, profit.

Aspects of the complex pattern of management by the Government of the WMS of the Level of Production, real capital expansion, its fiscal system, its expenditure systems, finance generally* have been mentioned in this Chapter, and will be discussed further elsewhere. At this point it is necessary to note that the Government must also manage the dependent organism itself. The capital units apparently function as independent units. But they are wholly controlled by the function of the dependent organism, and all aspects of the organism are under Government management. When the inherent dynamics of the ICE failed, most of its self adjusting mechanisms disappeared also, and inherent controls and mechanisms affecting price, wage rate, and profit rate, to a great extent, ended. The substitution of the fictive capital expansion for the real expansion of capital did not restore the older self adjusting mechanisms, but rather created an inherent instability in price, wage rate, profit rate, the wage profit ratio, the level of production and balance of production among the several sectors *at all times.*

* The fiscal policies of the Government, and its management of the money and banking system to maintain its fiscal policies, and the tax system, etc., *must* be coordinated and integrated with all the necessities of private production, exchange, finance, etc. It would be fair to say that public and private finance are not separable.

Price, in general:

Normal price is essential to the function of a pefcp; at the same time a pefcp makes normal price possible in a capitalist organism, i.e. by furnishing the necessary components of normal price, even though they are fictive. This is not a paradox. Of course, normal price is essential to equilibrium in the ICE, and capital expansion (constant type) ordinarily means that normal price will exist. But in the pefcp, the function and existence of the fictive forms themselves absolutely depend on the existence of normal price. Normal price must be established by the Government along with the fictive forms that make it possible. If price is not normal; the pseudo Profit B, money form, cannot be created; the WMS tax cannot be effective. Borrowing also will not be effective. Indeed, in the absence of normal price, inflation itself will not be effective to maintain the organism.

Particularly at the inception of the pefcp, the Government must act affirmatively to restore normality. *It must continue these efforts throughout the existence of the political economy.* The constant inflation, the constant depreciation of the paper money, always changes the price level, and since wage rate and wage-profit ratio depend on the price level, these are always affected. Furthermore, price power in any sector, which will always be found to exist, can not only derange normality in other sectors, but can force the Government to inflate beyond what is absolutely necessary. The WMS tax can easily be distorted when the price level changes, and this will further distort wage rates and the wage profit ratio.

At the inception of the pefcp: the Government acts directly to restore normality, by various means including the use of minimum price laws, or cartel agreements, marketing arrangements, production controls, etc. (Devaluation of the monetary unit is usually attempted, but this is not domestically helpful —Ch. II, Sections 14, 17; however devaluation of the monetary unit may be essential for foreign trade and foreign exchange in the pefcp—Ch. IV, Section 5). The Government must also raise the wage rate level, either by law directly, or by providing the wage earner with increased bargaining power. This must parallel the inception of the creation of the pseudo Profit B.

Maintaining normal price: high level economy

The Government must continue its efforts to maintain normal price in a high level economy. This is difficult when the high level economy is sharply expanding, and even direct price controls are only partially effective. But even in a slowly expanding economy, the price level is still always rising because of paper money depreciation, and wage rates tend to lag. Real wages may be rising because of increased productivity but nevertheless the actual wage must rise too. There are other problems: technology may be causing a price decline (despite the fact that this is concealed by the paper money depreciation). Furthermore, certain sectors tend to overproduce.

If the economy is slowly expanding there must be a constant increase in Government purchase to compensate for the expanding economy, and the technological advances. This may also be necessary to compensate for the decline in the number of laborers necessary in material production. And even though the severe pressures of rapid expansion do not exist, there should be some price control and some wage control exercised by the Government, as well as some degree of control over production in sectors without adequate internal control.

In wartime the Government is a major purchaser, and it must increase its revenue by borrowing and inflation to pay for its needs. Sectors with sufficient price power can push up prices that will force the government to increase its borrowing and inflation. Indeed, sector power can push up prices to obtain a greater part of tax revenues than it ordinarily would. That is to say the price power of certain sectors can disturb the congruence of the flow back of tax revenues to the dependent organism. If *wage power* is excessive, generally, or in certain sectors, and wage rates forced up so that the wage-profit ratio is distorted, the more powerful sectors simply push prices up to maintain the wage profit ratio (or exceed it). This increases the Government need for revenue—taxed, borrowed, inflated.

It is true that the increased tax can recover part of the money advanced by the Government when prices are above normal, but this generally comes too late, and the additional money becomes integrated into rising prices and often into spiralling wages. Furthermore, the tax can never recover all the additional money.

A falling price level is always harmful for the proper function of the pefcp. It generally means a reduction in the rate of profit, even though the mass of profit may remain the same. If wages would fall at the same time, the wage profit ratio could be maintained, but wage rates do not tend to decline.

The price level tends to fall because of technological improvements which certainly continue when the economy is in equilibrium at any level. Fortunately, as stated above, the fall in the price level because of this reason is counter-balanced by a steady monetary depreciation, and in actuality, a steady rise in price takes place. It may be said, therefore, that a depreciation of money is probably essential to the function of the system.

Recapitulation on Wage Rates:

The wage rate must steadily rise in the pefcp because of the constant depreciation of the paper money, including accelerated depreciation in periods of excessive inflation, public or private. But the power of the wage earners with respect to wage rates must never be so great as to injure the economy, by distorting the basic wage-profit ratio, generally or in any sector. In the pefcp there is a possibility of a wage-price spiral if the wage earners have an excessive power over the wage rate. In war time wage rate increases can be passed on to the Government by way of higher prices, which may force an additional inflation, an additional depreciation of the paper money, and further necessary wage rate rises.

The increased productivity because of technological advance must also be considered with respect to the necessity of rising wage rate. When productivity increases, the *real* wage may rise even if the wage rate remains the same. But, nevertheless, the wage rate should also rise as the price level rises. That is to say, it may be true that despite a price rise the wage earner may get as much or more for his money, because of technological advance. He must get this anyway; the wage rate must nonetheless rise because of depreciation of paper money and the general price rise. The wage increase consequently should not simply be a "productivity" increase; it is an illusion that the wage rate rise is a payment for "increased productivity."

Thus, with respect to wage rate, price, and profit rate, the Government should:

(a) preferably, at all times, maintain a system of *direct* legal controls over wage, and price, for all sectors of the economy; or

(b) at least maintain a system of informal controls over wage and price; attempting to balance power between unions and employers; utilizing its purchasing power to control large producers; utilizing selective taxation; all to maintain as great a stability as is possible, i.e., a slow, steady, rise.

CHAPTER IV

MONEY, BANKING, INFLATION

PART I

Money, Bank Credit Money, and Inflation of Bank Credit Money, in the Independent Capitalist Economy. The Collapse of the Banking System on the End of the Independent Capitalist Economy.

(1) The general form of the banking system, and the banking process, in the ICE. The banking system and process must be viewed as part of the capitalist organism.

.1 The banking system is composed of private commercial banks and a Government Central Reserve Bank.

The banking system (generalized form) has two interconnected parts:

There are a large number of privately owned *commercial banks*. They accept "deposits" of money, maintaining these "deposits" as book entries; the "deposits" are promises of the bank to pay money. These deposits are transferred among the commercial banks by check of the depositors, as means of purchase and payment. The commercial banks create "deposits," the money media, by loan and investment (that return interest to the bank). These money-media creations are the major part of the bank "deposits." That is to say, most of the deposits of a bank are money creations by other banks. The amount of money-media creation of all the commercial banks—all the "deposits" are a certain multiple of their "reserve"; for the most part this reserve is a deposit in another bank or banks (i.e. a promise of another bank to pay money).

The *Government central reserve bank*, (GCRB) owned or

controlled by the Government, (possibly very limited Government control during the ICE), accepts "deposits" of money from a substantial number of commercial banks, and from the Government. These are maintained as book entries. The deposits may in part be gold and Treasury Notes, but for the most part, are money created (deposits) of other bank, or the Government Bank itself. The money deposited by the commercial bank in the Government Central Bank is generally the "*reserve*" of the commercial bank. The commercial bank's "reserve" then, is generally a book entry of the Government Bank. (The conventional statement of this is that the Government Bank "holds" the reserve of the commercial bank.) The Government Bank creates money—*deposit type or currency,* also by loan or "investment," which are on some type of interest bearing capital paper. The volume and conditions of money creation of the Government bank, and its type, are controlled by law (although the law can be and is changed).

In general, the banking system as a whole, creates by paper instrument, promises to pay specific sums of money; the instruments themselves are used by the individuals who own them, as money for purchase and payment.*

The banking system and the banking process, when described apart from their context—as a part and essential mechanism of the capitalist organism in the production and sale of material goods—seems unreal; its terminology of "deposits," "reserve" "bank" (as money repository), "bank capital," "savings," "security" (all abstract relationships converted into pleasingly concrete terms) reveals little of its actual nature.

* Recapitulation, from Ch. II, Sec. 14: The bank credit money (bcm) created by the Government bank, or GCRB, whether deposit type or currency type, is called herein the *public* type of bcm; the bcm created by the commercial banks is called the *private* type.

The public form is the national (Government) paper money, although in the later ICE, some Treasury paper money still existed. The currency form, public type, is gold convertible (ICE) and is legal tender, but in actuality the deposit form is so managed that it is in effect gold convertible.

The private type is convertible to the public type, and then is theoretically, gold equivalent. For the sake of simplicity, it will be assumed that the private type exists only in deposit form.

But, however abstract the forms and processes may seem, the banking system and process is always ultimately based on the reality of the *material good,* and the universal form of value of the material good—*gold.* Even if the banking system is creating large volumes of its paper money for the buying and selling of capital papers and land titles and inflating money on fictive capital papers, which money is not used in the capitalist process of production at all—nevertheless the paper money forms created are still money. These creations are inevitably tied to the actuality of material goods, and, in the capitalist organism, thus inevitably tied to gold. Gold lurks behind all the mysteries of paper money creation by the banking process, at whatever the actual equivalency to gold that these paper money creations may have.

When we speak of material goods and their production, we are, of course, speaking of the capitalist process of production (Chap. II), wherein bank credit money is the major money form. In this process of production there is the advance by the capitalist of money to buy goods and pay wages, and the return of this money by the sale of the goods at normal price—which implies a profit and which implies capital expansion and constant new investment. In the banking process, paper money is created and then cancelled in the same context of constant advance and return, with interest as a share of the profit, if the price is normal and the economy is in equilibrium.

Since capitalist production is inherently on a "material good" standard, and all its relationships and ratios are on a "material good" standard, i.e., normal price, the wage-profit ratio—(and hence on a *gold* standard, since gold is the money commodity), the banking system and the banking process is itself fundamentally and ineluctably on a gold basis in all its relationships, at whatever the actual equivalency of its paper money to gold, or whatever the declaration of a Government with respect to gold convertibility. This is also true of the banking system of the pefcp, even though the Government sequesters the money gold, and the paper money is inconvertible to gold. (Sec. 4, below.)

It is true that the banking system and process have certain laws of function of their own. However, the banking system is always ultimately controlled by the function of the capitalist organism, (ICE), its dynamics and mechanisms. (Likewise, the basic laws of function of the pefcp will ultimately govern the banking system and process.)

Although the commercial banks are necessary for the capitalist relationship in the production of material goods, and supply a money media necessary for the public generally, they exist to obtain *interest*. The prototypical form of interest in the capitalist relationship is a share of the Aggregate Profit. The "Bank" is primarily monetizing a *capital* good, or a capital paper representing capital goods that will sell at normal price in the goods-money circuit. If all the material goods are not sold at normal price, then ultimately bank credit money (BCM) (on whatever basis they have been created) will either be worthless or will not represent the weight of gold they purport to represent.

The GCRB, however, follows only the forms of operating for interest; it will generally return to the Government the interest it receives above its operating expenses. It became a necessary part of the banking system of a developed capitalist organism, i.e., on the development of the financial system and mechanisms. Further, it creates a Government paper money, bank credit type, currency and deposit fom. A public bank credit money form is essential in an economy where the major money media are BCM. (The Treasury Note, for many reasons, is an unsatisfactory public paper money form in such an economy.) The bank credit currency form is legal tender; it is used to convert deposits of the commercial banks on request to a currency. The greater part of the public paper money form is of the "deposit" type.

The GCRB is a fundamental part of a pefcp, but in this political economy, its nature is transformed. (Part II, below.)

.2 *The banking process, restated and amplified.*

The banking process, in general form, consists of certain elements, which although separately stated herein, are all functionally interrelated:

(a) Recapitulation: The Banks create, by paper instrument, or some document, promises to pay specific sums of money. The instruments themselves are used by the individuals who own them, as money for purchase and payment, and they are generally acceptable as means of purchase and payment. ("Bank Notes," a currency passing from hand to hand.) The promise may be a book entry, called a "deposit"; this is used as a money media by the "depositor" by transferring it, by check, to another depositor" in the same, or another bank, as money for purchase and payment. The bank may pay its depositor in bank notes, thus cancelling the "deposit." (Assume herein that only the GCRB issues notes—see below.)

(b) These money media are created, almost entirely in exchange for an interest bearing capital instrument, itself a promise to pay money at a future date with interest (or discounted); the capital instrument *may* represent some material goods used in the process of production, or goods in circulation in the capitalist process of production. Almost all bank credit money exists because interest is paid for its existence. Thus, the banks either *lend* their credit, i.e. create these liquid promises to pay money, for individuals who execute these capital instruments, (or a Government), or the banks buy these capital instruments from their owners, by and with the creation of these liquid, generally acceptable, circulating promises to pay money (currency or "deposits").

(c) The banks may also create these media for individual who *deposit* actual gold with them, or Treasury notes, (see also below, creation of BCM by a bank on the deposit with it of *paper currency* of other banks, particularly Government bank notes).

(d) A bank can create such media by accepting the media (promises to pay money, of the book entry type) of other banks. In such case, the original bank must transfer to the bank the capital paper or other asset on which it originally created the money form, unless there has been a set off, or mutual interchange of media. Note: this set off, or mutual interchange of media, occurs in the process in which the depositors in each bank use their "deposits" as media of payment or purchase, transferring the "deposit" to another individual who maintains his account in another bank.

(e) The general assets of the banks are:
- —The interest bearing capital papers on which the "deposits" are created
- —Gold, Treasury notes and Government bank notes (almost all of which have been obtained by the creation of "deposits"; some may have been assembled as part of the bank's capital).
- —"Deposits" in other banks
- —Titles to realty

(A part of these assets are the *bank capital.* However bank capital is a relatively small part of the bank's assets. The bank capital thus may be gold, Government paper monies, possibly titles to realty, but it usually consists principally of capital papers, usually of a fictive type, and "deposits" in other banks.

(f) That part of the bank's assets that are money or money media—gold, Treasury notes, *"deposits" in other banks,* are called its *"reserve"* (including an excess reserve if the "reserve" is fixed as a percentage on deposits). A bank may keep almost its entire reserve in the GCRB; its reserve then being almost entirely the BCM, or the promise of another bank to pay money on demand. (See below, that this "reserve" on deposit in the GCRB may not actually be subject to draft, and, thus, in reality, may not even be a liquid asset, but simply a non interest bearing asset, perhaps not a "money" reserve at all.) The actual money "reserve" of a bank will be a relatively very small amount of money: some gold, some paper currency, and some coins.

(g) The individual bank must be *liquid*—have enough paper currency and gold, or "deposits" in other banks on which it can draw to pay any of its promises to pay (its "deposits") that may in practice be demanded. It is a fundamental premise of the banking process that, in practice, a very small part of "deposits" will be demanded in gold or currency, if the system is functioning normally, and that the transfer of "deposits" from "depositor" to "depositor" will balance themselves out in a time period. Liquidity consists, in major part, of keeping enough cash on hand to pay the demands that do occur. (Further with respect to liquidity: Banking practice requires that the bank keep part of its assets in types of capital paper that can be quickly turned into cash, and that there be a certain sequence of due dates in other capital papers).

—Refer further, with respect to liquidity, to (j) and (k) below, with respect to BCM creation as limited to a multiple of "reserve" and the relationship of this to gold.

(h) The individual bank, and the commercial banks as a whole, should be *solvent*. Solvency requires, essentially, that the interest bearing capital papers held by the banks (assets) do pay the interest required, and the principal when due, and could theoretically be sold at face value to the depositors of the banks generally (thus cancelling the deposit). But a bank and the banking system can function if not solvent, provided (a) the bank is liquid—has currently needed cash on hand, *and* (b) the transfers of deposits back and forth among all the banks are in approximate balance. And this can be true of the whole system of commercial banks. If enough interest is paid to cover expenses, insolvency is no bar to the continuance of the banking process. However: If the depositors of some, or many banks transfer their deposits to other banks, and there is no counterbalancing transfer to the insolvent banks, or if the depositors demand a great volume of currency (no confidence, etc.), the fact that the capital paper of the insolvent bank is bad, means the failure of the bank or banks. If the paper were "good," the Government bank or GCRB *could* buy it by creating BCM, and theoretically the Government bank can create money for any or all "good" assets (or for bad capital paper, for that matter also). See further in (3) below, however, as to the really very limited extent, in the ICE, that the Government bank may create media as "lender of last resort" on good or bad capital paper.

(i) The Central Reserve (Commercial banks reserve "held" by the GCRB, in the ICE).

Correlative: The GCRB as creator of bcm, book entry type, and currency type:

—Implicit in the concept of a central reserve

—Unilateral money creation by the GCRB in the later ICE.

When the commercial banks "reserve" is deposited in the GCRB, their reserve is then the bcm of the GCRB, a creation of bcm by the GCRB.

Whatever the professed theory or ideology of the GCRB once was, the GCRB was always a money creating institution; the centralization of commercial bank reserves was not the basis of this power, although it was a mechanism of this power. The real money creating power of the GCRB, even during the ICE, was not simply a multiple of the gold it possesses as reserve; nor does "centralization" of reserves of commercial banks increase the power of the commercial banks to create bcm.*

The GCRB was creating bcm on the "deposit" of the commercial banks reserves. (It may be argued that the part of this reserves that is a legally required percentage of the commercial bank deposits, is not money at all, since it may not be drawn upon). The GCRB was frankly creating public bcm by its loans to member banks, and this public bcm could become part of the commercial bank reserve, and be the basis for multiple expansion of bcm by the commercial banks (under the conventional or legal rules of money creation by the commercial banks). In the later ICE, the GCRB is clearly creating public bcm that enables the commercial banks to create money for the financial mechanisms to deal in and to monetize capital papers and fictive capital papers, and to inflate the bcm.

(j) Bank Credit Money creation limited to a certain multiple of

* At one time, under U. S. law, the amount of BCM that the GCRB could create was limited to four times the amount of gold it possessed. The law was changed, *first,* to remove the gold cover with respect to the book entry BCM, and then *second,* with respect to the amount of currency that could be created. The gold percentage restrictions are artificial, and the rules will be changed if they prevent the creation of money that it is desired to created. It is to be noted that the amount of gold that the U. S. possessed was extraordinarily great; other national PE's could practice no such restriction. (Yet in another sense the restriction is not wholly conventional and artificial. See section 4 below on gold in the PEFCP. Tying the volume of creation of bcm to gold, which *private* individuals possessed or could possess, or obtain through currency conversion, was a definite private control exerted over the Government's banking operations.)

the "reserve" (ICE). The increase of the "reserve" by money creation by the GCRB.

In general, the "deposit" creation by the commercial banks (by loan or investment), is limited by custom or law to a certain multiple of the commercial bank "reserve." Within this limit, the determination of the actual volume of deposits that will be created, is the volume of BCM that can obtain interest on a "safe" capital paper, or what is believed to be a good loan or investment.

Insofar as BCM were created for the production and sale of goods, and on capital papers directly involving the production and sale of goods, the actual volume of the BCM created is in actuality governed by the probability of production at normal profit, i.e., sale at normal price. But it is probable that the reserve could always be expanded sufficiently to provide a sufficiently great multiple expansion of BCM, for production and sale of material goods, in a prosperous, expanding system, without a GCRB. (Sec. 2.)

However:

A. The GCRB does create BCM which enables the commercial banks to create BCM as a multiple thereof. As indicated, this money creation by the GCRB was not necessary for the purpose of real capital expansion: It was the need of the financial system for money to deal in capital papers, land titles, or to engage in a public or private inflation of the BCM, that required money creation by a GCRB.
B. Presumably the GRCB creates sufficient money as "lender of last resort" when the commercial banks cannot do so, or the bank fail (cyclic depression). This power was actually very limited, and in the main, illusory (Sec. 3).
C. Presumably the GCRB controlled the money available for material production and capital expansion, through reserve requirements, the volume of its creation of BCM, the rate of interest, etc. In actuality such control, if exercised at all during the ICE, was not for the control of material production but presumably an attempt to control the function of the financial system and private inflation of BCM. In the ICE such control was fictitious; the GCRB was controlled by the financiers.

(k) Gold equivalency, and gold convertibility, of BCM, private type and public type, in the *ICE*. (Preliminary statement; refer to Sections 2 and 3 below.)

Whatever the bases and techniques of BCM creation, or the "multiple of reserve" restriction, and the creation of money by the GCRB, that becomes the "reserve" of commercial banks—the BCM presumably represents in the circulation the purported weight of gold of the monetary unit. This is true of the private form and the public form of BCM. And the BCM does ordinarily represent this purported weight of gold (ICE).

If the BCM were created only for the production and sale of material goods (capitalist system), and domestic production were the only concern, gold equivalency and gold convertibility would not be a problem, assuming the banks exercise reasonable care. The banks must always keep in mind whether the goods can be produced and sold at a profit, i.e., at normal price, the situation of capital expansion, wage-profit ratio normal, etc. But even if the goods are worthless, or if profit fails and interest payments fail, and there is a depression, the consequence ordinarily would be that a certain part of the BCM will become worthless. If enough of the bank's assets are involved, the bank will fail. If enough banks fail, confidence in the rest may be lost and payment of deposits generally demanded. But even in cyclic depression and bank failure (ICE), the question presented immediately is not the gold equivalency or gold convertibility of BCM representing the monetary unit, but the value of *some* specific BCM, or a large part of it. The test is whether the bank can convert its deposits into the more general paper form, i.e., the GCRB bank note. The gold convertibility of this is not in question, except under certain special conditions.

However, BCM are also created in large amounts for other purposes. There can be a public inflation of BCM by and for the Government. (This latter inflation can be a hyper-inflation also). And a great deal of this paper money can flow abroad. Gold equivalency and gold convertibility, become omnipresent problems, and must be considered at all times. In general:

A. If the organism is in equilibrium (capital expansion, normal price, prosperity) BCM can be created for production and sale, for dealing in capital papers, and even for a mild *private* inflation, or mild public inflation, and gold equivalency and gold convertibility *is not questioned,* and it can be assumed that the public and private BCM is gold equivalent. That is to say, the question of the amount of gold actually in the reserve, and gold convertibility in general, does not affect the banking process, and the amount of BCM is determined by the Level of Production, capital expansion, and the activities of the financial mechanisms. (Certain national economies, however, may maintain some artificial gold ratio limitations on reserve creation.) Furthermore: the BCM can depreciate if there is a mild inflation, and prices rise, even 2x or 3x, yet gold equivalency is not domestically questioned, and gold convertibility is maintained.

B. If there is a depression, gold equivalency and gold convertibility must always be considered in Government policy, and bank policy. The existing BCM must be deflated to maintain the gold equivalency of the rest. To maintain convertibility of the Government's currency, it not only may *not* be expanded to meet the needs of the commercial banks for currency to pay its depositors, but there probably must be a forcible contraction of reserves to reduce the BCM further. In short, the BCM generally, including the inflated BCM, if any, and the large volume of BCM created on capital papers and land titles, must be reduced as the capital papers on which the BCM were created, lose their value, and, if the gold convertibility of the Government BCM is to be maintained, these BCM cannot be increased to substitute for the BCM that should be destroyed, or for the private paper capitals that should be written off, or even for bank capitals of banks that fail completely.

C. In a public hyperinflation, the BCM depreciate to such point that they are not worth the weight of gold they purport to represent. This is patent. There is no gold equivalency and no gold convertibility.

D. Refer to Sec. 3.3 below on gold equivalency and gold convertibility in the ICE, where there is a foreign withdrawal of gold.

(2) Creation of money by the banking system of the capitalist organism (ICE).

—for the production and sale of material goods

—for the purchase and sale of capital papers, lands titles, etc.

—to monetize capital papers, including fictive capital papers, public and private, especially wherein part of the money so created is expended for personal and Government consumption, i.e. enters the goods-money circuit of the organism.

Herein a consideration of INFLATION of bank credit money in a capitalist economy:

—The inflated money as a pseudo Profit B

—Effect of a pseudo Profit B on the organism

—The theory of depreciation of inflated bcm as part of the pseudo Profit B

—Inflated money that does not become part of a pseudo Profit B; the theory of its depreciation.

—Distinction between a "demand" rise in prices because of inflated money, and a rise in prices because of depreciation of inflated money.

.1 Bank Credit Money created for the production and sale of material goods.

In general: the banking system described in general form (and even a less elastic banking system, without a central bank) can create and supply sufficient bcm at conventional interest rates for the production and sale of material goods, *including* capital expansion—

by direct bank loan

for non bank loan, (the money for non bank loans is held by lenders as bank deposits).

for money capital of individuals or corporations (also held as bank deposits).

when the economy is cyclically rising—capital expanding, price normal, wage-profit ratio normal. (This may not be true in certain sectors of the economy.)

The decline in the availability and supply of money for the production of goods is a consequence of the decline or failure of capital expansion, the decline in the Aggregate Profit and its rate, etc., not its cause. However, when the economy is extremely depressed, the effect of the depression on the banking system may be such (bank failure, etc.) that the supply of money may sometimes be inadequate for production. (Sec. 3, below).

It is an illusion that the fall in the Level of Production or the cyclic depression are due to a shortage of bcm, or because of high interest rates. (Refer to Ch. II. Sec. 12, that the illusion arises particularly from the fact that there may be a cessation of private inflation, which does affect the Level and Income; in general, the supply of money, interest rates, etc. are not the dynamic of the Level and Income.) In actuality there is usually an excess of bcm available for production and trade, but money is not advanced when it becomes obvious that production is an overproduction of goods or an overexpansion of capital. Money for production of goods is "scarce" in a depression because it is unreasonable to advance it for production on a falling level of demand. Interest rates are high because of the onset of depression, and money is scarce because the expansion of capital is imprudent. Even replacement of capital might be unwise at the moment.

When the economy is expanding, the tendency is to make money available for the overexpansion of capital. The financial system itself can be said to even force money into capital expansion, and not even because the capital expansion is patently reasonable and profitable, but because of the fact that money can be made on the new capital papers themselves. This money is easily created by the banking system. When there is an inflation of the BCM inducing the variable expansion of capital, there is a plethora of money seeking capital investment. This money actively seeks new capital, particularly as stated above, through the financial mechanisms. However new additional money could just as easily have been created for the new capital.

The exception to the general rule—that when production is generally profitable and the economy is in equilibrium—money can be made available at a normal rate of interest for production and sale of goods, is that certain very weak sectors of the economy (in a disparately concentrated economy) cannot easily obtain sufficient money as capital. The weakness of the producing units, the prevalence of below normal prices, and a low rate of profit, make the creation of money and the lending of money in these sectors risky, and the rate of interest is generally high. These sectors are first affected by a cyclic depression, and the banking facilities therein are weak, and first affected by depression. Rates of interest in these sectors are excessive with respect to the entrepreneural rate of profit, itself low.

It is also true that in the later ICE, with the full development of the financial control of the great capitals, the money for new capital (and capital replacement) becomes highly institutionalized, and both bank loans and nonbank loans cannot easily be obtained by the small businessman. This is not the result of shortage of money, although that is the appearance to the small businessman. It is the consequence of the structures of the capitals, and the risk and the low profit rate of the small business.

.2 Bank Credit Money created for dealing in capital papers, land titles, etc. The monetization of such papers.

In the later ICE, the money created for the financial system was probably as significant in the banking system and process as the money created for the production and sale of material goods. Great quantities were created for dealing in capital papers and land titles, in boom periods. The creation and maintenance of these large amounts of money profoundly affects the banking system itself. This body of money is also available as capital money for the production and sale of goods. The need for money for the purposes of the financial system is one of the reasons for the need for the GCRB.

The function of the banking system (in equilibrium, boom, depression, foregn exchange, the maintenance of gold equivalency and gold convertibility of BCM), is, of course, affected by the volume of BCM created for the financial system, and this must be considered in this Chapter. However, the major interest herein is the direct effect of this money on the Level of Production and Income. For some of this money will enter the goods-money circuit, not as a capital money for the production and sale of goods, but for the purchase of goods for a personal or Government consumption—goods that are not consumed in the process of capitalist production of other goods. As "profit" made on capital papers, realty titles, etc., i.e., income not arising from the production of material goods or a transfer of such income, it does enter the goods-money circuit. This "profit" made on capital papers and realty titles, etc., is monetized with existing money or new money. A part of this money is *inflated* money—money entering the goods-money circuit for a non-capital use, and remaining there. (Subsecs. .3, .4, .5, following.)

Indeed, one of the bases of the private inflation of BCM begins with the creation of this money for dealing in capital papers and land titles, and the creation of fictive capital papers, and their monetization by the banking system.

.3 *The inflation of bcm in the ICE. Prefatory: Government printing press money inflation in the early* capitalist *economy. (Archaic type of inflation.)*

The Government usually maintains a limited volume of Treasury Notes in existence, often convertible to gold, which serve usefully as gold substitutes in the circulation. This practice continued up through the late capitalist economy (ICE). However, Treasury Notes declined in importance in the whole body of the money media.

Inflation (of Government printing press money) by the Government is defined as the creation of new paper money as a *revenue* to the Government, generally done in a regular course, to be used to purchase goods and services for the use of the Government, substituting in part, for taxation and borrowing. The Government obtains material goods from private producers (assume herein capitalist producers) with this newly created money; the Government's consumption is almost invariably a consumption wherein other material goods are not produced for sale; it is a "non capitalist" consumption.

In exchange for the goods, the private producers have a media to spend, or keep. (The Government has not borrowed money to obtain the goods, or levied a tax; the money seems to be a creation ex nihilo; by means of this creation and purchase, goods privately produced have been obtained.) But the essence of the inflating process is that the new money passes into circulation, and remains in the circulation, increasing the volume of the paper money.

The inflation of Government printing press money has almost uniformly been considered a political and economic aberration, and in particular, contrary to the principles of the capitalist economy (and the Democratic State). However, it became archaic long before the end of the ICE. Bank credit money inflation on the basis of the Government bond or note became the standard type of a public inflation of paper money for the use of the Government.

A review of Government printing press money inflation for Government revenue can provide valuable insights into the basic nature of inflation, particularly the fundamental element in all inflation of paper money: the creation of the paper money by means of which the creator or the person for whom it is created obtains material goods privately produced, the producer of the goods obtains a paper money form which thereafter remains in the general circulation.

Consider, first, the effect on the production and sale of goods, particularly with respect to the first purchase of the goods with this paper money, and the price of goods. Assume two situations in which the Government prints money for revenue:

(a) Private production *not increased* to meet this additional demand; the demand satisfied out of the existing production. The available goods are then divided, at a *higher price,* among all groups of purchasers (wage earners, capitalists, and *Government)* each getting less goods for their money.

(b) The private production (capitalist) *increased* to meet the additional demand, and the demand of all those engaged in the additional production necessary. The production, then, is increased to such point that goods are produced for both the wage earners and capitalists who are producing the goods for the Government's new demand with the inflated money. That is to say, then, the Government purchases goods above the goods produced that reproduce the capital goods used up in the production of these goods and of all the goods produced, and above the consumer goods produced for the wage earners and the capitalists alike, not only for the goods sold to the Government for the inflated money but for all goods produced. The goods sold to the Government and the new paper money received are then *part of the Aggregate profit of the organism,* comparable to the goods produced for capital expansion for new additional capital advanced—the part of the Aggregate Profit called Profit B. (However, the good themselves are often not quite the same type as those purchased for capital expansion.) But the inflated money received by the producers, while part of the Aggregate Profit, is not the same as the "Profit B"—it is a pseudo Profit B that has yet to achieve a satisfactory capital form, which the real Profit B automatically does.

(In the (b) situation, assume a slow enough injection of the new money, that there is no "demand" type price rise.)

With respect to the first situation (a):

The price rise due to the additional demand on the first injection of the new paper money, is not per se a depreciation of the new paper money. The effective demand as a whole utilizes other money forms in addition to the new paper money injected: gold, bank notes, bank deposits, etc. The price of the goods *is higher to all* because of the additional demand. Prices rise in terms of gold, as well as in paper money. (A *depreciation* of the inflated paper money will take place, if the inflation continues, but as will be seen, it will be in the *further* use of the accumulating new paper money by the individuals receiving it, that causes the depreciation). For the moment, this new paper money is being absorbed into the circulation through the general (demand) rise of the price level, and it will be a necessary media in the circulation.

Assume that the Government continues to print and inject this money into the circulation by the purchase of goods (no additional production to meet this demand). Prices may continue to rise because of the additional demand, but the main factor now in the price rise results from the general use of this additional paper money in the general circulation. The paper money begins to *depreciate* and the prices of goods in terms of this paper money will rise. That is to say this paper money will represent less gold in the circulation than it purports to represent; gold will buy this paper money for less than the paper money purports to be in gold. In effect, there is a two price system for goods, a gold price and a paper money price. There may indeed be a further rise of prices in terms of gold, because of the demand, but the paper money price will be still higher, and indeed may reach fantastic levels.

The depreciation of this paper money must not be confused with the "demand" rise in prices. This is of great importance, because as will be seen in connection with (b) situation, where there is no demand rise in prices, the price level in paper money will nevertheless rise because the paper money depreciates, or the paper money will simply sell for less gold than it purports to represent. (The situation is more complex with respect to the inflation and depreciation of BCM; but again with respect to such inflation it is important not to view a general demand in rise prices as a depreciation of the paper money.)

The Government printing press money depreciates, as it accumulates in private possession (a continuing inflation) because of its volume relative to the monetary units (gold equivalent) needed in the circulation. If the usual volume of monetary units used and needed in the circulation is one million, and ten million paper units are created for the circulation, theoretically ten of the paper units will be worth one of the gold units, in the circulation, and the price level in these paper units will be multiplied by ten. The paper money will sell in terms of gold at one tenth of its purported gold weight. It is plain that the Government will be steadily inflating a steadily depreciating paper money, and to maintain the same level of its purchases, it will have to issue larger and larger volumes of the paper money. At a certain point the inflated paper money can become actually worthless. (Note again, that in the (a) situation, it is entirely possible that because of the demand, prices in terms of gold will also rise.)

In the situation (a) it should be noted also that the producers are really not getting anything through the Government Printing Press inflation. Actually, everyone is losing something; the wage earners and the capitalists alike will be losing part of the goods they could normally buy (at a lower price) with their income, and the "money" they get becomes worth less and less. As the paper money depreciates because of its volume (the price of goods in paper money rising sharply) they have a media that can approach the worthless.

In the (b) situation, which is hypothetical and except to a minor extent, unlikely in Government printing press inflation, the situation would be much different, and for the time being, desirable and beneficial to all: the creation of a pseudo Profit B, with all that follows therefrom, the higher production, Income, etc. Although unlikely (it is BCM inflation that can effectively create the pseudo Profit B), assume that the (b) situation takes place. It would be useful at this point to examine one aspect of this (hypothetical) process: How does this inflated money, which is a "capital" money, achieve a *capital* form? This it must and will do, since it does not represent actual capital goods, but is a pseudo Profit B. The money will not be used for the consumption of the capitalists (not a Profit A), but is going to be used as capital, and in no other way.

This can be accomplished in several ways. There may be an expansion of new capital proceeding. (This is possible, because an effective inflation, i.e., the creation of a pseudo Profit B—induces variable capital expansion and the new money can be used for new capital.) Or it could be used as capital money in the financial system to speculate in capital papers and land titles. (It may also be hoarded, and then the problem of achieving a "capital form" may not immediately arise.)

But if the inflated money (after crystallizing as the pseudo Profit B) cannot be so utilized, it can achieve the capital form by *depreciating*. That is to say, if there was, before the inflation, x capital money used for production and sale of material goods (capitalist production) with an Aggregate Profit of y, and because of the inflation the capital money becomes xx, while the return is the same y (again, assume no capital expansion) the whole paper money, as money capital, will be worth one half its purported gold weight, and thus as a capital money produce the same return. The paper money will represent in the circulation a lesser weight of gold, just as in the depreciation of the paper money injected into the circulation *for a fixed supply of goods*. Here the goods are likewise of a limited amount—*the capital goods that can function at a profit.* And again, in terms of *gold* (a two price system, a gold price, and a paper money price), these goods sell for a lower price, lower in gold than in the paper money seeking to become capital.

If the inflation (Government printing press money) resulted in the paper money supply 10 times the usual money capital, the money capital (as paper money), buying the same volume of goods will circulate at 1/10 of its purported gold value. The situation is not one of a demand rise in prices but rather that as a money seeking a limited investment opportunity. The goods are not scarce in the sense that there is a limited supply, but a limited amount that can function at a profit.

The net result of *all* inflation of Government printing press money is that the paper money will not represent the weight of gold it purports to represent, in the circulation. Either the paper money prices of goods are higher, or the inflated money sells for less gold. Undoubtedly, there may be an increase in the price level in gold money in the (b) situation, even when in this hypothetical case there is no demand rise on injection, for both the inflation and the depreciation process tend to raise prices.

It should again be noted that in the (b) situation, every one gains—capitalists and wage earners alike, *even if the paper money depreciates as money capital* as it enters the money capital circulation. Capital has expanded (constituting Profit B for the capitalists), the wage earners have additional employment, the depreciated paper money is an addition to the money capital. There has been a multiple expansion of the Level of Production. The entire production rises as a multiple of the new money injected that has become a pseudo Profit B plus the new actual capital (Profit B).

But, to repeat, the hypothesis of (b) is an unrealistic one and it is only with bcm that there are these positive gains.

.4 Inflation, continued. Episodic inflation of BCM for the Government, in the ICE. (War Finance.)

The inflation of bcm for the Government's use contains the same characteristic element as inflation by means of Government printing press money: a paper money form is created, which is exchanged for goods privately produced, the goods wholly consumed by the Government with no further goods produced for sale by the Government (non capitalist consumption); the money remaining in the possession of the capitalists (as a class) relatively permanently, and circulating further, and in some degree depreciating in the circulation. It is true that if this money is created by commercial banks on the Government bond (relatively permanently), the Government pays interest to the commercial banks to maintain the existence of the money; nevertheless this interest is only a transfer (by taxation) of part of the Aggregate Profit from one group of capitalists to another.

But there is a great difference between Government Printing press inflation and bcm inflation, for revenue, even in the crudest form of the latter, whereby a Government Bank creates bcm for the Government directly, deposit or currency form. (The interest on the Government's bond could be returned by the Government's bank, to the Government.)

The three fundamental aspects of bcm inflation that so markedly affect the mechanism of inflation, depreciation, *and* the consequences of the inflation on the organism, are:

(a) Bcm is itself a money form distinctively different from Government printing press money; it is almost always created as a "capital money" on a specific "capital" asset, an interest bearing capital paper. Theoretically, it exists because interest is paid for its existence. It is, theoretically, meant to be cancelled, when it has fulfilled its function, as when the "capital" paper is paid off. (Sec. 1, above.) The inflated money(for Government) is created on a *fictive* capital form; this interest bearing capital paper represents no real capital, and the money will not be used as capital. (Caution: the creation of bcm for the Government, in the pefcp, on a fictive capital paper which is *permanent*, and as part of a regular revenue to the Government, presents a different situation.) It is always important that the possessor of the inflated money (if it crystallizes as a pseudo Profit B, as a capital money to be used as capital) can theoretically cancel it by purchasing the Government interest bearing paper from the Bank, and the capitalists then, as a class, possess a fictive capital form. Thus, unlike Government printing press money there is the possibility of a "built in" capital form, although a fictive one, for the pseudo Profit B. As will be seen, all the foregoing affects the theory of the depreciation of bcm.

(b) What is being inflated, is not a separate, discrete paper money media, as in Government printing press money inflation, but the whole, great mass of the usual and typical money form —the bcm, the money media which is used in almost all transactions. No one knows the particular money for which goods are sold; there is no differentiation in the usual money of the economy between the inflated money and the rest of the money. It is obvious that a moderate inflation of bcm, relative to all the paper money, can be far greater than in the case of a (moderate) Government printing press inflation. The price level in the case of bcm inflation *ordinarily* remains a single price level for all goods—for consumption, for production, to the wage earner and capitalist, and Government, alike.

(c) The public inflation (in the ICE) has to be looked upon in the whole context of what is taking place. (Caution: it is *not* the same context as in the pefcp.) Basically, there will be a great variable expansion of capital, and inherently, *at least part* of the effective demand constituted by the Government's purchases with this newly created money is going to be met by an additional production to meet this demand. (This was assumed hypothetically, in the case of Government printing press money. It is the actual situation with respect to bcm). Furthermore, the Government is selling its interest bearing bonds, etc., to non bank investors to as great an extent as posible; the demand arising out of the expenditure of this borrowed money, is also, in part, at least, met by additional production. (The interest bearing capital papers are held by the capitalists as a class, representing the goods sold to the Government; unlike the situation of inflation on the basis of the Government bonds, the Government bonds immediately become part of the fictive capital.) Further, there will probably be a private inflation of bcm occurring at the same time as the public inflation takes place. Note also that bcm must expand for new capital advanced for the additional production.

The major problem that has to be considered is the depreciation of the inflated bcm, and the question of gold equivalency and gold convertibility. Depreciation will be seem to be both a money and banking problem, *and* a mode in which inflated bcm can achieve a capital form, when it crystallizes as pseudo Profit B. (The latter problem was considered above with respect to inflated Government printing press money). The depreciation of publicly inflated bcm does not always follow the same course as the depreciation of privately inflated bcm (considered in the following subsection). The episodic private inflation of bcm does not become the hyperinflation of bcm that may occur because of Government necessities in wartime, and the theory of the depreciation of hyperinflated bcm is somewhat different.

But before considering the question of depreciation, it is necessary to review the effect of bcm inflation on the economy—the fictive expansion of capital and the creation of the pseudo Profit B. It can well be assumed that production will be increased to meet the demand created by the Government expenditure with this money. (To repeat, unlike the Government printing press money, the new money is an indistinguishable part of the major money form; to meet the general demand, there will be a marked expansion of real capital.) Nevertheless, it is entirely possible, especially in wartime, that part of the inflated money is simply competing with other suddenly increased demands for a limited supply of goods, not readily increased in size, and all the inflated money does not become part of the pseudo Profit B. Because of the great demand for new capital goods, speculative buying, etc., a "demand" rise in prices may take place. (Note particularly, that this is not the ordinary course in the *pefcp*, where there is ordinarily no great pressure in the market; however, the same pressures may arise in wartime in the WMS, and the inflated money is not properly entering the market for newly produced goods in addition to the usual production).

Depreciation:

As stated above, if the inflated money is a part of the pseudo Profit B, it must achieve a capital form. Since, under certain circumstances, the bcm must depreciate, the nature of depreciation of *bcm* must be considered. Furthermore, since the bcm may enter the market without becoming part of the Pseudo Profit B, i.e., by competing in the market for the available production, the money may also depreciate in its further use. (This depreciation is something apart from the "demand" rise in prices that may occur on its first injection). However, since the inflated money is a bank credit money. there is always this preliminary question: Why is there not an automatic deflation of this inflated money, as it seeks a capital form, by the purchase of some of the Government bonds from the banking system? As stated in Ch. III, Section 1, the fact is that the Government bond is not an entirely desirable investment, and not only because its rate of return may be lower. Particularly in a time of prosperity an investment for new capital or replacement capital, or speculation in the financial markets, is considerably more attractive. In any event, a considerable part of this inflated money that is part of the Pseudo Profit B will for a time, at least, find its way into the capital market, the stock market, and the market for land titles, etc.*

But if the money does find its way into the capital goods market and the money is in excess of the money ordinarily necessary and available for the capital goods market, a situation somewhat similar to that of an excessive amount of Government printing press money that is part of the pseudo Profit B, will exist. But bank credit money is a money markedly different than Government printing press money and the theory of its depreciation is quite different. The concept of depreciation of bcm from a *monetary* and *banking* viewpoint must first be considered.

It was said that inflated Government printing press money will depreciate in the circulation and that the depreciated paper money does not represent in the circulation the weight of gold it purports to represent, i.e., it sells for less gold, or there is a two price system, a paper money price for goods and a gold money price. This is the situation either where the paper money is seeking a capital form, or in its further use in the circulation where there has been a demand rise in prices on its first injection and prices later decline.

* When the inflated money, crystallizing as the pseudo Profit B, finds a capital use by *foreign* investment, a new problem is added: preceding a depression, or in a depression, foreign holders of the bank credit money may demand conversion to gold (along with other BCM). This is a critical point in the banking system and process, and of Government monetary and banking policy. (sec. 3, .2 below.) While the question of conversion to gold by foreign holders of domestic BCM is periodically important in the ICE, it is a *constant* problem in the pefcp, always part of the general problem of foreign exchange and gold flow in the pefcp.

But it is only under *certain circumstances,* that each unit of the *whole* bcm can represent less gold in the circulation than the monetary unit it purports to be. These circumstances are a massive, and continued, public inflation ("hyperinflation"), where the Government is geometrically inflating a patently depreciating bcm. The volume of bcm, including the currency forms, can reach astronomical proportions. The Government's bonds and notes are not salable to non bank individuals. The bonds and notes already issued, bank held, for all practical purposes are becoming worthless as interest bearing capital forms. Depreciation, in the sense that the bcm is patently not worth the weight of gold it purports to represent, may become evident through the use of *privately owned* domestic gold but more likely it becomes plain because a reasonably "hard" foreign currency or foreign gold, buys the bcm, and the domestic capital papers, for little or practically nothing. Under such conditions, it is proper to say that the bcm, like the Government printing press paper money, does not represent the weight of gold it purports to represent. The Government must declare inconvertibility of its paper money.

But the meaning of depreciation of bcm is more complex when the inflation does not reach malignant proportions. (The following discussion will be of particular importance in connection with private inflation of bcm, considered in the following subsection, because private inflation does not reach the extent of a public inflation, and furthermore, is inherently brought to an end by the cyclic depression. The discussion is also of importance in the controlled inflation of the pefcp.)

It will be recalled that there is a relatively immense base of money that is being inflated; that the money base itself must expand anyway because of variable expansion of capital, and the need for money for dealing in capital papers, land titles, etc. But a depreciation of the bcm is nevertheless going to take place if there is, in the ICE, any significant degree of public inflation. The price level will rise, and this will be a rise in the general price level (unlike the situation in the inflation of Government printing press money, where on any significant degree of inflation, a two–price system becomes established).

But it is not proper to say in a *relatively* limited and controlled inflation, and a *relatively* limited depreciation (rise in price level) *that the bcm does not then represent in the circulation the weight of gold* it purports to represent, or even that it does not represent the established gold monetary unit. This sounds paradoxical, i.e. to say that the bcm is depreciated yet can be said to represent the same weight of gold as it purports to. However, recall the nature of bcm as stated above: BCM is a money media, and represents a certain weight of gold in the circulation, presumably that of the established monetary unit. However, there is a certain duality with respect to bank credit money as a paper money form. It is accepted as a paper money form to represent this weight of gold, because in the economy (capitalist) the particular bcm or each particular unit of bcm, *first* has a value because it presumably represents a *valid interest paying capital paper,* of a solvent and liquid bank. The *first* question is really whether it is any "good" at all—whether the bcm can reasonably on demand be paid in the *currency* that is the legal tender for the purchase of material goods. Is the *capital paper* good?—not whether the bcm is worth the weight of gold it purports to represent. Even if, through excessive demand in relation to the current production, *or* through the process of depreciation in a limited inflation of bcm, the price level of goods should rise to 2x or even 3x, this price level is as much a price level in gold, as in the bcm that represents the weight of gold (domestically, at least). At this point it cannot properly be said that the bcm represents less gold than it purports to. (See also, in this connection, Ch. II, 14, 17, on price and price level generally; it is not material to the organism whether the price level is x or 2x or 3x in gold, since the function of money, and gold as the money commodity, are to express the social demand for the good; the question is not one of equivalences of value between the good and the gold.)

It is plain enough that if the capital paper, or the bank itself fails (as in a cyclic depression), certain specific bcm becomes worthless (the bank cannot pay deposits in currency). Yet the question of gold equivalency of the bcm generally *still* does not arise. All that is determined is that part of the bcm is worthless (or worthless as money); not that the bcm generally is depreciated *in terms of gold weight.* Actually, in times of prosperity, where no possible question of gold equivalency or gold convertibility arises, parts of the bcm can still become worthless. In general, then, even if the process of depreciation takes place (moderate inflation), with a general rise in prices, gold equivalency and gold convertibility can remain unquestionned.

Gold equivalency and gold convertibility will be questioned, when, on a large scale, the interest bearing capital paper on which the bcm is created becomes worthless, *and* a considerable part of the bcm is *not* destroyed (deflated), and it then becomes simply a paper money per se (not a capital form of money based on capital papers). These are the possible situations:

a. The capital papers become worthless, but the Government simply obtains the creation of money by the GCRB, to make the existing bcm of all banks "good," and even creates large volumes of currency to make the deposit money of the GCRB "good."
b. The hyperinflation of bcm by the *Government Bank,* of money on the basis of the Government note—no longer a money really based on a valid capital instrument, no longer a gold equivalent money (certainly not gold convertible).
c. Hyperinflation of bcm, but the money created by all banks; the capital papers per se practically valueless insofar as they cannot pay interest that has any relationship to the Aggregate Profit. They may be exchangeable for Government currency created by the GCRB for this purpose.

Assuming, in these situations, that gold is privately held and available, (ICE) or some currency based on gold is available, the bcm can now clearly be said not to represent its purported weight of gold, and it is bought for little actual gold. (See below on the possible hyperinflation in a pefcp, or a very great degree of inflation where the economy is closely related, thru trade, to a foreign economy whose paper money is gold convertible or gold equivalent.)

Note, again, that in the ICE, where there is a private inflation, and depreciation is taking place, but there is no actual question of gold equivalence or gold convertibility, the question of gold equivalence does not arise even in a severe deflation, unless the Government attempted to make the existing bcm good—when it should be destroyed—by printing paper currency to prevent the deflation. If the Government did this, gold convertibility would have to be ended. And even if this were done (assuming a private inflation only) the inflation would not have been great enough in the ICE to cause a significant, permanent depreciation.

Thus: there are *two meanings* of "depreciation" of inflated bcm:

a. The rise in price of goods, as bcm depreciates, and the inflated bcm enters the circulation of capital money (see below on theory of the nature of depreciation) *but the bcm still represents the weight of gold it purports to in the circulation,* and probably the Government bcm is gold convertible.
b. The bcm does not represent the weight of gold it purports to in the circulation domestically—or even in foreign exchange. The Government paper money is inconvertible. This is the consequence of *hyperinflation,* or the creation of money to make "bad" bcm and "bad" capital paper good, on any significant scale.

Returning to the discussion as to why inflated bcm, that becomes part of the pseudo Profit B, depreciates:

Distinguish first, as stated, the "demand" rise in prices that will probably occur on the beginning of public inflation, in wartime. Production cannot expand rapidly enough to meet the demand of the Government, capital expansion, speculative buying etc. (In popular usage, the price rise is called an "inflation" or an "inflationary" price rise.) This rise in prices, it may be stated in passing, is in itself to some extent desirable in the ICE, since it is desired to expand capital and the Level of Production rapidly. But at a certain point it is self defeating, and does actually increase inflation since the Government must require the creation of further money to meet its needs. This type of price rise can be controlled by the Government; the subsequent rise in prices due to the depreciation of the paper money is difficult if not impossible to control. Rationing, allocation of materials price control, are measures that are needed.

This demand rise in prices is not the result of depreciation of the inflated paper money. And, as stated in the foregoing pages, the price of goods remains a gold price of goods. The "demand" price rise, absorbs into the circulation much of the new inflated money created.

Assume then, that the new inflated money is in volume, beyond that amount that can be utilized in the real expansion of capital, or in the financial mechanism and in dealing in land titles, capital papers, etc., all rising in price. The inflated money will then be simply part of the general capital money buying goods, paying wages, for material production generally. To repeat, from subsec. .3, the increased volume of bcm as capital money will be seeking a *relatively* limited investment opportunity with a *given* Aggregate Profit, and the BCM as a whole will purchase less capital goods, capitals, capital papers. If before the inflation x capital money used for production and sale of material goods produced a profit of y, and because of the inflation the capital money becomes xx and, assuming no capital expansion, the return is the same y, each unit of the money capital will have a lower rate of return.

Wages, too, should rise. As a practical matter, wages tend to rise after the commodity price rise, especially if there has been a "demand" price increase. The rise in wages reduces the profit: it seems that the depreciation which results in the higher prices of capital and capital goods and the lower profit per inflated dollar are the result of the wage increase, but this is not the case.

As was stated, the "demand" rise in prices at the outset, absorbs the inflated money into the circulation (it becomes necessary for the circulation because of the rising price level). The depreciation, per se, absorbs the money into the circulation, and it is the repeated inflation that causes the further depreciation.

Finally, if there is a hyper inflation of BCM, as stated above, the depreciation is very rapid and prices (In the ICE) again become dual, as in Government printing press inflation. There is a paper money price and a gold price of goods.

.5 Inflation, continued. The episodic private inflation of bcm in the ICE.

While an inflation of bcm as a revenue for the Government in wartime, in the ICE, was well known to have existed, the episodic private inflation of bcm for a personal consumption was rarely acknowledged. Nor was it frankly recognized that private inflation, and those private fictive capital forms that became a part of the pseudo Profit B—were of great, if temporary importance in the Level of Production and Income, of the ICE.

But if private inflation was one of the "mysteries" of the ICE (and of banking), its manifestations and accompaniments were well known, and eagerly sought. The booming stock market, the rapidly rising prices of land titles, creation of mortgages, capital papers on capital papers, mergers and "trusts" that tripled the amount of capital papers, all meant a prosperous economy, with production, income, and employment rising.

In this chapter, the analysis is concerned mainly with the money and banking aspects of private inflation (depreciation, gold equivalency of the paper money, the banking system in the depression and deflation phase of the business cycle). However, it is necessary to review briefly the basis for private bcm inflation: the private fictive capital form, especially those that are monetized, where the money enters the goods-money circuit for private consumption; the monetization of certain "profits" on all capital papers, including fictive capital papers, land titles, and mortgages, wherein these "profits" likewise enter the goods-money circulation for private consumption (Chapter III).

In the "public" fictive capital forms, the Government bond is created for the purpose of obtaining money for Government consumption, and it is fairly clear that the bcm created thereon will enter the goods-money circuit, and remain in the organism. But it is rare that a private fictive capital form is directly created so that the monetary equivalent is expended for a private, "noncapital" consumption, although this certainly does happen in boom periods. The usual situation is the creation, for their own sake, of fictive capital papers which are valuable, salable papers, and which also return interest or some form of profit (the latter being the basis of their value). But the fact is that in some way or another, part of them are sold, or part of them are used as the basis for creation of bcm, and this money does enter the goods-money circuit for a private consumption, and the money remains in circulation. The capital papers, or the money created thereon are used as a "profit" to some individual or group, and is expended as such, including expenditure as a business expense. The fictive capital paper itself becomes part of the pseudo Profit B, or the inflated money becomes part of the pseudo Profit B (and then in other ways achieves a capital form).

In the functioning of the financial system there is also episodically a large volume of "profits" on all capital papers, the rise in realty values, etc., that may be monetized with existing or new money. If these "profits" enter the goods-money circuit, the same situation arises. Actually, as will be seen, much of this money has been created for dealing in these papers, and when it enters the goods-money circuit as "profit" it is truly an inflated money. However, if it is not new money, some of these "profits" may represent simply a transfer of consumption from one individual to another, and thus there is no creation of the pseudo Profit B. But the fact is that the money that enters the goods-money circuit is to a great extent money that has been created to deal in or create these papers.

Thus the bases for private inflation of bcm usually begins with the creation of fictive capital papers *and* the creation of bcm on the basis of fictive capital papers (and other capital papers and land titles), wherein the money is generally at first used

(a) For the buying and selling and trading in capital papers, land titles, mortgages, etc., and to monetize "Profits" made thereon.
(b) For the creation of additional capital papers on existing capital and existing capital papers; for the creation of capital papers on land titles and mortgages; and fictive capital papers per se, representing expected profit, etc.

To repeat, the creation of money by the banks for buying, selling, dealing, and creating capital papers, etc., does not in itself constitute an inflation. It is an inflation when the paper money so created enters the goods-money circuit of the economy itself, (for private consumption, a non-capital use) and remains there. And a considerable part of all this money does actually enter the goods-money circuit, appearing in one way or another, as an "income" (an income not arising out of the production and sale of goods). The monetization of a land title, or of the rise in its value, may itself become an income which is expended for consumption; a mortgage created may likewise be such an income for consumption; a fictive capital paper itself may be created as an income which is expended for private consumption. Furthermore, in the financial system, a considerable part of these monies may take the form of "wages" or professional fees, or other expenses, the money entering the goods-money circuit. Part of these incomes are inflated money. Foundations, trusts, estate, that are constituted by fictive capital papers (or with capital papers created upon other capitals and capital papers very greatly expanding their volume) which sell these papers, and expend the money, may be part of the process. (Refer to Chapter II, Section 16, on financial profit generally.)

The most spectacular episode of private inflation of BCM occurred in the 1920's when it was the "secret ingredient" of the new economic era heralded at that time. An immense amount of money was "made" in the steadily rising stock market and in the real estate boom, and through profit arising from the creation of new capital papers based on other capital papers, etc. The "profits" on the issuance and the speculative rise of all these papers were steadily monetized by the banking sistem, and found their way into the goods-money circuit. Before this period, there were other periods of large scale private inflation of the bcm in paricular in the periods when all the capitals of the U. S. were being transformed into paper capital instruments, and there was a large scale creation of fictive capital forms.

The money created through private inflation and used to purchase goods for personal consumption, is almost invariably expended for goods *produced* to meet the new, additional demand. A private inflation is never a hyper inflation, a type of inflation which may occur in a public inflation. In a private inflation production will be increased to meet the effective demand.

(Refer to the foregoing section on public inflation with respect to the three aspects which make bcm inflation distinctively different from Government printing press money inflation: the capital nature of bcm; that bcm is not a discrete paper money that is being inflated, but the whole mass of the usual paper money, etc.)

The money will almost always be part of the pseudo Profit

B with the consequent effect on the Level of Production and Income. However, since the private inflation of bcm is almost invariably part of a "boom,"—a great over expansion of capital—and there *may* be some temporary shortages of goods, and there can be a "demand" rise in prices. Possibly this happened in the 1920's. But when the private inflation is paralleled by a marked public inflation of bcm for war purposes in the ICE, the *inflation as a whole* causes a "demand" price rise. Under such circumstances, part of the inflated money, privately inflated money or publicaly inflated money, does not constitute part of the pseudo Profit B.

Privately inflated money *may depreciate*, and the price level will rise just as in the case of public inflation. This is not a "demand" price rise. But the privately inflated money *need not* depreciate, for just as in the case of a public inflation—and even more so—a great deal of the inflated money (crystallizing as the pseudo Profit B, and seeking a capital form), seeks a use as capital money in the financial system, in speculating in capital papers, land titles, etc. It also has an opportunity to become capital money purchasing goods for capital expansion, because of the variable expansion of capital that is generally in process. Since the money finds a use as capital, it will not depreciate and raise the price level of goods, although the price of capital papers and land titles, etc. will rise.

But at a certain point in the private inflation, particularly when the real over-expansion of capital is ending, a certain quantity of this money must enter into the ordinary capital expenditure for capital goods in the process of production (reproduction of existing capital). Here it will be in competition with other monies for a relatively limited supply of goods. Refer to the analysis in .4 above that in the process of production the increased volume of money seeking investment in actual capital will be seeking a *relatively* limited investment opportunity (i.e., goods that will produce a given profit). The bank credit money as a whole, including the inflated money, then buys less goods to obtain the same profit. That is to say, the money depreciates and the price of goods rise.

In a private inflation, the bcm almost invariably remains gold equivalent and gold convertible. The banking system continues to function without gold equivalence, etc. ever coming into question. Furthermore, since the private inflation of bcm does not become a hyperinflation it is *only* the cyclic depression that raises the question of gold equivalency, (or the catastrophic depression). However, a private inflation may raise serious problems of gold withdrawal by foreign holders, etc.

In summary:

(a) A private inflation in the ICE is always temporary and episodic, usually occurring only in the rising phase of the cycle, and it terminates in the cyclic depression. It is a short term inflation. In the ICE, a public inflation is also temporary, and short term; it is a wartime inflation.
(b) The depreciation that *may* result from the private inflation is short term, and ends with the cyclic depression.
(c) In the cyclic depression, the inflated bcm is deflated, along with other bcm.
(d) The general deflation is the result of the depression, not the inflation.

Further comments:

An "excessive creation" of bcm for the financial system, realistically speaking, does not take place. The amount created can be very great indeed; but in the ICE it is a response to the activity of the financial system.

The reactivation of inflated money temporarily immobilized as "savings," which then enters the goods-money circuit, is properly part of the inflation syndrome. (Distinguish this from other deferred expenditures; also to be distinguished from the use of "savings" to monetize other fictive capital papers.)

The rising price level resulting from depreciation of inflated money, has itself a stimulating effect on the economy. Prices rise faster than the wage rate; the profit rate is temporarily higher. Rising price level due to depreciation also counteracts the general tendency for prices to fall because of technological advance in the process of production.

.6 Bank Credit Money in the goods-money circuit; in the money flow in the financial system; the interflow between the two spheres.
"Savings"; as Bank Credit Money, or claims easily remonetized (for use as capital, capital replacement, capital expansion, deferred consumption, inflation, etc.)

The money flowing in the goods-money circuit in the capitalist process of production and sale of goods, is, for the most part, bank credit money. The same BCM as money will move sequentially, in a large number of transactions. It may be advanced several times for capital. wages, Profit A, for new and expanded capital, and flow back and be advanced again. The same type of repeated advance and return is also found in the financial orbit. Of course, the BCM is not earmarked for either system, and the BCM moves between each sphere. The major part of the money in actual use is not created for the specific transaction, and although it may be created within one sphere, it may not stay there.

Some of the money advanced may temporarily come to rest as inactive deposits awaiting use for deferred consumption, or deferred use as capital (for capital replacement, or for new and expanded capital) and also for deferred use in financial transactions. Some of these deposits are called "savings," i.e., presumably arising out of non-expenditure of income paid out in the process of production—of wages, Profit A, and the profit B flowing back to the capitalists as a class, and monies held as deposits for capital replacement. There are also "savings" arising from profit in financial transactions, and the inflation of BCM. Money that may come into existence because of the monetization of pre-existing capital papers, a large number of which are fictive, is also often called "savings".

However, the major part of "savings" (presumably "money" held for deferred expenditure for consumer goods, or for expenditure as capital, and money arising as "profit" in financial transactions, including the monetization of pre-existing capital papers) are not held simply as BCM. At some point in the circuits, the money was used to create claims on various other financial institutions. Some of these claims are quite liquid, (almost money—as a saving bank deposit), others semiliquid, and others not liquid at all, being certain types of capital papers currently created. Insurance companies, saving banks, morgage companies, pension funds (many of which buy old, existing, fictive papers where the money created thereon has long since been spent), hold these claims.* These capital paper "savings," for the most part can be remonetized, as sources of capital moneys, both for production and sale, and for use in financial transactions (by way of non bank loans), and if necessary the banking system can create new money to remonetize these claims.

Current "savings" (whether arising out of the productive process, or out of profits arising in the financial mechanisms), may themselves be used to monetize capital papers, land titles, mortgages, etc., instead of a direct creation of money by the banking system for these purposes. These capital papers may be newly created or those created by former "savings." Part of this monetization of capital papers through "savings" may be considered inflated money.

Part of current money saving undoubtedly re-appear as "profits" in the financial system, and may then be expanded for personal consumption. It would be hard to determine what "savings" actually arise because of nonconsumption of goods, or because of deferred expenditure of capital funds for replacement. It is not unlikely that a large part of the funds that are current "savings" arise otherwise than in the goods-money circuit, i.e., because nonconsumption or non-investment.

(3) The critical points in the function of the banking system, as a whole (ICE).

—Cyclic Depression of the organism

—Withdrawal of gold from the banking system in foreign exchange (ICE)

—The final, catastrophic depression of the ICE.

.1 In the ICE, the business cycle dominates the function of the banking system; the depression phase of the cycle is its critical

* In prevailing usage, "savings" often includes, durable consumer goods purchased by individuals; all new capital paper created; even all existing capital papers. There is a certain absurdity in characterizing the immense mass of fictive capital papers, including Goverement bonds, as "savings."

point, with respect to existence of all BCM, including the inflated money. (The banking system does not, and cannot, in the ICE determine or control the Level of Production or the business cycle.) The inflation of BCM itself is determined by forces outside the banking system.

Summary propositions on depression and the banking system generally; and depression and inflation of bcm, in particular:

(a) On the cyclic termination of the expansion of capital, i.e. overexpansion of capital, a general depression sets in. There is then a *general deflation,* a reduction in the volume of bcm. The private inflation of bcm comes to an end; the creation of a considerable part of bcm for use in production and distribution of material goods ceases; and the creation of bcm for dealing in capital papers and land declines sharply. A considerable part of the existing bcm as a whole (created for production and distribution of goods, and the inflated money existing on the basis of capital papers, land, fictive capital papers), is *destroyed* in the general deflation. Individual banks fail; the banking system as a whole experiences difficulty. If the deflation is severe, and many banks fail, there may be a loss of confidence in banks generally, and the remaining banks function with difficulty. (Individual banks may fail before a general depression, and poor banking structure and management may cause financial crises, which also lead to loss of confidence in the banks.)

(b) It is not the question of gold equivalency of the bcm generally, or the question of gold convertibility of the Government bcm, that causes the cyclic depression and the general deflation. However, gold is of significance in the function of the banking system in the depression. (Also below, on gold withdrawal from the banking system by foreign holders of the paper money.)

(c) The termination of the bcm inflation is not the cause of the depression. Both the capital expansion, and the inflation, are ended by the depression.

(d) Gold equivalency and gold convertibility play a significant role in the mechanism of the decline in volume of the bcm (general deflation), and in the management of the banking system in a depression. This is seen essentially in the fact that in the ICE, the Government and the GCRB cannot, to any significant extent, create bcm to maintain all the banks, or all the existing bcm, if gold convertibility is to be maintained.

(e) The banking system and the banking process, and the GCRB, cannot halt a depression or cure a depression in the ICE, or be used to expand the creation of bcm, or to inflate the bcm, or raise the level of production, even if gold equivalency and gold convertibility are eliminated. If the depression is catastrophic, the banking system of the ICE will end also.

(f) Inflation, and depression:

A. Private inflation of the BCM is associated with the rise in level of production and is dynamically a part of the rising level, but only secondarily.

B. Private BCM inflation is always temporary in the ICE, since a depression always follows.

C. When the inflation ends in a depression, the deflation is of all BCM, including the inflated money.

D. The depression is not caused by the inflation, or by the end of the inflation; a deflation takes places whether or not there has been an inflation.

E. Any depreciation of the paper money that has taken place because of the inflation (even though gold convertibility has been maintained) is cured by the general deflation.

The first question in a cyclic depression is which (specific) bcm are good at all, not the gold equivalency of all, or gold convertibility of the Government's paper money. The capital paper on which the bcm was created may become worthless, and if enough of the issuing bank's capital paper becomes worthless, and it becomes both insolvent and non liquid, the specific bcm is not money at all—it becomes not only non money, but a bad debt.

The bcm as a whole may be somewhat depreciated, (if an inflation has taken place), but depreciation itself is of secondary importance in the deflation that follows. The deflation will cure the depreciation, if there has been any.

Beside the destruction of "bad" bcm, the deflation proceeds through the refusal of the banks to continue loans for production and distribution at the existing level, and to curtail existing loans; (i.e. production is not profitable at the pre-existing level). BCM created for dealing in capital papers and land, are likewise sharply curtailed. Higher interest rates by commercial and central banks also reduce the creation of bcm.

The deflation should properly proceed to the point where the banks are solvent and liquid; no more and no less. This will involve the writing off of assets by the "good" banks and the closing of the insolvent or "overextended" banks. After deflation to the proper point, the Banks are presumably able to pay their outstanding bcm, on the basis that their assets are valid, interest paying, capital papers, and the banks are sufficiently liquid to meet conventional demands. But it is still essential that there be no "run" on the good banks, i.e. a demand by most depositors for (Government bank) currency. A reasonable degree of confidence is necessary for all banking systems. Unfortunately, the course of a deflation is not a smooth one, and liquidity may become a problem even for "solvent" banks.

The question of gold convertibility arises if it is sought to have the GCRB create public bcm, either deposit type or currency type, to maintain the liquidity of the banks, or even to take over questionable assets, either in depression, or financial crisis. (In times of crisis, banking systems have utilized other paper money forms, such as clearing house certificates, to maintain liquidity.) If the Government should create bcm in any considerable amount, to maintain or make good the private bcm, or prevent the contraction of the bcm, thus preventing a *necessary deflation,* the question will certainly arise whether the paper money of the GCRB will be gold equivalent and gold convertible. This is a monetary question, a banking question, and a question involving the function of the organism. Certainly the Government can create such money up to a point, in a cyclic depression, especially if the deflation is proceeding too far, and the liquidity of sound banks is threatened, when the depression seems to have reached the bottom. It may only be necessary for the Government bank to state that it will create such money, if there is need for it.

Gold equivalency and gold convertibility of the GCRB paper money (either type) must dominate the Government bank's policy and conduct (ICE) when it considers *expanding* its bcm in a cyclic depression, to save banks, bcm generally, or individuals. The Government bank must recognize that it really cannot arrest a necessary deflation in a cyclic depression; it cannot "save" bad capital paper.

To repeat: the "gold standard" (convertibility aspect) does not create the cyclic depression; it is not the reason that the bcm and the capital paper become bad; the depression cannot be averted simply by creating or maintaining more paper money in existence. In the ICE, a continued creation of even inconvertible paper money would not enable the economy to function at the same high level. Such a course might possibly permit the existing overproduction of capital to continue for a time, and possibly even a private inflation of bcm (see below, on the course of the banking system in the inflation and boom preceding the final great collapse of the ICE), but in the usual business cycle, such conduct will ultimately lead only to a deeper depression, *and* the probability of the loss of gold equivalency and gold convertibility of the Government paper money. In the ICE, a boom cannot be indefinitely continued by means of private inflation, or even public inflation in wartime.

In summary then, in the ICE, the Government bank will not expand its bcm to maintain the volume of private bcm in existence. However, the cyclic deflation and depression does not necessarily require that Government bcm be contracted. The essence of maintaining Government bcm gold equivalency and convertibility is non expansion in depression. If absolutely necessary, the Government will *force* a contraction of private bcm to such point that the depositors will not demand conversion to public bcm (i.e. the existing bcm is necessary for the level of the economy). At this point it can be said that gold equivalency has been restored.

The creation of bcm by the Government bank, when private bcm should be sharply deflated, is tantamount to a public inflation of the paper money. It is certain that the Government paper money will then depreciate. In the later ICE, at least in the more powerful economies, the GCRB need be less cautious as to its actual gold position, but in earlier days such freedom was not possible.*

.2 Demand by foreign holders of domestic BCM for conversion to gold (ICE).

(Prefatory: The following analysis is not applicable to foreign exchange, foreign trade, in the *pefcp*. This is considered in Sec. 5, below. The discussion in Section 5 on the fundamental differences between foreign trade of the ICE and foreign trade of the pefcp, will amplify the conclusions stated in this subsection.

It is essential in the following analysis to keep in mind that the "foreign trade" and "foreign exchange" are that of the *capitalist organism* and must be examined in the context of the dynamics and mechanism of the capitalist organism. This trade and exchange is carried on in an organism wherein the Level of Production is cyclically rising and falling, as capital expands or fails to expand, and the capital expansion may well be an integral part of the foreign trade itself. The terms "trade" and "exchange" are simplistic; production and sale are carried on for profit, in the context of all that production for profit means in the organism. Foreign investment, either directly connected with the "trade" or independent of it, is generally part of the rise and fall of capital expansion, and hence the Level of Production of each economy, and the price level of each, etc. Furthermore: (a) it has been seen that the domestic money-banking-paper money gold equivalency–gold stock–gold convertibility, are irretrievably tied to the cycle and to depression. (b) the inflation of paper money, the function of the financial mechanism, are episodically part of the domestic dynamics, in each economy, and affect price levels, Level of Production, investment, etc. This inflated money enters into foreign trade and exchange, and enters into foreign investment, and it is not possible to separate the domestic and foreign aspects).

* There are of course, certain legal restrictions on the creation of bcm by a Government bank. These are artificial restraints that can be changed if necessary, and they do not govern the bank's conduct, especially in times of prosperity.

It has been stated that when the organism is in equilibrium, the banking system is not fundamentally governed, in the creation of new bcm or the maintenance of existing bcm, by the requirement of gold convertibility; that there can even be a mild depreciation of the paper money (usually caused by a private inflation of bcm) along with the continuance of gold convertibility. Furthermore: it is not until the cyclic depression that gold equivalency and gold convertibility really begin to determine the conduct and policy of the banking system, especially the Government bank, with respect to the creation of its bcm, and the volume of commercial bcm the Government bank can ultimately permit to exist.

The *constant test* of gold convertibility exercised by foreign holders of domestic bcm, seems to be an exception to the foregoing. (Indeed, this constant test seems to be, for all practical purposes, the reality of the actual gold (conversion) standard (ICE), since gold conversion is not generally sought domestically, even in the cyclic depression, when gold equivalence and convertibility could truly be questioned. The "conversion" that is sought is that of commercial bank deposits to Government currency.

However, it will be seen that in the ICE, the test of gold convertibility made by *foreign* holders, is, generally speaking, (among the developed capitalist nations with developed banking systems) also quite closely related to the cyclic depression.

> (To simplify the discussion, exclude the situation of the relatively undeveloped nation with a weak economy, whose Government is financing itself by the creation of paper money, either directly printed by the Government, or created by a Government central bank, or even by commercial banks on the basis of Government bank reserve creation. A fairly large scale public inflation is then always in process, but not necessarily a hyperinflation. If a considerable part of this money is ultimately used to purchase goods abroad, for consumption, public or private, or even for capital goods to be used for further production, it is plain that this paper money will not be accepted by producers of goods in foreign countries at the gold weight the paper money purports to represent. This paper money is almost certainly not con-

vertible to gold. In any interchange with foreign currencies, it will sell for far less than its purported gold weight in terms of the foreign currency—assuming the foreign currency is itself relatively "hard"—and its purchasing power in foreign goods is very low. This situation existed in many countries, and these currencies found a market at some parity based on the gold price of goods, Gold, then, the actual money of domestic and international trade, serves as the determinant of the value of such paper money.)

Returning to the situation among those nations which maintained a gold conversion standard: In the ordinary course in the ICE (equilibrium state) there will constantly be gold shipments back and forth among the nations, when the set-off of foreign paper currencies do not balance, being sometimes inadequate with respect to one national economy, sometimes excessive. An even balance is impossible to attain over a short period, and gold is then the money of the commerce among the nations, although it still represents a very small part of the total moneys actually used (which is paper money). Indeed, it is in the dealings of the producers-sellers of one nation with the producer-sellers of another that it becomes so clear that money is gold, and gold is money, and that the paper forms are only representations for gold, used domestically, and are money in foreign trade only insofar as these paper forms balance in the international exchange.

But it is not this back and forth movement of gold, performing its function as money, that is of concern here. Consider the situation where, despite an apparent domestic equilibrium (capital expansion), gold begins to move out of certain countries, or threatens to, in a marked and uninterrupted movement. It is actually leaving the banking system, generally the Government bank or the GCRB. (Assume that there is no domestic demand for gold conversion). This is a sign, a symptom of disorder or imbalance in the *domestic* organism; and it is not the cause of the disorder or imbalance.

The domestic disequilibrium or approaching disequilibrium should be viewed in two aspects:

(a) The production and sale of material goods. In connection with this domestic production, there will be a purchase and sale of goods in foreign countries. Furthermore, individual income arising from domestic production is spent to purchase goods for consumption that are produced in foreign countries.

(b) The function of the domestic financial mechanism—the creation of capital papers and fictive capital papers, their monetization, the domestic inflation of bcm.

If there is a considerable overexpansion of the domestic capital, one of the first signs that the goods cannot be sold at a profit (normal price), and that depression is imminent, is that purchases of goods abroad— either capital goods or consumer goods—begin to exceed exports. The purchases abroad ordinarily could be paid for by the sale of the domestic production abroad. The bcm (or bills of exchange) for the purchase of the capital goods and the consumer goods abroad, pile up in foreign countries, and gold is demanded, and has to be shipped consistently, and the domestic banking system loses its gold. The loss of gold is a clear sign of the approaching cyclic depression (overproduction, overexpansion of capital), just as if the domestic capitals cannot sell their production at home, and loss on capital papers must be absorbed by bank and non bank lenders.

In the later ICE, an equally important factor is that the gold loss indicates that the domestic bcm is being excessively inflated, or has been inflated (probably privately) and the money is being spent (or invested) abroad. That is to say, the inflated bcm, crystallizing as pseudo Profit B seeking a capital form, finds its way abroad as investment.

Actually, this domestic overproduction and overexpansion of capital, and domestic inflation, may be going on in many countries simultaneously, and a satisfactory balance of foreign exchange can be maintained, and there will be no real gold loss. All domestic price levels are rising. But when the imbalance occurs, the country that is overexpanding capital more than another, or is involved in the greater inflation, will have its paper money piling up in the foreign country. The gold loss can be severe, unless and until there is a sharp reduction in production and the end of the inflation; in effect a deflation and a depression. However, if the banking system is losing gold rapidly, it will or may have to act before the consequences of depression can make themselves felt, and it will have to take steps to stop the flow of gold abroad, and encourage the flow of foreign bcm and gold to it. A rise in interest rates is a step that is taken, and since this will also reduce domestic inflation, and possibly domestic production (although it is probable that other factors are far more important in reducing domestic production) it is though that the bank's action brings on the depression. This is not the case. The necessary steps to arrest the gold flow are but part of a chain of domestic events caused by the failure of domestic sales and inflation of the paper money; the gold flow was the symptom of the domestic imbalance.

Gold withdrawal from the banking system does not take place domestically; at worst, in the cyclic depression (above) the depositors of the commercial banks seek the Government currency form. The gold test is made only by foreign holders of the bcm, yet this is the warning that the domestic bcm may not be gold equivalent *and* unless curtailed, the Government currency may become inconvertible.

Domestic inflation, while one of the major causes leading to the gold outflow and the (foreign) gold test, is in fact a major cause of domestic prosperity (ICE), but it is more than likely that it is coming to its end apart from the fact that the bcm are piling up abroad. (See, Sec. 5, below, with respect to the pefcp, where the inflation *must* continue, gold outflow or not.)

It is probable that investment abroad, and the movement of inflated money abroad are the most significant aspects of an imbalance of payments. But the extent of foreign loans, the size of the gold stock, the relative importance of the foreign trade over the domestic trade, are all factors in creating, and taking necessary steps to deal with the imbalance. In the ICE, the problem is ultimately resolved by the depression of the business cycle.

.3 The banking system of the ICE came to an end in the catastrophic depression and collapse that ended the ICE.

The ICE came to an end in a catastrophic depression, during the period of the relative economic critical point. The depression was of such severity (because of the extent of the preceding fictive and variable expansion of capital) that the structure of the economy, including the money and banking system, could not endure, and a socially critical point was reached. (Ch. II, Sec. 18.) The Government closed the banks. The fact that the new money and banking system was then instituted obscures the fact of the real end of the money form and the banking structure of the ICE. There was not simply a declaration of inconvertibility and the institution of a banking process and system based on an inconvertible paper money. But this will be discussed in Part II: The new money and banking system as integral part of a pefcp.

In the great depression and deflation and continuing downward spiral after the 1929 collapse, almost all the capital papers were becoming worthless. An appearance of bank solvency could for a time be maintained by the creation of money by the Government to make good worthless bank assets and worthless BCM. This could not be continued. Even liquidity could not be maintained unless the Government created an enormous amount of Government BCM, which would, of course, soon be not equivalent to gold and would rapidly depreciate. In such a course the Government would have to declare inconvertibility. And such radical measures directed toward saving a banking system could not by themselves establish a socially acceptable ICE functioning at a very low level.

It was stated in Chapter II that the recp could theoretically result in a long slow decline of the ICE, culminating in a very low level, stagnant economy, and that it is possible that there be no socially critical point at this low level. If this were the situation, it would have been conceivable that after the great depression of the recp there could be a severe deflation, but the banking system of an ICE could continue, if not on a gold basis. (But if gold remained in private hands it is even hard to see how a banking system could function after so great a deflation and destruction of paper capital, with an economy at a very low level of production.) However, this is not what happened. The independent capitalist organism could not continue, and if the organism could not continue, a banking system for such an economy, even on an inconvertible basis, could not function.

As stated above, in a cyclic depression, with considerable

deflation and some bank failure, gold convertibility and gold equivalency can be maintained; the cyclic depression cures the inflation and the depreciation, and the rising phase of the cycle permits a return to ordinary bank functions. But there is no rise in phase of the cycle after the catastrophic depression; gold convertibility and inconvertibility are secondary aspects.

The requirement of gold convertibility was no more the cause of the catastrophic depression than it was the cause of the cyclic depressions. Ending convertibility of paper money to gold could not prevent cyclic depressions, and such a course could not prevent the catastrophic depression. The failure of gold equivalency or gold convertibility are only manifestations of the recp, the fundamental disorder of the ICE.*

* As indicated, the GCRB was truly powerless to save the ICE, or its banking system, despite all the ideology of the GCRB. Indeed, the GCRB had no power to prevent or cure cyclic depression. It could not "even out" the business cycle, and prevent depression by a liberal supply of money at low rates. It could reduce private inflation, but since this would prevent variable expansion, all individuals would view this as an abuse of power. When the pefcp came into being, doctrines that the GCRB has the power to provide full employment, price stability, etc., become popular again. But these doctrines are not true; the GCRB is an instrument of a pefcp, and the dynamics and mechanics of the pefcp govern the level of the economy.

PART II

Money and Banking in the Political Economy of Fictive Capital and Profit

(4) A new money form, and money and banking system, came into being with the WMS-pefcp. These are indispensable for the WMS Government's power to create the pseudo Profit B, as a regular course, i.e., maintain a political economy based on the fictive expansion of capital; thus to create and maintain the fictive capital and fictive profit forms as permanent, continually expanding forms, at the will of the Government; and to give the Government the power to cause the production of goods by the capital units for its effective demand.

The basic elements of the new money form and banking system:

(a) The sequestration of gold by the Government, the private possession and monetary use of gold forbidden. A unique money form then is created: a paper money created by Banks, inconvertible to gold, but gold exclusively held by the Government, the bcm being the exclusive money form (domestic).

(b) The transformation of the GCRB into a Bank that is part of the Government, no longer governed by the dynamics of the organism, as in the ICE, but by the Government.

.1 Prefatory

Refer to Ch. III, Sec. 1 on the elements of the pefcp. Reconsider, in connection therewith, the analysis in Ch. II, Sec. 14 on the nature of money, the monetary unit, and price generally; Price and normal Price, Ch. II, Sec. 17.

In the pefcp goods are produced by capital units, for sale, for profit. The money form must necessarily exist; money must be a material good. Money is the value equivalent for material goods produced for exchange. Gold is the money commodity; the monetary unit is a specified weight of gold. The monetary unit is the standard of Price of material goods. The question is still always present of the equivalency of the paper money form to the weight of gold it purports to represent. Since the relationship in the dependent organism is on a "material good" basis, and all its relationships and ratios are on a material good basis, and since gold is the money commodity, production in the dependent organism is still on a "gold basis." The banking system is then still on a gold basis at whatever the equivalency of the paper money to gold.

But the structure of the economy is now one in which the Government creates fictions to maintain the relationship in the units in material production.

While it is plain that the Government must have the power to make the question of domestic gold equivalency of the paper money irrelevant to the domestic producers of goods, bcm never escapes its inherent nature as value form, and money as general form of value, representing the value of material goods, and representing gold as the form of value of material goods.

In the pefcp, money is gold, the monetary unit is a weight of gold.

The new money form, and banking system, is based on the necessity for providing the WMS with power to create and maintain the fictive forms as permanent, expanding forms, and to cause the production of goods for its effective demand. The new money and banking system is not a "development," "outgrowth," "maturation" of the preceding money and banking system. But all the principles stated in Sections 1, 2 and 3 of this chapter, particularly with respect to the banking process, inflation, depreciation of the paper money, are all relevant in the function of the system, given the new basis: of the nature of the money, and the position of the GCRB.

.2 Fundamental bases of the money and banking system of the pefcp.

(a) The sequestration of gold in the Government's hands, and the prevention of its use, as a private bank reserve, or as money in the buying and selling of goods in capitalist production, or the buying and selling or creation of capital papers, or the buying and selling of any paper money forms, or as an *actual reserve* of the banking system as a whole.

In effect, the acquisition and sequestration of the gold by the Government under such circumstances is the *transfer of power* not only over money, but over material production, from private hands to the Government. (The essential basis for an *independent* capitalist economy is the private possession of gold or private access to gold.) With this power the Government can create a money form and system wherein the bcm is the sole domestic money form, invulnerable to any domestic attack, with its creation and maintenance without deflation in the absolute power of the Government. Furthermore, it will enable the Government to create and maintain, as a permanent, constantly expanding fictive capital form, its interest bearing notes and bonds as part of the pseudo Profit B. The real basis of the power of the Government to have a great mass of goods produced for it, as part of the Aggregate Profit of a dependent capitalist organism, also lies in gold sequestration, with this bcm as an exclusive money form in the control of the Government. Thus this money system is an essential basis for the existence of the pseudo Profit B, the fictive profit form, and the permanent fictive capital form.

(b) On the basis of the sequestration of gold and the establishment of the sole paper money form, the Government Central Reserve Bank can be transformed into the *Government's* bank for the maintenance of the political economy; and the *Government's* bank for the finance and management of the dependent capitalist organism. (In the ICE, the GCRB is in appearance a Government bank, but it is a bank whose function is determined (except possibly during wartime) by the dynamics of the capitalist organism, the expansion and contraction of real capital, the demands of the financial mechanism for dealing in stocks and land and the inflation of the paper money). The GCRB no longer *reflects* the function of a private system, but becomes the Government's agency in a system where the Government is the dynamic of the system, i.e. in creating the pseudo Profit B, its fictive capital forms, determining the Level of Production and the Income of the organism. The Government bank is either a part of the Government, or absolutely controlled by the Government (in a properly ordered political structure and economic system). The Government, through the GCRB, determines the volume of money, the purpose for which it is to be created, the constant inflation of the paper money, the maintenance of the fictive capital forms.

The monetary unit is still a weight of gold, and the standard of price, and gold is still the measure of value. The paper money created by the GCRB and the commercial banks purports to represent this weight of gold in the circulation. Gold is money in the pefcp, but only the Government possesses this money. The actual money media is the bank created paper form, which the Government and private individuals use exclusively (except in certain instances in foreign exchange—below). Although this paper money purports to represent a certain weight of gold, it cannot ordinarily be challenged as a standard of price of goods. Domestically, this paper money is always depreciating. However, except in certain political economies, where the monetary management is grossly incompetent, and there is a hyperinflation of the paper money, the domestic prices of goods are in effect, gold prices.

From the foregoing, it appears that the paper money of the pefcp is a new form; it is not the same as the paper money of the ICE when inconvertibility to gold has been declared, i.e. with private possession of the gold existing.

What weight of gold the paper money form actually represents in the domestic circulation cannot be domestically determined, but, just as in the case of any bcm (apart from the hyperinflation), this is not of any great importance. The paper money will depreciate; this is secondary to the function of the organism, so long as the Aggregate Profit (and the pseudo Profit B) are coming into being. (Note: as stated in Sec. 2, and 3, it cannot be said in the case of mild depreciation of the inflated bcm, even continuing over a very long period, that the bcm represents in the domestic circulation, less gold than it purports to represent. Furthermore, the price in paper money in many national economies is the price in gold, in terms of a foreign currency test or gold test of equivalency.)

Production of goods for the Government (as part of the Aggregate Profit—pseudo Profit B)

Since the Government has the real power of money creation of the *sole* circulating money form, it can purchase any goods it chooses, at normal price. Thus it can cause the critical mass of the goods to be produced for the Government and become a value, and part of the Aggregate Profit. All units must participate in the production for the Government, for the unit cannot make a profit unless part of the goods produced are sold at a profit, to the Government.

If the Government maintains the market at the given level of production (which, in the first instance is determined by the Government) then normal price of all goods produced will be maintained, and with the maintenance of normal price for all goods, the fictive *profit* form can be assured (at a certain level of production, and capital expansion, and inflation), and hence the pseudo Profit B at a high level. The WMS tax is absolutely predicated on *normal price*, at the single (paper money) price level, something that is solely within the power of the Government, because of the new money form.

The importance of having a single money form (no possible competition with gold, domestically) is not only with respect to the price of goods. The price of all capital papers, and especially of the fictive capital papers, Government, and private, is also a price in the same paper money, (hence the power of the GCRB to create and to maintain the fictive capital forms).

The Government Central Bank

Through the GCRB, the Government can create whatever volume of Government BCM, deposit form, or currency form, it chooses. The commercial banks then must in effect lend money to the Government or private individuals at a multiple of the reserves thus created. The reserve is not subject to private power, i.e., the demand for the convertibility of gold by banks and private individuals. The money created by the GCRB is not only the sole reserve money of the commercial banks but it is the sole money into which private BCM can be converted. Thus, the GCRB assures:

- –the constant flow of new money to the Government
- –the constant expansion of money, generally,
- –the constant inflation of money, for the Government and for private persons
- –the maintenance of all expanding fictive capital papers
- –an adequate supply of money for the production and distribution of goods,

and to accomplish all the foregoing without deflation, despite a process of constant depreciation of the paper money. The Government will be able, among other things, to create and maintain at its will, independent of any private unit or individual, the Government's interest bearing bonds and notes, as a permanent and constantly expanding fictive capital form (constantly re-funded).

The Power of Government, Supreme Over Any Private Financial Power

The possession of the gold, and the control of the GCRB, prevent any private power from hindering the Government in the basic function of the pefcp. (Of course the Government of the WMS has to have certain other powers, elsewhere noted.)

Ordinarily, the Government must be able to borrow (in the pefcp) constantly for its expenditure, from the commercial banks, as well as non bank sources. It must also borrow steadily to re-fund its outstanding bonds and notes. It is essential that most of the money creation be by the *commercial* banks, not by the GCRB. But since the Government (GCRB) can always create an *inconvertible* money reserve for the commercial banks, then the commercial banks will or must lend the Government whatever money it desires. If the commercial banks do not lend the money, they will then possess non interest bearing inconvertible reserves which they cannot use. If the Government money were convertible to gold, the private banks would have the power to refuse the Government, i.e. the banks or their depositors could ask for conversion to gold. When the commercial banks cannot convert their "reserves" to gold, or their "deposits" to gold (nor any individual convert bcm ultimately to gold) and the commercial banks do not even possess gold, the private banks and private individual lose power over the Government, its bank, the money, and cannot prevent the Government from borrowing what it wishes.

In effect all Government interest bearing papers become convertible into Government paper money, or into the bcm of the commercial banks (itself convertible into Government paper money).

It is only by obtaining a major part of the gold that private individuals or a foreign power can prevent the function of the pefcp domestically, (through establishing a two price system, for goods or for capital papers, i.e. a gold price and a paper money price). Foreign trade and foreign exchange, insofar as gold can be possessed by private holders or a hostile foreign central bank, can therefore be a source of danger.

The processes of a pefcp, then, as mechanisms, become, domestically, always workable. The Government bonds and notes, the primary FC forms, will always be absorbed, by private owners and by the commercial banks, and by the GCRB as a reserve. All existing FC forms can be constantly refunded and maintained, as the Government chooses, at their face value. And since the private producers will always sell at a profit for an effective demand, and they have no choice but to produce for and sell to the Government, the Government is in effect, by purchase, acquiring, as *goods*, part of the Aggregate Profit of the economy.

The Government should not attempt to manage the economy through the GCRB alone (i.e. manage the volume of real capital expansion, wage and price levels, the degree of private inflation to be permitted, and the degree of creation of private fictive capital forms that will be permitted; or the level of the economy, and the proportions in the Government's revenue mix). It is an error that "monetary management" is sufficient management for a pefcp. And apart from this, the practices and theory of central bank management developed during the ICE are inadequate for a pefcp.

In particular, rate of interest, and volume of money, should not be relied upon to regulate the level of the economy and the expansion of capital. On the one hand monetary ease will encourage private inflation; on the other hand monetary stringency will reduce the volume of money necessary for the production and sale of material goods. What is necessary is a direct regulation by the Government of all the incidents of the economy or a selective control over the creation of money, and the interest rates for specific purposes; and, above all, the proper use of taxation to make excessive private inflation, or the creation of private fictive capital forms less profitable.

Excessive private inflation, and the excessive creation of private fictive capital forms can become a serious problem in the pefcp, when the economy is permitted, or forced to operate at too high a level. In turn, the private inflation, etc. forces a still higher level for the economy. The Government bank can control this only to a limited extent.

It may be argued that in the ICE an inflation of bank credit money could take place, with the bcm slowly depreciating, yet the banking system could function and be maintained with gold convertibility, at least until a cyclic depression intervened. (There is no demand for conversion of the bcm to gold, so long as capital is expanding and price is normal, the paper money will be utilized in the economy.) Consequently, why should inconvertibility and sequestration be necessary in the pefcp, where there is no cyclic depression, and normal price can always be maintained?

The situation, however, is wholly different. The inflation, and the depreciation are always continuing in the pefcp; they are not interrupted by a cyclic depression, wherein a deflation takes place. Furthermore, what is involved is the maintainence of a constantly expanding, permanent (refunded) body of public fictive capital paper. The value of these papers must never be destroyed (as in the cyclic depression, where great volumes of private fictive capital papers are destroyed). Under these circumstances, in the pefcp there would always the possibility of gold price (for goods, for capital papers, for paper money) emerging, and this can destroy the pefcp. It is the fact that while the threat of demand for gold does not emerge in the ICE until a cyclic depression portends, (and it may then be dealt with without inconvertibility and sequestration by deflation, and other measures), the threat *always* exists in a pefcp, and it cannot be dealt with by deflation and related measures—that requires the inconvertibility and sequestration.

There is another aspect to the necessity for inconvertibility and sequestration. This has already been mentioned: the essential power that this gives the Government (along with control of the GCRB). In the pefcp the primary necessity is the *Government's* uncontrolled power to inflate, maintain the inflated money despite depreciation—not the private power to inflate. In the ICE, so long as capital is expanding, etc., the private power to inflate exists. But the existence of this private power also means that there is an inherent private power to prevent the Government from exercising absolute power over money, to inflate, etc., even if the private power is not exercised. There may be no such inhibitions on the Government's power in the pefcp.

(5) The money of the political economy of fictive capital and profit in foreign exchange and foreign trade.

Summary statement:

(a) The analysis requires, first, a consideration of the nature of international trade of the pefcp. This is distinctively different from international trade and exchange of the ICE. The dynamics and mechanisms of each economic system are different.

(b) Each political economy *must* seek an equilibrium in the trade of goods, and an equilibrium in the foreign exchange because of the inherent nature of the pefcp, as well as for other reasons.

(c) *All* the Governments must sequester gold as far as is possible, to maintain the protect their own political economy as a whole, domestically, and defend the others. This must be done also to protect their own paper money in international exchange.

(d) The foreign exchange of the paper money of each PEFCP (in trade, investment, etc.) is inherently difficult to manage, but it must be managed, and cannot be managed with complete effectiveness. Unilateral control over the gold weight of the monetary unit, over foreign exchange, and trade restrictions, must be retained, and sometimes exercised, but the inescapable difficulties can be ameliorated by international cooperation and regional cooperation with respect to imports and exports, rates of exchange, changes in the gold weight of the respective monetary units, the management of parities and market of floating currencies, and intervention in these markets.

(e) No pefcp can maintain the established gold weight of its monetary unit in international trade and exchange indefinitely, although the U. S. could do so for a much longer time than any other political economy.

(f) Gold in private hands is a danger to the power of *any* WMS-pefcp
- —to maintain itself
- —to maintain the domestic money, banking, expenditure, system
- —to maintain the position of its paper money in international exchange

(g) If the major part of the gold moved to private hands—even foreign private; holders,—*all* pefcp's, including the U. S., will be placed in a position of great danger.

(h) The U. S. money was unique, because of the size and power of the political economy, and its possession of the great mass of gold. The paper money of the U. S. became the "paper gold" of the political economies, and as a reserve money it also becomes a fictive capital form for the foreign political economy. The unique position of the U. S. paper money was of great advantage to the U. S., but also placed its paper money in a position of danger, both domestically and internationally.

(i) The domestic price level may have to be changed for foreign purchasers, by monetary devaluation or other means, because of the necessities of the domestic economy. But international and regional cooperation is essential for a high level trade, and to minimize the dangers of serious disequilibrium.

Foreign trade and foreign exchange, and investment of capital abroad, in the pefcp and the WMS, must be examined on the basis of the nature of this political economy and State. They cannot be understood on the basis of the nature and dynamics of the ICE and the "Democratic State."

The following are the premises and the necessary inferences on which the examination of foreign trade-exchange in a pefcp, must proceed (from Ch. III):

(a) The self expansion of capital—the constant necessity for new investment to expand the Aggregate capital, is not the dynamic of the pefcp, as it is in the ICE; the dynamism and basis of existence of the pefcp is in the level of Government purchase creating the pseudo Profit B, and the creation of the fictive forms therefor. However, where the system is at a high level, there is a degree of real capital expansion, and this may be a factor in the seeking of foreign markets for new investment, but it is not dominant (as in the ICE). Foreign trade, insofar as it relates to *expansion of capital* and the (economic and political) control of an undeveloped country as market and base for capital expansion, is not essential to the political economy. (On the contrary, the undeveloped country is more likely to be a place for commodity disposition. [Ch. V.]) However, inflated money crystallizing as the pseudo Profit B, will seek foreign investment as well as domestic investment. Furthermore, the trade may be essential because of the need for specific commodities by certain WMS's.

(b) The Government determines the level of production of the political economy. The Government will and must maintain as high level of production as possible. The level of the political economy is not inherently cyclic; this is fundamental with respect to foreign trade: that there is no inherent business cycle in the pefcp.

(c) Each political economy (WMS) must create the fictive forms necessary to its existence, a fictive capital form, inflated money that will achieve a capital form after it crystallizes as the pseudo Profit B, and a fictive profit form, and at a level for each in accord with the level of the economy, and in proper proportions. And these creations depend on the *whole* goods-money circuit, including any equal interchange with foreign political economies.

(d) Fundamental, with respect to the general theory of the pefcp: Any continuous purchase abroad in excess of sales abroad (by the nationals of any pefcp), assuming for certain reasons this is possible over a period of time, is inherently injurious to the pefcp. The Government (of these individuals purchasing goods abroad at a higher level than material goods are purchased by the individuals of the foreign countries) cannot obtain by *tax* or *borrowing*, that part of the Aggregate Profit of the producers of the goods, necessary to maintain the domestic goods-money circuit, at the given level of production, Aggregate Profit, and Wage Profit Ratio. Foreign producers of goods cannot be taxed (by the domestic Government), nor are they likely to lend part of their Aggregate Profit abroad. In the PEFCP then, a significant imbalance in purchase of goods abroad must result in increased inflation at home (i.e., the proper tax–borrowing–inflation mix is disturbed). Inflation is a consequence of trade imbalance as well as a cause. (Counterbalancing force: the special situation wherein U. S. paper money is held abroad as bank reserve, and as a fictive capital form of foreign political economies.) A fortiori, it is injurious to the domestic pefcp if the Government uses its revenues to purchase goods abroad (or lends money abroad which will not be used to purchase domestic goods). Corollary: The Government will use all means possible to maintain an equal balance, or a surplus of goods sold abroad. This is apart from the necessity of maintaining the balance in foreign exchange so that purchases can be made abroad.

(e) But, to a greater or lesser extent, certain goods must be purchased abroad—capital goods and consumer goods. Hence, an equivalent value of goods must be sold abroad to obtain the foreign exchange needed to purchase the goods. Certain goods must be purchased abroad because the goods themselves are essential for the function of the national political economy, at whatever level the Government determines the economy shall function. The goods are necessary for the productive and distributive systems, and possibly for the welfare and military systems. Trade therefore is essential for the existence of the political economy, and the level of certain political economies may be absolutely dependent upon their imports and exports. In general, there is a relationship between the Level of Production of the political economy, and the volume of goods that must be imported, and the volume of goods that must be exported in exchange. Corollary: Part of the Government's activity in determining the Level of the political economy, must be concerned with means and devices for obtaining goods from abroad, but to repeat, this is not fundamentally related to the expansion of capital, but to the dynamics of the Government's system of expenditure, etc. If a high domestic level of production is sought it will be necessary to increase both the export and the import of goods; this requires international cooperation with respect to trade and exchange. Regional cooperation and regional economic communities are probably also necessary.

(f) In each national political economy, the same fictive processes are proceeding, but the several elements in the process (the fictive capital forms—public and private, the inflation of paper money—public and private, the tax rate and its volume) are mixed in different proportions in each national political economy, and the proportions between Welfare and Military distribution may be different. The actual level of production in each political economy is probably rising, but the rate of rise differs among them. There are different rates of Government expenditures, real capital expansion, technological improvement. Furthermore, the domestic price level in each national political economy may be moving upward at a higher or lower rate than others. The wage rate in each political economy is always rising, and the wage-profit ratio may be changing (even within the context of the constantly depreciating domestic paper money).

(g) The monetary unit of the pefcp is a weight of gold, represented by a paper form, bank created. The paper money is not domestically convertible at its purported weight, or at any gold weight. The continued existence of the paper money is not controlled or determined by actual or theoretical tests of gold equivalency or gold convertibility (gold is sequestered domestically). The paper money is almost certainly domestically not equivalent to its purported gold weight, but this is essentially irrelevant to the domestic economy. The paper money of each domestic poliical economy is constantly and necessarily being inflated at all times (rate of inflation differing in each national political economy). The paper money is constantly depreciating and each national price level is rising, although not necessarily in equal step. The rise of the price level, however, provided there is a reasonable management of the economy and no hyperinflation, is not of domestic significance. (Refer again in this connection to the general theory of price, price level, money, and gold in Ch. II, Section 14. Whether the actual price level in gold is X or 2X or 3X is not domestically material if all ratios are maintained.) The degree of inflation and depreciation in each national economy depends on many factors, including the level of the Government expenditure, the mix of tax, borrowing, inflation, the degree of private inflation permitted and the degree of the real expansion of capital, etc.

In the context of all the foregoing, the foreign exchange arising out of foreign trade and investment, would be absolutely chaotic unless it were not only managed directly by the Government (and it will be managed in the interest of the domestic political economy) and unless the Government also entered into agreements and treaties with other foreign WMS's, and also entered into regional cooperation arrangements. The self-regulating dynamics and mechanisms of the ICE are gone. The cyclic expansion of capital in theICE and the domestic money-banking-paper money-gold equivalency-gold stock-gold convertibility sequence that was inextricably tied to the cyclic rise and fall of real capital expansion, no longer regulates domestic and foreign trade and exchange. None of these elements are tied together in the pefcp. Not only is the tie between gold and money creation broken domestically, but the tie between gold-money-level of production, and capital expansion is broken. In the ICE, both the imbalance in trade, and foreign trade generally, and the imbalance in the foreign exchange are automatically, or relatively automatically, adjusted, since both the trade and the imbalance, and the means to pay for the imbalance, flow from the causes of the business cycle, and they respond to all the manifestations of the cyclic decline.

The monetary units of each political economy could be exchanged at their declared gold weights, (i.e., declared at any particular time). They could also be exchanged at certain parity rates established by agreement, and the exchange at these parities could be supported by each Government in the market. There could also be a free or relatively free market for the exchange of currencies. The degree of imbalance in trade, the degree of foreign investment and the piling up of foreign currencies, will seriously affect any mode of exchange. Each Government must consider the domestic price level in relation to foreign trade. It can in effect reduce its price level in terms of foreign paper money by reducing the gold weight of its monetary unit. But each Government will inevitably first consider the need to maintain its own political economy at the highest level possible, in determining the weight of gold of its monetary unit, the parity rates it will establish, or its intervention in foreign exchange markets. However, no Government can escape the consequences of continuous marked imbalance of trade and foreign investment.

Many of the techniques adopted in the early pefcp (pre WWII) to conduct foreign trade and exchange will be found recurring after WWII, despite a greater effort in international cooperation. The licensing of the use of foreign exchange and gold in foreign trade, exchange controls, control of capital flow, the licensing of exports and imports, quotas, tariffs, special taxes, the sheltered trade areas, frank discrimination against those outside the trade groups, all re-appear in one form or another, often now concealed by a new ideology and terminology.

Nevertheless there is a considerable difference after WWII, particularly in that the U. S. completely reversed its position, and instead of withdrawing behind a high tariff, became an active participant and leader in the foreign trade. By loans, and grants of money, by its goods, it reestablished the economies, and the trade of the other nations of the world. Having accumulated the major portion of the gold, its paper money became the true "paper gold" of world trade and world banking, the money of international trade, the reserve money of the central banks, and to an extent, part of the fictive capital of other political economies.

After WWII, by international agreement, most of the nations established a gold weight for their monetary unit or pegged it in relation to the U. S. dollar. Each agreed to maintain the exchange rate so established (by supporting the currency in the exchange market; the U. S. by buying and selling gold). However, the peg was adjustable if there was a fundamental disequilibrium in the foreign exchange, and by agreement, the weight of the monetary unit, or the peg could be changed. The International Monetary Fund could extend relatively short term resources in foreign currency to those political economies which could not meet current balance of payment deficits. Longer term credits, for actual capital expansion, or capital replacement, or for personal consumption, or Government consumption, which required the import of goods, were provided for through an "International Bank for Reconstruction and Development." Furthermore, loans by the U. S., or a group of nations or central banks, provided foreign exchange for a national economy that could not maintain an equilibrium, by loans, swaps, etc.

Efforts were made to reduce foreign exchange restrictions and controls, quantitative trade restrictions and quotas, tariffs, dumping, import and export subsides, on a reciprocal basis. Regional groupings were again resorted to, and trade agreements, multilateral or with the regional groups. With the establishment of common markets, a complex discriminatory system still exists, and quotas and exchange controls still exist, and probably must continue.

But despite such agreements, a disequilibrium is inescapable. For most economies, trade-exchange equilibrium, over the long period, is simply an impossibility. Even to maintain welfare, and military systems, some national economies must import a large volume of goods. This seems bizarre, for it might be thought that such expenditures could be reduced. But this is not the situation. In any event, the maintenance of the productive level necessary for such systems of distribution usually requires the importation of certain goods.

There are many factors that may be mentionned that add to the disequilibrium. Some national economies determine to maintain a far higher level of production than others (greater capital growth, greater welfare and military systems). Some economies are enabled to undertake an extraordinary capital expansion because of a previous great capital destruction. Some economies have an extremely effective political structure, with adequate political power and an effective Government. Others cannot maintain a proper tax-borrowing-inflation balance in their revenue mix, or cannot maintain an adequate welfare or an adequate military system of expenditure. One of the consequences of all these disparities is that the several price levels of the national economies rise at an unequal rate.

With respect to disequilibrium, in general: The International Monetary Fund cannot meet the needs of a national economy in disequilibrium. Foreign loans, by the U.S. or groups of national economies are essential as a matter of course. Even with this cooperation, it would seem that periodic devaluation of the monetary unit is the only course for most national economies. To make such devaluation effective, there should also be some international agreement, to prevent a chain reaction. (Some national currencies may have to be revalued upwards). Speculative pressures, and the flow of money in expectation of a devaluation or revaluation, make the process a difficult one.

The situation of the U.S. is a special one.*

In the quarter century after WWII, the paper money of the U.S. occupied a unique position. This arose out of the extraordinary strength of the U.S. economy (one element of which was the possession of a great part of the world's gold). Furthermore, the foreign national economies, in the earlier years after WWII, were weak and disordered.

The position of the U.S. paper money was unique in three ways:

First: It was the paper money of a pefcp, and although constantly inflated, publicly and privately, and constantly depreciating domestically, the depreciation was kept at a low rate.

Second: At the same time, it was a true "paper gold" in international trade and exchange, circulating and held at its actual

* The discussion that follows was written before the action of the President on August 15, 1971, ending the convertibility of the dollar into gold at $35 an ounce, and freeing the dollar for devaluation against other currencies. Thereafter, the dollar was recognized as a floating currency. The United States officially devalued the gold weight of the dollar by 8.57% (December 1971), and on February 12, 1973, within 14 months, devalued the dollar by another 10%. (Although the official value of the dollar in gold was then $42.22 an oz., the price of gold on the London bullion market then reached $73.75. The price of gold has since risen to much higher levels.)

gold weight, and convertible to gold (abroad) at its established gold weight. In part it had this role through international agreement, since other foreign monetary units were pegged to it. But the practical basis for its international position was, in reality, the immense mass of gold accumulated by the U. S. which the U. S. stood ready to exchange for its paper money either to foreign central banks, or to foreign private holders.

Third: Insofar as it was obtained and accumulated by foreign holders by the sale of their goods of all types, and then held as a bank reserve, or by private holders, it was a *fictive capital* form for foreign producers. and as such, like any fictive capital form, and was one of the bases for the existence of the foreign pefcp's, and their Level of Production and Income, etc. This situation was of advantage to the U. S., and also to the foreign economies, as well as to the international trade. With respect to the U. S.: Its political economy need not be in a trade or exchange equilibrium, nor need it maintain a balance of payments of trade; and it can expand its capital abroad, and it can engage in welfare and military programs abroad without tying purchases to U. S. goods (although, of course, it does ship a large volume of domestically produced goods abroad in connection with foreign loans and grants). Furthermore, foreign holding of its paper money reduces domestic depreciation, insofar as the paper money is immobilized abroad. The advantage to the foreign countries, as has been indicated, is that they acquire, to an extent, a satisfactory fictive capital form for their own production. However, not all countries are able to maintain these dollars as reserves, and because of necessity, their reserves are lost to other national economies.

The advantages of the situation were so great that the U. S. pursued a somewhat dangerous policy of permitting its gold (after 1958, when the European economies became a surplus group) to flow abroad, not only to foreign central banks, but to private holders. Because of the size of its gold hoard, it was not compelled to reduce the gold weight of its monetary unit (which would have been necessary for any other national economy). Such a reduction, of course, would have been most unwelcome to those investing abroad, or purchasing foreign goods. The lowering of the American price level to foreign purchasers—ordinarily a basic incentive for devaluation—was not attractive to American producers either, since obtaining the foreign exchange not a matter of necessity.

But, as stated, the policy was a hazardous one. In the first place, there was a chance of the loss of all gold to foreign central banks, (which could be hostile), and to foreign private holders, (who also could be hostile). This could result in a disastrous depreciation of the dollar in foreign markets, which to some extent must ultimately be reflected in domestic markets. Furthermore, a worse consequence could follow: an attack on *all* U. S. capital papers, including fictive capital papers. This would threaten the possibility of maintaining a viable economy based on fictive forms. Actually, the private possession of the mass of gold would or could destroy *all* pe's based on fictive forms. The loss of the gold means that the paper money first loses value in international trade, requiring devaluation of the monetary unit; foreign and domestic depreciation will then increase, with the ultimate threat to the whole domestic fictive structure.

Fortunately the step was taken—late in the pefcp—to sequester monetary gold in all central banks, from private holders, and to prevent as far as possible, private gold being sold for newly issued paper currencies. This not only protected the United States, but protected the currencies of other national economies.

It is possible that the "Special Drawing Rights" created through the IMF can protect the United States, at least for the time being, from further gold loss. At the same time these SRD's as an international "reserve" can act as a new, and unique *international fictive capital* form, that can be accumulated by the central banks of the various national economies.

But all the inherent difficulties remain and for the United States they are now increasing. It would seem that there must be some reckoning because of the great pileup of American paper money abroad. And the United States cannot escape the ultimate need for the basic current equilibrium. What steps are to be taken and how the great overhang from the past is to be dealt with are subjects that at the present writing cannot be discussed. Each political economy fears to take the necessary steps, although they will be taken belatedly. The basic premises of the political economy based on fictive forms cannot be escaped.

CHAPTER V

"WELFARE" AND "MILITARY" SYSTEMS OF DISTRIBUTION AND USE OF GOODS

(1) a. The laws that govern the distribution and use of goods that constitute the pseudo Profit B can be stated as logically necessary principles flowing from the nature of a political economy based upon the fictive expansion of capital.

b. The "Welfare" and "Military" systems of distribution and use of goods, as they are in actuality, and when properly administered, conform to these laws. But the "Welfare" and "Military" concepts were not devised to suit the needs of a political economy based on the fictive expansion of capital; they are part of the dynamics of the new State. The Welfare and Military ideologies themselves are actualized into forms suitable for the requirements of the political economy.

.1 The general laws governing the use and distribution of the goods, stated in summary form.

The laws can be deduced from the nature of the political economy. It will be seen, that in general, the actually prevailing modes of use and distribution of goods by the State comply with the general laws, and that the laws are practical rules of management which the Government must and does follow.

Negative rules:

I. The goods, and the money, *may not be used as capital* to produce other goods (in a capitalist relationship). Nor may they be used to produce goods in any other economic relationship, as for example by Government production of goods for sale. Corollary: the goods should not be used by an individual to produce goods for the WMS or for any individuals in the society. (All goods in the economy are to be produced in the dependent capitalist organism.)

II. The goods may not be utilized for the personal consumption
  a. of the capitalists
  b. of the wage earners in material production
  c. of those whose income is derivative from capitalists or wage earners

III. The goods may not re-enter the market to compete with goods newly produced.

IV. The goods may not be used in such a way that the fundamental relationship of capitalist-wageearner in the capital unit is in any way impaired, or will reduce the availability of a class of laborers in capitalist production at the usual prevailing wage-profit ratio.

Positive:

V. The goods must be used in a way socially accepted as desirable or necessary. Corollary: No programs of direct, physical destruction of the goods is permissible.*

VI. The type of goods purchased by the Government and its distributees must be such that all capitals in the organism will be producing for the Government and its distributees; the purchases must be generally congruent with the sources of the WM tax.

* No society, no economic relationship, no political relationship, could exist if it were contemplated that a great part of the production of the society were produced to be destroyed. This is inconsistent with the nature of any economic relationship and a political relationship. Goods must be produced for a human need, even if this need or desire would seem to be an unnecessary luxury or something irrational, or a type of use rejected by many.

Even the destruction of simple, unprocessed foodstuffs, in limited quantity, in connection with the limitation of production in agriculture arouses resentment. Furthermore, if it were ever contemplated that technologically advanced products were produced to be destroyed, the technology, on which the economy depends, would be seriously injured.

VII. Some of the goods must be used to maintain at least a certain part of a welfare class (individuals available for employment that cannot be employed at a given level of production).

Two related corollaries:

1. The money disbursed by the Government for Welfare or Military purposes must be expended for goods produced for the demand created by the expenditure. That is to say, the money must not be expended for goods ordinarily in existence, simply raising the price of such goods. However, while the goods will ordinarily be produced for the Government's demand, in certain instances poorly administered programs will result in an expenditure that simply raises the price of the existing supply. To some extent this was true of the early medical, hospital and housing programs. A large-scale war creates so great a Government demand, raising prices, that the expenditure is in part wasted so far as the basic requirements of the political economy are concerned. Price controls and allocations will aid in assuring the proper use of the Pseudo Profit B.

2. The goods that will be used or distributed in the Welfare and Military systems should only be those represented by the Pseudo Profit B; i.e., the Welfare and Military systems of distribution should not be expanded to use and distribute goods that would ordinarily be consumed within the dependent capitalist organism.

.2 The actually existing "Welfare and Military" systems of distribution and use of goods, when properly administered, are suitable for the needs of the political economy based on fictive forms, and conform to the general laws of distribution and use of goods. Welfare ideology is actualized by the creation of forms of distribution and use suitable for a pefcp (the Welfare class). "Military" and defense concepts are actualized into forms for a State engaged in ideological warfare, but avoiding actual warfare. Reference to certain concepts in Chapter VI with respect to ideology, and the actualization of ideology in the political and economic relationships.

This chapter is primarily concerned with the description of the actual distribution and use of goods constituting the Pseudo Profit B, in the WMS. It will be seen that this distribution and use conforms to the laws of distribution and use of a PE based on fictive forms. Some of the actual distribution and use, in part, violates these laws, generally because the ideology is exerting too strong an influence, i.e., a partial failure of the general process wherein political ideology is ordinarily actualized into forms suitable for the needs of the economic relationship.

The existing patterns of distribution and use of goods constituting the Pseudo Profit B are dependent upon the ideology of this new State. (The laws of distribution and use, stated as logical principles flowing from the nature of the political economy, are not the dynamics of the actual patterns of distribution and use.) But at the same time it must be recognized that the ideology itself is actualized into forms that are somewhat different than what might be contemplated if the ideology alone were considered.

Thus, the description of distribution and use of goods in this chapter must also be considered in the light of the analysis of Chapter VI: (a) the nature of the WMS itself as a new State integral with the political economy; (b) its Welfare and its Military ideology; (c) the general principles of actualization of an ideology into forms suitable for the necessities of the actual economic relationship; (d) the general principle that the State will be of such actual form and structure as to be useful and necessary for the actual economic relationship.

As will appear, neither the actual systems of distribution and use, or the general Welfare, Military or Defense ideology, are devised for the necessities of a pefcp. The actual modes of distribution should not be regarded as being devised to dispose of goods in such a way as to meet the necessities of this political economy.

The primary meaning of "Welfare" in ideology of the State is that the State is an economic association to assure the *material* needs of each of its members (but it is not a "Communist" type of economic association). This Welfare ideology of such economic association is actualized into a political economy based on fictive forms wherein production, employment and profit are maintained by the use of fictive forms in a certain economic relationship. In this chapter the principal concern with respect to Welfare is the secondary meaning of Welfare in the ideology: that the *material* needs of all individuals who cannot obtain these needs directly within the dependent capitalist organism, will have these needs furnished by the State directly.

Where there is a dependent capitalist organism, there cannot possibly be a general distribution of goods (Laws of distribution, .1 above; the distribution must be of such nature that it is separate from the distributive systems of the organism, and does not injure the organism). Thus the actual system of Welfare distribution for the most part, will be to a carefully limited class, composed of those outside the distributive systems of the organism (the members of which are the capitalists, the wage-earners, and those obtaining goods and money derivately through their incomes). Most members of the Welfare class will be given an income at a lower level than those receiving their income through the capitalist organism directly or derivatively. They are not useful to the productive system; they function as consumers.

The major groups in the Welfare class are:

The unemployed. (In the pefcp, this group must always exist; the permissable size of the group is a difficult political-economic question).

The unemployable (relative to the level of the economy; the absolutely unemployable).

Old age retired (age limits arbitrary)

Children generally but especially of the "Poor."

The "Poor" generally including other welfare groups, plus some of the employed and marginally employed; the "Working Poor"; in particular add large parts of certain groups—Negroes, Indians, etc., Para Welfare groups: "Veterans", etc.

(The usual distribution is by way of money grants; under certain circumstances certain goods and services: housing, foodstuffs, medical and hospital care, education and special social services, etc. Certain of these distributions may go somewhat beyond the welfare class, under the theory that the goods and services will not ordinarily be purchased, or the services will not be privately produced. Refer to Sec. (2) on the "Welfare" theory of the latter.

The "Military" system of expenditure and use of goods of the WMS seems superficially similar to that of the "Democratic State." The important distinction is that in the WMS the expenditure is constant and at a very high level, as high constantly as the expenditure for the occasional war of the Democratic State. The "military" system of the WMS also is only in a superficial way similar to "military" systems and military States and societies of the past. The WMS is not a State based on war or conquest, nor is the Military class's existence dependent on its military power; nor is the military power of the class necessary to maintain the State.

The economy of the WMS is not based on the expansion of real capital; (which is the sine qua non of the ICE and the Democratic State). There is no real economic dispute among the WMS's that must lead to war, nor to war with Communist States.

Since the preparation for a technological war or defense can mean an almost limitless expenditure, the problem of the Government is to curtail the expenditure, so that a certain Level of the Economy can be maintained and a Welfare system of expenditure, equally important, can be maintained. The military class seeks greater expenditure, but in a properly conducted State it is not the controlling class of the State (Ch. VI) nor is it the controlling class of the economy. (In this respect, there is some similarity to the Democratic State.)

.3 *The Welfare system of distribution and use cannot be used alone; if an adequate Military Program is not in existence, the Welfare Program must be supplemented by a "public works" system of expenditure. But the latter will not permit a high level economy* or *a high level welfare system; The Military system of expenditure is essential to secure both a high level economy and a high level welfare system.*

The revenue obtained by the WM tax, and the money borrowed (even if the borrowing is from the banks, and is an inflation) cannot be expended solely on consumer goods. Refer to Ch. III on the goods-money circuit between the Government and the organism; if the major part of the money is taxed and borrowed from the "capital goods" industries or the recipients of income from these industries, the money *must* be returned thereto thru Government purchase, etc. The money that constitutes the pseudo Profit B must be used to purchase goods throughout the whole range of the capitalist organism, (Ch. III on the law of congruence). Actually the greater part of the purchases must directly, or indirectly be made from the capital goods industries. It is true that the purchase of a large volume of consumers goods must ultimately require the purchase of capital goods, and there may well be a degree of capital expansion also, but this is by no means adecuate.

If the law of congruence is not followed at least approximately, the effectiveness of the tax system will be seriously reduced, and the Government will also not be able to borrow from non-bank sources. Furthermore, a relatively excessive purchase of consumer goods usually requires an excessive inflation; too high a level in the welfare system when the military system is at a low level, means excessive inflation.

Even at a low level pefcp—as in the early U. S. pefcp—when welfare expenditure was the only major system of expenditure, the pefcp could not be sustained by the welfare system alone. In the absence of a military program of adequate size, a public works program is essential to furnish a market for heavy industry. Early public works programs often included the construction of power generating facilities, etc., which is inconsistent with the laws of use and distribution. However, this was necessary as an emergency measure to maintain the pefcp, in the absence of military expenditure on a sufficient scale.

Summary statistical note:

U. S., 1971: Federal Social Welfare expenditure, approximately $92.4 bns. (Compare, 1935, approx. $3.2 bns.)
National Defense expenditure,
approx. $77.6 bns. (Veterans included in Welfare)

(Add cost of Govt. administrative personnel for each system, insofar as not included in above).

Statistical data in this Chapter with respect to various Welfare programs, Military programs of expenditure, are approximations, indicating only the general pattern of expenditure in a developed pefcp. The Statistical Abstract of the U. S., 1972, is the main source of the approximations.

.4 There are modes of distributing goods that conform to the laws of distribution and use, other than those found in the established systems of distribution. They would be suitable if the requirements of the political economy alone were considered. However, they are outside the prevailing ideology of Welfare. Nevertheless, certain WMS's do maintain an "elite" class which possess themselves of a considerable part of the goods distributed.

The Welfare concept in ideology, refers to the provision of material necessities for those within the economic and political organization of the society (subsec. .2 above). The concept does not go beyond this; certainly not to provide a freedom from the demands of the economy on the individual. Thus, for example, a subsidy for the individual as artist, philosopher, religious, or scientist would not be acceptable Welfare distributions, although they would seem to be within the laws of distribution and use. However, such distribution in any event would be much too small to be adequate for a pefcp, which requires the existence of a large Welfare class to maintain a high level of economy. However, as part of a "make work" program for those in the Welfare class, it is conceivable that some distribution can be made to artists, writers, philosophers, etc. (Sec. 2.) This has been attempted before; it is somewhat doubtful if it can be revived.

There is another class, not a "Welfare class" which seems able in certain WMS's to obtain and consume a considerable part of the Pseudo Profit B. This is a so-called "elite" class, which has possessed itself of the Government power (not the capitalist class). As stated in Chapter VI, in certain nations the movements which led to the establishment of the WMS-pefcp utilized the concept of an "elite" class.

However, generally speaking, and certainly at the present time, this elite class will usually be found to be a Military class. Insofar as the distribution and use of goods is concerned, this Military class seems to substitute itself for a Welfare class. In these States, there is a signal lack of ordinary public Welfare distribution, and although Welfare ideology exists, it has little actuality.

Such a type of distribution and use does not exist in the United States, and it is not conceivable that it would exist. In those WMS's where it is found, it will be seen that the Government is essentially a military Government of great power. Such a Government is unsuitable for an effective WMS (Chapter VI).

(2) "Welfare" distribution and use of goods in the WMS. Welfare Programs: Early and advanced forms.

.1 The unemployed. The unemployable
–At the inception of the WMS; and at a low level of production
–At a high level of production
Types of distribution: general "welfare" money payments; made work programs; unemployment compensation. Non monetary distributions–housing, food, services, etc.

The unemployed and the relatively unemployable are a permanent major class who are outside the distributive system of the dependent capitalist organism. Its size depends on the Level of Production (which is primarily determined by the level of Government expenditure–Ch. III. At any level of production expenditure–Ch. III, and hence on the size of the military and welfare programs themselves). But at any level of production possible in the pefcp, there will always be a substantial group available for employment, for whom there are no jobs available in material production, or service employment derivative from incomes of capitalists and weageearners in the organism. Together with this group of prima facie employables, there is a large group of relatively unemployable, the size of which is also dependent on the Level of production. There are also the probably absolutely unemployable, physically or mentally disabled, or with such personality characteristics that there is no economic place for them in a technological society. It must be recognized that at an extremely high level (actual war economy) many relatively unemployable and disabled individuals can and will be employed. Many members of the whole class shift in and out of employment; it is the class that is constant.

At a very low level of production, the size of the class of unemployed will be massive. On the inception of the pefcp in the U. S. (almost exclusively a welfare—public works program) the class was almost 1/3 of the employable individuals. The need to maintain this class, at a socially critical point in the economy, was a major dynamic for the WMS. As stated in Sec. 1, the maintenance of such a class as a welfare class is necessary in a pefcp and WMS.

There are certain special conditions of payment for this welfare group, not particularly applicable to other groups in the welfare class. All in the welfare class are maintained at subsistence or below subsistence (i.e. the social concept of subsistence of an advanced technological society), but the special problem here is Rule IV—that the Government distribution must not impair the fundamental capitalist relationship of employer, employee, or reduce the availability of a class of employees for capitalist production at the prevailing wage-profit ratio. (The problem of Rule IV becomes acute when it is proposed to include in welfare payments the marginally employed etc., as where the "Poor" are constituted as a welfare class—subsec. .4 below).

In any event, these two principles must be followed: the payment must be substantially lower than the prevailing average wage rate, indeed as low as or lower than the substandard wage. There must also be a certain obloquy attached to the receipt of the payment, and a constant pressure of various sorts to compel the recipients to obtain some sort of employment. Yet the fundamental problem is almost insurmountable, since the "Working Poor" in many areas of the economy, may have an income less than the welfare beneficiary.

Because of the foregoing principles, it is necessary to establish a somewhat different system of benefits for that part of the unemployed group that is more likely to find employment; a program for the temporarily unemployed (unemployment compensation). This may be part of a "social insurance" program. There can be more liberality in the payments, and the program need not be managed with a design to attaching obloquy to the receipt of the payment.

Likewise, as part of a "social insurance" program a system of payment for the absolutely unemployable can be established. However, these are not particularly notable for any greater liberality of payment, even though the social obloquy is in part removed because the individuals are not properly considered a part of the labor class.

Types of welfare grants, other than direct money grant to the individual.

The payment may be made through a "made work" program, with a somewhat higher level of payment. Some of the work projects may be socially useful. However, to conform to the laws of distribution and use, neither the product, nor the enterprise may in any way compete with private production or private enterprise. Conservation projects, recreation projects, personal service projects *to members of the welfare class,* are suitable. These projects have fallen into disuse. However, in connection with community assistance programs, .10 below, some work projects are being revived. The public assistance grant is often directly dependent on the care of children. There may be other grants for the benefit of children—subsec. .3, below. The welfare grant may be goods and services, apart from, or in addition to a money grant (Subsec. .6- .10 below).

It has been proposed that the unemployed and unemployable be included in a welfare class constituted by the "Poor," generally, with the assurance of a minimum income. This will include the "working Poor" (subsec. .4 below). If investigation, a means test, etc. is eliminated, and the level of the welfare grant raised considerably, there will be a radical change in the nature of public assistance, and the amount of money expended. This may affect the laws of distribution.

The present extent of public assistance programs: 1971, Federal, State and Local expenditure approx $18 1/2 bns., including medical assistance costs. Of this Federal expenditure is approx.

$10 bns. This includes old age assistance, families with dependent children, disabled, general assistance. But see following section on old age benefits (Social Security), and disability benefits, Social security, also Unemployment Compensation payments (1970, approx. 3.8 bns.)

.2 *Old-Age Pensions. Survivors' Pensions.*

The old-age pension program, of the size and scale existing in the Welfare State, is probably the most important program of "welfare" distribution of the WMS. (A few Democratic States had such programs on a relatively small scale; the U. S. did not.) The recipients are for the most part outside the labor force, and the pension itself induces older people to withdraw from the labor force. The program ideally conforms to all laws of disposition of goods in the pefcp, insofar as consumer goods are concerned. (Welfare programs, in general, do not comply with Law VI—purchase of good produced by *all* capitals in the economy. Note particularly that with respect to old-age pensions, the main revenue source may be a wage tax, which in large part may be derived from heavy industry. See elsewhere on need for a parallel Military system of expenditure). But in every other way, a large scale old-age pension system, at a high level is particularly consonant with the laws of distribution. and use of goods in a pefcp.

The size of the class of recipients, intrinsically large because of increasing longevity, can be further enlarged by reducing the age of entitlement from 65 to 60, and for many occupations even to 55. The amount of payment can safely be increased to subsistence level. Indeed the problem is really not that of increasing the amount expended by this means, but of limiting it, so that there can be other dispositions of "Welfare" funds, and other "Welfare" programs. If there are 15 millions of individual eligible at a benefit of a thousasd dollars a year, this can easily be made 30 million individuals at a benefit of two thousand dollars a year. Payments of such scope can only be possible when the economy is functioning at a high level, i.e. in effect, one in which there is a large scale Military program of expenditure.

Where the economy is at a low level, an old-age pension system must be limited to a smaller group, and payments must be much smaller.

A proposed old-age pension program was one of the important elements in the dynamics leading to the new State, certainly in the U. S. It will be recalled that at the inception of the new State, there were movements to establish old age pension systems on a grandiose scale, but the plans were usually associated with absurd monetary schemes.

In the U. S., Social Security old age pensions are financed by earmarked taxes. and there is some attempt to proportion the payment to past earnings. This does not affect the general nature of this pension as a mode of commodity distribution and use, or the tax as a true WM tax, thru which part of the pseudo Profit B is created. (Ch. III.)

To some extent, recipients of such old age pensions may be receiving substantial income from investments, and thus are not outside the class of individuals receiving a distribution through the capitalist organism. The payment to them may not result in current commodity consumption to the extent of the pension. However, this is not significant in the overall distribution. Statistical note: 1970 U. S. Social Security old age retirement payments, approximately $21 bns. Add survivors, wives, husbands, widows, widowers, parents, children, lump-sum—$8 bns.
Total Social Security benefit payments old age, survivors. 1937-1969, approx. $217 bns.

.3 *Children, as a class of distributees.*

Children, in the modern economy, are ordinarily outside the labor class. Most children are supported through wage and income payments to their parents received through their work or position in the organism. Some of these parents are in the class of the "Poor" (which itself, as stated in the following subsection, may be regarded as a welfare class in the WMS). A very large number of children have parents in certain welfare groups; many have only one, or no parents (3.2 million in the U. S.)

Approximately one third of the children in the U. S. could qualify as being in a welfare class. These children would seem to be as ideally suited a group for welfare payments, as the group receiving old age benefits. The amount that is paid to them or to their parents (aid for dependent children, survivors benefits) is considerable, but it by no means approaches the amount of the old age pensions, or what would be theoretically proper and feasible under the laws of distribution and use. 1971, Aid to dependent children, which is included in Public Assistance, generally, $6.2 bns. Add payments for crippled children etc., survivors payments under the Social Security Act. Refer also to special programs for education, food distribution, health care etc. below).

There is a *tendency* to expand benefits for children, i.e. under family assistance plans, mentionned in the following section, on the "Poor." There has been, at least in recent years a steady increase in Federal expenditure for Education (.9 below) which in effect and often in express purpose is for the benefit of Poor children. Also refer to Social Services for youths, .10 below). Nevertheless, the low existing rate of expenditure for this welfare class is surprising in view of the fact that such distribution is so practicable in the light of the laws of distribution and use.

.4 The "Poor" as a welfare class, generally. (Income below "poverty level"; include most recipients of present welfare programs plus *the "Working Poor" and other groups.)*

The following discussion is in part theoretical since it is mainly concerned with proposed monetary benefits to the Poor as a welfare class, ,and the means by which this is to be accomplished. To clarify the discussion:

(a) A large part of the "Poor" are now receiving monetary welfare payments, in some program or other, and may also be receiving goods and services (listed in .6 to .10 below); some "Poor" may be receiving these goods and services although not part of present welfare groups.

(b) The primary question to be considered is the probable amount of *additional* welfare payments that will be involved, as

—amount to be added by payments to the "Working Poor" and others not presently receiving benefits
—increasing payments to existing welfare groups by their inclusion in the general class of the "Poor."

(c) The effect of different techniques of payment, with respect to laws of distribution and use.

(d) Effect with respect to special groups, as Negroes, Migrants, Indians, Appalachians, etc.

The proposal to constitute the "Poor" as a welfare class will, in the first place. considerably enlarge the number of individuals receiving "Welfare" payments. It is estimated (1968) that 25.4 millions or 12.8% of the population should be deemed to exist below the poverty level. An important aspect of this is that 1968 is a peak prosperity year; 10 years earlier the figure was much higher (39.5 millions, or 22.4% of the population).

Almost all welfare payment recipients, except some old-age pensioners, some veterans, temporarily unemployed higher income workers, fall within the category of the "Poor." But the addition of the "Working Poor"—which would include racial minority groups, Negroes, Indians, etc.—must substantially increase the size of the class and the volume of expenditure. But it is also contemplated that the amount of the payments to individuals or families be substantially increased over the present level.

If the "Poor" as a class is dealt with on a national basis, the standard of welfare payments in some areas where it is far below subsistence, will certainly be markedly increased. This would increase the stability of the welfare class, reducing migration to more liberal welfare areas, which has caused urban, school, and family disruption.

The significance of such an enlargement of the welfare class with respect to certain laws of distribution and use, depends in part on the level and techniques of the program. It has been proposed to set a floor on family income, and if the family income falls below this, the income will be supplemented. (Family assistance plan; negative income tax.) However, the floor proposed has wide variations—from $1500 to $7500. If the income minimum is set at a fairly high figure, there will be a serious disruption in the low paid labor market. Many of these individuals hold necessary jobs, particularly in the field of service. If the cut-off level is set very low, there will be difficulty in maintaining the system on a national scale. Furthermore, the elimination of investigation and the means test, not only for the Poor generally, but necessarily then for many others receiving present welfare grants, may tend to reduce the supply of labor for low paying jobs even further. All aspects of the problem revolve around the minimum level of income that can be established. If the Poor generally, become a welfare class, it can reasonably be contemplated that welfare expenditure can be increased ten to thirty bns. annually in the near future, depending on the family minimum established. Such an increase is of importance in the next few years of the WMS.

.5 Veterans' Benefits.

There are a variety of benefits paid to former members of the armed forces, including benefits to wives, dependents, survivors. These benefits consist of money and certain services. There are benefits for disability (service and non service connected), death benefits, old age; programs for education, hospital and medical care, etc. A degree of duplication exists with other welfare programs and payments.

In money volume, these payments and benefits have become extremely important modes of distribution and use. Annual benefits 1971, over $10 bns. in the U. S. (Contrast-1930 $675 mils.) Since WWII Veterans' benefits have amounted to over $150 bns. Such distributions are socially highly acceptable. The distributees are probably the most politically powerful sector of the welfare class. Veterans are not entirely a true welfare group. However, most who receive benefits are unemployable. In some instances, the payment is contrary to some law of distribution and use. It is possible to argue that veterans benefits should be classified as an adjunct of the military system of expenditure rather than as a welfare program.

.6 Food Distribution Programs; certain monetary distributions tied to food purchase. (To recipients of welfare payments; to the "Poor" generally; to children, students, others.)

Individuals in the groups receiving welfare payments, and often the "Poor" generally, are given foods directly by the Government, or may be given additional money earmarked for the purchase of additional foodstuffs. School lunch and school milk programs can be included in this type of distribution, although many of the children are not in the welfare class.

Although small in comparison with direct money grants, Federal Food Programs are not inconsiderable (in 1969 over $1 bn.) Food distribution is one of the earliest of distribution programs, and many billions of dollars of food have been distributed. (Also, Sec. 4, below, food distribution in foreign assistance programs.)

Closely related to the welfare aspect of the distribution, is the fact that the Government will acquire and store large quantities of certain foodstuffs in connection with its "price support" programs. The Government seeks to reduce the volume of foods held in storage. (See below. Sec. 5.3 of stockpiling and storage, as temporary modes of commodity disposition.)

The Government should not purchase food for the purpose of direct distribution to welfare groups, as this may injure the marketing system. A mode of distribution currently used, is the food stamp program, in which money grants are earmarked for retail purchase of food.

.7 Public housing; rent supplements.

Housing in publicly owned units is being furnished to a limited extent to low-income groups ("Poor," the elderly, Welfare program recipients) at a rental below the prevailing market price for comparable accommodations. The Government subsidizes construction and maintenance of these units by grants and loans (and also purchases and leases facilities from private developers and builders). This expenditure was of significance in the early days of the pefcp as part of Public Works construction, in the absence of an adequate military program of expenditure (Refer to "Public Works" below (3) on general considerations on the nature and necessity of Public Works programs in the WMS.)

Insofar as low rent housing constitutes a good or service for the welfare groups, it may be considered an additional distribution, or an increase in the payment, earmarked for a specific purpose. It takes this form, rather than a general cash payment, because the housing is not ordinarily privately available. It is a program of relatively small size when compared to the cash payments to welfare recipients, generally.

Strictly speaking, expenditure by the Government to build and maintain such housing is a violation of the basic Rule 1 of the Laws of Distribution and use of the Pseudo Profit B. It is an expenditure for a "capital" good and it competes with other housing. The Government is in effect providing housing for rent competing with private housing. However, in the level of the volume now furnished and existing: (a) there is no adequate housing available, being constructed, nor will it be constructed for the rentals that Welfare recipients can pay; (b) public housing does not constitute any significant part of the housing available particularly in view of the population growth. It is probably not even significantly competitive with slum housing; (c) at the price level there is no significant competition with privately produced privately rented housing.

But if the programs were greatly enlarged to include (a) most of the existing welfare groups including the elderly or (b) the Poor generally, it would be distribution of great scope and expense. There would be a significant production of goods competing with goods privately produced. It is quite true that private producers will not attempt to produce directly for this large class, and up to a certain point this could excuse the violation. But the market for the older and deteriorating housing will be injured. Furthermore, if the working poor are receiving the benefits and the lower middle class are not, it would seem that there could be a serious injury to the capitalist relationship (Rules 2, 4)). However, it is conceivable that because of the prejudice against public housing as a segregated institution economically and racially, the public housing may not really be competitive.

In view of the shortage of housing, the rise in the population, and the necessity for urban rebuilding, it is possible to say that a substantial increase in housing programs could be justified as exceptions to the laws of distribution and use, but not to the extent of providing housing for the welfare class.

Money supplements to tenants of private housing would seem at first sight, not to violate the laws of distribution and use, assuming they are restricted to existing welfare groups. But if the money supplements for rent were given to the Poor generally, the problem of competing with lower middle class families would again arise. But there are basic objections to rent subsidies, as to all subsidies. Will the rent subsidy really effect a consumption of the goods?

.8 Expanded medical, dental, hospital, and nursing care for the old age groups, or welfare recipients generally, or the "Poor" as a class. The possibility of furnishing such services to everyone.

The Government, particularly State and local Governments in the U.S., and non-Government voluntary agencies, provided such services on a minimal, possibly emergency basis, during the Democratic State and the early WMS, to those clearly in the "Welfare" class, the unemployed Poor. This was usually accomplished through direct service by City, State, and even private institutions (not by money grant to individuals or payment to vendors of services). The "Working Poor" and the lower middle class, generally paid for such services, and because of their cost, obtained them only to a limited extent, possibly even below the level of the publicly supplied services. Private prepay plans that began to be of significance in the early WMS, increased the volume of services that could be obtained.

The Welfare State, in general, proposes to provide medical, hospital, nursing care, etc. on a much wider scale, at least to old age groups, and the Poor generally. This was to be done either by expanding the public facilities, or paying individuals or institutions that supplied the services. It was also contemplated to utilize social insurance plans to pay part of the cost (prepay at a lower rate than actual cost). This is an expensive undertaking, representing a substantial outlay, and requiring a great expansion of personnel, facilities, education, etc. Nevertheless it is a mode of consumption of goods, suitable for a pefcp. So far as the recipients are concerned (Welfare class), it is an increase in welfare benefits, earmarked for medical, hospital, etc. care. In the U. S., this begins late—i.e., for a Welfare State. "Medicare" and "Medicaid" are still quite limited in their application (generally to the old-age group and welfare beneficiaries). However, this is supplemented by such care for "Veterans."

If these programs are expanded to the "Poor" generally there would still appear to be no real violation of the laws of distribution, *if* the sources of the services are rapidly expanding. Services, to the extent contemplated are not ordinarily obtainable by these groups, nor would they be purchased. Nevertheless, the cost would be very high, especially if dental care, psychiatric care, other types of care including custodial care of a humane type, were added.

The principal problems with respect to the laws of distribution and use, arise if it is contemplated to extend such services to the general public—i.e., outside the welfare class *or,* even if limited to the Poor and old-age groups, the available services remain private and are not rapidly and effectively expanded to meet the greatly increased demand. A premise of all welfare payments, direct monetary, and those that may be earmarked for a particular service, is that the goods and services are actually available on the market at normal price. More generally stated (Ch. III), the premise is that the production is being carried on for the Government's effective demand. This will almost always be true with respect to welfare expenditures generally, but it is not true for hospital and medical services (probably housing also). The supply *must* be increased, and the Government must pay for the increase in supply. It is erroneous to increase benefits, when the benefits have the effect of raising prices for goods and services in short supply. Even at the present time, the situation in the U. S. is deplorable; if the programs are expanded to the fullest extent, the immediate consequence will be a marked violation of the laws of distribution and use. It is not proper to simply increase the income of vendors and suppliers without an equivalent increase in services produced. From the point of view of the political economy (aside from the social welfare aspect) this is not a proper use of the Pseudo Profit B.

If the great extension of hospital and medical services takes place, and the vendors and suppliers generally remain private, and the extension is associated with a partial pre-pay plan (social insurance), the extension to the general public should not be regarded as an indefensible violation of the laws of distribution. The public subsidy part must still be regarded as being for services that might not be produced, except for an extremely small group of the general population.

Statistical Note:

1971 Hospital Insurance for the Aged (Social Security) $4.7 bns.
Medical Insurance (Social Security) $1.7+ bns.
Public Assistance, hospital, medical (Included in Subsec. .1 above–$2.1+ bns.
Veterans Medical, Hospital care,–included in "Veterans benefits," $2 bns.

.9 Education. Supplement of State and local expenditure for schools. Grants for higher education, and Research.

In the Democratic State, public primary education, and later, public secondary education, were regarded as a necessary cost of the function of the economy, and of the State, and properly to be paid for through taxation. To a limited extent, higher education was also included. State and local taxes, and borrowing, still pays for by far the greater part of the cost, despite the Federal subsidy. (1972, elementary and secondary schools, total expenditure in excess of $54 bns., most raised by State and local Governments. Contrast: in the 1930's the total expenditure was less than $2 1/2 bns. annually).

The expansion of the population generally, the marked expansion of schooling for the Poor, low income groups, the Welfare class, especially secondary schooling and some type of higher education (and a general expansion of the average length of schooling) provide a feasible and proper mode of expenditure for distribution and use of goods, well within the laws of distribution. It is an expenditure that is rapidly expanding; operating costs, including teachers' salaries, are constantly increasing, and new facilities are required. The expenditure is not simply a substitution for the conventional State and local expenditure (the later has been enormously expanded). The Federal expenditure is for the most part an expenditure arising from the nature of the political economy and the WMS and is an expenditure for the distribution of the Pseudo Profit B. The number of children to be educated, the nature and time duration of the education, are now much beyond the needs of the dependent capitalist organism. The Federal supplementary expenditure can steadily be increased in the future, even while the State and local expenditures are increased, and will constitute a proper mode of distribution and use.

Expenditure by the Government for higher education is in part a proper mode of distribution of goods. To some extent it is required by the Military and Welfare systems themselves; it is doubtful if the expenditure is needed by the dependent capitalist organism. It can be expected that grants for higher education will increase, and higher education will be extended to a larger part of the population. Even if the individuals benefiting are not within the Military and Welfare classes, the expenditure does not significantly violate the laws of distribution and use.

The large sums now expended for a considerable part of "Research" should be regarded primarily as a mode of distribution and use, associated with the Military and Welfare systems. The volume of these grants will be maintained, or increased.

.10 "Social services" for the Poor, as a class (include most individuals in the existing welfare groups). Community programs and community services, special education and job traiinng, special work programs.

In recent years there has been some expenditure for the welfare class professedly with a somewhat different purpose than the subsistence basis of most of the programs noted above. The concept is of the Poor as a community within an affluent society. The ideology is to "eliminate the paradox of poverty in the midst of plenty in this Nation by opening to everyone the opportunity for education and training, the opportunity to work, and the opportunity to live in decency and dignity." There is some expenditure to furnish job training and jobs (including publicly created jobs, "made work" programs) for the young. The community is assisted to provide more education and housing, and in particular to make a more effective use of the existing welfare programs and grants. Legal counsel is provided to assist the community, and the individuals, both to enforce legal rights of the Poor, and to establish new rights for the Welfare class.

The actual scope of the programs is such that they are a minor addition to welfare expenditure. It is not likely that the expenditure will be increased in the future. Elements of the program seem to antagonize the other economic classes. While conforming to the general ideology of the Welfare State, the programs go somewhat beyond the actual nature of "Welfare" in this State—i.e., in general, subsistence for a Welfare class.

.11 Supplement (unrestricted as to use) of State and Local revenues, by the Federal Government.

A considerable part of Federal welfare expenditure—public assistance, health, education, etc.,—and expenditure for other purposes, is disbursed by grant to State and Local Governments. The grant is often made with some provision for a matching fund by the State or Local Government. (1969 Social Welfare grants to State and Local Governments by Federal Government, $13.8 bns. Grants for highways, $4.1+ bns.) Recently it has been determined that the Federal Government would make most Welfare payments directly. The Federal Government now also makes unrestricted grants to State and local governments, presumably to assist in meeting the general expenses of States and Cities. It is estimated that total Grants-in-Aid and shared revenues to state and local governments in 1972 will be $39 bns.

It has been pointed out that State and Local revenues pay a major part of the cost of Education, hospital, health costs, and substantial part of public assistance costs; indeed half of the total revenues of State and Local Governments is so expended. Where the unallocated or unrestricted Federal grant will go, as a practical matter, may be uncertain—possibly for general Governmental services, and salaries of public employees, or public works apart from schools, hospitals, etc. However, it is probably that in large part the unrestricted grants will in effect be a distribution and use within the laws of distribution and use, i.e., for the most part will be an added welfare expenditure.

The deterioration of the cities and the increase in the welfare class in the cities, have increased costs of local Government. "Revenue sharing" will probably shift money from richer States to poorer States, with the ultimate effect of increasing services and welfare services in the poorer sections. Even if the supplement is in part spent for general Governmental services (local), and it cannot be considered a welfare class expenditure directly, since all members of the local community benefit, it is close enough to come within the rules of distribution and use.

(3) Public Works. Early WMS, and in later periods.

.1 Public Works, of various types, and on a scale beyond the customary public Works of the State, can serve as a mode of utilization of goods, especially the goods produced by heavy industry. Public Works are of particular importance if there is no substantial Military Program parallelling the Welfare Program of distribution and use.

Certain public works are undertaken by the Democratic State, and the WMS, that are necessary or useful to the function of the capitalist organism, paricularly with respect to commerce and transportation. In part, they are also used by all the members of the society, generally, and in part, they are necessary for Governmental functions. Roads, docks, harbors, canals, tunnels, bridges, dams, flood control, waterways, some power installations, etc. can be regarded for the most part, as facilities for the production of material goods, and used in the production of other material goods by private producers. The construction of these facilities is undertaken by the State, rather than by private producers, because this is most feasible. Their cost (paid for by tax, or amortized loan) appears as a cost of goods privately produced, and in the price of the products (Ch. III). It is a cost of production of the organism as a whole. Undoubtedly, however, many of these public works serve individuals other than in their function as producers. Normally, this construction is not paid for out of the pseudo Profit B, either in the Democratic State or in the WMS. However, the WMS may deliberately set out to construct public works of this nature, i.e. useful for the productive system. even public works that produce goods, such as power generating systems, for the immediate purpose of maintaining "capital construction" that utilizes the production of heavy industry. There may be no economic justification or need for such construction, and indeed it may not only be an absolute surplusage for the organism, but duplicate existing construction and facilities. It is a "Capital expansion" that is only possible because the State is initiating it. This was characteristic of the early U. S. Welfare State, and in the absence of any significant military expenditure it seemed to be a necessary expenditure to balance the welfare expenditures. Apart from certain of the laws of distribution and use, it can reasonably be conceived (at that time) to be a distribution and use of the goods constituting the pseudo Profit B. (It is significant that at that time these public works were regarded as a mode of providing employment; there was little understanding of the real significance of this expenditure, beyond the immediate employment furnished.

While, as stated. such public works at the inception of the Welfare State (U.S.) did violate the rule with respect to capital use of the goods, a use which, if continued would have been harmful to the organism, it is to be noted that at the time the goods, for all practical purposes, were not going to be used in the production of other goods. The organism is functionning at a very low level. (It is difficult, in any event, to determine to what extent many of these public works will actually be used by the orgainsm in production, and to what extent they will be utilities for the general population—in particular highways, etc.)

In the later, fully developed pefcp, large-scale public works of this nature, i.e. highways etc. (not military or welfare public works) are undertaken which in part at least, should be regarded as a disposal of goods constituting the pseudo Profit B. These constructions are considerably beyond the actual needs and use of the organism. In the last two decades an immense system of interstate highways was undertaken at a cost in excess of $40 bns., which in greater part are for the general use of the consuming public. This may be a violation of the laws of distribution, but it is a permissable violation; the products are not for sale or produced for sale (insofar as they are to be regarded as beyond the needs of the productive organism).

Public Works for the Government's use, public buildings, offices, and great monumental structures etc., are characteristic of all States. This would seem to be a peculiarly suitable mode of expenditure and use for the WMS, but in the U. S. this does not seem to have been a mojor mode of expenditure.

The public works that are most characteristic of the WMS (apart from the great highway system) are still in the area of Military expenditure, and Welfare expenditure. Military and defense construction, atomic energy facilities, facilities for space and space technology, have been proceeding at a rate of about $2 bns. a year for many years. Construction, etc. for the Welfare programs have been less, but are currently increasing:—for health, education, housing, community development, for veterans, etc.

The construction of public power generating and distributing systems require some further comment. This is clearly a productive enterprise in which the Government is competing with private industry (unless the output is wholly utilized for military purposes, including the production of atomic weapons). However our main concern is not the propriety of such conduct by the Government: the principal problems are (a) the expansion of "capital" for such purpose and (b) the use of the pseudo Profit B for such purpose. Both are highly improper, particularly the latter, violating the most basic canons of distribution and use.

However in the early pefcp in the absence of an effective military program, some "capital" construction was essential to balance the welfare programs. It turned out that in the very high level of production that followed a full scale military program, and the great expansion of the welfare and military systems themselves, power production actually became inadequate. (Note that nearly 13% of the capacity of all utilities producing power is provided by Federal electric utility projects. What has been said with respect to power generation, can probably also be stated with respect to rural electrificaion and rural telephone projects, also important as expenditures for capital goods in the early pefcp.)

.2 Continued: Recent trends in Public Works in the WMS. Urban renewal, mass transportation, sewage and waste disposal, water supply.
The repair of the physical environment.
Necessity of an increase in civil public works to balance increase in welfare expenditures for individuals, if military expanditures do not increase.

In the last few decades the great increase in the welfare class in the cities, the decay of the cities as a place of residence and business, obsolete housing, inadequate mass transportation, automobile congestion, inadequate water supply, water and air pollution, etc., invite a massive expenditure by the Government, for repair and restoration of the city.

Furthermore it has become plain that the land, the lakes, rivers, water sources have become seriously damaged. The pressure for production in the pefcp itself, the technology necessary for this political economy, the type of goods produced, and the inexorable pressure of the expanding population (itself in part a consequence of the political economy), are destroying the physical environment. A system of public works, and a new technology, will be required to repair some of the damage, and reduce future damage. Such expenditure will be socially approved and it fulfills all laws of distribution and use. Indeed, this seems to be the most logical means of increasing "non-Welfare" expenditure, if military expenditure cannot be increased. Repairing some of the consequences of this economy, can be the means of maintaining it.

(4) The goods exported, and used outside the domestic economy. (Foreign assistance programs.)

A considerable volume of goods has been purchased by the Government and exported to foreign nations, or grants and credits have been given by the Government to foreign nations, specifically or in effect tied to the purchase of the domestically produced goods. The three principal programs in which this is done, are:

(a) Welfare. War devastated areas; natural disasters and famines; relief of poverty, in undeveloped areas, including expenditures for health, education.

(b) Military assistance. Aircraft, vehicles, weapons, equipment, munitions, military installations, supplies of all types; technical assistance.

(c) Development of resources, industries, transportation, power facilities (including rebuilding of war devastated economies. (Distinguish this last from private foreign investment.)

These programs are still in function. At times they have been of great importance as modes of distribution and use of goods.

The export of goods in these programs seems to be a complete removal of the goods from the domestic economy, and highly suitable. Nevertheless certain of the laws of distribution and use require further consideration, in connection with these programs.

The first problem with respect to the export of goods in any of the three modes listed above is Rule V: that the goods must be used in such a way that is socially acceptable or socially desirable.

"Welfare" and "Military" distribution and use are accepted and dynamic for *domestic* distribution and use, but it is doubtful if the ideology of the WMS covers "foreign" welfare. So far as "Welfare" is concerned, if benevolence were the dynamism, there may be two billion people in the world in dire need, without evoking more than some shiploads of supplies. There is little more animation in furnishing free armaments to prospective warring countries.

The true key to foreign Welfare and Military programs, and to the third mode of distribution (supplying foreign national economies with capital goods, developing foreign economies) is *anti-Communism*, a basic dynamic of the WMS. These programs are first undertaken (and in very significant dollar volume) to restore those national economies seriously damaged in WW II, and which required capital reconstruction, welfare assistance, and military assistance against possible Communist invasion or subversion. The Marshall Plan (1947), under which some $12 bns. were authorized in the following 3 year period "to halt the march of Communism" was the pattern for the great expenditure in foreign aid that followed. Aid to undeveloped nations, and the extension of military aid to all friendly nations was set up and pursued in all the post WWII years thereafter.

U. S. Government foreign grants and credits post WWII (1945-69) were over $121 bns. The programs continue at nearly $4 bns. a year. Military aid is estimated during this period (1945-1969) at over $39 bns; economic and technical aid at over $55 bns. Farm products disposal, including famine and other urgent relief, at over $7 bns. The greatest part of grants and credits involved the export of domestically produced goods.

With respect to the restoration or even expansion of industries, transportation and communication, of foreign economies, and the development of productive facilities in undeveloped nations: Certainly Rule I of the Laws of distribution and use (forbidding capital use of the goods, money) has to be considered, although prima facie the capital use is in a foreign economy and would not seem to affect the domestic economy.

In the first place, even if there is a violation, the anti-Communist dynamic, overrides any objection. It was deemed absolutely essential to maintain the European national economies as viable (dependent) capitalist organisms, to prevent either domestic Communist movements from becoming dominant, or a take-over by the Soviet Government. And it was deemed essential to maintain a dominant upper class or classes—capitalist, military, or Government class in effective control.

The foregoing applies, in part, also to foreign assistance to undeveloped national economies. Again, the dominant ideology is anti-communism, and the fear of Communist assumption of power in the undeveloped country. Military assistance and capital assistance programs predominate in foreign aid to these countries. The welfare programs are utilized as adjuncts of the other programs, and they are not really comparable to domestic welfare programs. However, the foreign health and education programs are of importance ideologically. At this point, however, the main concern is the distribution of goods outside the economy and not the techniques and complexities of foreign policy.

In the second place (with respect to the capital use of the goods as a violation of the laws of distribution and use) the violation is not as serious as appears. It is entirely possible that foreign competition and foreign production will be reestablished by the assistance programs (Germany-automobiles, etc. Japan—textiles and a variety of other goods). Nevertheless this has to be looked at in a wider context. The various national WMSs are not competitors as were the national economies of the Democratic States (ICE). Refer, on this point to the analysis in Ch. IV, on foreign, trade and foreign exchange of the WMS. All the national economies, in one way or another utilize the techniques of the WMS-pefcp, and they are capable of consuming their production without resort to the expansion of capital abroad, or acquiring colonial possessions for that purpose.

The subject of the export of goods constituting the pseudo Profit B, and Government grants and credits tied to the purchase of goods, has to be considered also in the context of foreign trade, foreign exchange of the pefcp. (Ch. IV, Sec. 5).

It was stated that it is an impropriety for the Government to use the money derived from the WM tax, borrowing and inflation (that will constitute the pseudo Profit B) to purchase goods abroad, or permit the money to be so used. The money *must* be tied to the purchase of domestic goods; that is to say, the money must be returned in the goods-money circuit to the capitalist producers. The expenditure of this money abroad may *also* injure the balance of foreign exchange of the political economy. The difficulty usually arises in military assistance programs, particularly where the U. S. is maintaining its own military forces abroad.

There is also another aspect of the relationship of export of goods paid for through the foreign assistance programs, and the equilibrium of the foreign trade and the foreign exchange, so necessary for a pefcp. (Ch. IV, Sec. 5). There may be a considerable degree of excessive private foreign investment and expenditure of other money abroad, wherein foreign goods are purchased. However, it *appears* that there is an equilibrium in the balance of trade because of the great excess of exports over imports. Nevertheless, most of these exports are not being paid for by foreign exchange, and there is no real foreign exchange equilibrium.

Finally, the question should be considered of private, even Government *sale* of goods abroad, at a cost lower than production cost, with the difference made up by Government subsidy. This may come about in several ways. It may be absolutely necessary to obtain foreign exchange. Or it may be desired to maintain the production of certain industries at a certain level, but there is no domestic marke at that level, and if prices are reduced, the industry may operate at a loss. Thus the Government purchases the excess production and dumps it abroad at any price it can get. (Domestic dumping will injure the market; it is a violation of the Laws of Distribution and use.)

Assuming that the Government's action is economically necessary, the present question is whether the money expended by the Government is a distribution and use of the goods (constituting the pseudo Profit B). It may be in part, but it is certainly not necessarily such distribution and use. It may be simply an additional actual cost of production for the organism as a whole (see Sec. 7, below, on subsidies, generally), or a shift of part of the Aggregate Profit from one group of producers to another.

(5) Military and para Military Programs of distribution and use of goods.

.1 The defense requirements of the WMS (in which an immense, technologically advanced military establishment and armament is constantly maintained) constitutes a distribution and use of goods that can always be at a high level, always consistent with the laws of distribution and use.

An army, navy, airforce, ballistic system, equipped with the weaponry and devices of an advanced technology, and a personnel of say three million (peacetime) must draw upon the production of every sector of the economy (and every geographic area) and in particular on the heavy "capital" goods industries, and those most technologically advanced. The intricate and costly mechanisms required, the trained personnel necessary to operate them, the worldwide great bases, the complex installations required, demand the efforts and production of an advanced, constantly developing productive organism.

The equipment itself obsolesces rapidly, even with non use. If it is put to use, the rate of destruction in use even in a Little war, is fantastically high. There is no real limit on the amount of munitions that cannot be destroyed in a 24 hour period regardless of the military significance of the destruction. None of these goods can be utilized to produce other goods; the personnel are not engaged in the production of other goods, none of the relationships of the domestic organism are interfered with in any way by the use of the goods.

Ballistic and anti ballistic systems, with atomic weaponry, can be expanded in peacetime at a cost of tens of billions of dollars. Increasing the overkill-overdestroy factor, permits a factor increase in cost.

Assuming 1965 can be regarded as a year of peace (no significantly active little war) U. S. Defense Department outlay was over $45 bns. in that year. During the succeeding years of the Indo China war, this escalated rapidly. About $25 bns, a year average can be added for the cost of this war, and the total Defense outlay rises even further.

While the Welfare programs cannot substitute for the fully developed Military program, since the goods produced by the heavy and highly developed, technologically advanced "capital" goods industries cannot be purchased in adequate volume as part of the pseudo Profit B, the military system can *almost* take the place of the Welfare programs (Exception—Rule VII requiring the minimum welfare program for the unemployed and unemployable). However, while consumption by military personnel can reach high levels, adequate in most countries, it is not an adequate system of distribution in the U. S. It was noted in Sec. (1) above, that in some countries the welfare program is minimal, and the Military Program, plus a considerable expenditure for the personnel of Government is sufficient to maintain the political economy, as well as the WMS.

.2 *War itself. "Little Wars."*

An actual war is not necessary to the WMS or to its military system of distribution and use. A Great War is a disaster for the WMS. Even if fought without the use of strategic atomic weapons, another Great War will probably destroy the WMS.

The Little War is generally to be avoided, unless it can be effectively restricted. Even a Little War is so great a consumer of goods, that it tends to upset the balance of the pefcp. It creates a boom, an excessive capital expansion, an excessive creation of private fictive capital papers and private inflation, "full employment"—a sequence which injures the economy. Direct economic controls are necessary (and sometimes not provided) but a successful control of a war economy is difficult. The rate of monetary depreciation is excessive, and after a certain point, when capital expansion must cease, a recession must set in, along with continuing depreciation of the paper money. For political reasons, it is difficult to increase taxes adequately.

It may be that the Little War is unavoidable—given the ideology of the WMS— for in one way or other the ideology may force the war. But to permit the expansion of a Little War is an economic error. It is, of course, hard to resist this expansion. In this connection, the importance of a Government stronger than the military class, or certain military-industrial combinations, is evident.

If the Little War is small enough it will raise the level of the economy without disturbing the general economic pattern. It may be noted that the sharp increase in Military expenditure for the South East Asia Military operations in the last half of the 1960's, resulted in the highest, sustained, long term prosperity of the U. S., with a "gross national product" approaching a trillion dollars. And at the same time, it permitted the highest level of welfare expenditure ever achieved. The cost of the war to June 1970 is estimated at $110 bns. and the ultimate cost is estimated at $352 bns. Of the latter, $220 bns. is estimated as future veteran's benefits, which is extremely important for future welfare system expenditure. Thus the economic benefits of a Little War for a pefcp cannot be considered as confined to the immediate costs, and the immediate multiple effect on the Level of Production.

Another recent Little War—the Korean War is estimated to have cost $54 bns. The cost of benefits for the veterans' class (important, at the present time, for the welfare system) is estimated at $99 bns.

.3 *Stockpiling and Storage*

Many products of mines, and certain agricultural products can be purchased by the Government to be placed in storage, for an indefinite period. Mineral products are "stockpiled" as part of a program of national defense. The agricultural products are usually acquired in connection with "price support" programs for agricultural products.

This would seem to be only a mode of temporary "dispositioon of goods." But even as such, it is of some importance. Some $7 bns. of goods are now held in storage.

Since, as a practical matter these goods overhang the market, the problem of their ultimate use has to be considered, even though there may be a certain volume always retained in storage. A certain part of the agricultural products will spoil in long storage; (and the cost of storage of these goods and the building of storage facilities is in itself not an insignifiicant mode of distribution and use).

The general rule is that the goods may not be returned to the market to compete with newly produced goods. (Laws of distribution and use, Sec. 1.) The goods can ultimately be disposed of only thru the Welfare and the Military programs, and hence stockpiling and storage should be regarded as adjuncts of the military and welfare systems. Welfare distribution is either domestic (Sec. 2 above) or in foreign assistance programs (Sec. 4). But disposition thru the military system almost certainly requires a "Little War." The expenditure then rises so sharply, that the goods can even be returned to the general market with safety, despite the prohibition in the laws of distribution and use. In the absence of the Little War, it would seem that the storage itself, must be regarded as a "use" of the goods.

.4 *Exploration of Space, Man on the Moon. Research to advance military technology, and Research, in general.*

Expenditure for Federal Space Programs in the period 1960-1070 was in excess of $55 bns., and continues at the rate of approximately $5 bns. annually. Such expenditure can easily be expanded substantially. A voyage to the moon is a fantastically costly venture. (If one program is to be singled out as an ideal program of expenditure for a WMS, it could be this one.)

The close connection of space programs to military programs of expenditure, and military technology, should not be overlooked. Training and experience in manufacture and use of space ships, satellites, and propellants, is invaluable to the military system. This becomes of importance in the serious question of social acceptability of Space, Moon, and Planetary explorations. (Rule V, laws of distribution and use.) It is unfortunate that expenditure of this nature is contrasted with the seemingly more socially desirable expenditure for welfare, since if the military programs cannot be maintained at a very high level (cessation of active Little War) it would seem essential that a para military program be pressed. The expenditure is not at the expense of the Welfare programs; it ultimately makes the large scale Welfare expenditure possible.

The space programs, as well as research and development in space technology are of particular importance, since they utilize the same production facilities, and the equipment is similar to that utilized in military programs. The industries and personnel involved are in the most technically advanced part of the organism. There is no violation of the laws of distribution, even though some industrial application may be made of the development and research.

Research per se, as a mode of distribution and use funded by the Federal Government, is not confined to military technology, or space technology. But the military system, and not the welfare system is the real impetus for research expenditure. The cost of research has become a very important mode of disposition of goods (consumer goods, technical equipment, training of personnel, etc.) The importance of the military system in enlarging this type of expenditure can be seen by the fact that in 1940 Federal expenditure for research and development was $73 mils; in 1967, $17 bns.

(6) The cost of the personnel of the Government of the WMS (viewed as a mode of distribution and use of goods).

The number of employees of the Government of the WMS, is far greater than that of the Democratic State. (1969 civilian Federal personnel, approx. 3 million; total payroll in excess of $25 bns. Contrast: 1929 personnel 579 thou., more than half in the post office.) A great part of the personnel of the Government of the WMS administer the Military and Welfare systems of distribution and use; they should properly be considered, along with their cost, as part of these programs of distribution and use. A considerable expenditure and consumption is represented by the administrative costs alone. (1969 Civilian Defense employees, over 1,341.00; Vet. Admin. 175,000; Dept. Health, Educ. Welfare 112,000. Add certain other smaller Departments, Atomic Energy, Housing, Space, Security and Intelligence Agencies; add a substantial percentage of the cost of other Departments furnishing services, facilities, etc. to other agencies.)

The Government of the WMS has certain management functions with respect to the dependent capitalist organism (which the Government of the Democratic State does no have). The cost of the additional personnel (although by no means comparable to the cost of the employees needed by the Military and Welfare Programs), is properly to be considered a cost of Government, paid for through the conventional tax, and not part of the pseudo Profit B.

In these WMS, pefcp, (as in the Democratic State), the personnel of the Government should not be regarded as a class of beneficiaries, receiving part of the goods produced (whether as part of the pseudo Profit B, or transfer of a share of the Profit A) by virtue of their political position. The income of the administrators of the Welfare and Military systems of distribution and use, should properly be attributed to these systems.

While Government employees are not a distributive class in the U. S. and most WMS's, certain WMS's do have an "elite" or an elite "party" which directly or as party acquire Government power. These constitute themselves as a distributive class, and may be so regarded, although generally a part of the Military group. The distribution to them often takes the place of the true Welfare distribution. (Sec. 1 above.)

(7) Certain payments by the Government to farmers, industrial producers. (While not a direct purchase of goods, or a distribution of money for purchase of goods for consumption, certain of these payments may constitute a distribution and use of the goods representing the pseudo Profit B.)

Subsidies have been given (Democratic State, and the WMS) for various reasons to private, capitalist producers. It may be desired to maintain an unprofitable industry because it is necessary for the national defense; the development of certain industries may be felt to be necessary for the function of the economy. A whole sector of the economy, which cannot maintain itself at a profit because it is completely unconcentrated (agriculture) in the midst of a highly concentrated economy could theoretically be subsidized.

In general, such subsidy is a transfer of part of the profit from all other sectors, or a cost of production collected by tax, on all other sectors. A government subsidy to capitalist producers (independent or dependent organism) is almost always economically improper and unsound in either organism, and should, for many reasons, be avoided. (It is ideologically unacceptable in the Democratic State; it is only to a lesser extent ideologically unacceptable in the WMS.) It distorts the fundamental relationships within the capitalist organism. If undertaken to any extent, an uneconomic cost of production is being added in the capitalist organism, often serious in the ICE, and only possibly less so in the pefcp. Except in rare cases, no specific capital should be maintained by subsidy, nor should an industry or sector of the economy be so maintained. If, because of disparate degree of concentration or certain other factors, the price power of an industry or sectors becomes inadequate, other steps should be taken to maintain price and reduce production. Payments made in connection therewith should be of such nature that they are not a subsidy transferring part of the profit from other sectors, unless this is absolutely essential to the organism as a whole.

It may be argued that in the pefcp the subsidy to farmers or to industry is in effect a distribution and use of the goods (constituting the pseudo Profit B), if the subsidy payment can be shown to be expended (by the capitalists) for these goods to maintain the uneconomic production. But this is hard to show, for the money may not find its way to the market at all, but be dissipated in various charges and costs. This is especially true if the money is given to an insolvent company to maintain its existence. Subsidies given to *small* farmers not to produce, comparable to a welfare payment, are a true distribution and use of the goods. Such payments to large farmers and corporate farmers definitely are not.

CHAPTER VI

THE WELFARE-MILITARY STATE AND GOVERNMENT

(1) Recapitulation, and Preface to Part I and Part II of this Chapter:

The political economy (State as political economy) exists and functions because of the inherent powers of State and Government. These powers are the means of creating the essential elements of the new economic relationship (the fictive forms, their mechanisms, the distributive systems, etc.)

The nature of this State as polity and the constitution of its Government, must be examined. However, it is not possible to separate State as political economy and State as Polity.

It will be seen that this State and Government are new political-economic forms. The appearances of this State, and its ideology (the latter being fundamental to the existence and function of the State), reveal only in small part, its actual nature, its dynamic, and its actual constitution.

To examine "structure" "ideology" "dynamics" and actual nature of the political relationship, requires an explanation of the nature of social structure, the nature and significance of socially prevailing ideas (ideology), and the interrelationships of all social relationships and their ideologies. The procedure in this chapter is first to examine generally social structure and social change (Part I); in Part II the analysis is applied to the WMS-pefcp.

The "Democratic State," the predecessor State to the WMS, is also examined in Part I. This State differs markedly from the WMS in actual relationship, being a political relationship separate from the economic relationship. The constitution of State and Government differs from the WMS. There is a substantial difference in the ideology of the WMS and the Democratic State although part of the ideology of the Democratic State is found in certain of the WMS's.

Part I

Social Structure and Social Change
The "Democratic State"

(2) The Social Structure. (Relationships, Ideologies. The basic laws of social structure; the natural selection of elements of certain relationships, and of ideas.)

.1 —The actual relationships among the individuals of a society.
—The ideologies—ideas descriptive and imperative, prevailing among the individuals of the society.

In a modern society there are

(a) Four basic relationships among the individuals of the society—

—the economic relationship
—the political relationship
—the "family" relationship
—the "Church" relationship

and

(b) A pattern of ideas that prevails socially, believed and accepted by the members of the society, descriptive and imperative, with respect to each of these relationships. The ideology of the society also includes certain other ideas.

All of the first three basic relationships are a necessary part of the social structure; each relationship depends on the other; none is superstructure. Ideology is a necessary part of each relationship; the relationship and society generally, could not exist without the ideologies; ideologies are not a superstructure on the actual relationships, but express and embody the social relationships for individual man and move man to act in accordance with the requirements of the actual relationship.

The foregoing refers to relationships, and ideology generally. Each relationship will have, at a given time, a *particular* form and nature, and the ideology of each at a given time, will have a *particular* form and content.

The *economic relationship*

is that existing among the members of the society, in which material goods are produced and distributed. Individuals may relate to each other in the production and distribution of material goods in several ways, i.e., there are several different particular economic relationships. The particular economic relationships described in this book are the capitalist relationship (in the ICE, as an independent organism), and the political economy of fictive capital and profit.

The *political relationship* (State and Government), in general form:

The association of all the individuals in a territorial area with a relatively self-sufficient economy, who are under the power and dominion of certain members of the State—the Government; the Government compelling certain conduct by each member of the State towards each other and towards the Government.
(a) The power entity—the Government, is the essence of the State.
(b) The idea of those who possess the power that they are the power entity and have power and dominion over all members of the State to compel, etc., *and* the idea of submission to and acquiescence in a power entity, that the members of the State have, is the basis of State and Government, and is the basis of the actual, real, physical power possessed by the Government to compel, etc. Military organization is inherent in the State; its members acting under direction of the Government. (The essential element of any political *ideology*, is the idea of the power entity, and the necessity for its existence.)
(c) A fundamental aspect of the political relationship, and the primary area of conduct enforced by the Government, is in the maintenance of the economic relationship. However, there

are necessarily other areas of conduct enforced, and other activities of Government.*

(d) The actual relationships existing in a particular State and Government cannot be known unless the true nature of the existing economic relationship is known. The characterization "democratic" or "monarchic," etc., is inadequate to describe the *actual* structure of Government. The political ideology stating who has the power and dominion does not state who has the *actual* power and dominion, the number that exercise it, how they acquire or succeed to it, the actual scope of the power exercised. Particular States and Governments can be markedly different from others in actual relationship although the apparent form is the same. State and Government, or the particular forms that they take, are not planned constructions of man as a reasoning being. A Government is not constituted to enable each man to have a better life, to control the "passions" of man, etc.

The two particular States and Governments discussed herein are: the "Democratic State" and Government, a modality that existed during the ICE, the WMS, which is itself a political economy and a polity.

* Summary of the areas of conduct enforced, and activities and powers of Government:

a. The maintenance of the economy, and of the existing economic relationships of the individuals in the economy.

b. Maintenance of the State and Government; maintenance of the power of the particular incumbents of Government office.

c. Conduct of the political economy of the State (to obtain the revenues necessary for functions and activities of Government, per se, as stated in this summary): levy taxes, borrow money, coin money, print paper money.

d. Defense, War. Protection of territory, of the members of State, the economy. Expansion of economy, and territory, by conquest.

e. Performance of certain economic activities directly, necessary and useful for the productive economy, for the members of the State, or necessary for its own existence (roads, harbors, the post, etc.). Establishes standards of weights and measures, etc.

f. Maintenance of the prevailing ideologies of the society.

g. Maintenance of certain other relationships among the individuals of the society that may be necessary for the economy, or the society: "family," "Church."

h. Protection of individuals against assault, homicide; protection of personal property.

"Family" relationship:

The term is used herein in a wider sense than the word "family" now indicates: it encompasses the relationships of the individuals in the society in the reproduction of children, the maintenance and education of children for their place in the particular economic and political relationships; the particular type of family unit existing, the economy of the family. "Moral" ideology relating to the sexual relationships is of major importance in this relationship. A part of the moral ideology may be part of the religious ideology. Particular forms of the family relationship, and particular moral ideologies, exist in different social structures. This relationship, the ideology thereof, are not discussed in this book. The existence of a particular form of this relationship, and ideology, is always assumed; it is the basis for the creation of the human personality; it is the agency of communicating and teaching most socially prevailing ideas.

"Church" relationship:

The fourth relationship existing in a society (not an essential relationship to maintain a WMS-pefcp) is the "Church" relationship. It is an association of individuals professing a specific religious ideology, (a) wherein there is at least a certain minimum of control over the formulation, teaching and use of the doctrine, and over the membership of the Church, (b) that is possessed by certain members of the Church. However, the latter may have great power and dominion over the lay members of the Church and over doctrine, and constitute a power entity, often directly or indirectly associated with the economic and political power entities.

Ideology is of paramount importance in this relationship (i.e. religious ideology is of greater importance to the relationship than economic ideology is to the economic relationship). Religious ideology exists in all societies; a "Church" relationship is usually found in all societies, although a prevailing religious ideology can exist without a "Church" relationship. However, in such instance, the religious ideology will be a part of the economic-political-family relationships, and may be necessary therefore. (Caution: The subject under discussion is the socially prevailing pattern of ideas, and the specific "Church" relationship; not individual or private religious experience,or the specific teachings of Divine Persons or Prophets. Refer to subsec. .5 below, further on "Church" relationship and socially prevailing religious ideology. The main subjects discussed in this book are the economic and political relationships, and socially prevailing economic and political ideas. The three following subsections are concerned principally with these relationships and ideologies. However, while "Church" relationship and prevailing religious ideology do fall within the general laws stated in the following subsections (and indeed "Church" may be a relationship essential to the economic and political structure), at first sight, the laws stated in the following subsections do no seem entirely applicable, for certain reasons set forth in subsec. .5

Ideology—preliminary definition.

As used herein, the term refers to the body of ideas that can be said to be socially prevailing at a given time; principally concerning the nature of the four social relationships of the society. These ideas are descriptive and imperative, and include beliefs, myths, outlooks, aesthetic images, creeds, rituals.

"Socially prevailing" does not mean that all members of the society have all the ideas. Each individual may possess a fragment of the total; many ideas may be inchoate or in the unconscious of individuals, but they will be assented to if stated. Furthermore, there are at least two levels of ideology (subsec. .2) and a social class may have a pattern of ideas apparently inconsistent with those of another class, yet the *whole* is the socially prevailing ideology. There are also aberrant ideas; vestigial ideas from older social structures; new ideas coming into social being that may serve to revolutionize the existing social structure.

Almost all socially prevailing ideas are inadequate ideas, and do not describe the relationships as they exist in actuality.

The term "ideology" is used herein for the body of social ideas, because, as appears in subsec. 3, and subsec. .4, this body of ideas is not a fortuitous concourse of ideas and modalities. It is a coherent, interconnected pattern, wherein the social prevalence of each idea, and the relationship of each idea to the other and to the whole pattern, and to all relationships, is explicable pursuant to the laws of social structure and natural selection. However, this can only be seen when the whole structure of actual social relationships is known. It can then be seen also, that although the ideas are false or inadequate in themselves, they are a necessary part of a whole pattern, and necessary to the whole social structure, and the ideas exist by the same necessity as an adequate or true idea, or the actual relationships themselves.

The usage of "ideology" herein differs from other common usages, particularly the usage that refers to a specific, highly systematized and integrated body of thought of intellectual content with respect to society. In the usage herein, ideologies in the latter meaning may be parts of the whole socially prevailing pattern of ideas, and may be necessary to the function of the actual relationship. (They may be private systems, not part of the ideology of the society.)

.2 —*The true nature of any particular relationship is not known to the members of the society. The members of the society believe an ideology that describes the relationship (socially prevailing ideas of the nature of the relationship).*

—*The ideology, as description, is either false or inadequate to describe the actually existing relationship.*

—*But nevertheless,, ideologies are essential to the existence of the particular relationships, and to society.*

—*The particular ideology is always congruent with and useful for the actual relationship, supports it, and may be a functional part of the particular relationship.*

—*Ideologies must be viewed as phenomena of the social relationships, explicable through the social relationship.*

The members of the society do not need to know the true nature of the relationships in which they live and act in order for the relationships and the society to function, any more than a person needs to know the laws of biology and physiology to live and function. (It is possible that the ICE and the pefcp would not function well if the nature of the actual relationships were socially known.)*

However, man thinks, and he must have a body of ideas acceptable to him and believed by him, that seem to describe and explain his relationships in society, his conduct therein, and stating what is required of him in society. These ideas are descriptive and imperative. As a thinking thing, man's ideas are the basis of his actions; a particular idea moves man to act in a particular way. Many, or even most socially prevailing ideas are emotions. In a particular form of society (as constituted by the several particular relationships) these ideas must have a certain specific content and form. For society and social structure in general, or a social structure of a particular type, man must act affirmatively in a way that maintains the given social structure. Social man is thus a participant or actor in a society where a certain pattern of ideas prevails. In practice, man passively adopts the socially prevailing pattern of ideas (he is taught them; they are enforced). Social man does not ordinarily create these ideas. He cannot ordinarily know if they are true or false.

In summary, a body of specific ideas is necessary for a society and for a particular social structure and particular pattern of relationships; the body of social ideas must have a particular content and form. If the ideas are adequate for proper conduct in the several relationships, this is all that is necessary (knowledge of the actual relationships unnecessary). Ideas, and the ideological pattern socially prevailing are the primary motive force for particular conduct of social man in the particular relationship.

However: The ideas socially prevailing (with respect to the nature of the social relationships), are always inadequate to explain or describe the actual relationships, and are usually completely false or so incomplete and partial as to be essentially false. This can be seen only when the relationships, economic, political, etc., have been discovered and stated. The statement

* The *managers* of a pefcp should know the true nature of the political economy. This complex economy cannot function well unless it is carefully managed. The managers should not be guided only by the ideology of the WMS.

of the actual relationship is the first, the primary task of the scientist.

It is difficult to discover the nature of the actual relationship. There is one relationship that must *first* be discovered and stated: this is the economic relationship. It is the key to disclosing the true nature of the other relationships. Unless this sequence is followed, the true nature of the other relationships cannot be known. The reason for this will be seen in the basic law of social structure, and of natural selection, etc. (subsecs. .3 and .4, following).

When all the relationships are stated as they actually exist, and all ideologies stated (this itself having its own difficulties), it will then also be seen that the ideology is logically related to the actual relationship. And since each relationship is congruent with and supportive of each other, all ideology is interconnected, and congruent. (Again, this anticipates the discussion in subsecs. .3 and .4, following.)

Ideology itself, because of its nature, is a major source of difficulty in discovering the actual relationship. Ideology is deceptive as well as false. It is extremely difficult to penetrate a good ideology, especially an upper class ideology. Ideology at the lower class level, usually has a greater emotional content rather than logical complexity, but this too tends to prevent the discovery of the actual relationship, and the role the ideas and the emotions play in the actual relationship.*

* An effective ideology is a believable ideology. It does not have to be logically consistent or demonstrable. The good ideology tends to express or use universal elements in human personality or universal experience in inter-personal relationships. Furthermore, a good ideology will ordinarily utilize the *appearance* of things. What appears to be true and reasonable to the individual, i.e., simple common sense, although it is false in the whole social context, is characteristic of good ideology. Certain ideologies may consist of complex patterns of thought. They appear completely logical, only a few concealed premises containing the false or inadequate concepts.

A useful rule, in seeking the nature of the actual relationship, is that a social relationship is never what it appears to be (i.e., as it may be described in an ideology).

Further, with respect to ideology, and the appearance of things: At one time ideology was a major difficulty in the effort to discover the actual

The falsity or inadequacy of ideas that describe the actual relationships is probably inherent in the nature of ideology as phenomena of the society. What is required in ideology is utility and power. True ideas of the nature of the relationships have no social utility or power. Socially prevailing ideas are not overthrown by true ideas but by other, more useful, congruent ideas, of the same or a lesser degree of "truth." (A new economic relationship rising to power will require a new ideology, and part of such an ideology will include an attack on existing ideologies, as false.)

Certain ideas are knowingly created as false ideas; facts may be deliberately misstated to support or maintain an economic, political, or religious power entity. Most socially prevailing ideas are not so created. A deliberately created false idea must be treated, in the social process, as any other idea of the general ideology.

Ideology as phenomena of the actual social relationship.

To recapitulate: First: the ideology is false or wholly inadequate to describe the actual relationships; second: the ideology is necessarily logically connected with the actual relationship, and the ideas have a content and form that are useful to the actual relationship. The ideas exist (socially) by the same necessity as the actual relationship, and by the same necessity as true ideas. Socially prevailing ideas are completely explicable through the actual relationship. The ideas do not prevail socially by accident, or because they are "true," nor are socially prevailing ideas false because of human inability to arrive at truth. Mundus vult decipi. The ideas will be of a nature that is

---

nature of the physical universe. The ideology stated a believable appearance of things. The ideology was enforced (the ideology was a part of the ideas necessary for Church structure and religious doctrine). However, the difficulty presented by such ideology in seeking to discover the nature of the universe, is not comparable to the role of ideology in the discovery of the nature of social relationships. Ideology is not a necessary part of a system of natural science; but it is a necessary part of a society and social relationships. In the latter, ideology plays a more powerful role in resisting the discovery of the actual relationships.

congruent with the actual relationship; usually *supportive* of the actual relationship, and sometimes *necessary* to the particular relationship (i.e., functionally necessary to the mechanism or structure of the actual relationship). The foregoing, again, requires the analysis of the basic law of social structure and the law of the natural selection of elements of relationships, and particular ideas.—.3 and .4 following.

That socially prevailing ideas are to be examined as phenomena, is itself a concept contrary to the ideology. Further, the concept that it is the economic relationship that is the ultimate basis for explaining the congruence, natural selection of socially prevailing ideas, is contrary to ideology. Corollary: the basic law of social structure and the law of natural selection, in .3 and .4 following are ideologically unacceptable to the society.

The two levels of ideology:

There are at least two levels of ideological patterns: in general, that of the lower economic class, and that of an upper class.* Many of the ideas, attitudes, outlooks, at the upper class level are markedly different from lower class ideas, even when referring to the same relationship, rule of conduct, etc. Upper class ideology is more sophisticated and is usually more logically organized. It may reject lower class ideas (although these are recognized to be socially necessary) and it may appear to be contradictory. But the ideas at both levels are the ideology of the society; everything stated in this subsection with respect to the nature of ideology is applicable to each level. Both levels will be congruent, supportive, and possibly functionally necessary to the relationship; both levels have to be examined as phenomena of the actual relationships. The ideology of an upper class is as important to a society as the ideology of the lower class.

* It is possible to have only one level of ideology. When there is simple, personally directed slave labor, without the necessity of a family organization for the slave (i.e., family relationship to reproduce a lower class) there need not be a lower class level of ideology.

The fact that ideology is formulated and taught on two levels is one of the reasons for the need of professional ideologists. The ideology on each level must be reconciled and co-ordinated with the other; contradictions ideologically explained; and both levels constantly updated. The professional ideologist must also co-ordinate the ideologies of the several relationships. There may be highly technical ideologies also, theological, philosophical, political, economic, that have to be co-ordinated. (Moral ideas, especially, are difficult to reconcile with the actual customs of the society. Stated as absolute rules, they may, in the first place, be much different than the actually prevailing custom of either class. Yet they must also be applied differently, in practice, for different social purposes. The moral ideas may not be untrue in themselves, but in the way they are used in the whole social context, they may be false or inadequate. Refer to subsec. .5, below, on the transvaluation of true ideas in a religious ideology).

.3 *The basic law of social structure:*
The particular political relationship, and the particular forms of other relationships in the society (actual relationships, not as described by their ideology) will be such that they are congruent and consistent with the existing economic relationship, and serve to support and maintain it, and the ideology of each relationship will be congruent with and support that relationship, and all relationships and ideologies, prevailing in a society will be consistent with and congruent with each other, and will serve to support and maintain the economic relationship.

Prefatory:
(a) It must be assumed that prior questions have been answered: what determines the form of the particular economic relationship that is in existence; and why has this particular economic relationship prevailed socially as against a prior one? (Sec. 3 on social Change, subsec. .2)

(b) It is the economic *relationship* that is referred to, not *individual economic motivation.* Economic motivation exists in *all* forms of economic relationships, and in all societies, but the structure of the *particular* economic relationship can be markedly different from another (and all congruent and supporting social relationships, and ideologies, will be markedly different too), despite the same "economic motivation" operating; economic motivation is not the cause of the *particular* economic relationship. Economic motivation of individuals is the significant factor in making the economic relationship the primary and dynamic one of all relationships; there is a powerful economic motivation to be a member of the upper economic class of a *particular* economic relationship.

(c) The basic law does not mean that the economic relationship *creates* the other relationships, or creates the particular form that they will achieve, or creates the particular ideologies that will prevail. Particular forms, particular ideologies are created through other dynamics. The elements of relationships, and the ideas created or in existence are *selected, shaped,* etc. into a congruent social structure. (subsec. .4, following). Nor are these other relationships, ideologies, etc. the result of individual economic motivations. (They have dynamics other than economic.)

(d) The fact that the nature of the actual economic relationship is socially unknown is not material to the function of the basic law:—The elements of other social relationships and the content of all ideologies are naturally selected—.4 following. Although the nature of the political relationship and other relationships are not socially known, their actual form and nature will be congruent and support the economic relationship.

The basic law of social structure can be deduced from observation, if the actual economic relationship, and all other relationships of the society are set forth, and their ideologies. That is to say it will be seen that all relationships support and maintain the economic relationships; all ideologies are congruent with, and supportive of each relationship, and the economic relationship. More generally: the reason for the law is that the economic relationship is the primary and dominant one of a society.

The *need* and the *desire* for material goods by every member of the society is the primary and dominant force operating in the society. It is the overridingly powerful individual drive. This need and desire must be satisfied in a *social relationship* in production and distribution of material goods (the economic relationship of the society).

But although the need and desire for material goods by *everyone* in the society is primary and dynamic, it would be unrealistic not to recognize that the desires and need of the *upper economic class* in the particular economic relationship, is more significant than the *general* need and desire for material goods, in the dynamism that the economic relationships exert over all other relationships, and over all ideology. That is to say, the maintenance of the flow of material goods to the upper economic class (in the *particular* economic relationship) is a primary aspect of the dynamics of the particular *economic relationship*. The maintenance of this economic pattern will be of supreme importance to the members of the upper economic class. The other relationships must be of such particular form and all the ideologies must have such particular content that they will maintain this particular economic pattern, in which this particular upper economic class exists. The individual economic motivation to maintain the specific particular upper class relationship, is *functionally*, the most powerful economic motivation of the society.*

Invariably then (a) the other relationships in the society will have an upper class structure, and the power entities will be found to be in alliance with, or an identity with the upper economic class of the existing economic relationship; and (b) the ideology of the society, in general, and including the political and religious ideology in particular, will be of such nature to

* "Economic class" in an economic relationship, generally (not only in the capitalist relationship): Certain individuals, singly or collectively, have such power over other individuals directly, or over land, or instruments of material production, that part of the material goods produced by the direct physical labor (of the lower economic class) flow as income to the members of the upper economic class, individually or collectively, without the members of the upper economic class engaging in the process of material production directly.

maintain, assure, reinforce an upper class dominance. With respect to the latter, it will be noted that political and religious ideology conceals the dominance of the upper class economic relationship in the society and its controlling power, as well as the supreme importance of the economic relationship per se, and the class structure of the economic relationship.

In brief, while the need and desire for material goods, operates on all member of the society, in reality that need and desire of the lower economic class has less significance than the demands of the upper economic class, in assuring the congruence of all relationships, and ideologies. The motive and desire of the upper economic class to maintain its position and to maintain the adjuvant relationships and ideologies that are necessary for the economic relationship and their position in that relationship, will be found to be the powerful social force. This is the true significance of individual economic motivation in a *given economic relationship*, but, to repeat, it is the form and nature of the economic *relationship* that is the basis for the selection of structures, ideologies, etc. (Below, on Natural Selection, etc.)

.4 A. *The Natural Selection*

—of the *elements* that will ultimately constitute an effecive, supporting political relationship (State, Government), "Church," and "Family" relationships (i.e. necessary for the dominant, existing economic relationship);

—of ideas, etc. that will socially prevail with respect to each of these relationships, that will create an ideology that is congruent with these relationships and hence is congruent with and will support the economic relationship.

—of elements, relationships, ideas and ideologies that will form a consistent pattern as a whole, congruent with an supporting the economic relationship.

B. The *pragmatic test* (in the choice of *elements* of relationships and the ultimate relationship as a whole; in the choice of ideas, etc. for each, and the ideology of the relationship and of the society as a whole), is *utility* in the function of the economic relationship, and the effectiveness of its function.

C. The existing economic relationship exerts a positive and dynamic force that will *maintain* a congruent, supporting pattern of relationships and ideologies, useful and necessary for it. This is true even though the true nature of the economic relationship is not socially known, nor the nature of the other relationships, nor the actual role of the ideas selected for the whole structure.

D. The upper economic class of the existing economic relationship has a dominant role in the dynamics of the economic relationship, in selection and maintenance, etc.; again, this is true even though the nature of the relationships, ideologies, the social structure as a whole is not socially known.

Although the true nature of the relationships (and particularly that of the dominant and dynamic economic relationship) are not socially known, the members of the society proceed to construct the whole, with the essential ideologies, without any "master plan"—the latter term being used in the sense of conscious construction of the society and its relationships. This does not mean that some unseen mystical or meta-social force operates in the formation of the social structure, and in the selection of the elements and ideas that will prevail socially.

The elements that will constitute the relationship, and likewise the ideas that will constitute the ideology of the society, are selected *if they work* within the framework of the *actual* economic relationship as it actually functions, and if they support (or are functionally necessary to this economic relationship). The *elements* are selected and fitted into a whole, and if the whole is then workable, the elements continue. An unworkable element is discarded, and a new one substituted. There may be a process of trial and error, or chance. The end result is a synthesis, usually of elements formulated by many individuals who do not know the ultimate use of their creations. The whole is not conceived as it will be by any *one* contributor of a part. *But the result in function* (of element, of idea) is socially perceived. There is a constant pragmatic test of elements and ideas (and of particular relationships as a whole, as to the form necessary for the economic relationship). *Utility, Power,* are the tests of natural selection; it is an illusion that truth has any dynamic force in the formulation of an ideology.* The process of natural selection in which the ultimate structure and the ideology of the society are formed, is centripetal. The particular social structure is formed out of a great mass of ideas, most usually not new, and tentative relationships actually existing or being formulated, elements of old relationships, new inventions.

(In this connection, it should be repeated that the creation of ideas and ideologies themselves, and elements of certain structures, have their own dynamics, which may not be at all economic. They have to be themselves first created, and have a vitality, before the social shaping process uses them. It is in this social shaping process that the economic relationship exerts its power. The dynamism of this economic relationship, with respect to other relationships and ideologies, is only a selective force, or a force maintaining the practicable and useful and necessary parts of the structure. But note, again, that whatever the original dynamic of an idea, or element, the social use to which it is put may be quite the opposite of that contemplated in its original creation. The ideas an individual newly formulates may be true, but they are socially used to create structures and ideologies unknown to the creator, and will not be true ideas in the social structure.)

In the creation of the particular relationship and ideology, man believes he acts out of consciousness and free will. But the idea of freedom is man's ignorance of the cause of his action; the idea of conscious creation of actual relationships, and ideologies, is due to ignorance of their true nature. "Social man" is not a free man in the society in which he lives and which he creates. In any established economic relationship, political relationship, Church relationship, social man thinks and acts in accordance with the established relationship and ideology. (Refer to Ch. II, on capitalist economic relationship, wherein it is shown that man believes he is free economic man, but he is governed by the function of the capitalist organism.)

* The Natural Selection of the useful idea means also the natural selection of order and emphasis of ideas in a body of ideas. Order and emphasis may totally change an ideology, even though the same elements are used. Subsec. .5, following.

The relationships and forces in which social man acts are not unknowable; they are unknown to him. They can be discovered by the scientist. But it is probable that only an existing or past society can be understood and described through the laws of social structure. The future form of a society, or the nature of a social structure that may come into being, cannot be predicted, except possibly, negatively. Chance plays a part in social change; the laws of social change are indeterminate. (Sec. 3, following.) Only the laws of an existing or past social structure and ideology are determinate.

Ancillary to the laws of Natural Selection:

State, Church, and Family, teach the prevailing ideology to the young, acquiescence therein, and fear to dissent from prevailing ideas. The family is the principal teaching institution. Refer to "C" in headnote, to the effect that here is always a positive, dynamic force that will maintain a congruent, supportive ideology. Teaching is an essential mechanism of the society. Refer, elsewhere, to direct enforcement of belief, by Government, Church; the use of direct and indirect sanctions.

.5 Amplification on "Church" relationship and socially prevailing religious ideas (ideology).

It was stated in subsec. .1 that at first sight, the general principles set forth in subsecs. .2, .3, .4, (inadequacy or falsity of socially prevailing ideas; their necessity nonetheless for the existence of the prevailing social relationships; the laws of congruence of ideology, etc., with the prevailing economic relationship, the natural selection of ideas, etc.) do not apply to religious ideology and the "Church" relationship. True ideas of God and teachings of Divine Persons seem often to be contained in a socially prevailing ideology, or the "Church" itself claims to be founded by the Divine Person or Prophet and embody His teachings. Furthermore, in apparent contradiction to the general laws, a religious ideology or a Church itself may seem to be the same in different economies and polities. Finally, a religious ideology or most of its elements might be considered as universal phenomena of human personality, rather than of the existing social relationships.

Religious ideas (of God, His nature, man's being and conduct; the universe, the society and the Godhead; rituals, sacraments) exist in all societies, in primitive form or as the fully achieved ethical monotheism or monism. They are inherent in man. But at any one time a socially prevailing pattern of religious ideas will be found. There is usually a "Church" relationship, and the prevailing religious ideology is usually formulated within this relationship.

However, the specific "Church" socially prevailing, and the socially prevailing religious ideology will be found to be congruent, or may be necessary to a particular economic-political relationship. The law of natural selection does apply. The true ideas of God that may be present, are transvalued in the prevailing ideology, and particularly by a socially powerful Church, into modalities that make the ideology and the Church a support of the existing social order—the particular economic and political relationships. The true ideas become forms or pretences; they are not experienced or understood as true ideas. The true ideas can be manipulated in the social process as easily as false ideas. The teaching of the Divine Person can be used to maintain a particular social structure. This may even be a structure thoroughly alien to the teaching. It is probable that the actual social relationship could not exist if these teachings were the real essence of the prevailing Church relationship or the prevailing religious ideology.

With respect to the seeming continuance of the same Church and the same ideology in different political and economic structures: By certain processes the same religion (apparently) or the same Church and religious ideology can become a markedly different one. The techniques of the transforming processes are beyond the scope of this book. The change in order, selection, emphasis, and actual use of an element of the whole ideology, can create a markedly different ideology, or Church relationship. That is, if there are five elements represented by digits 1 2 3 4 5, a sequence and emphasis of 12,345, will mean something much different than 54,321. The addition or deletion of one element can radically transform the whole, create in effect, a different religion, although all the other elements seem the same. (Refer to Note at end of Sec. (4) discussing the separation of Church, State, Economy, in the Democratic State—ICE. A Christian religion becomes quite a different religion by the addition or deletion of the idea that the godhead is represented by some power entity on earth.) The significant change in a religion might not be apparent, but can be seen through the use of the law of social structure and the law of natural selection.

It has been noted that religious ideology may also be examined as a phenomena of human personality. (It is usually formulated in terms of universal human relationships and needs—father mother, child; food, sexuality, the sources of human existence; dependency, fear, guilt, etc.) The elements in the formulation of the ideology may remain constant in different economic and political structures. But again, a particular religious ideology cannot be viewed simply as a phenomena of human personality: it will be nonetheless a phenomena of the *particular* social relationships. That is to say, it will be seen that although the elements may be the same, nevertheless the same processes (change of order, emphasis, addition or deletion of a simple element, etc.) that transform a Church and a religious ideology into a new form congruent etc. with the prevailing social structure, will be at work, and the ideology, as a social form, is actually a different one. Nevertheless—whatever the social use of the ideology—the basic ideas and the rituals, and the symbols will remain personally meaningful and necessary to the individual. (Some of these ideas, myths, rituals, are the product of great genius or spontaneous group creation, and have a power, depth, perception and imagery far beyond any individual's power to create for himself.)

In summary: The socially prevailing religious ideology, and "Church" relationship must be examined as phenomena of a particular economic and political relationship, in accordance with the laws of congruence, natural selectioon, etc., (a) even thought the ideology may seem to contain true ideas of God; the true ideas are transvalued into socially useful forms; (b) even thought the ideology, "Church" is seemingly the same in different social structures; (c) even though the elements of an ideology constantly re-appear in ideologies.

(Note: the discussion has been of social structure. In social change (Sec. 3) where ideology plays a more dynamic role, religious ideology, and true religious ideas, have a greater importance, in effecting a change in the social structure.)

(3) Social Change. The dynamics and process of Change of the Whole Social Structure.

.1 The Basic Laws of Social Change:

I. The whole social pattern (economic relationship, political relationship, "family" relationship, "Church" relationship) and the whole ideology of the society, will change if the economic relationship changes; and conversely, the society will not basically change if the economic relationship does not change. (There may be an appearance of change; there may be minor change resulting from the slow decline of surviving old forms, or because of quantitative change in the same economic relationship.) This general law is a corollary of the basic law of social structure, and the natural selection of elements, ideas, etc.

II. A *new* economic relationship *may* become the prevailing economic relationship (displacing the existing economic relationship, or succeeding it, if (and because) it is *more productive of material goods* than the existing economic relationship, or rival economic relationships. But it is not *general productivity* alone that constitutes its dynamism: economic relationships almost invariably have an economic class structure (of a type wherein there is a power possessed by the upper economic class to obtain part of the current material production because of individual or group ownership of some property form) and it is much more important that the new economic relationship would result in a wealthier and more powerful new upper economic class, than that general productivity be greater, although both seem to exist together. Superior productivity in general, and particularly for the new upper economic class, is *the dynamism of the new economic relationship* to effect a change from an existing economic relationship.

III. This dynamism is not a determinism: the new economic relationship does not necessarily prevail even though it has this dynamism, (and, to repeat, without the change in the economic relationship, the social structure will not basically change).

IV. A new political ideology and movement, and an effective political relationship that will maintain the new economic relationship is absolutely prerequisite to establish the new economic relationship. The actual (new) political relationship develops of itself, if there is an effective new political ideology with sufficient force to displace the old political relationship, and if necessary, old adjuvant relationships, and ideologies, including, in some instances, the older "Church" relationship and religious ideology. However: the success of the revolutionary political ideology and movement is not determined by the dynamism of the new economic relationship; there is no necessity that it succeed. Note that any revolutionary political movement inconsistent with the existing economic relationship, and not supported by a dynamic *new* economic relationship, wil fail.*

V. The formulation of new political ideologies, movements, other relationships and ideologies, have their own dynamics. These are not the dynamics of the new economic relationship, and the motivation of individuals to make such ideologies and relationships prevail, are generally not economic. (Repeat: what-

* Thus ideology, the revolutionary ideology for a political (or religious change) plays a more affirmative, positive role in social change, than ideology does in social structure, necessary as it is to the existence of the social structure. In social structure (Sec. 2), the form and content of the ideology is determined by the economic relationship; when the new economic relationship is established, it will again determine the form and content of all ideologies. But in social change, the revolutionary ideology is a moving force, without which the dynamic of the new economic relationship will not be effective. Of course, the revolutionary ideology and movement must be supportive of the new economic relationship, but this aspect is not created or constituted by an economic motivation. As stated in V. following, the motivation, etc. of the revolutionary ideology and movement is rarely economic. Refer again, to the distinction made in Sec. 2 between economic motivation within any particular economic relationship, and the determining and dynamic force of the economic relationship itself.

ever power the new ideologies and movements have, they will not succeed without the prerequisite dynamism of the new economic relationship; whatever dynamism exists for the new economic relationship will not cause it to come into existence without an effective revolutionary political ideology).

VI. In view of the indeterminism indicated in III, IV, and V, the occurrence of social changes cannot be predicted, nor can the form of any future society be predicted. Certain probabilities can be stated; chance plays a part therein. However, there are negative rules—V above, unless an economic dynamism for the new economic relationship exists, ideologies and movement seeking revolutionary change do not succeed.

A note on relatively minor changes in an existing social pattern:

The above laws refer to major social change. Relatively minor changes may take place in political, Church, and "family" relationships, although the social structure remains substantially the same. Furthermore, ideologies may seem to be undergoing constant reformulation, although there is no real change in the economic relationship. However, a change in the scale of an existing economic relationship, can bring about more than nominal changes in the other relationships, and ideologies.

In any case, the relationship and ideological changes, whether minimal, nominal, or moderately substantial, will be found still to be congruent with the existing economic relationship, and support it. In assessing the significance of all relatively minor change in a social pattern, it is important to note that older forms and ideas that have survived, may be dying, or quite commonly, are being transmuted into socially useful forms. The social structure and the ideologies, at any point of time, do not present a monolithic appearance.

.2 —*The new economic relationship may prevail socially because it possesses greater productivity of material goods in general, but especially greater productivity for an upper economic class.*

—*The basic cause of such increase in productivity is technological development.*
—*Restatement of sequences and dynamics in economic change and general social change.*

A new economic relationship may come into being, and may prevail generally in a society, when a method or techniques of production of material goods, or an organization of individuals in production of goods, (usually both together) are developed that is generally more productive than the former system, technique, organization of individuals; but in particular, provides a greater volume or value of goods for an upper economic class, making a new upper economic class wealthier and more powerful than the upper economic class of the earlier relationship.

It may be that in some new relationships of individuals, the actual physical process or production is the same, but that the new social organization of individuals results in a marked quantitative increase in the volume of goods available for an upper class. (However, it is probable in this situation that there will be some technological advance in some particular area of production, at least.) This latter change in organization of labor will result in and constitute a very real change in the economic relationship for the society, as a whole. Such a change in organization of individuals in production that results in the quantitative change will usually involve a change in the upper economic class also, and to make it viable, there will probable have to be a political change and possibly a change in "church" and "family" relationships.

But the major factor in increase in productivity (in general, and for an upper economic class) is the development or creation of a new technology in the production of material goods. A new technology in itself usually requires a different organization of individuals in the direct productive process itself. (Note: the primary subject of this book is the capitalist system of production, in the ICE, and in the dependent capitalist organism, both based on the increasing development of machine technology and mechanical power technology, and division of labor and automation of machine processes, etc.) A marked rise in productivity because of radical technological development (and, to repeat, this itself necessarily involves a different organization of individuals in the productive process), definitely means a *new* economic relationship, which *may* be able to prevail socially, because of its dynamism.

The economic relationship existing; the new economic relationship.

In stating the basic law of social structure (Sec. 2), the existence of the prevailing particular economic relationship was simply assumed. If it be enquired what has determined the nature of the particular economic relationship prevailing (passing for the moment, the question why it may have been able to supersede an earlier one), it will be seen that the determinants are both physical, and social (cultural). The latter herein refers to the structure of the society, although, since technology and the state of the arts has much to do with the latter—a sharp distinction cannot be drawn between the social structure as a whole and the state of the arts and sciences.

Physical conditions plainly must affect, establish limits, and sometimes even formulate the nature of the economic relationship possible; i.e. climate, natural configurations, natural resources, size of territory, size of population possible, water and land communications, etc. And it is entirely possible that social and cultural, structures and ideologies, can change the physical conditions to a considerable extent. An aggressive culture (Government, Church) can change the territorial, natural resource base very considerably. Each interacts on the other.

The same determinants (physical, social, cultural) exist for the new economic relationship. But it is the change in each of the two factors—physical and social—and here the effect of the one on the other is particularly important-that are the *bases* for the change in and creation of a new economic relationship. These bases for changes thus develop within the framework-economic, political etc. of an existing society, wherein a new technology, system of production, and even physical conditions are changing.

This new economic relationship can conceivably be a less productive one than the existing one, and it may necessarily prevail because, in view of existing conditions, there is no alternative. But it may be a more productive one, especially for the upper class, and then it will tend to prevail. This is the basic law of social change stated above. However, as stated, in the general laws, the new economic relationship alone does not have sufficient power to establish itself. The new economic relationship must supersede an existing one in a society where the whole established structure supports and maintains the existing one. It is not only that a new political, or religious, etc. pattern is necessary to the function of the new economic relationship, but the situation is that revolutionary movements for the new relationships and ideologies must move to establish themselves if the new economic relationship is to prevail. The new ideologies and proposed new relationships must be congruent with and *supportive* of the new economic relationship.

The same forces that may be providing the *bases* for the new economic relationship may be providing the bases for powerful movements for political and social change etc. That is to say, the dynamics may be parallel and contemporaneous and the movements likewise.

Restatement of sequences and dynamics in economic change and social change generally; indeterminancy and unpredictability of social change.

The great rule is, as stated, that the society will change if the economic relationship changes, and if this new relationship is more productive than the old, it will strongly tend to establish itself and prevail socially. However the dynamics for other social change must exist in the society and effectively assert themselves. It is true that the bases for economic change do arise in the existing society itself, and the dynamics, movements and ideologies for social change likewise. But the predicates of the total change are definite, if the actual sequences or parallelisms are not too clearly discernible. The power, primacy, and dynamic of a more productive economic relationship i.e. for the upper class arises from the same reason that the economic relationship has primacy in the social structure—the desire, and need for material goods is an overriding individual drive and motivation. (Note that the new economic relationship may itself not be able to function at all without the other social changes, since a certain, new political, religious or family structure may be *functional* elements of the new economic relationship. This is true of the pefcp; it is true of certain precapitalist economic systems.) As to the ICE, even if the new political, religious, etc. patterns are not an integral part of the economic relationship, the older relationships may have to be destroyed in order that the new economic relationship can function.

There is no determinism, no predictability as to whether (a) the bases for economic change will be laid (b) the economic change will be more productive, or will be able to establish itself (c) the general social movements can be formulated and be effective. The general laws of social change stated above can only explain the past. At the point of "now" no prediction can be made; only negative rules stated and probabilities assessed. If the new economic relationship is established, then according to the law of social structure the nature of the whole can be delineated: a pattern congruent, and supportive.

.3 The revolutionary political movement and ideology. The necessity of establishing a new political relationship to establish the new economic relationship. (In certain instances a religious movement and a new Church relationship may be necessary to establish the new economic relationship.)

It was stated above that a prerequisite for the change to the new economic relationship is a revolutionary political movement and ideology to establish a political relationship suitable for the economic relationship. This is not to say that the actual form of the new political relationship is clearly contemplated or stated: The actual political relationship will develop of itself (Sec. (2), the natural selection of elements, ideas). The actual political relationship that develops is generally not contemplated in the ideology of the political revolutionist.

The necessary function of the revolutionary movement (political, religious) is the overthrow of existing relationships— Government, sometimes the Church, and the existing ideologies supporting the existing economic relationship. The whole existing social pattern is usually hostile to the new relationship or incongruent with it. Until these relationships and ideologies are eliminated, the new patterns necessary to the new relationship cannot develop. Social change usually appears as political or religious revolution, sometimes dramatic and socially convulsing. (Refer to Sec. (4), Note, on the Protestant ideology and movement, as dynamic in the establishment of the capitalist relationship.)

A society may be unable to develop or sustain an effective political movement and ideology. Furthermore, even if there are revolutionary movements, the existing social fabric, economic, political, ecclesiastical, may be strong enough to resist all change. Or the society may not be able to develop the necessary political institutions.

The existing economic relationship might even be a failing one, yet the establishment can remain sufficiently powerful to resist economic change. However, if the existing economic relationship is failing, the new economic relationship and the revolutionary ideology stand a greater change of succeeding; the old ideology has less power to sustain the existing social order.

The new political ideology, and even a new religious ide-ol-ogy, are seldom newly created as a whole as revolutionary ideology. All, or most of its elements, political and religious, are already in existence, as existing deviant ideology, or as private philosophies, or the basis may even be true religious experience. The new ideology will be synthesized from existing idea, heresies, old and new private philosophies. The dynamism of the new economic relationship often serves to coalesce various idea into an ideology of social power, or permit the emergence of basic religioous ideas seeking to overthrow or reform the prevailing religious ideology.

With respect to revolutionary political ideologies: these often contain primary ideas of great power over individuals (although these will be transvalued in the established ideology, if the revolutionary ideology succeeds). The revolutionary ideology wil have a greater degree of truth than the existing ideology. An important part of the new ideology is an effective criticism of the old.

It is probable that there will be a leader, who can move and shake the old institutions and their ideology, and persuade the society to adopt the new. He will be a man of great force, as speaker, writer often as political or military leader. It is not necessary that he be an originator of the new ideology, or a great thinker, or a great religious figure, although this is possible.

Prospective followers for these revolutionary movements (political, religious) will exist in surprising number in any society. Although existing relationships seem to be effective, and ideologies seem to be believed, a great many are always dissatisfied with their own status, with the existing relationships, with the ideas they must accept. There is certainly much injustice, falsehood, dishonesty, evil, in existing societies and their power entities. Any ideology breeds dissent and heresy. This is ordinarily forcibly repressed, and repression is effective if the economic relationship and the other relationships are viable. Most dissenters and heretics sincerely object to the ideology, declaring it false, probably without any idea that they want to change a basic relationship, or without recognizing that the ideology is in effect supporting the other relationships in the society. New ideas and many dissenting ideas seem to offer a closer approach to truth.

The principal point, herein, is that the motives, and the underlying dynamics of those who seek revolutionary change in political, religious relationships, and ideology—especially the leaders—are not usually economic. They may have a true, prophetic call. There may be simply a motivation for power. "Patriotism" and "Freedom" can be powerful moving forces. Hatred of oppressors, of those in power, is characteristic of revolutionists; almost all movements incite violence towards some group, sometimes an innocent one.

Some direct economic motivation in individual political revolutionists may exist. Members of a prospective new upper economic class, may directly seek political change for their own economic purposes. They may seek to place themselves in political power in a new type of State and Government. Usually they will be participating in a movement and ideology that seems suitable for their economic interests. In any event these individuals do not believe they are acting out of economic motivations. While direct political revolutionary action by the new upper economic class has existed, it is not typical. The new economic upper class are not per se the political revolutionists, nor are they the persons who effect a religious revolution. Actually, they do not want the political (or the religious) structures that the revolutionists seek. The political structure must be one that will be suitable for the new economic relationship, and this will be a form that develops through the principles of natural selection and will be quite unlike the forms that are contemplated.

It is possible that there may be a direct economic motivation to political change among the existing lower economic class, or the poor or destitute. They can be induced to undertake direct action to secure political change, believing that it would relieve their poverty. They are usually deceived; the new political relationship does not change their level.

Most "economic interpretations" of history tend to view revolutionary political and religious change as the result of individual economic motivation. This is reductionist. In the first place, individual economic motivation itself is not the dynamic for social change. It is the new economic *relationship* that is the necessary, indispensable dynamic force that makes revolutionary change possible. In the second place, it is the political movement or other movement that may effect the change to the new economic relationship, and the dynamic of these movements is not primarily economic.

.4 An economic dynamism for a change to Communist economic relationship and State (herein referring to a large scale, technologically advanced system of production carried on by the Government itself, with distribution determined by the Government) may *exist. Its nature will necessarily be somewhat different than the economic dynamism for change to economic relationships that have an economic class structure.*

- —Such economic dynamism (for a Communist economic relationship) if it does actually exist, requires a powerful political-economic movement, and ideology, to accomplish a social change to the new economic relationship (just as a change to any new economic relationship requires an effective political revolutionary movement, and ideology, etc.
- —That the economic dynamism for a Communist relationship, if it exists, does not determine the success of this revolutionary movement and ideology (just as the success of any new political ideology and movement is not determined by

the economic dynamism for social change).

–No revolutionary movement for a Communist economy and State will succeed in the absence of an economic dynamism to such economy and State.

The terms Communist economic relationship and Communist State herein mean a new State and Government which is also an economic relationship—an economic relationship of a particular type. State and Economy are integral. The particular type of economic relationship is one wherein the productive enterprises, the land, all goods used for production of other material goods, are owned by the State; and all labor in the production of material goods is performed under the direction and control of the Government and its agents. The production itself is carried on in large units, technologically advanced. The Government determines the distribution of the current production, either to all the members of the State generally, (equal distribution or some other formula) or to certain groups, or classes (a labor class, a military class, a Government class, possibly welfare groups, etc.) There is theoretically no ownership or dominion over any type of property by individuals, or groups of individuals, of such nature that a share of the current production can be obtained thereby.

There is a complete political relationship, a true State and Government (Sec. 2). The Government has dominion and control over the members of the State, etc., performing all activities and functions of Government. The Government maintains all relationships and ideologies necessary to this State and economy. (The Government's form, the nature of the power entity, the ideology of State and Government are not discussed herein. The *actual* relationships, and the ideologies that prevail in *particular* Communist States and political economies also will not be discussed.)

The laws of social change heretofore set forth (subsecs. .1 to .3) and the economic dynamism of a new economic relationship, refer to economic relationships that have an economic class structure. The new relationship will be more productive generally, but the essential part of the dynamism is that the new economic relationship will be more productive for the new upper economic class.

It is possible that a Communist economic relationship can be more productive generally, than any existing one. However, this alone will not create an economic dynamism for such an economic relationship, as against any viable, existing economic relationship with an upper economic class. The powerful individual economic motivation to become, and remain a member of the upper economic class of any viable economic class relationship, and the consequent economic dynamism of that relationship, is of superior force to the fact or possibility of a general increase in productivity, in a non economic class economy. The economy that has the class relationship will prevail, if it is at all viable, and, pursuant to the laws of social structure, the relationships, and ideology of the society will conform to the class type economy.

The foregoing does not mean that there can never be an economic dynamism to a Communist economic relationship, and it does not mean that any type of economic class relationship has a superior economic dynamism, per se. The general rule with respect to economic dynamism to a Communist economic relationship and State, is as follows:

An economic dynamism to a change to a Communist economic relationship will exist if

(a) The *general productivity* in this type of economic relationship is *far greater* than in the economic relationship it seeks to displace, or any other economic relationship (class type) that may seek to follow, any other possible economic relationship of an earlier type with economic class,

(b) the productivity *for the upper economic class* of any existing or reasonably possible economic class type relationship is extremely low (i.e. principally, that the existing class type relationship is in a state of permanent decline or collapse).

General considerations with respect to the foregoing:

A. The poverty of the mass of the people, employed or unemployed, is not the fundamental factor in creating a possible economic dynamism to a Communist economic relationship. (Refer to general rules of social change—that such poverty is also not significant in creating a dynamism to a new economic class relationship). The income, wealth, of the upper economic class, existing or possible, is the more significant factor. However, the importance of general productivity increases as the population increases.

B. An economic dynamism to a Communist economic relationship is only conceivable where an advanced technology comparable to the productive processes in an advanced capitalist relationship, prevails, or can be instituted.

C. Repeated from the general statement in the headnote: Even if the economic dynamism exists, it is not a determinism, and it is entirely possible that any type of class economy may still prevail.

Whether an economic dynamism to a Communist type economic relationship and State has ever existed.

If the general technology is of small scale production, essentially not based on machines and mechanical power, with agricultural production predominating, there can be no economic dynamism to a Communist economic relationship.* A Communist economic relationship with such a technology, could not in the first place be as produtcive as one where there is a small upper economic class, and a large laboring class, and the compulsion of slavery, poverty, low wage and threat of unemployment compel an individual to produce far more than the minimum necessary for his subsistence. But more important than the fact that an economic class relationship in such a technology would be more productive generally, is the fact that the motivation to upper economic class is so powerful a force, that the economic class relationship will be maintained. To repeat: before the development of the modern machine-mechanical power

* However, Communist movements and ideologies did exist before the modern technology. Small, quasi religious communist sects have been established where a simple technology of production has existed. These were outside the mainstream of society, and had little significance.

technology, there was no *possibility* that a dynamism to a Communist State, etc. or any type of Communist economic relationship could exist. (Even if strong Communist movements existed, they could not succeed.)

With the development of the highly productive machine technology, the *possibility* of an economic dynamism for a Communist economy and State can reasonably be contemplated. If all are employed in material production, using a modern technology, it is possible that productioon could be greatly increased. (Yet it is only a possibility. It would still have to be shown that production would actually be higher. Furthermore, it would have to appear that the increased productivity would be of such extent that it could overcome the power of an upper economic class in a viable, effective economic class relationship.)

From the foregoing it must be concluded: in a functionning ICE, there will be no economic dynamism to a Communist State and economic relationship. Thus such a relationship will not come into being even assuming the existence of a powerful Communist movement and ideology. During the 19th century, *despite the depressions of the business cycle,* there was no such dynamism, and no possibility of the success of any Communist movement. (The Marxist ideology, discussed below is to the contrary. It stated that the periodic depressions, and the poverty of the unemployed and the employed alike, created a powerful dynamic for the Communist economy.) The fact was that so long as the productive ICE could function, with a rich and powerful upper economic class, it possessed the basic economic dynamism. Temporary periods of depression and unemployment did not materially affect this. Depressions did not create a dynamism for the Communist relationship, for while the income of the upper class was temporarily reduced, the level of capital expansion and the volume of profit subsequently rose to higher levels. The poverty of the lower class was an irrelevancy, as was the fact that under a different economic arrangement they would be better off. The fact that the technology created great wealth for an upper class strengthened the dynamic for the ICE, rather than the contrary.

Actually, it is questionnable that a Communist type relationship would be more productive generally, than an ICE in periods of prosperity. The threat of unemployment, pressure of competition and threat of loss of capital to the employer, compels a high productivity and constant advance in technology.

Even the approaching end of the ICE, in the early 20th century, created no economic dynamism for a Communist relationship. (Refer, however to Note in Sec. 7, with respect to Russia). The wealth of the upper economic class was increasing. If the ICE was approaching its end, it was not because of any Communist threat.

Conclusion: The answer to the question posed in this subsection is that only on the final collapse of the ICE did the possibility of an economic dynamism for a Communist economy and State come into being. If the ICE could not function, a Communist economic relationship would be a far more productive one than the disintegrated economy.

However, at this point it was not the Communist economic relationship that possessed the economic dynamism. (Sec. 7.)

Communist ideology and movements.

- —If the movement succeeds, the State and Economy will not be the one set forth in the ideology. (Furthermore, as stated in the general rules of social structure, the State and Economy will not be the one set forth in the ideology of the established State.)
- —The "Marxist" ideologies and movements.

The Communist movement and ideology will be directed against the entire existing social structure—all relationships and all ideologies. The existing society is one where all relationships and all ideologies support and maintain an economy of class structure generally, not only the particular type of class economy prevailing. State, Church, and family relationships and their ideologies, have long been of such nature that they are congruent and supportive of an economic class relationship.

Fundamental to the ideology is (a) the attack on economic class structure, (b) the declaration that economic class is the source of evil in the society, (c) the idea that a society is possible without an economic class structure, and that this will be a good society, (d) that the existing State, Government, Church relationship, ideology, should be overthrown. A criticism of the entire existing social structure and the entire existing ideology, is an essential part of a Communist ideology. The ideology contains little by way of presentation of the future actual relationships of the new society.

The important Communist movements and ideologies for well over a century are those that use as an ideology a body of doctrine, and social and economic analysis called "Marxism." The greater part of this doctrine and analysis was stated, or presumed to have been stated by Karl Marx. Marx was a scientist who was the first to describe fully the true nature of the capitalist relationship, the significance of capital expansion, and the dominance of the economic relationship in the social structure. He was also a revolutionist who sought the overthrow of the entire economic, political, ecclesiastical structure of the capitalist society, and an ideologist for such a revolution. It is important to recognize that as revolutionist and ideologist he was moved by an ideal of a society which could achieve excellence by freeing man from want and exploitation, and man himself freed from the power of acquiring economic dominion over others.

Marx, as scientist, recognized and taught the significance of technology in social structure and change; that it was the modern technology that could make a Communist economic relationship possible; that it would be the economic dynamism of the Communist economic relationship with this technology that would enable that relationship to come into being. But it is fair to say that he knew that a revolutionary movement and ideology were essential, and that the economic dynamism of a Communist economic relationship would not by itself establish this economy. Despite (ideological) statements of an evolution to "higher social forms" Marx did not confuse organic evolution with social change; if he spoke of "determinism" he spoke as revolutionary ideologist.

Marx was a great ideologist; he formulated the modern Communist ideology. The ideology contains the fundamental ideas of good revolutionary ideology: Communism as irresistable social force that must succeed; that it must overthrow the capitalist economy, the State, etc. (In the revolutionary ideology, State, Church, were not powerful entities, but scarcely relationships separate from the capitalist relationship; he called the entire ideology of the society simply a "superstructure.") Inevitability of success, an irresistable social force, an ideal society to be created, an evil enemy already fatally stricken, the force of history on its side, were the components of this ideology. Furthermore: the Communist movement was stated to be the movement of an economic class (proletarians) which is declared to be the revolutionary class, presumably comparable to the "bourgeois" class that overthrew the preceding economic structure. The ideology presents social structure and social change in terms of class warfare.

Actually, the Communist revolutionary movement was far from an irresistible social force. There was no determinism that it must succeed; actually it must fail while the ICE was viable. There is no significant class struggle in an established social structure. The proletarians are not a revolutionary class, and the revolutionists are not proletarians. The movement itself was constituted by a small group. Labor unions and international associations of workers are not revolutionary. The proletarians will not establish a new State, and in any new State they will not be the dominant class. The State will not and cannot wither away when it coalesces with the economic relationship; actually it becomes more powerful and necessary, and the Government will achieve supreme power.

It is an irony that when the ICE did fail, the Communist ideology and movement was ineffective. All its "science" and "determinism" fell before the superior economic dynamism of the pefcp and the several ideologies that supported it. Another irony is that the Russian State and the Communist ideology became the vital counterpart ideology for a WMS; it is the ideological and military enemy that creates the Military ideology of the WMS.

(4) The "Democratic State" and Government.
The two primary aspects of this State and Government, in ideology, and in actual relationship. (Contrasts with the W M State and Government.)

The Democratic State (herein described in prototype, principally as represented in the U. S.), is the name given herein to the political relationship that developed and prevailed during the existence of the ICE. It is a specific political form that once existed. It is not to be confused with the "Democracies" of other periods, or the democracies described by the political philosophers, i.e. as a form of polity generally, to be distinguished from aristocracy and monarchy. (Some of the concepts of the political philosophers, particularly in the 17th and 18th centuries, with respect to the nature of democracy, and the nature of sovereignty, became important elements of the *ideology* of the "Democratic State" of the ICE, and also of the ideology of the revolutionary movements that led to the establishment of the "Democratic State.")

The actual nature of this State and Government appears only when the nature of the economic relationship (ICE) has been set forth. As stated in the basic law of social structure (Sec. 2), the actual political relationship that develops is one that is congruent with the economic relationship, and is necessary for it, supporting and maintaining it. The elements that constituted the actual relationship were naturally selected to create a State that was suitable for the capitalist relationship.

The ideology of this State does not reveal the actual relationships existing. Nor does this appear in the revolutionary ideology that established this State; the State and Government contemplated by the political revolutionists were not the State and Government that eventuated. But the basic ideology has a direct connection with the actuality of the relationship. (Sec. 2). With respect to this ideology, and the actual relationships:

The two basic ideas or rather the two bodies of ideas in the "Democratic State" ideology are:

(a) Man is a free individual, with the power of private judgment, with a right to his own life, to liberty, and to pursue his own happiness; he exists as such free individual apart from and before the State. These rights are inalienable; but by free compact, free men create the State and Government for certain limited purposes and with limited power, for their own benefit and advantage.

(b) The Government: Certain limited powers are bestowed on the Government. The Government can exercise no more power than the specific powers given and must act in accordance with due process of law. The individuals who constitute the Government will be chosen periodically from the members of the State. The right of existence of any Government can be revoked by those who bestow the power (the sovereign people) if it exceeds the limits set upon it, or acts contrary to the interests of the people.

Paralleling the foregoing, the two major actualities of this State and Government are:

A. Man's freedom is primarily that of a free, independent, *economic* person. The basic operative freedom is the freedom to function in a certain, specific economic relationship, the capitalist relationship. It is fundamental then, that the State is an association or relationship *separate* from the economic relationship of the individuals who constitute the State. (State not part of the economy or economic relationship; State not a political economy.) Membership in the State creates no economic obligation or economic duty to another member, and the Government has no economic duty to any member, nor any economic right against anyone except to levy a very limited tax. Man owes no economic duty to another and has no economic obligation to another except as arises out of free contract in the economic (capitalist) relationship. The foregoing is the actualization, the reality, the essential operative aspect of the general ideology of man's freedom, equality, private power and private judgment (the free "economic" man). The *actuality* of the ideological right to life, liberty and the pursuit of happiness is that all of these will be ultimately dependent upon man's position and power in the economic relationship. The actualization of the idea of the compact of free men to maintain each other's rights, powers, freedom, etc. is the creation of a political form wherein the primary function of Government is the maintainence of a specific economic relationship, and for this purpose the Government will maintain private property, enforce contracts, maintain individual liberty to contract. The power bestowed on the Government is fundamentally limited with respect to the economic relationship: The Government must not control the market, wage, the labor contract, or profit. The doctrine of minimum Government—that Government best that governs least—is primarily a doctrine demanding that the Government not interfere with the economic relationship. Furthermore: The State (Government) shall not take any part of a man's property or income (except the absolutely minimum tax for the minimum of Government activities), and this taxing power shall itself be under the control of the capitalist class—B, below.

(Further on the actualization of the basic ideology of individual freedom, equality, etc.: 1. Despite the ideology, there can be a direct and open violation of the ideology. Thus, there can be human slavery, even though the "rights of man" are constitutionally stated and guaranteed. Furthermore, certain classes can be openly excluded from political rights. 2. Economic position tends to determine the extent of civil rights that will be legally afforded in practice. However, in the "Democratic State" there seems to be a greater degree of civil rights, generally, and almost complete religious freedom, the latter being inherent in the Democratic State (refer to Note, below). 3. The concept of economic freedom is most realistically applied to the capitalist organism, i.e. as Independent Capitalist organism.

B. The Government: The idea that power and sovereignty reside in the people, generally (power being periodically entrusted to certain members of the State generally), has this actuality: The Government represents a certain economic class of the ICE, the capitalist class, or the more powerful part of this class.

The foregoing is accomplished by a complex of mechanisms and institutions and Government structure, all superficially consistent with the general ideology. The *political party* is a basic mechanism by means of which the political power is exercised by the capitalist class. The party itself is a small group of individuals controlled by an oligarchy. The oligarchs are or are controlled by the capitalist class, generally by the dominant part of this class, the large scale producers or the operators of the financial mechanisms. Party ideology itself is to the contrary; the party represents itself as a mass of individuals democratically organized. Control by party oligarchs is the essence of Government power. This is not an aberration of the "Democratic State," but essential to this State and Government. It is an essential mechanism whereby the Government can pursue its primary function of maintaining the Independent Capitalist organism without controlling it. It is not unlikely that an actual control of the Government by the "people" generally (including "labor") would have seriously damaged the capitalist organism, either by legislation affecting the wage-profit ratio, or affecting the ability of the organism to steadily expand capital, or by the utilization of the tax for improper purposes (redistribution of wealth).*

The *structure of Government* is also of great importance in (a) maintaining power in the capitalist class directly, and through the political party. (b) maintaining the separation of political relationship and the economic relationship, and preventing any political control of the economy and restricting the tax on Profit A. In general, power is divided, as well as limited. The *Legislature* (Congress, Parliament) is the dominant organ of Government of the Democratic State. In effect, the Legislature controls the Government, and the party controls the Legislature. (Fundamental contrast to the Government of the WMS—Sec 5.) But the Courts and lawyers, also have great power, and this branch of Government can ultimately be utilized by the capitalist class if party cannot control the legislature.

The Legislature, the dominant organ of Government of the Democratic State, is usually so organized that a few members control the whole (committee control). The bicameral structure also checks the exercise of Government power, and prevents escape from party control. A crisis may temporarily shift power to the Executive from the Legislature. (Government by legislature is essentially negative Government). Any shift of power to the Executive, in the Democratic State, also usually means an attempt to increase Government control over the economy. A rise in Executive power over Legislative power is a sign of increase in popular power. (The prevailing ideology on this is to the contrary.)

* In the Democratic State only the smallest part of the Income may be taken by tax. The restrictions on the power to tax is a major aspect of revolutionary ideology leading to this State. The ideology is specific: no taxation without representation (i.e. control), etc. The structure of the Government and the restricions on fiscal procedures assures control over the tax by the capitalist class.

Despite certain aspects of the ideology of this Democratic State and Government (i.e. that it is a Government of limited power; that the consent of the governed can be withdrawn at any time; man's freedom and independence of the Government, etc.) and the fact that the function of the capitalist organism is independent of the Government, this is a fully sovereign and powerful Government. To begin with, it is not a weak military State, or unwarlike (as aspects of its ideology would indicate) but a definitely *expansionist* State, and this to an extraordinary degree. It freely uses military force for expansion. This State frequently wages war. Many of these States are *imperial* States; and even the smaller ones aspire to this status. However, it is fundamental to observe that war is not essentially ideological; war is waged for direct economic purposes (capital expansion, acquisition of territory and other semi-States for capital expansion, "markets.") Furthermore, war is not waged for the benefit of a military class, nor for the Government as a military power. The military is subordinated to civil power, i.e. to the power of Government as in the control of the capitalist class. Ordinarily, there is no great standing army (except in a state of tension with a neighboring expansionist power). This too, is not an ideological warfare; the patriotic ideologies are of a different nature. The world is one of comparable States, with comparable economic interests. A successful war is an economically profitable war.

Reviewing general Governmental powers, (as listed Sec. 2 Subsec. 5) it will be seen that the powers of Government are quite the same as in all Governments. It maintains the existing economic relationship. It maintains its own existence. It will resist any attempt to overthrow it or divide it. It will suppress any movement against it. Treason is a constitutioonal crime in this State, as any other State. It carries on direct economic activities (roads, bridges, harbors, sometimes railways, telephone). It has the essential power of all States, to tax, borrow, cooin money and print paper money.

Note: On Church, Religious Ideology—Democratic State.

—Separation of State, Church, Economy (ICE); Religious freedom.

—General Note: Christian religions, Church relationships, in different economic and political structures. Church, as necessary to Economy, State, in precapitalist economies. Separation of Church, State, Economy, each from the other, is the consequence of the capitalist relationship.*

The major points in the foregoing discussion are: the separation of the State and the Economy (ICE); that the actual political relationship, although related to the ideology, develops in the form necessary, and supportive of the economic relationship.

It should be added that inherently the Democratic State (typical form) is separate from the Church relationship (as it is separate from the economic relationship) and that there is freedom with respect to religious ideology and Church membership. The Church relationship is probably not a necessary one for this State and Economy.

There were many variations in the actual Church-State relationship during the later ICE, although the basic separation did take place. It is not feasible to describe these variations. Some States supported a Church financially; some Churches retained power over education and family relationships.

In general, even though a complete separation is effected, and there is religious freedom, the religious ideologies will be found to be congruent with the economic and political relationships.

* The Protestant Christian religion was the religion (Church relationship, ideology) congruent with the capitalist economic relationship, the political forms associated therewith, and the ideologies of each. Furthermore, the Protestant doctrine and movement was a necessary force leading to the establishment of the capitalist economic relationship, and the necessary political change. Nevertheless, as stated in Sec. 3, although the Protestant movement and doctrine was an essential element of the social change, it was the dynamism of the new economic relationship that enabled the new religion to prevail; it is the capitalist relationship that is the essential dynamic for the political change, the ultimate separation of Church, Economy, State and religious freedom. (Corollaries: Protestant doctrine and movement are not the cause of the capitalist relationship; nor the cause of the new State form; nor the cause of the separation of Church, State, Economy.)

It is proper to characterize the Protestant religion as a different religion than Primitive Christianity, or papal Christianity (papal Church, or ceasorapapal forms), despite the fact that all have the same Divine Person, and the same basic doctrine of original sin. However, change in emphasis, etc., and in particular the addition or deletion of another element of doctrine (Sec. 2, above) so change a religion that it becomes qualitatively different. Primitive Christianity, in which the significance of salvation is otherwordly (the real evil from which God delivers man is an evil society —the economic-political structures), is not even a socially useful, socially congruent religion, and it will be suppressed as destructive to the existing social order. However, such a religion can be absolutely transformed into a Church relationship and ideology that is not only congruent and supportive of a *certain type* of economic-political structure, but may be necessary to it. This is accomplished by the addition of the idea that the godhead exists in or is represented by a certain person on earth, where this person is either the political power entity, (and the political power entity represents the upper economic class) or, if the religious power entity is within a Church that does not have economic power and political power directly, the Church is directly and intimately associated with the existing economic and political power entities.

The addition of such doctrine changes the meaning and significance of the basic elements of doctrine, and even changes the nature of the godhead. A religion comes into being wherein Emperor, as religious power entity, has power to maintain the specific (pre-capitalist) economic and political relationship. In other (pre-capitalist) economic and political structures the religious power entity took the form of papal Church. Church papalism must create power for and in itself, since the Church (papacy) is not itself primarily a political and economic power entity. It must achieve such power that the Church becomes essential to the political-economic power entities with which it allies itself (i.e., power to make a symbiosis with these latter power entities useful to each). To achieve this power certain other doctrines and practices are "naturally" selected. (Sec. 2.)

The rejection of this element of doctrine (religious power entity as representative of the godhead, and doctrines and practices associated therewith) and, in effect, the transvaluation or transformation of other elements of doctrine creates a religion and religious movement that attacks a basic support of the pre-capitalist economic relationships and their polities, and the actual economic relationship itself. As stated at the outset, this new Church and ideology is one that is congruent with the new (capitalist) economy and its polity, and the separation of Church, State, and Economy will follow. It is also congruent with the ideology of the capitalist relationship and the ideology of the Democratic State. The ideology of capitalism is that the expansion of capital is due to "saving"—which is a benefit to others. The presumed ethic of Protestantism of an asceticism that results in the accumulation of capital through "savings" is in accord with this ideology. Man cannot be more innocently employed than in making and saving money and accumulating capital. The basic new religious doctrine of individual judgment, responsibility, and power to achieve salvation, becomes actualized in the new economic-political structures as individual freedom and power in such economic relationship, just as the ideology of the Democratic State is actualized into an economic freedom for the individual.

While the Protestant doctrine and movement was probably essential to establish the capitalist relationship originally, the capitalist relationship then spreads, however,because of its inherent power and dynamism, even though papal forms and associated political forms continue. The papal or ceasaropapal Church cannot prevent the spread of the capitalist relationship, although they can delay it. The papal Church itself changes substantially, and as a Church separated from Economy and State, tends to become more congruent with the capitalist relationship and State.

PART II

The Welfare-Military State

(5) The Welfare-Military State:
—The actual relationship: political economy and polity. The general form of the Government.
—Ideology: —The "Welfare" and "Military" components.
—The whole political ideology. The two forms of general political ideology of the WMS.

.1 The actual relationship: the WMS as political economy and as polity.
Recapitulation and amplification.

The keys to the actual relationships constituting this State are
—The State is a political economy—i.e., the State itself is an economic relationship, (a relationship among the individuals in the society in which the material goods are produced and distributed). Alternative statement: the State is an integral and functional part of the whole economic relationship of the society.
—The peculiar nature of this economic relationship: the political economy based on the fictive expansion of capital.
—The economic relationship (the political economy), is necessarily based upon State as Polity. That is to say, certain powers of Government (although now moving in a new context, and transformed in this context) are the means of making the political economy possible.
—The Structure of State as Polity and the constitution of the Government arise out of the distinctive nature of the political economy.

The discussion in this Section and the following section is principally concerned with this State as Polity, an association, etc., of individuals under the power and dominion of Government (certain members of the State), which has power to compel certain conduct and power to undertake certain activities. The ideology of the State and the nature and constitution of Government must be examined.

But it is not possible to really separate State as political economy and State as Polity. Whatever the appearances and ideology of this State are (and here we necessarily have regard primarily to the "Welfare" and the "Military" aspects of ideology and Welfare and Military activities) their real nature and dynamic will be found in the political economy. The ideology of the State as Polity is profoundly important to its existence and function (and, to repeat, State as Polity is the basis of State as political economy), yet this ideology and activity are at the same time the functional parts of the political economy.

The Government is the dominant factor in the production of material goods. It causes the production of a great quantity of goods in an economic relationship of privately-owned capital units, which it purchases, uses and distributes. The Government pays for these in effect by certain forms it creates, which when analyzed, will be seen to be fictions of capital forms and profit forms that the capital unit seeks and *must* have; the capital units cannot exist as such, without these fictive forms; furthermore, the level of their production is determined by the volume and value of these fictive forms. "Purchase" of goods from the separate capital units is an act of Government (not comparable to the purchase by private persons or capital units) within this context, and the context is of a new political economy existing by virtue of Government power. The activities of Government, then, provide the return to the capitalists who own the units (by way of actual goods to consume, new and expanded capital if any, the fictive capital and profit forms) and State and Government are the basis also of wage and the consumption of labor and the possibility of their existence in this economic system. State and Government directly furnish subsistence of a Welfare and Military class created by Government. The nature of the economic association is such that the Government, although apparently not directly participating in the physical process of production, is the operative force causing all goods to come into existence, in this economic relationship. This is not the Communist economic relationship, or the Communist political relationship. There is a semblance of such a relationship; there is a closer semblance to the capitalist relationship of the ICE; it is a simulacrum of the latter relationship.

Although the actual relationships constituting this State are not apparent, nor are they socially known, nor stated in the ideology of State and Government, the idea that this State is an economic association of some sort and has an economic purpose, does appear in its ideology. Herein is the radical change from the ideology of the Democratic State as well as the actuality of the Democratic State. It is found in the "Welfare" idea in the "rationalist" form of the ideology, and it is implicit and explicit in the mysticist form of the ideology of the WMS. In the "Welfare" ideology the basic idea is that the State is an association to provide and assure the economic, material needs of all of its members. This ideology is actualized, primarily, into a political economy based on fictive forms, wherein a certain level of production and employment are maintained in a certain economic relationship by means of these fictive forms. The secondary meaning of "Welfare"—in its actualization in this State and Economy—is the creation of a Welfare class of distributees. It has been seen that the actualization of both the Welfare and Military components of the ideology are into forms useful and necessary to the political economy (Ch. V).

The Government

The actual nature of the Government and its typical constitution does not appear in the ideology of State and Government (although to some extent it is stated in the mysticist form of the ideology). The prototype form, government by a Chief of Government (subsection .3) is one that is suitable and necessary for a State which is both an economic association an a political association, and the economic association is one that is dependent on government power for its existence. The Chief of Government must be above each economic class and control each of them, and act for the political economy as a whole, centralizing all power necessary to create such a political economy and enable it to function.

However, the prototype form is only an ideal. Often the Chief is not in good control of the economy and cannot manage it properly, primarily because he is too closely associated with one of the economic classes, or a certain part of them, and the tax system is inadequate, and there is an improper encouragement of the creation of private fictive capital papers and the private inflation of bank credit money. Or the Chief may in effect be operating the Government for the Military class, a deviation from the ideal form. It is possible, too, although unlikely, that the Government be under the control of labor and Welfare classes.

This Government—the Chief of Government, performs all the general Government functions of a State: maintains the State and all other relationships socially necessary, and maintains all ideologies necessary for its existence and the existence of all relationships; provides for the personal safety of all State members, and their property, etc.

.2 Ideology of the State: Two general forms—the "rationalist" form and the mysticist form.

—The Welfare and Military components in each.

—The ideology of State as economic association; the actualization of this ideology.

At first sight the "rationalist" form of the ideology and the mysticist form seem to be describing two different States and two different economic relationships. However, each form is actualized in a State and political economy that is the same: the political economy based on fictive forms. The Government form of each State follows the prototype of a Government of a WMS, but there are significant differences in the way the Government of each is constituted, and in the techniques of Government, and the nature of exercise of Government power over individuals and the scope of this power. The fundamental point is that the "rationalist" form is as congruent with the political economy as is the mysticist form. The "rationalist" type is now of principal importance: it is the dominant, successful one.

The "rationalist" type of ideology utilizes certain parts of the ideology of the Democratic State (Sec. 4). It had its origin in those countries where this State prevailed, but following World War II it was transplanted to other countries. Although parts of the ideology of the Democratic State are still of importance, the addition of the "Welfare" concept really makes a fundamental change in these parts. Yet two basic patterns of ideas of the Democratic State seem to continue: free man with power of private judgment, inalienable rights, etc., the State as compact of free men for limited purposes; Government of limited power with sovereignty always in its members, the personnel of Government selected by them periodically to represent all the members of the State, etc. These two basic patterns of ideas, with the addition of the Welfare concept and the Military concept (below) will become actualized into a form of State and a form of Government quite different from that represented by the ideology. The actuality will be as different from the ideology as the actual Democratic State-Government differed from its basic ideology. And the actual new State and Government will be different from the actual Democratic State and Government, although there are similar elements in the ideology of each.

The New Components of the Ideology: "Welfare State."

The State is conceived to be an association to provide and assure the economic and material needs of all of its members (among other basic political purposes). However, the WMS is not to produce material goods directly; it is not a Communist relationship. To some extent the concept from the older ideology of "free enterprise" continues, as ideology in the WMS, but with little emphasis on this since it is conceded that the Government must order and control the productive system to assure the necessary level of production of goods, and to directly provide material goods for those who cannot obtain necessary goods through employment by the capital units or through Profit arising from the capital units. The Welfare ideology often contains the idea (more explicit in the mysticist form of the ideology) that the production of material goods is carried on for the "needs" of all the members of the State, and the needs of the State for its defense. That is to say, production is not "for profit," but "for use."

The addition of the Welfare concept is not entirely inconsistent with parts of the ideology of the Democratic State incorporated into the ideology of the WMS, although it must enlarge and change it. The free, independent man can enter into an association to provide the economic welfare of each member of the State. Although this must change the meaning of limited powers of Government, the idea of Government with great powers over the economy is not inconsistent with the idea of sovereignty of the people. Yet the "Democratic" elements of the ideology were utilized in the early days of the WMS-pefcp, to attack the State, and particularly the actual Government form.

"Military State"

In the present form of this ideology, the State is conceived to be one in a constant, ideological war, to preserve itself, its institutions; it must be in a posture of constant defense requiring at all times an immense armament. It faces dangerous, heavily armed ideological enemies. It is under constant threat of attack by Communist foes, (who have allies within the State). who would destroy it, its way of life, Churches, religion, its ideology, the economic welfare of each member of the WMS. The Communist ideology is itself destructive to the WMS. Foreign powers which profess this ideology have the military power to destroy the WMS. There is a state of actual war on the peripheries of the great Powers.

In the "rationalist" ideology this essential aspect (constant defense and large-scale armament) does not have its inception with the "Welfare" aspect of the State. It originates somewhat later, first as anti-Fascism, in response to the actual aggression of the Fascist States. (The mysticist ideologies, discussed below, were highly aggressive, seeking world domination.) It was after the victory over the Fascist states that the basic anti-Communist aspect or the rationalist" ideology developed. It should be noted, too, that the State is not presented as a "Military State," but rather as a State that must be in a posture of defense.

The scale and extent of the military structure of the WMS is very great. One of the functions of the Military establishment is to maximize constantly the threat that is presented.* However, it seems at the present time, that the ideology of the nature of the threat is changing somewhat, and a new aspect of this part of the ideology is developing.

The effect of this part of the ideology of the WMS on both the ideology and the actuality of Government form and power, has been noted elsewhere.

The ideology of the WMS characterized herein as mysticist is historically important. This is generally the ideology of the Fascist State of the first decade and part of the second decade of the pefcp.* Its typical form can be described in more detail than the "rationalist" form, since it has been stated more consciously and definitively. The elements of the ideology had been in existence since the late 19th century. (Sec. 7 on movements that led to the WMS. The early forms of the ideology are not exactly the ideology of the WMS in function. The movements and their ideology were congruent and suitable for a WMS-pefcp, but they could only become effective when the ICE failed.)

These ideologies, as parts of powerful WMS's, are moribund. However, they need to be examined for several reasons: The ideologies, and their utilization by aggressive WMS's were the basis for the full development of the WMS that has a "rationalist" ideology. Furthermore, the analysis will serve to illustrate the difference between ideology, and actual relationoship; the way ideology conceals the actual relationship; the congruence of

* The ideology of each—the Communist State and the WMS—and the conduct of each, creates the actual military structure of the other. The ideology of each is necessary to the actual economic structure of the other.

* The word "Fascist" is used herein to describe these States, and their ideologies, for want of a better term. It is not entirely appropriate. A particular ideology and a particular State and Government that called itself "Fascist" existed during this period. Its ideology was of a mysticist type. However, the "Nazi" ideology, both in the revolutionary movement and in the established State, was more characteristic of this ideology. The tendency is to use "Fascist" to describe such Governments, ideologies, movements.

ideology and the actual relationship. Finally, if the "rationalist" ideology becomes inadequate, a mysticist type may be revived in some States, provided the pefcp is itself viable.

The State. in this ideology, is conceived as a mysticist community arising out of "blood" "race" "soil," perhaps the "national will"; it is an entity not created by individuals. The Government, which is conceived to be under the total direction and control of a "leader," is the consummation of the State. "Blood" and "race" which is realized by this State and Government, is that of a pure race and blood, superior to all other races. The State and Government of this superior race is superior to all others; other races, degenerate mixtures, are to be the natural slaves of this superior State.

The State is conceived as the supreme community, and the supreme relationship. The economic relationship is of secondary importance, and is certainly subordinate to the State, or can be conceived as a subordinate part of the State. The Government will control all economic matters. It is not a capitalist economy, but a State Economy.

In this State, the Government will be constituted by the leader as Chief of Government. The leader and Chief is not dependent on the "people" for his power and existence. The Legislature is not a dominant organ of Government; Government by Legislature, and all other aspects of the Democratic State, and its ideology, are rejected. The Democratic State is conceived to be a degradation of the true State.

"Welfare State": The supreme State, inherently having power over the economic relationship, will provide the economic welfare of each of its members. The economy will be so ordered that there will be subsistence and more, for each; more important, the power of the State will be increased. Welfare will be of a "Socialist" type, not a "Communist" type.

"Military State": The State is definitely conceived to be a Military State seeking territorial expansion. The destiny of the State is to overcome inferior peoples and their States. War and aggression are the attributes of a superior race. They are the necessary means of achieving the economic welfare of the members of the State.

The fascist ideology is a suitable ideology for a WMS-pefcp. (Sec. 7: it is also an effective revolutionary movement for a WMS-pefcp.) The ideology provides for a suitable Government form and constitution; includes a "Welfare" concept suitable for a pefcp, and of course, a system of military expenditure. The Government is in a Chief of Government above all economic classes; the party of the Chief seems to be an effective administrative mechanism.

The ideology was more suitable for a pefcp than the early ideology of the "rationalist" type, which did not contain an effective military component. In this latter ideology there were anti-fascist and anti-communist components, but they were confused, and it was not possible to actualize them into an effective system of military erpenditure. It is also fair to say that the "rationalist" ideology in its early stages, was not quite as suitable for an effective Government form, although ultimately the "rationalist" States did develop a superior Government structure. Some States, however, could not develop a suitable Government structure on the basis of the rationalist ideology (Sec. 6, France) and were in effect destroyed by the Fascist propaganda. But the element of Fascist ideology that made it more suitable and effective than the early "rationalist" ideology—the aggressive military element—also led to its downfall.

In actuality, the seemingly well organized, monolithic, Fascist State is not so well organized below the surface. The terror and violence that seems to be focussed on only a relatively few, infects the whole society, and damages it as a State and a society. The tendency towards irrational conduct in a State with this ideology is very great; ideology soon runs the Government, rather than the Government using the ideology.

.3 General form (prototype) of the Government of the WMS (actual relationship).

The Government is constituted by a *Chief of Government,* who exercises the legislative, fiscal, as well as the executive and managerial power (and even the judicial power within the political economy). He functions through an administrative and executive staff constituting an immense bureaucracy. The Government power is not in a Legislative body. The Chief of Government of the WMS possesses the real legislative power. As part of the legislative power generally, the Chief of Government has the basic *fiscal* power, managing the entire political economy—tax, loan, money, banking, Government distribution level and type of good distributed, and their proportions. He controls the Welfare system and the Military system. He controls the dependent capitalist organism, as to real expansion of capital, price, wage, profit. He controls the foreign affairs and foreign economic relationships. The Chief of Government likewise controls the armed forces and can dispose them anywhere in the world.

The primary function of this Chief of Government is to maintain the political economy. The Chief of Government must obtain or compel the support and suffrage of the four economic classes of the political economy (dependent capitalist, labor, welfare, military). He must not be under the control of any single economic class. The Government must be "above" any economic class. How this is accomplished is the major practical problem of the WMS.

(It may be noted, in passing, that the scope and complexity of the Government's managerial function, would make a legislative or Parliamentary type of Government not feasible. Administration, and power over basic policy, must be in a Executive. But the reason for the change in the constitution of the Government lies deeper. It is necessary to centralize power to make a pefcp effective—for the creation of the fictive forms, the mechanisms to make them workable, the Welfare and the Military systems. Any significant opposition by the separate economic classes must be overcome. The Legislature is an impediment to such centralized control. The centralization of the executive, the legislative, and in part the judicial power can be accomplished through a Chief of Government, who, as will appear, leading his own partly, is not dependent on any one economic class).

To achieve and maintain the prototypical form of a Chief of Government free from the control of any particular economic class, is a matter of great practical difficulty. The two greatest danger (deviations from the prototype) are inadequate separation of the Chief of Government from control of certain parts of the capitalist class, and from military control. If the Chief is too dependent on financial groups, there is a tendency to provide an inadequate tax system, a tendency toward encouraging financia manipulation and the creation of private fictive capital papers and the private inflation of banks credit money. These activities are hurtful to a pefcp when carried to excess. Control by the Military invariably means a poorly functioning pefcp.

But the direct popular control of Government is no more feasible in a WMS than it is in the Democratic State. The Chief of Government must have means of maintaining his power, seeking only popular acquiesence. This is not a difficult problem in the States with a mysticist type ideology. In these States there is no ideology of popular constitution or control of Government. There is only one party; the party of the Chief of Government. All other parties are suppressed. The "people" "ratify" the party-leader's (Government), acts. The Government is above any class; the real power, and the succession, is in the hands of the leader who becomes Chief of Government. Nevertheless, it will be seen, that the party still has the major function of obtaining and maintaining some consensus of all economic classes, and in particular the capitalist class, without being under the power of that class.

In the WMS with the "rationalist" ideology (which ideology includes the idea of Government representing the people generally, etc.), the Chief of Government commands a party that will support and maintain his power. The party is not the same type of party as in the Democratic State. The Chief of Government of a WMS is the party leader and as Chief of Government constitutes the party into an instrument of the Government of a WMS. The party does not represent nor is it controlled by an economic class; control resides in the Chief. As his instrument, the party is used to obtain a consensus of the economic classes. Specifically, the party of the WMS, may not represent the capitalist class, as in the Democratic State.

One of two existing parties, or one of more than two existing parties, can become the party of Chief of Government. But it is not the party that is the moving force in making itself the Government's party (WMS, rationalist ideology). The Government form is first established; it is the Chief of Government that creates or constitutes his party. An oppositioon party may become a Chief's party, generally when it adopts the basic ideology of a WMS. A Chief of Government may maintain an effective coalition of parties. This is a weaker Government than a Chief with his own party.

The Chief of Governments should (ideally) be the spokesman for the ideology of the WMS. He should be able to obtain a consensus of all clases. His power will depend on his practical success in maintaining a high level economy for all classes: a high level of production, a high level of employment and a high level of Profit A, a highly developed Welfare and Military system.

(6) The Welfare-Military State (continued).
—The Government of the U. S.
—The Government of certain European WMSs (prewar WWII, and postwar)

.1 *The Government of the United States.*

The general form of the Government of the WMS exists in the U. S. The fact that the WMS developed in two stages in the United States delayed the complete development of the Government form, but the main elements of the prototype form, existed at the outset. The following discussion however, for the most part, refers to the fully developed form beginning with WWII.

The *Presidency*—the Office of the President—was transformed into the office of Chief of Government—the Government of the WMS. *Presidential Government* became the Government of the U. S., not Government by Congress as dominant organ of Government, as in the Democratic State. However, Congress remains as an important adjunct of the Presidency.

The Government power is not a personal power of the President, but is the power of the Presidency. Seemingly the structure of the Government—in Executive, Legislative, Judicial branches, is the same as in the Democratic State. But it is the Presidency and its immense administrative machinery that has the legislative, even the judicial power (the last with respect to the political economy), and it is the Presidency that has the fundamental fiscal, monetary, banking, welfare, military and war power. And it is the Presidency that manages the entire political economy, including the dependent capitalist organism.

The statement that all these powers are not personal powers, but the powers of the Office, means, among other things, that all the foregoing powers exist and are exercised regardless of the particular person that holds the Office. Even if the President himself is inactive, and even if he does not effectively express or embody the ideology of the WMS and the pefcp, or does so inadequately, the Presidency functions to maintain this State and political economy, once it has been established. It is better to have a strong President who is an ideological leader of the welfare, military, anticommunist concepts, and who is an active positive force in the function of the WMS, pefcp. An inactive President can impair the functions of State and economy, yet the basic power of the Presidency cannot now be destroyed, nor can the course of a WMS and pefcp be interrupted by any individual.

The transformation of the Office of the President to the Office of the Chief of Government of a WMS took place at the same time as the creation of the pefcp and WMS. The creation of the WMS-pefcp is the context in which the meaning of the immense expansion of Government power, the President's power, and the nature of his role as Chief of Government, must be examined.

The actual change in the Government of the U. S. was not clearly perceived in the U. S. at its inception, as the change was clearly recognized in the emergence of the fascist States. (The change in the Government form is the subject discussed at this point. It is also true that the nature of the political economy and State that came into being was also not socially recognized.) The same attitude towards the elements that constituted the revolutionary change—i.e., that they were "emergency" measures, existed with respect to the change in the Presidency. It was some time before it was even recognized that "emergency" measures were permanent measures, and emergency powers were permanent powers that changed the nature of the office. In the prevailing ideology all the institutions of the Democratic State, continued. The fact that much of the ideology of the Democratic

State was adapted to the ideology of the WMS, permitted the erroneous views of the nature of the Government to continue, even to the present. No such error could be made with respect to the fascist States, where a new ideology came into power with the inception of the WMS-pefcp.

Furthermore, it seemed, superficially, that the expansion of power and function of the office of the Presidency was the same thing as the expansion of power of that office in wartime. The fact was however, that past episodes of expansion of power (wartime) were quite different from the change that occurred on the inception of the pefcp and the WMS. The scope of power exercised was not only greater but utilized in a way never before known and never contemplated. It was exercised in a new State and a new political economy. For, as stated above, the Presidency is transformed pari passu as the State and the political economy.

There was some early opposition to the change from Congress, and the Court. However, even before the full development of the pefcp-WMS, (WWII), the legislative resistance was ineffectual, and legislative dominance had really ended. The Court did attempt to veto basic legislation. After a threat by the President to end the Court's power, a so called "constitutional revolution" took place, and thereafter the legislative power of the Presidency becomes the actuality.

WWII, which brings about the full development of the political economy and the WMS, with both the welfare and the military pattern, also brings the complete development of Presidential Government. The President achieves and exercises full power over the *whole* economy, including the dependent capitalist organism (level, capital expansion, price, wage. etc.) and the fiscal control becomes fully institutionalized. And in particular, with the full development of the military ideology (antifascism, and then anti communism) the complete Presidential power over foreign affairs, and the power to commit and use the military force anywhere in the world, is established.

The President's Party:

It was stated in Sec. (4), with respect to the Government of the Democratic State, that he political party was the key to the oligarchic control of the Government by the capitalist class (or the most powerful element of the capitalist class at any time). The party becomes the means of control of all "branches" of the Government, although it is in the Legislature, the dominant organ of Government of the Democratic State, that the party operates most effectively. This party (of the Democratic State) has roots at the local level, and is centralized at the national level.

In the WMS, the party that becomes the major instrument of Government is no longer the representative of the capitalist class, but rather is itself the party of the Chief of Government of the WMS: herein the *President's party*. The President is the party leader, and controls the party; the party is no more controlled by the capitalist class than the Presidency itself. Nor is the party under the control, or the representative of *any* economic class of the pefcp-WMS—labor, military, welfare. In a certain sense, this party is more "democratic" than the party of the Democratic State, since it must represent most classes. But again, just as the Chief of Government is not the representative of any economic class interest per se, but only the economic interest of a class as part of a pefcp—WMS, the party will not represent any economic class interest per se. The party becomes one of the President's instruments in securing the consensus of all economic classes. As a *national party*, the President's party is somewhat different than the party at a local level. The President may use the party at all levels (when it becomes the President's party) to obtain a consensus of the four classes.

A party, even in its choice of a President (if it is not the President that names his successor) must act for the WMS, and must act as a "President's party." That is to say, the party can usefully nominate for President only one who will operate the Government as a part of a pefcp, and will be acceptable to all classes of the economy. The party must really support both the Military and Welfare programs.

In the U. S., the Democratic party became the President's party, and it maintained this position for many years. It was originally a Welfare party but actually the capitalist class was significantly represented. It then became a true Welfare-Military party. The Republican party could not achieve national power until it also adopted the Welfare programs and the techniques of the pefcp. The Republican party was finally able to become a President's party, first, because General Eisenhower was regarded as "above" class and party, and finally by adopting the new ideology and the techniques of a pefcp.

Congress; the "Court."

In the Presidential Government of the WMS, Congress is more than a powerless vestige of the Democratic State, (as might seem to be the situation from the description of the prototype of the Government of the WMS, wherein the Legislative body not only loses its dominance, but becomes vestigial). It is true that the President as Chief of Government now possesses the legislative power in actuality, as well as the executive power, and it is he who established and executes the basic fiscal policy. It is he who has the real power of waging war, the conduct of foreign affairs, etc. Nevertheless, in several ways Congress plays a significant role in the Government, i.e., in Presidential Government.

As an investigative and consultative body, which represents many diverse interests from all the economic classes, it does affect details of policy formulation, and the actual administration of the Government, although within the basic requirements of a WMS-pefcp. The influence of individual members of Congress on the function of the bureaucracy (the President's administrative staff as a whole), is considerable. In a sense, it can be said that the Congressman becomes a representative to the Administration (Chief of Government).

Congress also has another role in Presidential Government. This arises out of the fact that the political structure of the U. S. still contains Federal elements, despite the fact that Presidential Government itself, and the nature and function of the WMS, marked the end of any significant state power. Congress can act to suppress certain manifestationos of State power that may be injurious to a pefcp, something which may be difficult for the President to do directly. The "Court" also serves in this connection. In general, i.e., with respect to the political economy, the "Court" acts to support Presidential Government.

While Congress and the Court are not the power entities in

the Government of the WMS, and the Government is Presidential Government, it should not be overlooked that Congress and especially the Courts are the major means of the realization of certain parts of the ideology of the Democratic State that are adopted into the ideology of the WMS, in particular with respect to individual civil rights. Indeed, Congress and the Courts have in the WMS taken a more active and effective role in the realization and establishment of these rights than in the preceding Democratic State.

The Government of the U. S., as a WMS, is a stable one, although the quadrennial elections give an appearance that the WMS and Government are under attack. This Government is more stable than most of its foreign counterparts. It is an illusion that it is weaker (and less efficient) than the earlier "Fascist" Governments. Its excellence should not be minimized. It is probably superior, in efficiency and competence, and justice, to the Government of the pre-existing Democratic State or to any other existing State.

.2 The Governments of certain Europeans WMS's (pre-World War II; postwar). All Governments tend to approximate the prototype form of Government of a WMS.

Germany:

The prototype form of Government is found in the postwar Government (rationalist type of ideology) and it existed in the pre-war Government (mysticist type ideology).

The Nazi political movement was successful in establishing a WMS in Germany. sec. (7).) Adolf Hitler, the leader of the revolutionary party, was elected Chancellor in the final election of the Democratic State. After the 1933 election he procured passage in the Reichstag of an enabling act giving the Executive (the dictator) the power to issue decrees and legislate independently of the Reichstag and President. Subsequently he assumed the office of President and Commander-in-Chief. The Government thereafter was constituted by the Chief of Government, and with all powers centralized in him. The legislature (Reichstag) had no real function. The inmmense bureaucracy characteristic of the Government of the WMS was under the absolute control of the Chief of Government.

The Nazi party, the revolutionary party, became the sole party of the established State. In this instance, the party became a part of the Government itself. It had police and military functions. However, its main function was to obtain the support of as large a number of the members of the State as possible, and enforce the support of the rest. Actually it did obtain the almost complete support of four main economic groups: capitalist, labor, welfare, military. The Government was "above" the economic classes.

This totalitarian Government exercised an extraordinary degree of control over individuals. It utilized terror, psychological techniques, secret police and tribunals. The institutions and the concepts of individual freedom of the Democratic State were done away with.

The *post war* German Government was one of the many established by new constitutions. The true nature of these Governments—the actual relationship—cannot be ascertained from reading the constitutions. The constitution should be considered an ideological representation of the Government. These constitutions are generally constructed on an American model, restating the classic ideology of the Democratic State. They pretend to establish, or re-establish, Governments of separation of powers, dominant Legislatures, separate Executives and Judiciaries, and free elections by members of the State who purportedly choose the representatives who will govern.

But these Governments, in actuality, are generally forms of the Government of a WMS. They are executive-administrative in form, with a powerful Chief of Government, controlling the Legislature. Party oligarchs and the Chief of Government, whose actual power is in some sort of coalition of welfare-capitalist, and labor interests, are in control.

The Federal Republic of Germany (1949) functions under a Chancellor, a practically irremovable Chief of Government. The Chancellor, in effect, is the dominant officer of Government, determining who the ministers will be, and controlling the bureaucracy. The Chancellor determines the general policy of government. He may request the declaration of a state of "legislative emergency," and secure the legislatioon he wishes. The Parliamentary bodies have no effective control over the Government.

The Chancellor has his party (CDU) which is basically a party for a welfare state (the "social market economy"), and the party's doctrine is to maintain a strong central government with a Chief of Government controlling all agencies of the Government. The "Federal" aspect of the Government is part of the ideology, and of no actual significance.

It is said that the "Chancellor principle" is inherent in the German culture, and it is for this reason that such a Government was instituted after the Weimar Republic, and then again (despite the Allied indoctrination of the ideology of the American constitution) in the Federal Republic. But a Government controlled by a Chief of Government is inevitable in a pefcp.

Italy:

The control of the Italian Government by the Fascist party in the 1920's preceded the establishment of the WMS. The Fascist movement was originally not a typical "elitist" movement. It was a reactionary political party, in a nation of many irreconcilable interests—economic, political, and ecclesiastical. Secretly backed by the Monarchy, by large and small capitalists, by the semi-feudal land owners, and probably by ecclesiastical leaders, the fascist party obtained power within the existing political structure. Mussolini obtained appointment as Prime Minister, and for a time maintained the same type of Government as had been in existence. There was really no new distinctive political or economic ideology at that time. Mussolini utilized all existing political forms, with the full support of the existing power entities. The Government was a corrupt "Democratic" Government.

But in the 1930's, on the final collapse of the ICE and an international economic collapse, the Fascist ideology, the Fascist State, and the Fascist Government came into existence. The Government was that of a Chief of Government, and all forms of "Democratic" Government were abandoned. The State itself, ideology aside, was actually as little a welfare State as could be conceived of (indeed, in Italy, throughout the fascist period, despite a pretentious "welfare" ideology, welfare features were minimal). The ideology was based on concepts of force and military exploits as expressing a nation's virtue. The Abysinnian war in 1932 marked the inception of the formulated ideology, and the WMS in function.

The doctrines for an authoritarian central Government were developed. In 1934 the mechanisms of a "corporate State" were established, presumably as a means of economic control, but this was more ideology than anything else, since the Government bureaucracy had established totalitarian control. The single party became part of the Government and was utilized as a means of totalitarian control by the "dictator." Violence, terror, psychological manipulation, became established means of maintaining the power of the Government.

The *postwar Government,* (the new republic, 1948) *seems* to be a return to Italian Parliamentary Government. The Government must have the support of a majority in Parliament, or an effective coalition of the parties, and the Executive cannot govern without Parliament. But the Prime Minister does direct the general policy of the Government, and controls the ministers and the bureaucracy, and has considerable legislative power. There is no genuine "Federalism": (it is a true, central Government). While the Prime Minister must have the support of the Parliamentary majority, in effect he controls his party or the party oligarchs, and the Parliamentary majority. There is a workable prototype form of Government because of certain special conditions (which may not continue). The party that is more powerful than any one other party is a "Welfare" party, and it obtains power as a welfare party, and is supported by the Church. It is effective because it opposes and maintains itself as the opposition to the Communists. Fear of the latter maintains the party, the power in Parliament, and a Government strong enough to function as a Government for a pefcp.

France:

French political history, pre WWII and postwar, demonstrates the consequence of inability to develop an effective Government form for the WMS. Out of absolute necessity, a change finally took place in 1958, and the prototype Government form of the WMS was established.

Prewar: Far from achieving the effective Chief of Government form, the Government remained the traditional unstable one, with impotent executive and a dominant, yet fragmented, Legislature. The French political tradition is one of constant struggle between "aristocratic" groups and "democratic" groups, with a weak, unstable Government. This tradition was not unsuitable for the "Democratic" type of Government appropriate for an ICE. But the tradition, and other factors were strong enough to prevent political progress. The "elitist" movement that existed could not establish an effective executive Government, but weakened the existing Government further. Some of these movements were treasonable. After 1932, the average life of a Government was four months. The German attack resulted in the fall of the Government, with scarcely a token military resistance.

In the years following WWII, the Fourth Republic (1945-1958) had the same pattern—a strong Legislature and a weak executive. It managed to survive by means of temporary party coalitions, but mainly because France has always had an effective bureaucratic structure which could function from day to day. It is possible that the Government of the 4th republic was weaker than the Government of the 3rd republic, except that the treasonable elements had been removed.

In 1958 a modern executive type WMS Government was established (the Fifth Republic) under the leadership of Charles deGaulle, who had sufficient personal power to establish such a Government. DeGaulle became President, with power to appoint the Premier, and control the Parliament, the cabinet, and his party. The President can assume full emergency powers. He controls foreign and domestic policy, military and welfare policies, and has full economic control. He has adequate legislative power. With this constitutional change, the executive at last overcame the Parliament. But nevertheless there is still a serious internal weakness, and the question remains whether effective Presidential Government will long survive deGaulle.

Britain:

It seems an anomaly that the Labor Government, which was in power in 1931, and, on the collapse of the ICE, presented with the opportunity—really the necessity—of putting into effect its long contemplated welfare program, should dissolve itself, and a coalition Government succeed it. (It was not until 1945 that the "Welfare State" was professedly established.) It is an anomaly also that the coalition Government that succeeded the Labor Government in 1931 did not undertake a policy of massive re-armament and heavy military expenditure, (this was not begun until 1935) when faced by obvious Nazi aggression.

Nevertheless: (a) the pefcp and the WMS are in existence in Britain in the 30's, (b) an effective and prototypical Government form for a WMS was likewise in existence in the 1930's. The program of welfare distribution established in 1945, the economic planning and control, etc. were actually only a fuller development of an earlier start. The 1945 program of the Welfare state did not make the basic change. The war itself had brought full employment and a generally raised standard of living. With respect to the characteristic form of Government of the WMS: Before the collapse of the ICE, the British Government was already shifting towards a Government by cabinet and bureaucracy, and not essentially by Parliament. The Prime Minister exercised power (in practice) greater than that of the U. S. President of the Democratic State. This does not mean that the Parliament was simply an electoral college for a strong executive Government, but it is fair to say that the cabinet controlled Parliament, and not the reverse. The necessity for any marked change to create an effective Government for a WMS, was less in Britain than in other countries.

With the full development of the pefcp and the WMS, it can be observed that the residues of power in Parliament shifted to the cabinet, and more important, the powers in the cabinet concentrated themselves in the hands of the Prime Minister. The Government achieves the prototype form, with an immense, self-activating administrative machinery and a powerful Chief of Government.

The Government—the Prime Minister and the bureaucracy—maintains power through party. (This, of course, is not a new development in Britain, where the rigidly disciplined party was the basis of *Cabinet* Government and Cabinet control of Parliament.) There is also a distinctive aspect to the British party system. In other countries, the Chief of Government leads a party that will support a WMS and its ideology, and represent a sufficient part of the four classes of the economy, to maintain a Government of a WMS. But in Britain both existing major parties, the Conservative party as well as the Labor party, accept the principles of the WMS. A dependent capitalist organism, completely controlled, is accepted as a necessity, and the welfare system, and in part the military system, and the system of close economic control are likewise accepted by two major parties.

(7) Economic dynamism for a WMS, —pefcp. Movements, and their ideologies, that led to the WMS.

Upon the collapse of the ICE, there was a powerful economic dynamism for the establishment of the *pefcp* in those countries where the Independent capitalist economy had been fully developed. It was a far stronger economic dynamism than that towards the Communist economy and State. The WMS-pefcp in its fully developed form (i.e. embodying both the "welfare" and the "military" systems of distribution) is

(a) more productive generally than any other reasonably possible economic relationship; specifically it is more productive than a Communist economic relationship, *and*

(b) provided for the existence of an upper economic class based on property rights enforced by the Government.
On the collapse of the ICE, there *seemed* to be only two reasonably feasible economic relationships that might succeed the large scale ICE:

(a) a small scale capitalist system of production, localized, limited market—the advanced technology and very large units abandoned. (A doubtfully viable relationship.)

(b) A large scale, large unit, technologically advanced productive system, based on direct Government "ownership," Government employment, and Government controlled production, and some sort of system of distribution of goods determined by the Government.

(Note: the possibility of an agrarian, semi-capitalist system, as variant of (a) above can be dismissed as unrealistic. The population, so great in number and so concentrated in urban centers, cannot possibly be maintained by so relatively unproductive an economy. A socially critical point would soon be reached, and the social and political organization could not be maintained; the nation-State would fragment itself into regional or individual "state" units. On a regional basis in the U. S. (in the South, perhaps in some other individual "states,") such an economy might be practicable, but the national economy would dissolve, and the cities would be in chaos. The same criticism could almost be made of the first of the two possible alternatives: the small scale localized capitalist system of production, with a definitely retrograde technology. Even if production be adequate for minimal needs, it is not likely that a national economy and a nation-State could be maintained. A political fragmentation would also follow. The question always remains if any such economic relationship is viable, since capital expansion, the sine qua non of any capitalist structure would not be feasible. Even with a retrogressive technology, the degree of capital expansion necessary for function would not be possible. It should also be noted that the very existence of a rapidly developing Communist State-a powerful Russian State, with a developing modern technology, makes the first alternative wholly impractical, even assuming that a nation-State, and a national economy could be maintained.)

Upon the collapse of the ICE the second of the two seeming alternatives -a technologically advanced large scale productive system based of State "ownership," State distribution, would have possessed the economic dynamism, and not the first, or its variants (assuming that the first pattern was economically viable).

This is so despite the fact that the first alternative or variants could maintain an upper economic class. A Communist State economic relationship would be *far more* productive in material goods than any localized small scale, capitalist or quasi capitalist relationship. Furthermore in the localized or retrogressive capitalist or quasi capitalist system, production for the upper economic would be extremely low, and the class very weak. The contrast in the two situations—between a generally high productivity (Communist economic relationship)—and that of a lower class of great size, very low productivity, and a low productivity for the upper economic class itself, would have destroyed any economic dynamism for the class type economic relationship in favor of that for the Communist economic relationship.

(It should be repeated, that as stated in the general theory of social change, even if there were an economic dynamism for the Communist economic relationship as against a possible small scale retrogressive economic system, there would have been no necessity, no determinism that the Communist economic relationship would have actually prevailed, even if there were an effective Communist movement and ideology. In the U. S. at least, there was no reasonably effective movement for a Communist State. The Marxist movement attracted only a small group in the United States in the 1930s, and these were not working class. In European countries, the Communist (Marxist) movements were stronger, but as will appear, it was almost certain that they would not succeed.

There are more than two economic structures possible on the end of the ICE: there was the pefcp. This political economy was certainly not socially known as a political economy based on the fictive expansion of capital, integral with the State. But the idea of an economy in which the State would determine the distribution of goods (not undertake their production directly), and could determine the level of production was clearly enough contemplated by all ideologies. Such an economy was thought to be feasible without any idea of what was implicit in such an economy. Such an economy could exist once the ICE came to an end, on the basis of a State becoming a political economy based on the fictive expansion of capital. In simple appearance this could be created if the Government maintained the level of production by purchasing goods produced by the creation of its bonds as permanent forms and the inflation of money thereon, with an immense distributive system for Welfare and Military purposes. This new political economy was the one with the *actual economic dynamism,* an economic dynamism far superior to that of a Communist economic relationship and State.

The pefcp-WMS possesses the economic dynamism because it is ultimately more productive than any other economic relationship, including the Communist one, *and* it provides for an upper economic class based on property rights, and this class can also acquire great wealth in the form of private and public fictive capital forms. The pefcp also creates other economic classes (Welfare, Military), which are fundamental in creating the WMS itself.

Seemingly the share of the capitalist class is diminished by the shares of the new economic classes. This is in actuality not the situation, and it is soon recognized that the absolute size of the share of the capitalist class increases. When fully developed, the pefcp is far more productive than the *ICE,* even at boom level.

Some further comments on the productivity of the pefcp should be made: Even at a low level (the early "Welfare" system in the (U. S.) this economic relationship possesses the economic dynamism, because of the maintenance of an upper economic class. It is probable that at this low level this economy is more productive than the contemporary Communist economy. But even if productivity in an advanced technology in a Communist type relationship would be greater than in the early Welfare type pefcp, the class aspect would outweigh the possible greater productivity.

Movements and ideologies leading to the WMS.

Assuming the existence of an economic dynamism for a pefcp:

A new State must come into being. To establish this State there must be an effective movement and ideology. The actual nature of the State that eventuates, will not appear in the moving ideology (Secs. 2, 5), but the idea of State as economic association of some sort (Welfare), and as Military State of some sort, will be present. The movements and ideologies that established the fascist type of WMS were plainly visible. The movements and ideologies leading to the early "Welfare" State ("rationalist" ideology) were more amorphous.

(Statement of the general ideology of each form, in the established States, Section (5); Sec. (6) on the Governments of certain of these States.)

Elements of each ideology existed for several decades before the final collapse of the ICE. There had even been miniscule movements embodying many of the ideas that finally prevailed as ideology, in each category.

In the U. S., the basic "Welfare" concept of State and Government responsible for the economic needs and material welfare of all of its members, existed during the Democratic State-ICE, but it was weak and unorganized. It was so at variace with the powerful and prevailing "Democratic" ideology of complete laissez faire, and the idea that the Government owed nothing to anyone, that it had little significance. "Welfare," ideology is not to be confused with the ideology of "progressive" movements of the early 20th century, and even the earlier "populist" movements. These were essentially concerned with public regulation of utilities, businesses—especially large scale units; they were movements of small business men, farmers, etc., who felt injured by "monopolies," "trusts," international bankers, etc. However, the idea of a public regulation of business and an increase in Government power implicit in progressive and populist movements are not entirely to be dismissed as contributing something to the movement and ideology that led to the WMS. Likewise, while labor movements and unions were not in themselves a significant forerunner of the "Welfare" ideology, certain aspects of movements to increase the power of labor in wage negotiations became of importance in this ideology. (The suggestion that a Rousseauean philosophy of the equality and perfectability of man which Government can assure, was a significant factor in the ideology leading to the Welfare State, is more than doubtful. Such doctrine was of significance in the ideology of the "Democratic State," and some of this doctrine does reappear in the ideology of the WMS of the "rationalist" type, but it was not a moving force.)

The main source of Welfare ideology was probably in the Socialist movements, weak as they seemed to be in the U. S. The significant part of Socialist ideology was the idea of State responsibility for the material, economic needs of the members of the State. More immediate sources of ideology were the many schemes of "social distribution" that flourished directly after the collapse of 1929. These proposals for production for use and distribution (many based on "crank" monetary schemes, Social Credit plants, etc.) and miniscule parties seeking radical social change, did have a marked effect in the formulation of the "Welfare" ideology, particularly among the great number of unemployed, poor, etc.

The ideas coalesced in the Great Depression 1930-1932, and, to an extent, in the Presidential campaign of 1932. It was the President himself who became the leader of the movement, and effective formulator of the Welfare ideology that established the early Welfare State in the U. S.

The Military component of the ideology of the "rationalist" WMS is of later development. It began as a direct response to the aggression of the Fascist States (which ideologically and actually were inherently militarist). The focus of the ideology later becomes anti-Communist.

Early mysticist ideology and movements

The mysticist ideologies and movements (later Nazi and Fascist) can be more easily discerned in their earlier stages. In the late 19th and arly 20th centuries a peculiar type of anti-Democratic, anti-capitalist, ideology began to develop in European countries. Its rise coincided with the full development of the ICE (in particular the large scale, technologically advanced system of production; the later banking and financial systems).

While this ideology seems to resemble the ideology in the precapitalist economy and political structure (of kings, an aristocracy, and Church as religious power entity allied therewith), and *seems* to seek to restore this older economic, political, and Church structure (by eliminating the capitalist economy and the Democratic State), it has quite a different meaning. The difference lies in this: The main line of these ideologists (and the miniscule movements too) did not reject the wealth and goods of the modern industrial society, or the modern technology that creates them, or the social and economic pattern of a great mass of poor wage earners in the relationship required by the technology. These ideologists attacked the ideas and the social relationships of the capitalist society: individualism, freedom in personal relationships, equality and social mobility, the ideal of rationalism, private judgment and power, all consequences that necessarily flow from the capitalist relationship and the Democratic State.* Presumably these ideologists sought to revive the tradition of old institutions, rituals, hierarchies, all arising out of "natural" inequality and inherent evil of man.

This antinomy—the acceptance of the technology, wealth, etc., of the capitalist industrial sociey, and the rejection of all that is associated with such a structure, and the turning back to pre-capitalist and medieval concepts of the social order and relationships, really means that the ideologists have something new in mind with respect to the nature of the social order they seek. They are by no means "conservatives." It is to be a social order in which the "framework" and the technology of modern material production is maintained, but the political, social, and personal relationships inherent in the modern industrial society are to be abolished. The individual relationships of the older societies—or what such relationship are conceived to have been—will be superimposed on a modern industrial society.

The structure and form of this fantasied new society is set forth in mysticist, non-rationalist terms. For most of the ideologists the focus is in the mystique of the State. (Sec. 5, above, on idea that State constitutes the primary relationship of society). The State is deemed to arise out of a mysticist community of pure blood, race, national will. The "race" or "blood," etc., is superior to all others. The natural leader, or Head of State, represents an elite of this superior blood and race. The

* The ideas of money, interest ("usury"), banking, capital, etc., in these ideologies are the ideas of the precapitalist economy. There is no understanding of the nature of money, interest, banking, etc., in a capitalist relationship.

elite will exercise a supreme power over the community. (It would appear that they are also the natural beneficiaries of the economy.) The economy is the creature of the State. These mysticist concepts, to repeat, are not those existing in the pre-capitalist society, which also envisages a mysticist community, and an order and hierarchy therein. In actuality, this older mystique is truly based on an economic structure, although the actual economic structure is different than in the mysticist conceptions. In fact, the new mystique rejects the old mystique;* it is now a "scientific" mystique. The new society contemplated is certainly not the same as the actual old society. Production will be based on a modern technology, but distribution will take place according to a different scheme.

In summary, the essential thrust of the 19th and 20th centuries mysticist ideologies and movements is towards a State and Government in a modern industrial society, wherein the State is in the absolute control of an "elite," who are not the capitalists or any older upper class. The State will absolutely control the economy and distribute wealth to an elite. The elite, among others, includes a dominant military class which will conquer decadent States and inferior peoples. The elite are ultimately the believers in this ideology; they are the natural "superiors" of the mass, i.e., the working class. It is an extraordinary concept of an elite, not really based on any upper economic class, either that of the modern technology, or of an older economic relationship.

A basic element of this ideology and movement is anti-semitism. The myth of the evil Jew (in the revolutionary ideology as well as in the ideology of the established mysticist type WMS) is indispensable. It is more than a clever tactic to utilize the hatred and passions created by this basic myth of Western society. Antisemitism, and the exclusion of the Jew from the social order seems to be a major basis for the fundamental idea of pure, superior blood and race, which culminates in the mysticist community of the State, and the elite. Anti-Semitism

* Nevertheless, this ideology appealed to the survivors of the older relationships and ideologies: aristocrats, monarchists, prelates, etc. They saw in this ideology an ideology the same as their own, or at least an ally in the attack on the Democratic State, the capitalist economy, the separation of Church and State.

is also utilized in ideology to attack the capitalist relationship and the Democratic State ("inventions" of the Jews to overthrow the old order that excluded them from society). It is the nexus, or the apparent nexus, i.e., the common element in the pre-capitalist, feudal society, and the new society to be created. It is a basis for rejecting rationalism, and ideology and relationships based on rationalist concepts. The ideas of the power of the individual, the idea of private judgement, of equality, of concepts of free, ethical man, are indeed antithetical to the mystique necessary for this ideology. Of course, these are not Jewish concepts alone; they are embodied in Protestantism. Actually, the new ideology really rejects Christian doctrine, insofar as it embodies these ideas. The "Fascist" ideology seems to embody a new religious doctrine, not the doctrines of ancient religions, or Christian or Jewish religions.

Infused in this ideology, especially when the collapse of the ICE becomes imminent, are many Socialist concepts. These are reformulated and adapted to the mystique of the ideology. Communism and Marxism were characterized as further Jewish inventions, part of the Jewish conspiracy against the Aryans.

The social relationship contemplated was a fantasy that could have no real existence. (And the ideology and movement could not prevail socially as long as the ICE was viable.) But it has already been pointed out how congruent, supportive, such an ideology could be for the actual *WMS* and a *pefcp*. Once the economic dynamic for a pefcp is operating, the ideology and the movement could succeed. Of course, the actual State and the actual economy that eventuated are not those of the ideology.

The conflict preceding the establishment of the WMS-pefcp, appeared as a great ideological conflict; Welfare concepts, Fascist concepts, Communist concepts. It could be predicted that the Communist ideology and movement would not prevail, since the basic economic dynamism was for the WMS. But it may also be remarked that Fascist ideology had almost as great an appeal to the lower economic class as the Communist ideology.

Note: The establishment of a Communist relationship in Russia *before* the final collapse of the ICE; in China *after* the rise of the WMS.

The ICE was moribund by the end of WW I. It was sustained in the following decade only by the great capital overexpansion in the U. S., itself the result of the destruction caused by the war, and by the extraordinary fictive capital expansion and inflation. (Ch. II). However, it would seem, since the ICE was not dead, that the economic dynamism for a restoration of a capitalist relationship in Russia would be superior to an economic dynamism for a Communist relationship.

But there was a conjunction of circumstances in Russia that makes it possible to say that a strong economic dynamism to a Communist relationship did then exist. The greater part of the upper class was still essentially feudal; the nation and its people were still primarily agricultural. It was only in very recent years that the agricultural pattern began to approach a capitalist form. But both capitalist and surviving feudal patterns were weak. And of great importance was the fact that no suitable political relationship for a capitalist economy had ever been developed. The anachronistic Czarist autocracy, maintained by Church and Army, was not only unsuitable, but had destroyed the bases for a political form that could maintain a capitalist economy. The survivors of the upper class, and the Church, would have as soon overthrown a Democratic Government, as a Communist Government. There was not even the political background to establish an effective military dictatorship. The Communists moved into a political vacuum, scarcely aware how complete the vacuum was.

It may be said that a Communist pattern, economic and political, was feasible and would be more productive in material goods than the existing conflicting patterns, or any other pattern immediately possible, and that an economic dynamism for a Communist economic relationship existed. It is true that an effective intervention by foreign (capitalist) powers could have restored and sufficiently strengthened the capitalist relationship, and a suitable Government form. But WWI exhausted the capitalist powers. (Actually, it was the Communist movement that was aided by a foreign power.)

It is nevertheless remarkable that after the establishment of the Communist State, it survived during the next decade. It functionned at so low a level of productivity, that it would seem that a capitalist pattern could displace it. It is probable that the reason it continued during this decade was the moribund condition of the capitalist structure.

As to China: A strong economic dynamism to a "Communist" economic relationship and State existed at the time of the change to the present structure. The feudal economy was moribund; the disintegration of the social fabric was marked; there was no significant capitalist economy in being, and even if there had been a somewhat more advanced one, by that time it would not have been viable. Certainly after WWII, only a WMS could have existed, but it was not likely that this could be established without a more advanced industrial base. The ideology for a WMS, while not absent, was not effective, or at least not sufficiently supported by the U. S. On the other hand a strong Communist movement existed supported by the Russian State, a factor of great importance in economic and ideological dynamics of change.

Indeed, after WWII, the dynamics, and the movements, and the course of history have to be viewed in the context of the military and economic power of the Russian State, and the military power and the political economy of the U. S. Supported by the military and economic power of the Russian State, a Communist movement could have succeeded in the dying economies and disintegrating societies of the former combatants, or the undeveloped economies of other nations; it is equally true that the military power and economic aid furnished by the U. S., can establish a WMS.

After WWII, the Communist movements had no life of their own. Their activity and power were determined by the policies of the Russian State. The ideology, as revolutionary ideology came to have little appeal. The direct military and economic power of the two great nations determined the course of the minor powers.

(8) The end of the political economy based on fictive forms, and of the Welfare Military State.

For reasons inherent in the nature of the economic relationship this political economy cannot continue to exist indefinitely. Leaving aside gross mismanagement, (i.e. a disastrous great war, a grossly excessive level of production and excessive inflation, etc.) certain developmental processes are taking place which will make it impossible to maintain the pseudo Profit B, the fictive forms, and hence an economic relationship based on fictive forms. This ultimate, inescapable failure of the political economy and the State will take place in the most effective and successful of the political economies and WMS's, not alone in those whose economic basis is so inadequate as to make them totally dependent on the powerful WMS for survival.

The basic cause of the ultimate failure of this political economy is the resumption of the process that exists in all capitalist relationships, i.e. the steady advance in techonological development that reduces unit value of goods (although this is concealed by the depreciation of paper money) and reduces the rate of Aggregate Profit and entrepreneural profit. A point can be reached where the Aggregate Profit itself must always decline, and the Aggregate Capital itself must always shrink, and there can be no market whatsoever for any new additional capital goods. (Ch. II, Sec. 18.) It was this tendency that produced the relative economic critical point in the ICE, wherein constant expansion could no longer take place in sufficient volume to maintain the economy, and a variable, episodic, expansion could no longer fill the gap. But the fictive processes introduced and maintained by the WMS, and the creation of a *pseudo* Profit B made it possible for the relationship of individuals in capital units to continue. Yet the same tendency still continues, to the point where any real capital expansion become impossible. This is the absolute economic political point of any capitalist relationship, even if mainained by a pseudo Profit B.

What then occurs, stated generally, is the beginning of the failure of the *fictive Profit form* (WMS tax), the return declining, and the rate reduced in an effort to maintain entrepreneural profit. Inflation then must increase. A rapid depreciation of the paper money and all fictive capital forms sets in. The pseudo Profit B becomes more difficult to maintain, and it declines, and then the declining spiral in the pseudo Profi B, induces a declining spiral in the level of production; value begins to decline faster than volume. The Level will decline to the point of a possible socially critical point, with collapse of State and Economy.

That is to say the fictive forms (fictive capital, fictive profit, inflated money as capital money, the private fictive capital forms) can no longer maintain an equilibrium at any reasonably acceptable level of production (acceptable for labor class, welfare class, military, capitalists themselves), and as a corollary, the fictive forms themselves lose all acceptability. The actual, approximate sequence is:

I. The real expansion of capital, whether involving technological advance or not, comes to an end, including any possible "reactive" expansion of capital for Government demand. (Note, however, that this does not mean that technological advance terminates.) There is, of course, an end to the creation of new private fictive capital forms and private inflation.

II. Parallel: The continuous fall in the fictive profit form—WM tax in amount of return and usually in the overall tax rate.

> The steady increase in the issuance of the fictive capital public forms.
> The steady increase in the public inflation of the paper money.

III. The beginning and continuance of the spirally increasing decine in the Level of Production, as the pseudo Profit B begins to decline.

IV. The spirally increasing fall in the WM tax return. The continuing increase in the issuance of fictive capital forms and inflated money.

V. Loss of acceptability of new and existing fictive capital forms, almost final loss of value of the paper money. Level of production insufficient to maintain Government distribution—welfare—military systems. (Note: if gold reaches private possession in sufficient amount, the fictive capital forms and the paper money are the sooner destroyed.)

VI. Final spiral. (Note: before final spiral, it is likely that the final Great War intervenes. This will appear as an attempt to maintain an *"ideology."* In view of the needs of the Government, which cannot be met thru the dependent capitalist organism, it is possible that a Military Government system of production—production directly undertaken by the Government for military purposes, something like existing so called "communist" States, comes into being.)

If the end is not in the devastation of war and collapse, the point of the declining spiral will be such that the economy is socially unacceptable to any class. Note that the welfare distribution would have to increase as the Level of Production declines.

The inability to expand real capital, and expand the pseudo Profit B is really made critical by the lower tax return, (and the fall of the tax and of the whole Aggregate Profit will be precipitous because of spiral effects). Thereafter, the Government bond will not be privately purchased; the Government must rely on inflation to obtain money, and this will destroy the political economy. The Government will not be able to arrest the spiral.